MASTERING INTENSIVE SHORT-TERM DYNAMIC PSYCHOTHERAPY

To our parents—Johannes de Labije, Karla de Labije-Ottenhoff, Peter Bernard Neborsky, and Edith Lavy Neborsky—who each in their specific ways of loving us taught us the treasure of love and how to deal or not to deal with the pain of trauma

MASTERING INTENSIVE SHORT-TERM DYNAMIC PSYCHOTHERAPY

A Roadmap to the Unconscious

Josette ten Have-de Labije
and Robert J. Neborsky

Routledge
Taylor & Francis Group
LONDON AND NEW YORK

First published 2012 by
Karnac Books Ltd.

2 Park Square, Milton Park, Abingdon, Oxfordshire OX14 4RN
52 Vanderbilt Avenue, New York, NY 10017

Routledge is an imprint of the Taylor & Francis Group, an informa business

First issued in paperback 2019

British Library Cataloguing in Publication Data

A C.I.P. for this book is available from the British Library

ISBN-13: 978-1-85575-821-6 (pbk)
ISBN-13: 978-0-367-32553-4 (hbk)

Typeset by Vikatan Publishing Solutions (P) Ltd., Chennai, India

CONTENTS

LIST OF FIGURES

Note to reader

The figures are given in black and white. Therefore, the red and green traffic lights used in figures throughout this book will be denoted as follows:

green traffic light: ●

red traffic light: ●

LIST OF TABLES

ABOUT THE AUTHORS

Josette ten Have-de Labije, registered psychologist-psychotherapist and clinical psychologist, studied at the universities of Groningen and Amsterdam (at the Netherlands Institute for Brain Research). She started her professional career in 1972 at the Department for Neuro- and Psychophysiology of the Free University of Brussels, Belgium. Thereafter, she worked in the Netherlands at a public mental health centre for ambulant (non-residential) patients as coordinator of the Behaviour Therapy Department and member of the diagnostic staff. Since 1990, she has been working in private practice. As a qualified psychotherapist and clinical psychologist she was trained as cognitive-behaviour therapist (individual and group setting), Couples therapist, therapist for psychodynamic group psychotherapy and she was trained and supervised by Professor Dr H. Davanloo as a therapist for Intensive Short-Term Dynamic Psychotherapy. She is editor of the Ad Hoc Bulletin for STDP: Practice and Theory. She is a member of the Board of Directors of the International Experiential Dynamic Psychotherapy Association.

Robert J. Neborsky, MD, is a psychiatrist in private practice in Del Mar, California, and a Clinical Professor of Psychiatry at UCSD School of Medicine and the UCLA School of Medicine (Hon.). A member of the Board of Directors and Vice President of the International Experiential Dynamic Psychotherapy Association, and a founding member on the Editorial Board of the *International Journal of Short-Term Dynamic Psychotherapy (Wiley)*, he currently serves as guest editor of the *Ad Hoc Bulletin of Short-Term Dynamic Psychotherapy.* In 2003, Dr Neborsky was honoured by the UCLA School of Medicine clinical faculty association as the Distinguished Psychiatric Lecturer of the year for 2002. In 2003, he helped to found the Southern California Society for IS-TDP and was elected as President of the Society. In 2011, he was appointed a Distinguished Life Fellow of the American Psychiatric Association.

PREFACE

Dear colleague,

You are reading this book because of your interest in making acquaintance with intensive short-term dynamic psychotherapy. Perhaps you acquired this book because of your wish to enter an ISTDP core group training in order to become an ISTDP therapist. Or perhaps you already are an ISTDP therapist but you find yourself still struggling with some ISTDP concepts and/or techniques.

Becoming a competent and mature psychotherapist is a lifelong and difficult job. Why? Because no matter what kind of psychotherapy school, all psychotherapy is supposed to be tailor-made to the particular patient's variables and problems who comes for help. To become a competent and mature psychotherapist, one needs a lot of therapy experience. Mainly because of the fact that no two patients are the same—notwithstanding the fact, for instance, that they both enter with the same problems on the DSM-IV, Axes I and II. Further, let's not forget that we, psychotherapists, live in the same imperfect world as our patients. It is not only the patient who brings his own personality, his past experiences, and his own problems to the therapy. Let us hope that the therapist has—at least—an awareness of his own intrapsychic conflicts and intra- and inter-psychic dynamics, and an awareness of where and when his own intrapsychic conflicts and dynamics prevent him from making the appropriate interventions at the appropriate time with the appropriate duration. And, let's be honest, it isn't easy to keep our motivation high to understand and assess our own intra- and inter-psychic dynamics and those of the patient at the same time. Psychotherapy is also a lonely job. It is a job where the focus is mainly on the needs of the other. Thus, no matter what the theoretical differences with other colleagues may be, it is important to have colleagues with whom one can exchange opinions, failures, successes, concerns, doubts, tears, anger, laughter!

Learning in general, but particularly to do ISTDP as a therapist and as a patient, requires, amongst other things, that the student (therapist and patient) will be able to construct a conceptual framework that allows organization and integration of new knowledge into a coherent structure. Thus in order to stimulate real and deep learning, it first will be necessary that we help ourselves/our students/our patients to build an intellectual curiosity out of intrinsic motivation (or attentive ego). In the meantime, we have to park our earlier ways of thinking and expression in the garage of our minds while understanding constituents of new conceptual structures. Having accomplished that, we have to integrate these constituents into these new conceptual structures and, last but not least, we have to be able to place these conceptual structures into larger and meaningful patterns.

Intellectual curiosity can make us look to improve and perfect our ways of dealing with problems, looking for new methods or techniques, and mastering these. The effort to understand new concepts, to look or to listen in another way than one is used to, can be great fun—especially when this process can be shared with others.

Let us not forget that failure is a normal part of the process of learning. The possibility of failure is inherent in all learning, and the further one has progressed in a process of learning, the greater the risk of failure can become. An intellectual curiosity, while taking pleasure in a search for perfection (and being fully aware that perfection never can be accomplished), is at the base of real deep understanding. Because of the fact that perfection never can be reached, failure is a normal and realistic part of this enthusiastic strive for perfection, and as such it could be used to increase and deepen our understanding of why a particular step/path did not lead us to a desired outcome; it could be used to feed our intellectual curiosity.

We certainly need our intellectual curiosity on our road to mastering psychotherapy, and mastering ISTDP, especially, is a very challenging yet demanding job.

That it is such a challenging job is mostly because the method of ISTDP asks moment-to-moment precision from the therapist. This requires a moment-to-moment precision in assessment of the patient's variables, a moment-to-moment precision in deciding for an intervention, a moment-to-moment decision in assessing the effects of that intervention, and so on.

Therapists are mostly trained to listen to the contents of their patients' problems. To become a competent ISTDP therapist, we also have to learn to use our eyes: which anxiety manifestations do we detect? At what moment do we observe this change? When do we see a decrease of anxiety manifestations, when an increase? Which non-verbal defences do we notice, at what moment? When do we see the manifestations of a mobilized feeling? We have to learn to use our ears. Oh, the pitch of a patient's voice changes. Is that a sign of anxiety or of anxiety and helplessness? Between a subtle smile or a frowning of eyebrows and the outright verbal statement of love or anger or any other feeling lies a large range of cues that shape and control our reactions.

This book evolved from the First International Meeting of the Experiential Dynamic Psychotherapy Association which was held from 10 to 12 May 2001 in Milan, Italy, and the subsequent symposia, workshops, trainings, and supervisions on ISTDP which Josette ten Have-de Labije and Robert J. Neborsky did together. This book also evolved from the various contacts the authors had with colleagues of other theoretical orientations.

From our non-ISTDP colleagues, we came to learn that theory and method of ISTDP had been sometimes misconceived because of prejudice/bias: "ISTDP is a harsh kind of psychotherapy, where the therapist has to crack the resistance of the patient. ISTDP is only suited for patients with massive character and superego pathology. The aim of ISTDP is to go for a breakthrough of sadistic rage. ISTDP is only about experiencing of emotions."

From our ISTDP colleagues and student/supervisees, we came to learn that many concepts of psychodynamic psychotherapy and of Davanloo's ISTDP had remained very abstract and therefore had been the basis for their discouragement in achieving mastery of theory and technique. For example, although students often seemed to use an apt psychodynamic vocabulary or could often give a correct theoretical definition of concepts like transference, resistance, defences, superego, ego-adaptive capacity, conscious and unconscious working alliance, they did not understand their exact meaning, significance, and function. One of the consequences is that the many faces of these concepts are not recognized at all, are misperceived, or are wrongly assessed in the therapeutic practice of ISTDP, leading to mistaken interventions or faulty application of an intervention. We also witnessed that often our supervisees were so preoccupied with the results to be achieved that they missed the purpose of the moment-to-moment assessment of their patient's response to that particular therapist's intervention, and therewith missed the purpose of the moment-to-moment assessment of the status quo of the conscious/unconscious working alliance with the patient. And of course, without an optimal conscious/unconscious working alliance being established, therapy will only lead to failure.

Establishing an unconscious and conscious working alliance with the patient and keeping this working alliance optimal—session after session, moment to moment—is at the basis of a successful ISTDP. As it is the therapist who has to establish such a working alliance with his patient, it is essential that the therapist is at each moment able to assess which patient variable(s) obstruct such an establishment, and which patient variable(s) can be seen as factors in favour of such an establishment. From moment to moment, the status quo of this unconscious/conscious working alliance determines the focus and task of the therapist and the desired focus and task of the patient. From session to session, from therapy phase to therapy phase, it is this moment-to-moment assessment that characterizes the charm and challenge of doing ISTDP. From session to session, from therapy phase to therapy phase, it is this moment-to-moment assessment that determines the moment-to-moment decisions, which intervention should be selected and applied, with what timing, duration, and "dosage".

These moment-to-moment assessments and decisions are at the base of the quantity and quality of the patient's and therapist's successes.

Like so many other psychotherapists, the authors, as well as their students, are used to audiovisually recording their sessions (with their patients' consent). First of all, it is done to safeguard the optimal quality of our working alliance with the patient. It provides us with a second chance to assess the dynamic processes that are put into operation by the patient and to assess at each moment which of the patient's variables was selected by the therapist as targets for his interventions. Was it the right target? Why? Did the therapist select the right intervention? Was the timing of the intervention OK? The duration—the "dosage"? Did the intervention result in a desired response of the patient?

Audiovisual recording also gives the therapist the opportunity to assess why the session did not work out as was hoped for. Was it because the therapist had theoretical/technical problems? Or, was it because of personal problems that, for example, the therapist failed to recognize his patient's specific defence? Perhaps it was because of the syntonicity of the therapist's own defences; or, perhaps because of other countertransference problems?

Peer supervisions and student supervisions become more objective and fruitful when we can make use of the audiovisually recorded sessions with our patients.

It is an empirical reality that the very areas where supervisees need the most help are often those particular areas, of which they are unaware, resulting in the supervisees being unable to articulate the relevant information about the therapy process, and problem in establishing/maintaining the working alliance, to their supervisors.

Last but not least, these audiovisually recorded sessions put us in a better position to conduct each psychotherapy as a N = 1 study and, therefore, will hopefully provide a point of departure for process and outcome research of ISTDP.

Some of the transcripts you will find in this book are taken from our sessions with our patients. We are grateful to our patients for having given us their involvement, their partnership, their courage. For having shared their problems, their doubts, anxieties, tears, anger, unhappiness, happiness, failure, success, laughter. We are also grateful for their having given us the possibility to learn, to be humble, and to become mature.

We are grateful to our students/supervisees for taking a vulnerable position, for letting us not forget that we made similar mistakes when we began. For keeping us awake and alert, for their companionship and loyalty, for their tolerance in keeping up with us. Ultimately, we are grateful for them teaching us to become better therapists and supervisors.

We thought it could be of help to end each chapter of this book with a "Steps in the Chapter"section. You could interpret each step as a title for "giving words" to your own summary. We hope such a summary feeds your curiosity to read the next chapter, and if it does, then that would be a desired outcome—at least to us!

We hope that this book will be of some help in correctly unmasking the patient's superego pathology, to assess the quality and degree of the patient's (and your) observing capacity, to help the patient (and you) to increase the acuity of his (your) observing ego, and to acquire an attentive ego.

We hope that this book will help you to make use of the conscious working alliance with the patient to establish and increase the unconscious part of the working alliance. We hope the book will help colleagues to understand that and when the patient's ego-adaptive capacity needs to be strengthened on the way to the patient's unconscious. We hope it will be of help in conquering the patient's (and the therapist's?) sadistic superego in order to go for uncovering and understanding feelings, impulses, longings, values, opinions, with love, precision, and scientific honesty. We hope it will be of help to the colleagues repeating this process over and over again.

Dear colleague, we hope that this book will become your friend, we hope this book will be of help to you to stay motivated to achieve mastery and to allow for imperfection!

Josette ten Have-de Labije, PsyD, The Netherlands
Robert J. Neborsky, MD, USA

CHAPTER ONE

Davanloo's ISTDP, psychoneurosis, and the importance of attachment trauma

In the early 1960s, Davanloo decided to break away from the traditional psychoanalytic approach. In 1980, in his chapter, "A Method of Short-Term Dynamic Psychotherapy", Davanloo briefly presented his method of ISTDP which was based on three systematic studies, involving psychotherapy with respectively 130, 24, and 18 clients with psychoneurotic problems.

His work, which from the start was all audiovisually recorded, was received with enthusiasm as well as with scepticism and criticism.

Now, more than thirty years later, we have many clinical studies and outcome research confirming the efficacy of this method.

Davanloo's modification of analytic theory

Davanloo (1990) describes that Freud believed that the superego establishes itself relatively late in developmental history and comes into operation after the resolution of the Oedipus complex. Evidence from his work with patients and from his clinical case studies has led Davanloo to modify analytic theory in emphasizing that it is already in the early months of life that the superego may play an active role in the causation and maintenance of neurosis. Neurotic disturbances arise as a result of a variety of possible traumatic experiences, involving damage to or disruption of the affectionate bond between the child and his caretakers. The child unconsciously reacts to this damage/disruption with a sadistic, murderous rage. It is this sadistic, murderous rage and the consequent loss (of the beloved murdered person(s)) which leads to guilt and grief as well as to punitive, sadistic reactions of the superego towards the child's ego. The traumatic experience(s), murderous rage and its result(s), guilt and grief, are repressed into the unconscious. Various symptom patterns and character pathology develop as the ego of

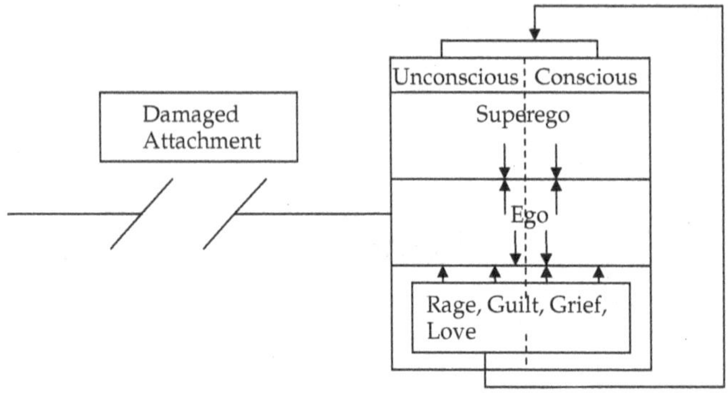

Figure 1. Davanloo's view on the development of neurosis.

the developing child attempts to keep functioning under the mandate of the punitive/sadistic superego in such a way that it will not be overwhelmed by the impulses and feelings themselves, by anxiety, nor by the defences. The earlier, the more intense, and the more frequent the traumatic experiences, the more sadistic the impulses, and the more the ego will be trapped between the sadism of the id and the sadism of the superego, and the more the ego will become paralysed in managing the resistance of repression and the resistance under the mandate of the superego. Davanloo's view on the development of neurosis is depicted in Figure 1.

The attachment bond and our mental health

Although Davanloo explicitly mentions the importance of the nature and quality of the attachment bond between child and caretaker in impacting the nature and quality of our mental health, he does not elaborate on this relationship.

Thanks to Ainsworth (1978), Bowlby (1969, 1980, 1988), and many other great minds of scientists and colleagues, we all know that the emotional bond, or attachment, formed between a (prenatal/postnatal) infant and its caretaker(s), is of considerable influence on the structure and functioning of the developing infant's brain and the individual's functioning in relationship with himself and others.

In the literature, four patterns of attachment are often distinguished: secure attachment, insecure-avoidant attachment, insecure-resistant/ambivalent attachment, and disorganized attachment (see, e.g., Hesse, Main, Abrams & Rifkin, 2003).

A secure and stable attachment lays the base for the developmental tasks of differentiation, separation, individuation, and the internal structure of object constancy from which our sense of self emerges. A secure and stable attachment will thus positively impact brain structure and functioning, thereby setting the basic requirements for the individual:

1. to understand our own and other people's longings, feelings, norms, values, opinions, and behaviour with love and care,
2. to explore the outer world in a constructive way,
3. to engage in meaningful interpersonal relationships, and
4. to deal constructively with painful/harmful events of different interpersonal involvement.

Although there is a basic lifelong need for secure attachments, it may be clear that these attachment bonds will undergo changes in object, nature, quality, and intensity over the course of their development. Also, attachment bonds may develop with others such as siblings, extended family, teachers, friends, colleagues, lovers/partners, and pets.

An insecure, unstable, or disorganized attachment, whether caused by physical/emotional abuse, neglect, or emotional unavailability on the part of the caretaker will negatively impact brain structure and functioning, setting the basic requirements for the individual's developmental and neurotic disorders (of course, the reverse is also true: neurological dysregulation, for example caused by birth, can also interfere with an attachment bond). The relationship between a) the features of a particular attachment bond, b) the particular phase of the individual's development, and c) a later capacity of the individual to constructively regulate emotions, adapt to new situations, and learn is amongst other things due to the fact that the early social environment/caretakers has/have a direct impact on several neurobiological structures mediating the regulation of anxiety and emotions. For example, the first two years of life are critical for the growth of subcortical limbic areas and, because of the fact that the different structures of the limbic system are involved in mediating anxiety and emotions for the rest of the individual's life, early harmful attachment events during such a critical period may have long-lasting effects.

The symptoms of untreated (attachment) trauma worsen over time and become more complicated as time passes, and it becomes more difficult to link present behaviours to the original (attachment) trauma. Feelings and behaviours linked to past traumatic (attachment) experiences are reinforced by new traumatic (attachment) experiences, and symptoms and destructive coping behaviours become more severe. Over time, acting out, repetition compulsions, and episodes of dissociation can become severely debilitating.

As mentioned above, it is in the interaction with our caretakers that we learn how to look at ourselves, to look at other people, to understand our own longings, feelings, behaviours, and those of others.

This implies that

1. the specific features of the harmful/traumatizing attachment bond,
2. the particular developmental phases experienced, and
3. the subsequent specific neural dysregulation and memories of the several harmful interactions with each of the particular caretakers will become the basis for the specific (harmful) ways the adult person will have with respect to
   a. expectations of himself and of the outer world,
   b. understanding one's own and others' longings, feelings, norms, values, behaviours, and
   c. interaction patterns in intimate and social relationships.

The neurodevelopmental impact of violence in childhood

According to Perry (2001) and Schore (2003), a growing body of evidence suggests that exposure to violence or trauma alters the developing brain by altering normal neurodevelopmental processes. Bruce D. Perry's clinical research (2001) has pointed out that trauma influences the pattern, intensity, and nature of sensory perceptual and affective experiences of events during childhood. The human brain develops and, once developed, changes in a "use-dependent" fashion. Neural systems that are activated in a repetitive fashion can change in permanent ways, altering synaptic number and micro-architecture, dendritic density, and the expression of a host of important structural and functional cellular constituents such as enzymes or neurotransmitter receptors. The more any neural system is activated, the more it will modify and "build" in the functional capacities associated with that activation. The more threat-related neural systems are activated during development, the more they will become "built in".

Thus,

- exposure to violence activates a set of threat responses in the child's developing brain,
- in turn, excess activation of the neural systems involved in the threat responses can alter the developing brain,
- these alterations may manifest as functional changes in emotional, behavioural, and cognitive functioning.

The degree and nature of a specific response to threat will vary from individual to individual for any single event and across events for any given individual.

In animals and in humans, two primary but interactive response patterns have been described: hyper-arousal (fight or flight responses) and dissociative response patterns. Dissociation is a broad descriptive term that includes a variety of mental mechanisms involved in disengaging from the external world and attending to stimuli in the internal world. This can involve distraction, avoidance, numbing, daydreaming, fugue, fantasy, derealization, depersonalization, and, in the extreme, fainting or catatonia. (See also Chapter Three on emotion regulation and Chapter Four on anxiety.)

If a child dissociates in response to a severe trauma and stays in that dissociative state for a sufficient period of time, it will alter the homeostasis of the systems mediating the dissociative response (i.e., opioid, dopaminergic, HPA axis). A sensitized neurobiology of dissociation will result and the child may develop prominent dissociative-related symptoms (e.g., withdrawal, somatic complaints, dissociation, anxiety, helplessness, dependence) and related disorders (e.g., dissociative disorders, somatoform disorder, anxiety disorders, major depression). If the child exposed to violence uses a predominately hyper-arousal response, the altered homeostasis will be in different neurochemical systems (i.e., adrenergic, noradrenergic, HPA axis). This child will be vulnerable to developing persisting hyper-arousal-related symptoms and related disorders (e.g., PTSD, ADHD, conduct disorder) (Perry, 2001).

Early trauma of course is not only synonymous with physical violence. What about emotional neglect or other kinds of emotional violence? The trauma of neglect is often cumulative and when an infant is experiencing chronic physical and/or emotional neglect (and we do see this neglect often in combination with physical abuse, this will not only result in impaired psychological functioning but also—as is the case with physical abuse—in changes in brain function (Schore, 2003).

We as humans can be tolerant and can love. But we can also humiliate, neglect, ignore, hate, destroy, and kill. There is violence across history, across cultures. Thanks to advances in technology our world has become small and we all have experienced or witnessed (e.g., via papers, broadcast, television) the horrors of violence and despite the wish of many amongst us, we have never been able to say a final goodbye to the violence that surrounds us and the violence of which we are a part.

Sadly enough the reality of our history, as well as the reality of this present time teaches us that we don't need the violence of wars, natural disasters and so on to be confronted with traumatizing events on a daily basis.

Nevertheless, many people, including many therapists may underestimate the heterogeneity and complexity of violence, may underestimate the prevalence of physical and/or emotional violence in the home. Emotional violence may take the form of e.g., humiliation, devaluation, intimidation, neglect, ignoring, threat of abandonment or physical assault, blackmail etc. Taking care that a child is properly fed, clothed and is going to school doesn't make one into a parent! Nor are schools providers of structure and safety from emotional/physical violence, which is exerted at school or at the homes of their students.

There is violence which is not recognized as violence, there is trauma which is not recognized as trauma nor recognized as violence and trauma by other family members. It is also not recognized as violence and trauma by neighbours, schools, therapists, health organizations, governments, the United Nations (see chart below). We all know that under the pressure of unresolved trauma we can "freeze" into an impaired ability to regulate anxiety, to regulate emotions, an impaired ability to develop and maintain healthy relationships, and even worse to engage in the same abusive behaviour towards others of which, we ourselves once were victim.

We therefore think it important to focus here on some factors of violence from which to examine the impact it has on our mental health.

Classification of potentially traumatic events

The concept of psycho trauma refers to an individual's psychologically and physiologically damaged condition as a result of having experienced extremely threatening and harmful events.

In the literature, traumatic events are often classified as degrees on a continuum: big-T trauma, little-t trauma, and cumulative trauma (also called chronic unremitting stress).

Big-T traumatic events are generally considered discrete, identifiable events such as rape, severe childhood abuse, catastrophic illness or injury, unexpected loss of a friend, witnessing of violence, war. Little-t trauma and cumulative traumatic events are considered continual or recurring situations like continuous neglect or racism.

We ourselves think this terminology confusing because it suggests that big-T trauma would generally exert more debilitating physical and psychological effects than little-t and/or cumulative trauma.

All potentially traumatic events that are mentioned in the literature reflect some kind of violence. This violence can be directed towards victims in a random way, in a systematic way, or even in an institutionalized way. Here, we give you only one or two examples. We are sure you can think of far more examples.

- *Violence directed towards victims in a random way*
  In these cases, the victim was there at the wrong time and place. The victim could have been anyone who happened to be at that time and place. For example, a woman walks home. It is after sunset, she passes a park. She is attacked, dragged into the bushes, and raped.
- *Violence directed towards victims in a systematic way*
  What about marital rape? Or a child witnessing the assault of his/her mother by father? Or what about systematic humiliation or degradation by one or both of the parents, or by other students or teachers at school?
- *Violence directed towards victims in an institutionalized way*
  The Holocaust was exerted on Jewish people, gypsies, and homosexuals by the National Socialists Genocide was recently committed in Rwanda and Darfur by one group against another—sometimes racial, other times religion as an excuse to exterminate Catholics, Protestants, Jews, Hindus, or Muslims.

Research and clinical findings from working with traumatized patients indicate that the impact a psycho-trauma has on the life of the individual is not only determined by the nature and degree of interpersonal involvement with the traumatized individual, the age of the traumatized individual, and the way the traumatized individual is able to deal with the traumatic event and its effects; it is also determined by the presence of an emotional support network and the society's acknowledgement of the trauma.

Nowadays, a train accident, an aeroplane crash, a tsunami, for example, are immediately acknowledged by society as traumatic events.

Immediately following a disaster, religious and social support, mental and physical health care (and sometimes also economic support) is organized for the victim-survivors. Of course, this is not only to help the victim-survivors to deal as constructively as possible with the effects of trauma, but also to prevent or reduce economic damage in the long run. Such support prevents longer hospitalization of victims when they would not immediately have been taken care of, prevents loss of jobs, and so on.

But what about those children, who have a chronically ill mother … or a depressed mother … or a mother regularly suffering from severe migraine attacks? Their father has to earn money, so he leaves the house early in the morning to return in the evening. "Please take care of mommy, you are doing such a great job, you are daddy's darling and please do not forget to buy bread and groceries. Here is the money." Often, neighbours, aunts, and uncles join the child's father in praising the child, therewith denying the fact that the child is being parentified, denying the violence of emotional neglect, and denying that the child is not being helped to take his/her own longings, feelings, needs seriously, not being helped to regulate impulse, feelings, anxiety in a constructive way.

And what about those children, who had the courage to tell mother, aunt, uncle that their father sexually abuses them and subsequently are punished and obliged to apologize to their father because of telling lies?

What about those children, who as a consequence of chronic neglect, withdraw into their rooms and are praised for being so self-supporting and never causing any problem to the parents? These are only some examples of violence that is not recognized as violence. Not recognized as such by family members, neighbours, teachers. Not recognized as such by mental health care workers.

Events that may be considered as potentially traumatic events range from a single incident to repetitive or to enduring events. All these potentially traumatic events, whether of a single, repetitive, or enduring nature, include a degree of interpersonal involvement and interaction with the potentially traumatized individual. This interpersonal involvement may range from events where there is practically no personal relationship with the prospective traumatized individual (e.g., the victim of a natural disaster) to intimate interpersonal relationships (e.g., witnessing a loved one being a victim of a natural disaster, witnessing a sibling being a victim of incest, or being oneself the victim of prolonged incest or of emotional neglect).

Table 1 represents possible traumatic experiences.

Table 1. Traumatic experiences: relation between aggressor and victim can range from impersonal to intimate.

Single event	Repetitive events	Enduring events
Natural disaster	Natural disaster	Natural disaster
Serious accident	Serious accidents	Serious accidents
Serious sports injury	Serious sports injuries	Serious sports injuries
		Life-threatening disease (e.g., cancer) and treatment
	War	War
	Concentration camp	Concentration camp
	Refugee	Refugee
	Refugee camp	Refugee camp
Human trafficking	Human trafficking	Human trafficking
Hostage		Hostage
Kidnapping		Kidnapping
	Discrimination	Discrimination
	Physical/emotional assault at school	Physical/emotional assault at school
Physical/sadistic assault including murder, rape, incest, molestation, other domestic abuse	Physical/sadistic assaults including murder, rape, incest, molestation, other domestic abuse	Physical/sadistic assaults including murder, rape, incest, molestation, other domestic abuse
Emotional/physical neglect/abuse	Emotional/physical neglect/abuse	Emotional/physical neglect/abuse
Prenatal experiences	Prenatal experiences	Prenatal experiences

The spectrum of psychoneurotic disorders and the spectrum of patients with fragile character structure

Based on clinical research data, Davanloo (1995) has introduced a spectrum of five groups of patients with psychoneurotic disorders and a spectrum of three groups of patients with fragile character structure for which the indication could be ISTDP.

Ego fragility, ego-adaptive capacity, superego pathology

At the extreme left are patients with high ego-adaptive capacity and absence of superego pathology, at the extreme right patients with low ego-adaptive capacity and high superego pathology.

As in trial therapy, it is the therapist's first task to assign the patient to his correct position on the spectrum of psychoneurotic disorders, one could also say that the first task is to assess patient's level of ego-adaptive capacity and superego pathology. It is specifically on the basis of the quality and degree of ego-adaptive capacity (including the degree and nature of resistance) that the implementation of the central dynamic sequence (CDS) is custom-made.

Ego-adaptive capacity could be defined as the extent to which the ego mediates constructively between the external (the subjectively interpreted and/or objective demands of various persons in different situations) and internal demands (the instinctual demands of the id and the moral, punitive ones of the superego).

As the processes of the inner interactions of id, ego, and superego cannot be observed directly, Malan (1979) in following Menninger's triangle of insight (1958), operationalized the experience of the patient's intrapsychic conflict within the interpersonal context by means of the linking the two concepts: that is, the linking of the triangle of conflict and the triangle of persons (see also Chapter Seven on the working alliance).

In Davanloo's ISTDP, the two triangles constitute a crucial part of his techniques. Among other things, they serve as a diagnostic tool, and as such they provide means for assessing the quality and degree of ego-adaptive capacity.

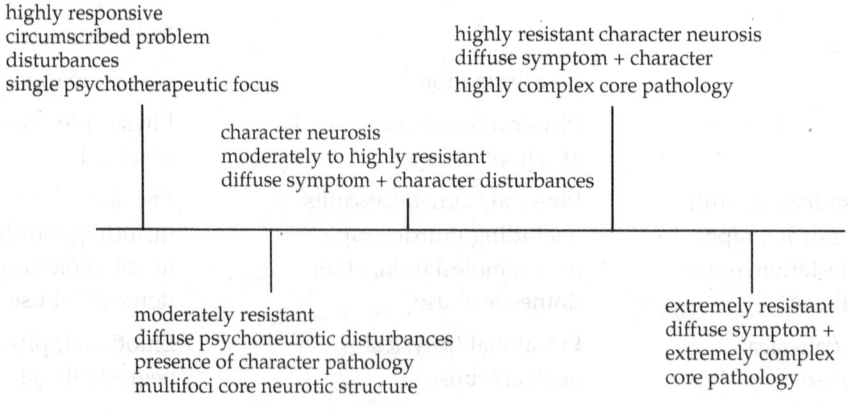

Figure 2. The spectrum of psychoneurotic disorders.

Next to the spectrum of psychoneurotic disorders, Davanloo distinguishes a spectrum of patients with a fragile structure.

Davanloo considers three major groups as located on this spectrum:

- patients with mild degree of fragility,
- patients with moderate degree of fragility,
- patients with a severe degree of fragility.

What precisely is considered as mild or moderate degree of fragility is not defined by Davanloo (at least not in his writings). Patients with severe fragility (according to Davanloo) cannot withstand the impact of their unconscious during the initial interview. These patients do not have the capacity to experience and tolerate anxiety and painful feelings, and they have a life-long access to a spectrum of primitive defences such as temper tantrums, explosive discharge of affect, poor impulse control, projection, projective identification, and double projective identification. These patients become easily flooded with a high degree of anxiety and a major disruption of their cognitive and perceptual functions with hallucinatory experiences. They easily become light-headed, and experience the phenomena of drifting, drowsiness, and dissociation (Davanloo, 2000).

The concepts of ego strength and ego fragility are static concepts. They give a state description of the ego's supporting power in relation to its burden. In fact, with this state description only a value (mild, moderate, severe) of the ego's supporting power is specified at some given point in time. Such a description, which covers the momentary state of the ego's supporting power, is important, but it doesn't tell us anything about the operations of the ego in order to bear its burden or to collapse under the burden. State descriptions give us still pictures, a photograph instead of a motion picture. For the latter, a process description is needed. As the (ISTDP) therapist is motivated to discover what may be discovered/uncovered, he will be interested to investigate the interconnections among his patient's psychological status/structure, the therapist's interventions, and the in-session consequences of these interventions. The therapist (and the patient) will be interested to achieve progressively more insight into the operations of the ego to 1) withstand the forces of the id, the superego, and 2) the external demands as they are perceived by the ego, and 3) to mediate between these in a constructive way. The dynamic concept of ego-adaptive capacity permits us to come to a process description. If the procedural steps, such as devised by Davanloo, are taken, this concept permits us to take base-line measurements as well as to specify the causal relationships between our interventions and the subsequent changes in the quality and degree of patient's ego-adaptive capacity. (For a more elaborate view on assessment and restructuring of ego-adaptive capacity, see Chapters Five and Eight.)

As pointed out above, one may notice that within Davanloo's spectrum of psychoneurotic disorders, the five groups of patients are placed along a five-point scale of level of ego-adaptive capacity and superego pathology. The level of superego pathology has an inverse relationship with the level of ego-adaptive capacity. The more a patient is located on the right of this spectrum, the higher his superego pathology, the lower his ego-adaptive capacity.

We therefore think Davanloo's spectrum of patients with fragile character structure superfluous as it is already incorporated in his spectrum of psychoneurotic disorders. In this book, we will only make use of the spectrum of psychoneurotic disorders.

ISTDP as therapy indication and as a contra-indication

ISTDP can be indicated for all patients who are located on the spectrum of psychoneurotic disorders.

ISTDP is contra-indicated for patients with

- psychosis,
- severe depressive episode (with or without psychotic symptoms),
- severe physical dependency on alcohol and/or drugs,
- life-threatening psychosomatic diseases,
- incapacity to live without a social/medical support system,
- severe psychopathic character traits.

Length of the therapy

ISTDP is considered to be of "short length". For patients located on the extreme left of the spectrum of structural neurosis, one or two sessions would be enough—at least according to the data Davanloo brings forward in his teachings. The further patients are located on the right of the spectrum, the more sessions are needed. In the literature, length of ISTDP therapy with patients located on the right half of the spectrum and the relation with the cost-benefits are regularly mentioned. The number of sessions mentioned ranges from six to forty. It is, however, not always clear whether the ISTDP with all of these patients resulted in 1) an increase of their complex transference feelings, 2) an unlocking of their unconscious, 3) a breakthrough of their complex transference feelings, 4) a conscious experiencing of impulse, guilt, grief, damaged love, unlocking of past traumas, and working through.

Allan A. Abbass (2002) is more precise in investigating and describing the outcomes of different patient categories, the length of their therapies with him (fourteen to forty sessions), the cost-effectiveness and relation with the number of unlockings: the number of major breakthroughs of complex transference feelings, partial breakthroughs, and no breakthroughs at all.

Of course, the length of a therapy is also determined by the therapy goal of the patient and therapist. In our own experience, most of our patients are located on the right half of the right side of the spectrum. All of these patients have personality disorders (Axis I, II of the DSM-IV). With these patients, it takes the authors about forty to fifty sessions (of ninety minutes) to resolve the patients' Axis II problems.

Many of our supervisees doubt their capacity as ISTDP therapists and the quality of their therapy because "I did not manage to reach the patient's unconscious in the initial interview, the therapy lasts already fifteen sessions and the patient only had his first major/partial breakthrough in the fourteenthth session". At this point, we encourage our supervisees to set aside their concerns with yes or no, having attained breakthroughs or with the number of sessions. We encourage our students and colleagues to focus instead on the process of establishing (and maintaining) a conscious/unconscious working alliance with the patient. The quality of this working alliance is of great influence on the quality of the ISTDP process and the quality of the therapy results.

Steps in the chapter

- Davanloo's modification of analytic theory
- The attachment bond and our mental health
  - *secure, insecure-avoidant, insecure-ambivalent, disorganized attachment*
  - *insecure, disorganized attachments negatively impact brain structures and functioning, setting the base for the individual's neurotic disorders*
- Neural systems regulating the neurobiological response to violence
- Trauma that is not recognized as trauma
- Classification of traumatic experiences
  - *single, repetitive, recurrent violence*
  - *random, systematic, institutionalized violence*
- Variables that influence the impact of trauma on emotional health
  - *specific features of (attachment) trauma*
  - *during which developmental phase(s)*
  - *specific neural dysregulation*
  - *acknowledgement of the trauma*
  - *social support system*
- Spectrum of psychoneurotic disorders: five clusters of patients
- The inverse relation between superego pathology and ego-adaptive capacity
- Contra-indications
- Length of the therapy

CHAPTER TWO

The neurobiological regulation of emotion and anxiety

Any of our functions, be it perception, or thinking, feeling, behaviour, involves the integration of an unknown number of neurons in specific brain areas and in the nervous structures outside our brain.

Therefore, we think it will be helpful to the ISTDP therapist to have at least some basic knowledge of the process of neural transmission and of specific brain regions and neuronal network systems that are thought to be involved in the regulation of our feelings and anxiety. Regarding the neuro-anatomy, we base ourselves mainly on Carpenter (1972) and on Netter's *Anatomy of the Nervous System* (CIBA, 1994).

The limbic system

The structures of the limbic system are largely interconnected with the rest of the brain, and they are believed to play an important part in the regulation of our feelings and anxiety.

First, however, we want to give you a warning, as in the literature the definitions of structures belonging to the limbic system may vary.

The term "limbic system" is used to include 1) cortical and 2) subcortical parts of the brain:

1. The limbic lobe, a region of the cortex on the medial surface of the cerebral hemispheres, consists of: the subcallosal, cingulated, and parahippocampal gyri, the hippocampal formation and dentate gyrus. (Some authors include the cortex of the posterior orbital surface of the frontal lobe, the anterior insular region, and the temporal polar region because of cytoarchitectural and functional similarities.)
2. The following subcortical nuclei: the amygdaloid complex, the septal nuclei, hypothalamus, parts of the thalamus (anterior thalamic nuclei), parts of the basal ganglia.

The amygdaloid complex

The amygdaloid complex is divided into a corticomedial nuclear group and a basolateral nuclear group. The central nucleus is sometimes regarded as a separate subdivision, but is frequently included as part of the corticomedial nuclear group. The central nucleus of the amygdala receives input from the basolateral group of amygdaloid nuclei and activates a number of brainstem and hypothalamic effector sites, resulting in the anxiety response.

The septal nuclei

The septal area, a nuclear region, is located in the anterior medial depths of the forebrain. The septal area receives fibres from the hippocampus and the amygdaloid complex, and connects to the thalamus, hypothalamus, hippocampus, and brainstem.

The hypothalamus

The hypothalamus, together with the pituitary gland, constantly adjusts the body to keep it optimally adapted to the environment. The hypothalamus is the chief subcortical centre for the regulation of both sympathetic and parasympathetic activities. These dual activities are integrated into coordinated responses which maintain adequate internal control of the body. Control of *parasympathetic* activities is related to *the anterior and medial hypothalamic regions and the ventricular portion of the tuber cinereum.* Stimulation of this region results in increased vagal and sacral autonomic responses, characterized by reduced heart rate, peripheral vasodilatation, and increased tonus and motility of the alimentary and vesical walls *The lateral and posterior hypothalamic regions are concerned with the control of sympathetic responses.* Especially the posterior portion from which most of the descending fibres arise, activate the thoracolumbar ouflow. This results in increased metabolic and somatic activities characteristic of states of emotional stress, combat or flight. These responses are expressed by dilatation of the pupil, piloerection, acceleration of the heart rate, elevation of blood pressure, increase in the rate and amplitude of respiration, inhibition of the gut and bladder (Carpenter, 1972).

The hypothalamus is located just below the thalamus on both sides of the third ventricle and just above the pituitary gland. It stands in functional relation with both the forebrain and the brainstem.

The hypothalamus receives inputs:

- from the vagus nerve, it gets information about blood pressure and the stomach,
- from the reticular formation in the brainstem, it gets information about skin temperature,
- from the optic nerve, it gets information about light and darkness,
- from neurons lining the ventricles, it gets information about the contents of the cerebrospinal fluid, including toxins that lead to vomiting,
- from the other parts of the limbic system and the olfactory nerves, it gets information that helps regulate eating and sexuality,
- from amygdala to the ventromedial hypothalamic nucleus.

The hypothalamus has direct connections with the orbital portions of the frontal lobes. Indirect connections:

- with the prefrontal areas through the medial thalamic nuclei,
- with the gyrus cinguli through the anterior thalamic nuclei,
- with rhinencephalic structures via fornix and stria terminalis.

The hypothalamo-pituitary axis

The hypothalamus controls pituitary secretion via two separate pathways:

1. The hypothalamus controls anterior pituitary secretion by the selective secretion of humoral "releasing factors" into the portal circulation (blood supply of the pituitary gland). There are at least five releasing factors:
    corticotropin-releasing factor (CRF) (controls the activity of the adrenal glands)
    thyrotropin-releasing-factor (TRF) (controls the activity of the thyroid gland)
    somatotropin-releasing factor (SRF) (controls tissue growth)
    follicle-stimulating hormone releasing factor (FSHRF) (controls activities of ovaries and testes)
    luteinizing hormone-releasing factor (LRF) (controls the secretion of luteinizing hormone)
    prolactin-inhibiting factor (PIF) (holds the secretion of prolactin in check)
2. There is a neuronal pathway from the supraoptic and peraventricular nuclei to the posterior part of the pituitary. The hormones oxytocin and vasopressin, manufactured in the cell bodies of the supraoptic and peraventricular nuclei of the hypothalamus, pass down to the pituitary, and with appropriate stimulation they are released into the bloodstream. The peripheral endocrine glands (e.g., adrenal glands, gonads) can function as long as they are fed by the pituitary substances of the general blood circulation that control their activity.

The thalamus

The thalamus is the relay for virtually all sensory pathways to the cortex. All sensory impulses, with the sole exception of the olfactory ones, terminate in the grey masses of the thalamus, from which they are projected to specific cortical areas by the thalamocortical radiations. It seems certain that the thalamus is the chief neuronal sensory integrating mechanism, but there is also evidence that certain parts of the thalamus play a dominant role in the maintenance and regulation of the state of consciousness, alertness, and attention through widespread functional influence upon the activity of the cerebral cortex. The thalamus is concerned not only with general and specific types of awareness, but with certain emotional connotations that accompany most sensory experiences (Carpenter, 1972).

Thalamocortical radiations

The cerebral cortex receives its afferents exclusively from the thalamic nuclei. Several of these relay sensory messages. Not all the thalamic nuclei send afferents to the cortex (Netter atlas).

The basal ganglia

The following subcortical nuclei are often regarded to represent the basal ganglia: the caudate nucleus, the putamen, the globus pallidus and the substantia nigra.

Because the caudate nucleus, the putamen and globus pallidus contain a combination of grey and white matter, they have a striped appearance in post-mortem brains. This causes them to be referred to as the corpus striatum. LeDoux (1996) suggests that the prefrontal cortex (and the basal ganglia) are essential for emotional action. It is considered pivotal for planning, decision-making, working memory, and executive functions and also for emotional consciousness and feelings.

Functional imaging studies

Data on the processing of different emotions suggest a common neural network.

Emotional stimuli activate sensory pathways that trigger the hypothalamus to modulate heart rate, blood pressure and respiration. Physiological inputs to the hypothalamus act on the brainstem and the autonomic nervous system. In turn, this information projects to the cerebral cortex from the peripheral organs, whose homeostatic state has been changed, and gives rise to the conscious perception of the particular emotion.

The functional imaging studies of the last years have given a boost to research on cognitive control processes that are involved in the regulation of emotions. However, there remains still much to learn about peripheral and central mechanisms that are involved in the conscious and unconscious regulation of our emotions. Ochsner & Gross (2005) describe functional imaging studies on two types of cognitive control processes, that is, 1) attentional control (e.g., selective inattention to emotional stimuli, ignoring of stimuli, or attentional distraction to limit attention to emotional stimuli), and 2) cognitive change (this concept refers to selecting which meaning will be attached to a situation, for example as with anticipation or as with re-appraisal—(transforming the meaning of a situation so as to alter its emotional impact).

These studies found that these two control strategies of emotion regulation depend upon interactions between prefrontal and cingulate cortical control systems and cortical and subcortical (limbic structures) emotion-generative systems. The prefrontal cortex is divided into a dorsolateral area and an orbitofrontal region. This orbitofrontal region receives input from the amygdaloid nuclei via the dorsolateral thalamus and projects, in turn, to several regions of the limbic system including the cingulate cortex, hippocampus, lateral hypothalamus and amygdala (Wickens, 2005).

Mauss, Bunge & Gross (2007) reviewed the neuroscientific literature on two types of automatic emotion regulation, i.e., "antecedent-focused" (attention that is paid to a situation or appraisal of a situation) and "response-focused" (cognitive engagement or disengagement after an emotional response has been triggered). These studies suggest the involvement of the orbitofrontal, the lateral, and ventromedial prefrontal cortex, the anterior and posterior cingulated cortices, and the basal ganglia that interact with the structures of the limbic system to be involved in the regulation of antecedent-focused processes. The subcallosal cingulate cortex, the dorsal pathway and the cerebellum operating on the subcortical limbic system and brainstem are found to be involved in the regulation of the response-focused processes.

Emotions, including anxiety, are elicited by essential stimuli from the outside world or from inside (internal mental representations, thoughts). The essence of these stimuli is determined via cognitive/perceptive processes: the essential stimuli are analysed and interpreted in the context of earlier experience in order to establish their significance and meaning. It may have become clear that it takes the involvement of the frontal cortex to experience consciously.

The neurobiological regulation of anxiety could be depicted by means of the following simplified steps:

1. We construct our knowledge and understanding of our world with sight, sound, touch, pain, smell, taste and the sensation of body movements. When we perceive a threat, this information is processed via our sensory pathways, the spinal cord, brainstem to the thalamus, the brain's major sensory relay station. From the thalamus, sensory information is transmitted to a) the amygdala and to b) the cortex.
   1a. The thalamus passes in about twelve milliseconds rough sensory information to the amygdala. (This quick and direct thalamic input may mediate short-latency, primitive emotional responses and prepares the amygdala for the reception of the more sophisticated information from the cortex.) The existence of this quick and direct pathway from the sensory thalamus to the amygdala suggests that emotional responses can occur even without the involvement of the higher-level information processing systems of the brain, systems believed to be involved in cognition, thinking, consciousness. These low-level neural mechanisms, including the autonomic, endocrine, skeletomotor, and arousal systems, mediated through the amygdalae, prepare the organism to cope with the situation involving significant change (LeDoux, 1998).
   1b. The thalamus sends the more sophisticated sensory signals to the cortex (this takes about 30 to 40 milliseconds) to analyse and process what is happening exactly.
2. If these cortical regions, and the amygdala (in cooperation with the hippocampus, involved with the regulation of memory), have analysed this information as dangerous, then
3. The amygdala signals the hypothalamus directly and indirectly via the locus coeruleus in the brainstem, and it signals the cortical association areas (this pathway is important for the conscious perception of emotion/anxiety).
4. The locus coeruleus functions as a kind of neural relay station. This group of neurons a) coordinates the short arm of the stress system along multiple nerve pathways and b) it links the CRH-producing brain regions with the autonomic nervous system.
   4a. The short arm: the amygdala signals the hypothalamus, and brainstem regions that regulate autonomic responses to the threat. The hypothalamus integrates the information from cerebral cortex, amygdala, brainstem into a coherent response. And it acts on the autonomic nervous system by modulating feedback information from the viscera.
   4b. The locus coeruleus signals the hypothalamus, which runs the long arm of the stress system (also called the hypothalamus-pituitary-adrenal axis). Corticotropin-Releasing Hormone (CRH), the most important stress hormone, is secreted in the hypothalamus and via the bloodstream (the pituitary-hypophyseal-portal system) it is transmitted to the pituitary, which in turn releases the hormone ACTH (adrenocorticotropic hormone) into the blood. ACTH stimulates the adrenal glands to produce glucocorticoid hormones,

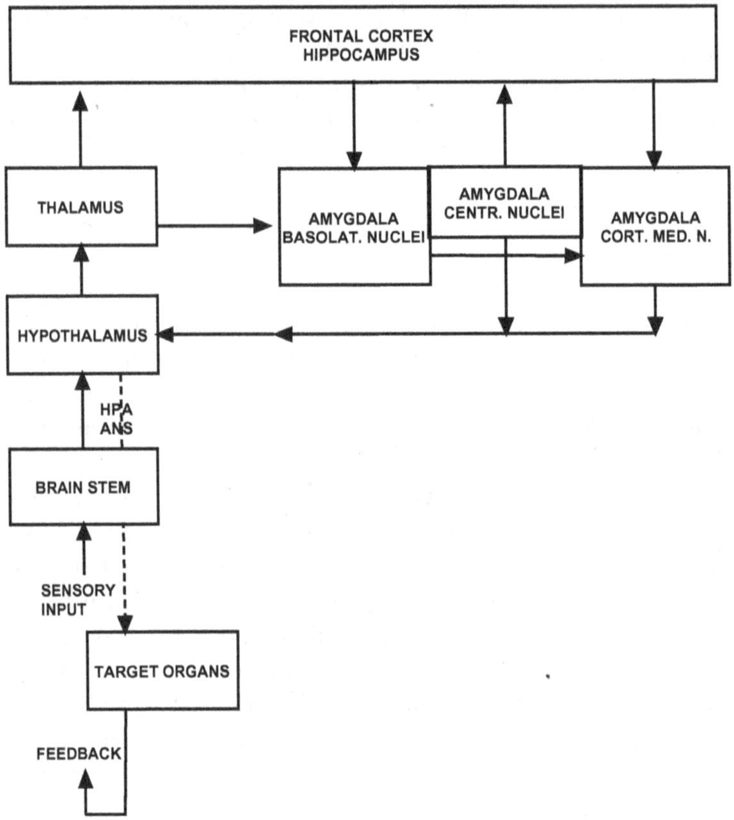

Figure 3. The neurobiological regulation of anxiety.

> which put the body on alert, increase glucose in the blood to provide energy for muscles and nerves. In acute stress, the hypothalamus secretes vasopressin as well, to further activate the adrenals. The system regulates itself down after a threat is over via a negative feedback loop in order for the hypothalamus to suppress the CRH secretion and the pituitary to suppress ACTH.

When (the perception of) a threat ends, the system, involved in the regulation of anxiety must quickly be turned off so that the affected organs can recover.

However, under chronic strain, this anxiety-regulating system will be repeatedly stimulated and will leave many tissues vulnerable to damage. Davanloo frequently warns his trainees to take diarrhoea, dizziness, jelly legs as an alarm to further investigate other signs for low ego-adaptive capacity or ego fragility. Obviously, such a patient has paid his price in his coping with stressful stimuli. His arousal in anticipation of or in response to (prolonged) challenges has resulted in pathological consequences for the functioning of his organs and tissues. It can be surmised that at least the normal balance of sympathetic and parasympathetic systems has broken down and that these two systems are not longer operating within their normal limits (see also ten Have-de Labije, 1999).

Englert (2004) refers to research, indicating that when the hypothalamus-pituitary-adrenal axis is too active (e.g., under chronic strain) and levels of CRH in the brain are simultaneously too high, signals on the vagus nerve are blocked (the vagus nerve is a major thoroughfare of the autonomic nervous system and controls contractions of the stomach and digestive tract and it sends nerve impulses to the heart and motor muscles). Some studies suggest that irritable bowel syndrome is caused by too much CRH.

The principle of interaction and feed-back, operating in neurobiological systems is often underestimated. Although much of the neurobiological regulation of anxiety remains still to be investigated, it may be clear from the above that at any given time, the pattern of manifest autonomic and endocrine activity within an individual is reflecting the momentary balance between functioning and interaction of cortical and subcortical structures, endocrine activity and sympathetic and parasympathetic arousal. The regulation of a person's visceral state and the maintenance of homeostasis is greatly dependent on the afferent feedback system, conveying information regarding the momentary state of the peripheral target organs to the brain areas. In turn, these brain areas interpret the afferent feedback and exert control over their output back to the visceral organs and other peripheral target organs.

From the above, and from Chapters Three and Four, you will understand that:

- Disruption in biofeedbackloops can lead to physical and psychological disorders (and that restoration of biofeedbackloops between the body and the brain and within the brain can help the patient to modify his psychobiological state for the sake of his physical and mental health)
- Defences have the capacity to keep our emotions out of our awareness and that they have the capacity to block the cognitive/perceptual processing of information both at the level of the stimulus (front door: see Chapter Three) and/or at the level of the response (cellar door: see Chapter Three).

In our view, this could specifically mean that defences have the capcity to block the flow of cognitive/perceptual processing between the thalamus and prefrontal cortex (front door) and between the central amygdaloid nuclei and cortex (cellar door) (ten Have-de Labije, workshops).

Undoing a patient's defence that is operating at the front door by taking care, during the therapeutic process, that a patient describes in a precise and concrete way what the other person (in the C, P, or T) in that particular interaction exactly said/not said, did/not did (the evocative stimuli) forces in the first place the cognitive/perceptual flow of information to reach the patient`s cortex. Thereafter the processing of information from 1) cortex to amygdaloid nuclei, 2) from amygdaloid nuclei to hypothalamus, pituitary gland, and brainstem, 3) from pituitary gland, brainstem, to target organs in the body, 4) from target organs to brainstem, thalamus, cortex, etc.

Undoing a patient's defence that is operating at the level of the cellar door by taking care that the patient's cognitive and perceptive system is explicitly directed at the particular physiological manifestations in the body and to label them correctly as anxiety or as anger or as, for example, sadness and to make them explicitly aware of the action tendency forces the processing of information between 1) the body, brainstem to the thalamus, the prefrontal cortex, 2) between the prefrontal cortex and the central amygdaloid nuclei, 3) between the amygdaloid nuclei—the hypothalamus—brainstem—body, etc.

The hypothesis is then that in due time a patient´s anxiety is regulated again in a healthy way (mainly somatomotor and sympathetic manifestations) and that feelings are experienced to the full extent and can be expressed in a constructive way (see also Chapter Four).

Steps in the chapter

- The limbic system (structures and interconnections)
- Hypothalamo-pituitary axis
- Functional imaging studies (cognitive control processes)
- Neurobiological regulation of anxiety
- Disruption in biofeedback loops
- Undoing blockages caused by defences

CHAPTER THREE

Emotion regulation and the role of defences

The road to the patient's unconscious is in the patient and not in the book (not even in this one!), and establishing a conscious and unconscious working alliance is dependent on the therapist's expertise to assess the nature and degree of the patient variables that function as red and green traffic lights on this road. Thus, we first want to elaborate on such patient variables as how healthy versus unhealthy is the regulation of the patient's emotions, and what is the function of the patient's defences in the patient's particular emotional regulation process? All of our patients who come for help have a certain degree of unhealthy regulation of emotions.

The consequences of failures in a healthy regulation of emotions range from personal distress and unhappiness to socially maladaptive and self-destructive patterns of behaviour. The more our patients are located on the right side of Davanloo's spectrum of structural neurosis, the more their emotions and anxiety are regulated in an unhealthy way, the more these patients exert self-destructive patterns of behaviour in their interactions with themselves and with important and unimportant others.

We all know that a great part of all of our ISTDP therapy sessions is focused on helping the patients to overcome their unhealthy, (self-)destructive regulation of emotions, of anxiety, and to change it into a healthy, constructive one. Therefore, it is extremely important that the therapist has a complete understanding of emotion and anxiety regulatory processes and of the specific role/function of defences in the regulation (and generation) of emotions. If not, then the consequence will be that the therapy process will get stuck.

Defences can be put into operation in the realm of the resistance against the experiencing of the impulse and feelings (including anxiety) (REI) and/or in the realm of the resistance against the emotional closeness (REC) with another person in the present or past. If the level at which a defence operates (REI or REC) is unclear to a therapist, the process to unlock in cooperation with the patient his painful past is doomed to fail. Therefore, a sound understanding of a process-oriented approach of emotion regulation is a basic tool for each ISTDP therapist. This understanding is specifically important in the phases of helping the patient 1) to allow the therapist to be of help, 2) to change syntonic defences into dystonic ones, and 3) to quit the defences out of intrinsic motivation, in order for 4) uncovering painful past and associated impulses and feelings in proportion to a patient's anxiety tolerance, and 5) experiencing these impulses and feelings.

This chapter will first focus on the assessment of degree and quality of a patient's healthy regulation of emotion, then the chapter will focus on the role of defences in emotion regulation.

Emotions/feelings—moods, states, affect

Among ISTDP practitioners, the terms "affect", "emotion", and "feeling" are sometimes used interchangeably. In the literature, sometimes "affect" is used to refer to the experiential components of emotion; at other times, it is used to refer to the behavioural component of an emotion or as the superordinate category for valenced states such as emotions, emotion episodes, and mood (Gross, 1998).

The authors suggest not using the concepts of emotion and affect interchangeably as this creates only confusion. Instead, the authors suggest to use the terms emotion and feeling interchangeably and to distinguish emotion/feeling from mood (depression, euphoria) and state (for example, hate). The authors suggest reserving the term "affect" exclusively for the umbrella concept to which the separate categories emotion/feeling, mood, and state are subordinated.

Emotions and emotion regulation

Emotions are elicited by essential stimuli from the outside world or from inside (e.g., internal mental representations, thoughts). The essence of these stimuli is determined via cognitive/perceptive processes. The essential stimuli are analysed and interpreted in the context of earlier experience in order to establish their significance and meaning. The functions emotions serve may vary from providing the individual with information about ongoing interpersonal processes, ongoing intrapsychic processes, to facilitating decision-making and behavioural responses.

Emotion regulation refers to the conscious and unconscious processes by which human beings influence at what time they have which emotion(s) or impulses, with what intensity and duration, and how and when they are experienced and expressed (Gross, 1998). In other words: these conscious and unconscious regulatory processes determine whether and how essential eliciting stimuli are perceived, how they are appraised, and how as a result of that these regulatory processes influence several aspects (and their inter-relations) of our emotions such as:

- timing
- intensity
- duration

- physiological manifestations
- behavioural and expressive manifestations.

It will be clear that these processes, with which we regulate and create our emotions and impulses, can enrich but also restrict our capacity to enjoy life, to engage and enjoy intimacy with ourselves, our loved ones, our friends, our colleagues, our capacity to function in a constructive way, and so on.

Assessment of internal physiological manifestations of an emotion and experiencing an emotion

From the neurobiological regulation of emotion and anxiety (Chapter Two), we understood that only when information from peripheral organs has reached the cortex is the patient able to assess his internal state. For the emotion to be experienced, conscious perception of external demand characteristics and conscious perception of physiological peripheral reactions are important, but the conscious awareness of action tendencies in combination with the feedback of behavioural (somatomotoric) reaction is crucial (Frijda, 1993).

An action tendency is the *state of preparedness* to execute a certain action. A certain action and hence an action tendency is defined by the intended and realized end result. According to Frijda, the concept of action tendency refers to the presence (or absence) of the internal disposition to execute actions and to attain relational changes. So the experiencing of an emotion can be seen as being composed (in part) of proprioceptive feedback of expressions (e.g., I am aware that my arm is stretched forward) in so far as the expression confirms the action tendency (e.g., I want to hit with this arm). In the awareness of the action tendency, the proprioceptive feedback has a confirmative and informative function.

Assessment of degree and quality of emotion regulation

Davanloo obviously has a psychobiologically based orientation to the interacting neural and endocrine system underlying the regulation of feelings, impulses and anxiety. And although he never elaborated upon the underlying complex system of interacting neural and endocrine mechanisms that is ultimately responsible for the observed psychobiological components of feelings, impulses and anxiety, he obviously considers each of them as a total integrated response of cognitive, behavioural and physiological components. This means that when assessing the degree and quality of a patient's healthy regulation and experiencing of his feelings and impulses (or anxiety) a comprehensive approach should be taken. Assessment of the total integrated emotional response should include: assessment of (several aspects of) manifestations of 1) the somatomotor, 2) autonomic and endocrine, 3) cognitive and perceptual patterns, as well as assessment of 4) the extent to which the three subsystems are involved (see also ten Have-de Labije, 1999).

Thus a person, who regulates his emotions (and anxiety) in a healthy way, is able to tell you:

- exactly what the other person in an interaction did/didn't do, said/didn't say that functioned as a trigger for his emotion that was evoked

- the meaning he adhered to these stimuli
- the specific emotion that was evoked
- with which physiological concomitants
- and action tendency
- the precise cognitive contents of the evoked emotion.

See, for instance, the following interaction:

Pt My mother and I telephoned and I told her I had been disappointed that I didn't get the job that I had wanted so eagerly. She said she was sorry for me but her next sentence, and all the sentences thereafter, were about herself: how she had once been bypassed for a job she had wanted, that life hadn't been easy to her, that she often had to deal with her disappointment, that there had been so many persons that had hurt her, etc. (description of essential evoking stimuli). I felt very angry (evoked emotional response).

Th How did you notice your anger physically?

Pt I noticed that I straightened myself in the chair, I felt an upward motion of power in my body, there was a slight increase of my heartbeat, my chest widened, my voice grew louder (physical concomitants of anger). I really wanted to assert myself in my anger (action tendency).

Th And what was your anger precisely about?

Pt Well, I said, Mum, you say that you are sorry for me not getting that job but you don't really want to know how that is to me. You immediately switch to your own experiences and then it is all about you. This makes me really angry. I don't get the impression that you are genuinely interested in me. You don't inquire what I feel or think how I deal with this disappointment. For a long time, I complied when you turned the spotlight immediately on yourself, telling myself that you are lonely, that you deserve all the attention. But I have had it and I don't want to continue like that. I would appreciate it if you would make some effort to listen to me, to be curious of what is going on inside me. I felt very satisfied with myself. (contents of anger)

Of course, such a patient we would never see at the time of an initial interview. But hopefully, most of our patients have this capacity of dealing with their emotions by the time their therapy has come to an end.

When helping a patient to experience a feeling or impulse, we want the patient to experience the full extent of that feeling (in accordance with his momentary state of ego-adaptive capacity). If we would depict duration and intensity of a feeling into a graph, we would get the shape of a skewed curve. The intensity of the feeling grows relatively slowly to a maximum and thereafter drops relatively fast. See Figure 4. This is important to keep in mind because whenever we witness a sudden drop of the patient's feeling, we know that this was due to a defence.

In order for determining the degree to which a patient still has the capacity to regulate his emotions in a healthy way, the therapist should be able to understand an emotion as a total integrated response (see above), and therefore assessment should include (several aspects of) manifestations of 1) the somatomotor, 2) autonomic and endocrine, 3) cognitive and perceptual patterns, as well as assessment of the extent to which the three subsystems are involved (ten Have-de Labije, 1999).

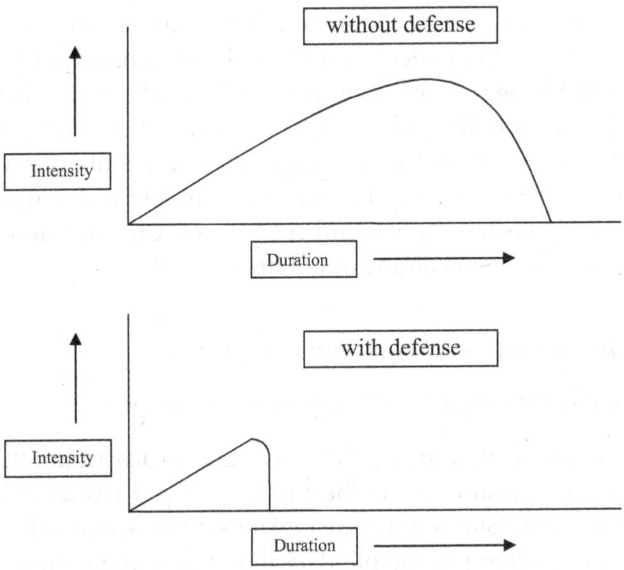

Figure 4. Development of emotion intensity without and with defence.

Assessment of anger and the sadistic impulse

Manifestations of somatomotor patterns

Both anger and the sadistic/murderous impulse have the same pattern of somatomotor (striated muscles) manifestations. Passage of anger and the impulse is described by Davanloo as a distinct pattern of up and down movement of muscles in the pelvic area to abdomen to chest. The breakthrough of anger and of the impulse is characterized by an upward force, resulting in an upright to forward position of the body.

Manifestations of autonomic/endocrine patterns

No sympathetic, parasympathetic, or endocrine patterns are described by Davanloo. However, increase in diastolic blood pressure, heart rate, and cardiac output, dilatation of blood vessels (flushing), dilatation of pupils, and tearing of eyes, focused vision, sweating, suppression of immune response (effects of sympathetic adrenergic stimulation) is regularly described in the literature as well as by our patients.

Manifestations of cognitive/perceptual patterns and action tendency

In order to have direct access to the experience of anger, the patient also has to know what exactly triggered his anger, what the anger is about, and he should not only be aware of the proprioceptive stimuli (the upward force in the body as, for example, in the outstretched arm), but should also be aware of the internal disposition to action tendency (e.g., I would like to underline my words and to set my boundaries). In order to have direct experience of his sadistic/murderous impulse, the patient also has to know what exactly (such as the fact that he had no influence on his aggressor's behaviour) triggered his reactive sadistic/murderous impulse. He should be aware of the proprioceptive stimuli, of the internal disposition to action tendency (I would like to destroy/kill and seek revenge). He should be aware of exactly how he wants to destroy/kill/avenge (I want to hit with this arm and kick with my right leg), and he should be aware of the results he wants to inflict by his sadistic/murderous actions (my father is lying on the floor, there is blood coming out of his head, etc.).

Problems with the assessment of the patient's anger

The patient does not indicate what exactly triggered his anger

Some colleagues fail to assess that their patient is vague in describing the trigger of his anger and they mistakenly put pressure/invite their patient to put words to his anger. The consequence will be that the therapist is joining the patient's defence and colludes with the patient's superego. This kind of "working in the blind" will not help the patient (nor the therapist) to adequately cope with his anger and to express it in a precise and constructive way.

Pt When he devalued me like that (defence of vagueness), I became very angry and I told him so
Th What did you tell him?
Pt That he shouldn't (defence of giving behavioural instructions) behave like that and that it pissed me off (still all very vague)

It would have been better:

Pt When he devalued me like that I became very angry and I told him so
Th Do you realize that you are rather vague in describing what exactly was his wording when devaluing you?
Pt No ... anyway I thought he was devaluing me ... to me that was evident
Th Yes, but you don't do yourself a favour if you keep his words that were so painful to you vague. We are here to understand you with love, care, and precision, and keeping vague what hurts you so much will not help us to understand you in a precise way. It is important you understand me.
Pt I do understand you but the problem is that I don't remember ... I often forget what exactly the other person did or said when we had an argument.
Th So you tell me in fact that there is a part in you that tells you that you and I shouldn't take your eyes, your perception seriously and you have accepted that or am I mistaken? ... etc.

The patient fuses anger with a defence

Some colleagues fail to assess that their patient (con)fuses anger with a defence and as a consequence the patient's ego-adaptive capacity will be insufficiently restructured and the patient will not a) gain access to constructive anger. and b) unlocking of the patient's impulse will become irresponsible.

Pt When he told me that he had better things to do than spending time with me I became very angry
Th How did you notice?
Pt I was so angry that I did not want to see him anymore and I left the room.
Th And what would you have done to him if you would make a mental picture?

It would have been better:

Pt When he told me that he had better things to do than spending time with me I became very angry
Th How did you notice?
Pt I was so angry that I did not want to see him anymore and I left the room
Th That you did not want to see him anymore and left the room is the consequence of your anger. It is important that you understand me. Anger and subsequently leaving the room
Pt Exactly ... that is often the case ... when I am angry I go away
Th But it is important to understand that feeling angry is not the same as going away, leaving the room. Anger is a feeling, and subsequently going away is what you do. How do you feel anger in your body?

Problems with the assessment of the patient's impulse

A purely cognitive account

A mistake we frequently encountered with our supervisees is that they put prematurely pressure on the patient to make a mental image of his impulse. After having restructured their patient's ego-adaptive capacity, they put pressure to the patient's impulse although there is zero mobilization of anger or impulse. Whenever a patient complies (which is not recognized by the therapist), the consequence will be that the patient will give the therapist a hundred per cent cognitive account of some aggressive actions towards his victim and (perhaps of) the inflicted damage. It may be that with this intervention no harm has been done to the patient (the ego-adaptive capacity being restructured), or that in a few cases such a procedure could be of some benefit to the patient. However, to assess such a patient's account as a breakthrough and subsequent conscious experiencing of his impulse is certainly a big mistake!

A physical mobilization but sloppy mental image of deeds and/or inflicted harm

There is mobilization of the patient's impulse, and the patient has told the therapist that he is furious.

Pt I kick him in his ass and I throw him out of the door
Th and then?
Pt I don't care, that's all, I don't need to do more
Th But if you open the door and look how he is lying there, what do you see?
Pt Nothing. I don't care. He is too unimportant

Or:

Pt I take a knife and I stab him, I stab him everywhere. I kick him and push him, I throw him against the wall ... etc.

Th And how, in the meantime, he is lying there?
Pt Oh he is lying in a corner
Th And where do you see wounds or blood or …?
Pt He has no wounds
Or: He has no blood
Or: You can't see blood or wounds
Or: He has changed into a rag/a doll

Of course it is mostly due to the mobilization of a patient's guilt (grief and love) that the defences are put into operation in order for the patient to avoid the full contact with his lust to revenge/inflict pain/torture/kill and the guilt that accompanies this lust.

Therefore the therapist could continue e.g.,

Th Guilt is not the reason to stop investigating your rage, your lust to revenge and to inflict pain. Guilt is the reason that we continue investigating your murderous feelings because we want to understand what exactly of your murderous feelings make you so guilty.

Assessment of grief and sadness

Manifestations of somatomotor (striated muscles) patterns

The mobilization of grief is characterized by a short immobility of the body. According to Davanloo and to our observation of European, American, Canadian, Asian, and Australian patients, the passage and breakthrough of grief and sadness follows a distinct upward pattern, starting with the muscles in the abdominal region (deep sighs), to the muscles of the chest (widening the chest), the vocal cords, to the shoulders (shaking motions), to the muscles of the head (downward position of the head). The grief comes in waves. We witnessed in our practice with our patients how the deep sighs that accompany the grief succeed each other with regular intervals. These intervals grow longer as a wave of grief approaches its end. The length of these regular intervals depends on the particular patient. With one patient, these intervals are four seconds long, with another five, and so on. We advise the therapist to silently count these intervals. When they suddenly grow shorter, the therapist will know that the patient has used a defence to suppress the remainder of his grief. Also, in our view, sobbing needs to be differentiated from crying. As sobbing requires convulsive inhaling with spasms of many respiratory muscles, the therapist could infer that his patient's grief has become fused with anxiety and/or helplessness.

Manifestations of autonomic and endocrine patterns

Apart from tears, Davanloo doesn't describe underlying autonomic and/or endocrine changes.

Perhaps this is the moment to point out that there are tears and tears and tears. But whatever the cause of these tears, they are produced by the lacrimal glands, which are situated above the cranial orbits, laterally to the eyes. The lacrimal gland that produces tears is fed by the parasympathetic branches of the seventh cranial nerve.

There are three types of tears, all different in composition, and all with different function. We distinguish basic (or basal, or continuous), reflex, and emotional (or psychogenic) tears.

Basal tears lubricate our eyes. They are excreted continuously in small amounts, spreading across the exposed surface of the eyes with the help of the eyelids. Reflex tears are stimulated in larger than normal amounts by irritation/trauma to the eye and have a protective function. Psychogenic or emotional tears flow in response to alterations in our mood and emotions (Cardoso & Sabbattini, 2002).

Manifestations of cognitive/perceptual patterns and action tendency

In order to have direct access to the experience of grief and sadness, the patient has to know what exactly triggered his grief/sadness, what the sadness is about, and he should not only be aware of his proprioceptive stimuli but should also acknowledge that he wants to cry and that the content of his grief/sadness is irrevocable (action tendency: to acknowledge that what has happened cannot be changed).

Problems with assessment of the patient's sadness

Sometimes it is hard to differentiate between tears out of helplessness, tears out of sadness, and tears out of sudden overwhelming anxiety. A patient's tears may be assessed as a parasympathetic manifestation of anxiety when the onset of anxiety is sudden, spread of manifestations is fast, the intensity is high, and when there are more parasympathetic manifestations and/or some cognitive/perceptual disturbances. In all these cases, the therapist may notice that his patient is doing effort to withhold the tearing. Often, the patient (and the therapist as well) takes his tears that accompany defensive weepiness as evidence of sadness. Underlying autonomic and endocrine changes with weepiness might be similar or might be different from those with sadness. However, if a patient is not able to tell the therapist what the sadness is about, the therapist may be sure that his patient's tears are accompanying defensive weepiness. See the following examples:

The patient has a good access to her sadness/grief

A patient is crying, her head is bent downward, her sighs are starting in the abdominal region (deep sighs), interval between the sighs is six seconds, then gradually these intervals grow longer and the therapist waits till this wave of grief has ended and the patient has dried her tears.

Th What was going on inside you during this grief?

Pt I hadn't realized that I had still so much sadness in me about the sudden death of my first love. I saw him again lying in the hospital. The day he died. I held his hand and he looked at me with his sweet brown eyes. He couldn't speak but his eyes told me that he loved me, that he didn't want to die but that he was losing the battle. And I was crying and I kissed him and I told him that I loved him so much and that I would never forget his love and support. In fact, at that moment,

> I didn't think I could live without him, but I didn't tell him because I knew he would be worrying about me.
>
> I am also sad because I realize that I never really accepted his death and he leaving me all alone. Since then, I only have chosen the wrong men. Either they were married, or freshly divorced and not ready for a new relationship. This is so self-defeating ... etc.

The patient's tears as manifestation of helplessness

> A patient is crying, her head is bent downward. The therapist isn't sure whether these tears indicate sadness or helplessness.
>
> Th Are you crying out of sadness or out of helplessness?
> Pt I don't know. (now the therapist is almost sure that patient is tearing out of helplessness)
> Th What is going on inside you during these tears?
> Pt Nothing.
> Or: I feel so powerless.
> Or: I think it has something to do with my mother/father/friend/dog, etc.
> Or: I am just vulnerable, that is all.
>
> (In all these four cases, the therapist is sure the tears indicate helplessness.)
>
> Or: a patient has described a concrete interaction and tells the therapist he was/is angry with his boss/relative/friend/partner.
> Th If you would give words to your anger, what would you say?
> Pt I would say ... the patient starts tearing.
>
> (In this case, the therapist is immediately sure that the patient's tears indicate the defence of helplessness.)

Assessment of guilt

Manifestations of somatomotor, autonomic, and endocrine patterns of guilt

Although Davanloo repeatedly points to the fact that guilt is the most painful feeling and that the experience of guilt is a necessary prerequisite in order to experience grief, he is vague in describing the physiological concomitants of guilt. "There is a breakthrough of a major wave of guilt-laden unconscious feelings, with heavy sobbing. The guilt-laden unconscious feelings come in waves and involve the upper respiratory area" (Davanloo, 2000a, p. 79).

As a result, there is no clear physiological differentiation between guilt, on the one side, and anger, rage, and grief, on the other side. However, as said before, sometimes the patterns of somatomotor, autonomic, and endocrine manifestations may be difficult to assess by introspection and the therapist's observation, and obviously more refined measurement is needed.

We ourselves have noticed that the mobilization of guilt (as well as the mobilization of sadness) is often accompanied by a stillness of the upper part of the body and a downward bent head.

Manifestations of cognitive/perceptual patterns and action tendency

In order for the patient to have direct access to his guilt, he has to be aware that it is especially the lust with which he executes his destructive/sadistic actions onto his victim, the awareness of his desire to revenge, the awareness of the distress/suffering/destruction he inflicts upon his victim, that makes him feel guilty. The action tendency will be his wish to undo the harm he inflicted, to repair if possible the damage that was caused by the aggression.

Problems with the assessment of guilt

Not differentiating between shame and guilt

Many patients, as well as therapists, confuse shame with guilt. The experience of shame—according to Helen Block Lewis (1971)—is directly about the self, which is the focus of negative evaluation. In guilt, the self is not the central object of negative evaluation, but rather the thing done or undone is the focus. Shame involves judgement of an internalized disapproving other (Neborsky, 2003). With guilt, by contrast, the internal evaluation system originates from within a person's own sense of self. Helen Block Lewis (1971) pointed out that empathy is a key marker for differentiating shame from guilt. A person who has access to his guilt has an empathic awareness of someone's distress and has at the same time an awareness of being the cause of that distress.

A person who has access to shame will *conceal* issues due to projection of negative evaluation onto others, who as a consequence will mirror the patient's negative self-evaluation. Davanloo does not deal with a patient's shame as if it would be a feeling. He deals with shame as a defence: the patient is concealing something in the relationship with the therapist or with another person.

> Davanloo could have the following interaction with a patient:
>
> Th What do you feel towards me?
> Pt I feel shame.
> Th So you want to hide something from me, something negative you want to conceal. What do you feel?

Not differentiating between guilt and guilt

Many patients, as well as therapists, do not differentiate between (unhealthy) "externally imposed guilt" and (healthy) "guilt that originates from the own sense of self and love, empathy and compassion". In psychotherapeutic practice, it occurs often that a patient tells the therapist that he "regularly feels guilty". Upon investigation, while in the process of undoing the patient's identification with his internalized former aggressor, it will become clear that "feeling guilty" refers to the blaming, accusing, or punishing voice of his internalized former aggressor. As a response, the patient will be obedient and go for self-blaming, self-devaluing.

The more a patient will get access to his longing to understand himself with love, care, and precision, thus with increasing separation of ego and superego, the more a patient "feels guilty" because of his disobedience to the dictate of his punitive superego.

As we have mentioned above, (healthy) guilt originates within a person's own sense of self, and it is based on the person's capacity to love and to have empathy. This is also what we frequently witness when our patients experience their guilt that accompanies their murderous impulse. They all (without exception) tell us that there is this other part, in which they don't WANT to inflict this harm onto the other person. They all tell us that if it would have been possible, they would wish they could undo the harm they inflicted. When asked whether they say this because of penal code, they will all say that penal law has nothing to do with it.

During the therapeutic process, it is important to help the patient differentiate between this "unhealthy" and more "healthy" guilt feelings. To help him understand that what he calls guilt is in fact unhealthy guilt that once was imposed on him by his aggressors-caretakers and that he now imposes on himself in obedience to these aggressor-caretakers, and which he has internalized. It is the therapist's job to help the patient make a choice whether he wants to accept the imposed guilt, "yes or no?" The aim is to help the patient differentiate between these two kinds of guilt and to quit his unhealthy, imposed guilt; to help the patient to be proud of his capacity to have guilt because of empathy/love, and to accept this healthy guilt, coming from his heart, as a compass for continuing dealing with himself and others with love, honesty, and respect.

See, for example, the following patient–therapist interaction after the breakthrough of a patient's impulse, guilt, grief, love:

Th So we have seen that you are more complicated than only one feeling. More complicated than only having this murderous rage. You said you felt guilt, you were very sad, and you felt love towards your mother.

Pt Oh yes, I felt this love very deeply. Up till now I knew I had this love, but I never felt it. I suppose this rage and this guilt were in the way to feel my love.

Th This guilt you mention ... about what exactly was this guilt ... or did you say it because you are afraid of what I might think about your rage?

Pt Oh Nooo ... that has nothing to do with it .... I felt this guilt because I realized very clearly and intensely that at the same time I don't want to do such sadistic and hurtful things. I don't WANT to. I don't want to express my aggression in such a way ... not towards my mother ... in fact, not towards anybody ... it would make me a cruel person. No, I want to express my aggression with the help of words.

Th You often mentioned here you feel guilty. For instance, last session you told me you felt guilty because you had spent so much money on yourself. Do you remember?

Pt Yes, my mother, and in fact my father too, they wouldn't approve of that and they would say I was just idle and vain.

Th So what you call guilt is in fact a guilt that is imposed on you by your parents. And until now, you agreed with their norms and said yes, I am guilty of being idle and vain. What is it you want: guilt out of own norms and values or guilt out of imposed norms and values?

Pt Ooh ... (patient gets tears in eyes)

Th What is happening right now?

Pt	This is so important … . now I finally understand … I was so confused … . I thought of myself as very bad also whenever I felt this rage. … I am happy and sad.
Th	Just cry.
Pt	(cries)
Pt	I always want to keep this guilt (about the impulse) … it makes me proud … . I will never accept again that guilt that both of my parents impose on me. It really is sooo unhealthy. Oh thank you, this is so important to me.

At the beginning of therapy, often after the breakthrough of the sadistic impulse, pressure from the therapist is sometimes needed in order for the patient to reach his guilt, which in turn serves as a transition zone to experience grief. As soon as the patient is aware of the action tendency of his guilt, his wish to undo the inflicted harm, and as soon as he is aware that this harm cannot be undone nor repaired (the action tendency of grief is to acknowledge that, what is irrevocable), then we will witness the transition to deeply felt grief. Pressure from the therapist comprises confrontation with the fact that nobody else but the patient himself is responsible for the destruction of his object, that this destruction was experienced as pleasant and confrontation with the destructive *effects* of his impulse on his object. In fact, the therapist's interventions are aimed at the patient's evaluation of his intentional act to destroy, at the patient's evaluation of the action tendency of his impulse, resulting in the patient experiencing his guilt. With therapy progress (and thus the stronger client's ego), the impulses become more sadistic and the patient almost immediately feels guilty. Thus, the patient's guilt moves forward as soon as the patient is aware of the action tendency of his impulse.

In our experience, whenever our patients had a breakthrough of the sadistic impulse, followed by an unlocking, they experienced their guilt and grief both as very painful. However, when asked specifically for the physical concomitants of their guilt, patients described it as a diffuse sensation within their body. We take the opportunity here to raise the question whether guilt should be considered as a feeling to be distinguished from anger/impulse, and grief/sadness, or that it should be considered as a cognitive structure, accompanying and determining the full experience of the impulse. The evaluative awareness (which is a cognition) that in experiencing the impulse, the person is aware of and feels (a degree of) pleasure in his intention to destroy (which is an action tendency) and that nobody else but he himself is solely responsible for its irreversible result may be what we call healthy guilt.

Pt My little girl is jealous of her brother and as a consequence she was nagging me. Therefore, to distract her, she and I played in the swimming pool. I would throw her up and catch her as she fell, letting her sink into the water. However, she continued to nag me and suddenly I couldn't control myself, and I threw her up, then pusher her completely under the water. I saw how she was shocked. I realized that she would never forget the incident. I thought, Christ, what have I done. I felt so terribly guilty that I had not controlled my temper and that I caused her to distrust me.

A healthy regulation and conscious experiencing and expression of emotion

At this point it might be evident that for a healthy regulation, conscious experiencing and expression of an emotion and/or anxiety, a patient's cognitive/perceptive system must be able:

- to detect eliciting essential stimuli from the external or internal world (current situations and persons), to analyse them and to interpret the information in the context of earlier experience (past, transference) in order to estimate the significance and meaning of the eliciting stimuli
- to detect, analyse, and interpret the physiological manifestations of that particular emotion and to give these the correct emotional label
- to know the cognitive contents of that feeling and to give adequate words to what the feeling is about
- to be aware of the proprioceptive stimuli and the action tendency
- to establish the causal link with the preceding essential stimuli
- to detect, analyse, and interpret whether and how the patient will express his feelings and whether he is herewith fulfilling what he really wants.

The concept of defence and classification systems of defences

The concept of defence stems from Freud. He originally conceived of defences as intrapsychic mechanisms that mediate the internal struggles between the internalized societal expectations of the superego and the instinctual drives of the id (Brenner 1991). Therewith the function of the defences was seen as mainly protecting the person from internal threat. Nowadays the function of defences is expanded to also include protection from external threats, as e.g., protection from actual or psychic loss of relationships. Thus nowadays defences or defence mechanisms are commonly conceptualized as managing anxiety from both internal and external threats (Cooper 1998). This anxiety would occur if the person became aware of unacceptable thoughts, feelings, impulses, wishes (Cramer & Davidson 1998).

In his earlier writings, Freud used terms such as "mechanisms of defence" and "repression" synonymously. Later, he outlined other defences such as denial, displacement, dissociation, and so on. After his death, others contributed to conceptualize defences. The list of specific defence mechanisms is huge and there are several classifications of defence mechanisms.

In a number of classifications, the defences are related to their emergence in a certain developmental phase, see, for example, the division of defences into categories such as immature, neurotic, and mature. Immature defences emerge early in life and they reduce anxiety by distorting the occurrence as well as the salience of the event (Olson, 2008). Neurotic defences occur in adulthood and result in acknowledgement of the occurrence of an event but the meaning and impact of the event are managed by distorting the meaning. Mature defences emerge later in life and result in the fullest acknowledgement of the nature and extent of the threat. Vaillant (1992) classifies defences along four levels, i.e., level I (Childhood—"psychotic" defences, e.g., denial, distortion, delusional projection), level II (Adolescence—immature defences, e.g., projection, acting out), level III (Adulthood—neurotic defences, e.g., intellectualization, reaction formation), and level IV (Adulthood—mature defences, e.g., sublimation, humour).

Davanloo's classification of defences into tactical and major defences is based on his finding that rapid mobilization of the unconscious instantly mobilizes a repertoire of defences, which he has called "tactical" defences. According to him, "these 2 categories of defence form a continuum, and any attempt to draw a sharp distinction between them would only result in hair-splitting". "In highly resistant patients, those with complex pathogenic unconscious; tactical defences are aspects of major defences and they can be considered the front-line defensive structure of the major resistance. While in patients with no major resistance, the resistance predominantly consists of a series of tactical defences". According to Davanloo, tactical defences are not major defences such as repression, projection, and so on. Although Davanloo is fairly explicit in what he calls tactical defences, he is not that explicit in what he calls major defences.

According to the author this classification of Davanloo only creates confusion because of the fact that a so called tactical defence can be at other times a major defence, like denial, stubbornness, defiance, weepiness. On top of that, it is the author's opinion that some of Davanloo's examples of tactical defences must not be understood at all as a defence. Davanloo gives some examples of patients, suffering from character neurosis, who describe they became "nervous and agitated" when they were asked how they experienced their anger. Davanloo gives this as an example of "the tactical defence of describing anxiety rather than anger". To the author, this example is not evidence of a defence in operation (tactical or not) but mainly referring to a patient's realistic incapacity of experiencing anger as a *consequence* of their defence, i.e., their character defence mechanism of instant repression (see also ten Have-de Labije & Neborsky, 2005).

When growing up, in each developmental phase, we all bring a repertoire of defences into operation.

Sometimes, circumstances can be such that we bring some of these defences so habitually and automatically into play that they become part of "our character". Character defences are habitual, rigidly fixed, and usually ego syntonic. Often the patient even approves of his character defences and he isn't aware of the different aspects of their self-defeating function. One could say that the character defences serve the purpose of enabling the ego to resist taking an active cognizant and perceptive position towards the external and internal demands.

Not understanding where the defence operates in the emotion-regulation process: one example

Above it has been already implicated that a correct assessment of a specific defence's target of operation (at the level of the stimulus, response or at both levels at the same time) is crucial in different phases of the therapy process, such as e.g., in the phases of helping the patient 1) to allow the therapist to be of help, 2) to change syntonic defences into dystonic ones, and 3) to quit the defences out of intrinsic motivation, in order for 4) uncovering painful past and associated impulses and feelings, and 5) experiencing these impulses and feelings.

Here is an example that may illustrate why a faulty assessment may block from the very beginning the therapy process:

Phase 1: allowing the therapist to be of help

A patient enters an initial interview with anxiety at the forefront. There is immediately massive spread and storage of anxiety in the striated muscles, a very dry mouth and frequent clearing of the throat, breathing pattern is high and superficial, the patient is avoiding the eye contact with the therapist, and upon the therapist's invitation to give insight into her problems, the patient starts speaking in a galloping way. The therapist interrupts by asking whether the patient notices her high anxiety manifestations. The patient admits she is "nervous", is still withdrawing from the eye contact and continues in a galloping way the course of her disclosure. The therapist confronts the patient with her defence of neglecting her anxiety in labelling it as nervous (thus confronting the patient that this defence operates at the level of the response) but fails to confront the patient with the defences that operate at the level of the stimulus (withdrawing from the eye contact, galloping, and dismissing the therapist by continuing the course of her disclosure).

Th May I interrupt you. Do you notice you are highly anxious, you are tensed from head till toes, your breathing is superficial and you frequently have to clear your throat

Pt Yes, that is true, I am nervous ... and when my boyfriend told me ... etc.

The therapist continues to confront the patient again with her defence of minimizing, identifies it and asks the patient whether she could report other anxiety manifestations. The patient answers she is tensed in the stomach region and continues the course of her disclosure. In dismissing the therapist again, the full and precise assessment of the patient's anxiety has become impossible as long as the patient's defences that operate at the level of the stimulus are not assessed.

Th When you say you are nervous, you are neglecting and minimizing the intensity of your anxiety. How do you notice your anxiety physically?

Pt It feels tensed here (points to her stomach) ... and in fact I didn't like what my boyfriend said but somehow I couldn't react.

Of course, it is evident that if the therapist would have understood and assessed correctly the patient's defences that operate at the level of the stimulus, thus at the level of the front door, the therapist would have understood that the first target of the therapist's interventions should have been these defences.

In a therapy session, front door defences always have the priority over cellar door defences. After all, for the working alliance to be established and/or maintained, a patient has to open the front door and allow the therapist to be of help.

It would have been better:

Th You know, I noticed that when I speak you look at me. But when you want to give me insight into your problem, you become anxious, you avoid the eye contact with me by looking away and you start speaking in a galloping way. Obviously, the intimacy with me evokes your anxiety and you start galloping and looking away. If I say so, do you understand me?

Pt Yes that is true, then I can better concentrate. My boyfriend ....

Th Let us first assess that you want my help in understanding your problems. Avoiding the eye contact with me, is the same as avoiding intimacy with me and in that case I will be of little help. Galloping will prevent us from understanding your problems in a precise way. Not letting in what I explain to you by continuing telling me about your experiences with your boyfriend is also keeping the front door closed to me and with all these mechanisms of looking away, galloping, dismissing my interventions by continuing your story, you prevent that I can be of help. It is very clear to me that you are not aware that in continuing to do so you prevent me to be of help. Do you understand me?

Defences block the regulation and generation of emotions at the level of the stimulus and/or response

As defence mechanisms can be seen as operations/strategies of the ego to block/avoid a full awareness of unpleasant situations, thoughts, feelings, anxiety, and behaviour, we could say that defence mechanisms block the cognitive/perceptual processing of information, either at the level of the stimulus, or at the level of the response (Frijda, 1993).

For therapy purposes, One of the authors, (ten Have-de Labije) herself conceives a person as a house. One part of the cellar can be compared with the unconscious storage for impulses and painful feelings. These impulses and feelings are stored via an entrance cellar door. The living room could be envisaged as a part of the conscious, a place for investigating and experiencing impulses and feelings with love, precision, and honesty. The cellar has two doors, an entrance and an exit door. The cellar exit door connects the cellar with the living room. The living room gives directly on to a corridor, leading to the front door. The front door could be conceived as representative for the defences, that are antecedent-focused and operate at the level of essential eliciting stimuli or, in other words, that operate in the realm of emotional closeness with another person in the present or past. The cellar exit door could be compared with the defences that are response-focused and operate at the level of the response (thus after an impulse or feeling has been triggered/mobilized) or, in other words, that operate in the realm of the resistance against the experience of impulse and feelings. Upstairs is the superego's room, filled with monitors and other spy equipment. The superego has put a camera on the head of the ego and an auditory receiver in the ego's ear. In this way, he can constantly monitor the ego's behaviour and instruct the ego about behaviour that is allowed and that is forbidden. The person's obedient ego part is only allowing intimacy with himself and with others upon instruction of his superego part, who

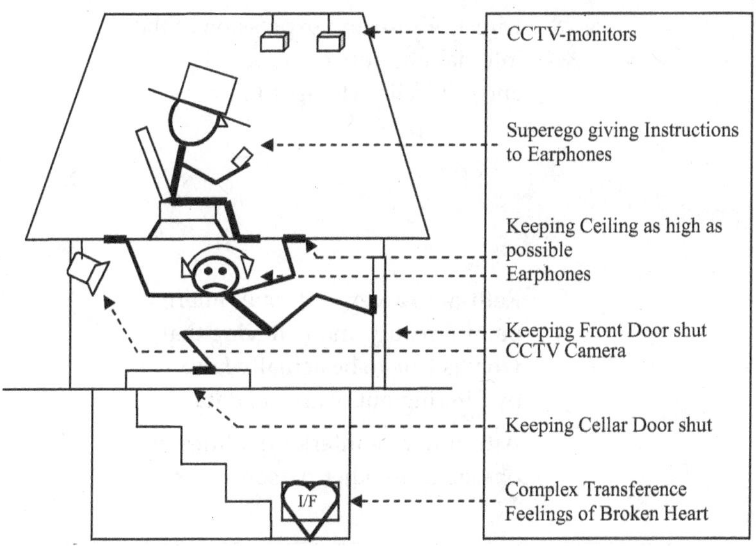

Figure 5. Ego's obedience to his superego: defences.

is constantly watching all his moves. The more this person's house is located at the right side of Davanloo's spectrum of structural neuroses, the fuller the cellar storage, the emptier the living room, the more massive the cellar exit and front doors, the heavier the equipment of the superego, the weaker the forces of the person's ego part, who is all the time desperately engaged to keep these two doors closed.

Figure 5 depicts the front door and cellar door defences that are put into operation out of the ego's obedience to his superego.

Assessment of defences for ISTDP purposes

For ISTDP purposes, the author suggests to assess defences into verbal and non-verbal ones according to their level of operation: defences that operate at the level of the stimulus, at the level of the response, or at both levels. Or, in other words: the verbal and non-verbal defences can operate at the level of the front door, the level of the cellar door, or at both levels (at the same time or at alternating times).

Table 2. Verbal defences.

		Stimulus level	Response level
Accusations			X
name-giving			
complaining			
playing the victim			
Acting out	Direct release and expression of the internal pressure of an impulse and/or feeling; temper tantrum	X	X
Ambivalence		X	X
Compliance		X	
giving the other priority			
Defiance		X	X
Denial	Refusal to accept external/internal painful reality and believing that what is true to be actually false by filtering out of crucial data	X	X
Devaluation	Attribution of inferior qualities to oneself or to other persons	X	X
Dismissiveness		X	

(*Continued*)

Table 2. (*Continued*)

Displacement Not confronting the real source of pain (stimulus) Redirecting aggression to a substitute, less menacing or irrelevant person (response)		X	X
Dissociation Minimizing awareness of incoming information (stimulus) Losing track of space, time, identity (response)		X	X
Distortion	Reshaping of external reality to meet internal needs	X	
Distraction	Distracting attention away from essential eliciting stimuli	X	
Fantasy (narcissist) Day-dreaming	Distract attention away from source of unpleasant reality	X	X
Helplessness Passivity/constatation		X	X
Humour	Expression of painful ideas/emotions in a way that gives pleasure to others	X	X
Hypochondriasis	Transformation of painful feelings towards others into oneself by preoccupation with illness		X
Idealization Omnipotence	Attribution of unrealistic superior traits/characteristics to oneself and to others	X	
Identification Introjection		X	X
Ignoring Neglecting		X	X
Intellectualization		X	X
Isolation of affect	Separating cognitive content from the specific physiological manifestations of that emotion		X
Minimizing		X	X
Negation		X	X

(*Continued*)

Table 2. (*Continued*)

		Stimulus level	Response level
Normative		X	X
Paranoid ideation		X	
Passive aggressiveness	Aggression towards others expressed indirectly or passively		X
Pleasing		X	
Projection	Attribution of characteristics, thoughts, feelings, behaviour of one's self or of an internalized person with whom one is identified onto another person	X	
Projective identification		X	X
Rationalization			
Psychologicalization	To justify, explain one's own or others behaviour by resorting to logical, socially acceptable, psychological explications and excuses	X	X
Reaction formation	Taking a position or behaviour that defies personally unacceptable thoughts, feelings by expressing diametrically opposed ideas, opinion, behaviour		X
Repression Selective memory loss: what happened in a situation (stimulus) or what was emotion about (response)		X	X
Ignoring/neglect			
Denying		X	X
Sexualization		X	X
Somatization			X
Speaking in general		X	

(*Continued*)

Table 2. (*Continued*)

vagueness		X	X
story telling		X	
Splitting	Inability to integrate contradictory qualities of same person into a coherent picture. Adhering positive qualities to one, negative to another person	X	X
Cycles of idealization, devaluation of self and others		X	
Sublimation	Channelling unacceptable feelings into positive actions and socially accepted behaviour		X
Suppression	Consciously forcing unwanted information out of awareness	X	X
Undoing	Trying to get rid of feelings/guilt by compensating the injured person symbolically or actually	X	X

Non-verbal defences

Most non-verbal defences, such as immobility, sitting with crossed legs, moving the legs (discharge), sighing, pacing, are operating on the level of the cellar door (response). However, defences such as avoiding eye contact, smiling, slouching, sitting with crossed arms, are operating at the level of the stimulus/front door.

As mentioned above: defences may block a patient's healthy experiencing and/or expression of emotions at various stages in the emotion regulatory processes. It may be evident that a defence, operating at the level of a stimulus/front door is very effective. Right away information processing of eliciting, essential stimuli is blocked or changed and its impact in the emotion-generative and emotion-regulatory process is at a very early stage. Defences operating at the level of the response (experiencing and/or expression of an emotion) have their impact relatively late in the emotion generative and emotion-regulatory process In case a patient uses a defence both at the level of a stimulus and at the level of the response, the therapist should first focus on undoing the defence that is operating at the level of the stimulus. Front door defences always have priority!

Defences at the level of the front door/stimulus

Defences in service of attentional control, at the level of the front door/stimulus, may be put into operation to a) ignore/neglect eliciting essential stimuli from the external and/or internal world (current situations/persons and thinking of situations/persons) b) to distract attention from these stimuli or c) to change the meaning of eliciting essential stimuli from the external/internal world. According to common sense one can expect that defences that fall under a) are far more effective in blocking incoming information than those that fall under categories b) and c). In case of b) and c), information must first be perceived in order to go from distraction (b) or for changing the meaning (c).

A few examples:

Imagine the following therapist–patient interaction:

(ignoring a stimulus)

Th So, instead of postponing, what you used to do, you immediately tackled the problem of ... I understand that you took our work of last session seriously, I am so proud of you
Pt Yes, but today I want to discuss the following ... with you
Th I was giving you a compliment but obviously you choose to ignore my compliment

(ignoring/neglecting a stimulus: selective memory loss)

Th You tell me you had this argument with your wife
Pt Yes, that's right but I cannot remember what she did or said that started the argument.
Th So suddenly you have selective memory loss whereas in other situations you have an excellent memory

(distracting attention from a stimulus ... avoiding eye contact)

Th You are looking away, suddenly you avoid the eye contact with me. Could we understand that
Pt I cannot concentrate when I look at you
Th So you change one defence for another defence. Look at me ... what do you see in my eyes? (changing the meaning of a stimulus ... rationalization)
Pt My mother did very sarcastic when I told her that I passed the exam as one of the best. But of course, she was never allowed herself to follow any education, so I can understand her reaction.

Defences at the level of the stimulus and at the level of the response

Th I notice that you are angry, now that you are telling me about this interaction with your father. Do you notice that too
Pt No, I am not angry (denial at level of response) but I don't think that very important, I prefer telling you what happened afterwards (dismissal of therapist/defence at level of stimulus)
Th You and I are here to understand your emotions with love, care and precision and when I focus your attention on to the fact that your anger, here with me, has been mobilized, you dismiss me. Are you aware of that? How do you perceive me when I focus your attention to your anger?
Pt I suppose I perceive you like I perceive my father ... judgemental.

Hopefully, this example makes it clear that in case a patient uses defences that are both operating at the level of a stimulus and response the therapist should give priority to tackling the defence at the level of the stimulus.

Defences in the realm of instant repression

Last but not least we would like to give some extra attention to the concept of instant repression. The concept of instant repression stems from Davanloo's clinical observations with patients, suffering from depressive, functional and psychosomatic disorders. According to Davanloo, one of the characteristics of these patients is that they have access to the unconscious defence mechanism of instant repression, which is responsible for the direct and instant internalization of the sadistic impulse. The consequence is that the impulse never reaches consciousness. This explains the clinical observation that these patients often are unable to distinguish between the poles of the triangle of conflict. Specifically they are unable to differentiate between anger and the sadistic impulse, on the one hand, and anxiety and defence, on the other.

Apart from postulating this concept of instant repression, Davanloo did NOT elaborate on a more theoretical view of this concept of his. His approach has been more pragmatic in elaborating on the specific steps of the treatment protocol when working with these kinds of patients.

In our view, a more elaborate understanding of the concept of instant repression may help the (I)STDP therapist to recognize it in a timely manner and to act accordingly upon it. Patients suffering from depressive, functional, and psychosomatic disorders often have severe superego and character pathology. We all know that the array of character defences, utilized by our patients, may interfere with the therapist's ability to conduct a trial therapy. This is because these defences are automatically put into operation and the degree of this automatism reflects the degree to which they are unconsciously put into operation. It goes without saying that, the more defences are syntonic, the more automatically, and therefore the more unconsciously, the patient puts his defences into operation. The defences of instant repression are thus considered as both unconscious defence mechanisms, as well as character defence mechanisms.

During therapy it is, of course, mainly the patient and not the therapist, who has to observe and to assess his own functioning and problems in several *in vivo* and *in vitro* (thinking of a situation) interactions by using his cognitive/perceptive system. Roth (2004) states that any effort to understand consciousness must begin by noting that it comprises various states. At one end of the spectrum is the so-called alertness (or vigilance) state. States of lower consciousness include drowsiness, dozing, deep sleep, and on down to coma. By logical thinking, it becomes obvious that defences, which instantaneously block the cognitive/perceptive processing at the level of the stimulus (or in ISTDP terminology, at the level of the triangle of persons) are, for example, denial of the painful significance of a situation, ignoring a painful significance of a situation, making the head empty/blank, or selective memory loss of painful situations. These defences block the flow of information right at the source, and phases of analysis and interpretations in the context of earlier experience are prevented.

The consequence, of course, is that these defences are at the same time instantaneously blocking the cognitive/perceptive processing at the level of the response (or in ISTDP terminology, at the level of the triangle of conflict). Defences that instantaneous block the cognitive/perceptive processing at the level of the response are thus denial, ignoring, empty head, but also motoric retardation or immobility. Other defences such as e.g., "understanding" the other person (at the level of the stimulus, e.g., "person X is impatient, undoubtedly he will be tired") or e.g., rationalization (at the level of the response, e.g., "I have no right to be angry because I often do the same") are used at a later stage in the processing of information (i.e., in the phases of analysis and/or interpretation) and therefore—compared to the instant repressors—they are "slower repressors".

Table 3. Defences instantaneously blocking the cognitive/perceptive processing of information.

At the level of the stimulus: overt or covert situation	**At the level of the response: internal state**
Denial Ignoring	Denial Ignoring
Making head empty	Making head empty
Selective memory loss	Selective memory loss
	Motoric retardation, immobility

Steps in helping the patient to overcome instant repression

Of course, in all ISTDP with patients, suffering from all kinds of character pathology, the therapist has to some degree to function as a provider of biofeedback in order to restore internal feedback loops and to take care that information reaches cortical regions and can be processed by the associative regions of the cortex. This is done by the therapist's decision to drawing the patient's attention /his cognitive/perceptive system (the process of focused attention in itself causes cortical and subcortical synaptogenesis (the formation of new synapses) (Fossella, Sommer, Pfaff, Fan & Posner, 2003) to the particular defence in question, particular feeling and/ or anxiety and keep it under scrutiny till the patient himself will be on the alert to recognize himself the particular defence, feeling, or anxiety correctly. So to speak, the therapist "obliges" information to reach the patient's cortex and therewith—in repeating this—internal feedback loops will be restored. In case of depressive and/or psychosomatic patients, it is of utmost importance for the therapist to be such a provider of "biofeedback" and to recognize at what level (stimulus or response) and with what duration.

1. From the above, the reader will understand that after having established some degree of working alliance with depressive and/or psychosomatic patients, the therapist will assess if and to what degree his patient has access to the defences of denial, ignoring, empty/ blank head, selective memory loss (at the level of stimulus and response) and motoric retardation and immobility (at the level of the response).
2. The therapist will do this by asking the patient for concrete situations in the C in which the patient encounters his problems but,
3. in the relation with the therapist, the T, the therapist will confront the patient with each of these defences by drawing his attention to them, identify them, clarify their function and after that the therapist will return again to the particular situation in the C,
4. subsequently the therapist will challenge the patient to relinquish his defences at the level of the stimulus by inviting the patient to make a mental picture of the particular situation, give words to the particular concrete situation and to describe precisely which behaviour/ words of the other person were perceived as painful to the patient,

5. having a mental picture and describing it to the therapist triggers of course some emotional response in the patient (which of course he will repress in a split-second),
6. this gives the therapist opportunity, at the level of the response, to draw the patient's attention to his (split-second) physical reactions, helping him to label them correctly and helping him to differentiate between the physical manifestations of impulse, feelings and anxiety,
7. of course, in-between the patient will repeatedly take refuge in his defences and the therapist will repeat steps 2, 3, 4, and 5,
8. in a growing cooperation the patient will progressively be able to describe painful situations properly, painful feelings will be progressively longer contained, and the therapist will continue drawing the patient's attention to the physical manifestations of the patient's feelings, its causality with the mobilization of anxiety and the patient's escape in defences. As soon as the patient is able to label the physical manifestations of feelings and anxiety correctly and understands their causality with taking refuge into defences,
9. the therapist will put more pressure on experiencing the feelings by inviting the patient to a) label his feeling correctly and to give words to the contents (e.g., what is the anger about). This will result in more mobilization and rise of the patient's complex transference feelings,
10. the therapist will repeat steps 8 and 9 and if necessary, the therapist will heighten his dosage of power of interventions to motivate the patient to quit all of his defences by using a head-on collision with reference to the patient's superego pathology and to the intimacy with the therapist until the patient will be able—out of intrinsic motivation—to allow his impulse, guilt, and grief to be contained, experienced, and investigated in his conscious and to unlock traumatic experiences (see also the chapters on depression and on psychosomatic complaints).

Steps in the chapter

- Quality of healthy emotion regulation and location on spectrum of structural neuroses
- Defences in the realm of REI and REC
- Affect as umbrella and distinction between emotion/moods/states
- Assessing is not experiencing an emotion
- Complete and correct assessment of anger, impulse, guilt, sadness
- Problems with assessment of a particular emotion
- Classification of defences: verbal/non-verbal and level of stimulus/response
- Assessment of and dealing with defences
- The concept of instant repression

CHAPTER FOUR

Assessment of a patient's anxiety

When there is anxiety at the onset of the therapeutic encounter, we could say that the patient's anxiety is somewhere on the continuum between anxiety as a transference reaction and anxiety as a sign of generalized anxiety.

In patients with a high capacity to regulate anxiety, signs of anxiety will be reflected by a pattern of facial muscle behaviour and by tension of other striated skeletal muscles, by a pattern of sympathetic reactivity and sensory vigilance. The proportion of somatomotor manifestations would be higher than the proportion of autonomic manifestations. The rise of the respective manifestations would be slow, and the duration of the manifestations would be relatively short. Such a patient would report various concerns in terms of (subjectively) perceived reality and cognitions, and he would accurately perceive the internal state of his periphery and label it as anxiety.

In practice, we seldom meet such patients at the initial interview. Mostly, we meet patients whose pattern of physiological anxiety manifestations reveals that they are less or not at all capable of adequately regulating their anxiety for their own benefit. In these cases, the proportion of autonomic manifestations is higher than somatomotor manifestations and/or there is cognitive and/or perceptual dysfunctioning. The rise and spread of physiological manifestations is fast and high and the duration of the respective manifestations is relatively long and the velocity of fall of anxiety manifestations is slow. Often, although they suffer from their symptoms, such patients do not report anxiety because they are not (accurately) processing their internal state, and in this way—of course—they maintain their inability to self-regulate their anxiety and, in due time, their anxiety will continue to grow worse and will eventually generalize.

We already understood in Chapters Two and Three that patients who are not processing or inadequately processing their internal state do so because they put defence mechanisms into operation that serve, among other things, the function of keeping the ego's cognitive/perceptual system dormant. Of course, having determined that the person's cognitive/perceptual system is dormant is not the same as assessing the abilities of the person's cognitive/perceptual system or what is left of these abilities.

Complete and correct assessment of a patient's anxiety is important because it gives the therapist clues about 1) the degree to which a patient is capable of regulating his anxiety for his own benefit, 2) the nature and degree of a patient's ego-adaptive capacity, and 3) the degree of a patient's superego pathology.

Mistakes in the assessment of anxiety are easily made. Common errors are: incomplete assessment of the patient's specific pattern of anxiety manifestations, underestimation of the intensity of a patient's anxiety, overestimation of the patient's ability to regulate his anxiety for his own benefit.

One of our aims is to help our patients to experience their painful feelings without anxiety (or with a tolerable amount of anxiety). But when, on the basis of incorrect assessment of anxiety, the road to the patient's unconscious is taken too hastily, the result may be that a patient's anxiety has only uncontrollably increased!

When patients enter an initial interview with anxiety on the forefront, one of the first tasks of the therapist will be the assessment of the patient's specific pattern of anxiety manifestations. In Chapter Two, we have seen that the regulation of a person's visceral state and the maintenance of homeostasis is greatly dependent on the afferent feedback system, conveying information regarding the momentary state of the peripheral target organs to the brain areas. In turn, these brain areas interpret the afferent feedback and exert control over their output back to the visceral organs and other peripheral target organs.

When (the perception of) a threat ends, the system involved in the regulation of anxiety must quickly be turned off so that the affected organs can recover.

However, under chronic strain, this anxiety-regulating system will be repeatedly stimulated and will leave many tissues vulnerable to damage.

Davanloo frequently warns his trainees to take diarrhoea, dizziness, or jelly legs as an alarm to further investigate other signs for low ego-adaptive capacity or ego fragility. Obviously, such a patient has paid his price in his coping with stressful stimuli. His arousal in anticipation of or in response to (prolonged) challenges has resulted in pathological consequences for the functioning of his organs and tissues. It can be surmised that at least the normal balance of sympathetic and parasympathetic systems has broken down and that these two systems are no longer operating within their normal limits (see also ten Have-de Labije, 1999).

Assessment of the patient's specific pattern of anxiety manifestations

Assessment of the patient's specific pattern of anxiety manifestations should include:

- assessment of manifestations of a) somatomotor, b) autonomic and endocrine, c) cognitive and perceptual patterns
- assessment of the respective proportions of a), b), and c) patterns
- assessment of the velocity of rise, duration and velocity of fall of the respective manifestations.

Assessment of a) somatomotor manifestations (striated muscle patterns)

Rise, spreading, and storage through the somatomotor system follows a distinctive pattern (according to Davanloo's clinical data).

Anxiety begins to channel into the muscles of the hand (moving of the thumb), the mouth (rabbit-like movement), or in the preorbital area (tics), then channels into the flexor and extensor of the forearm (clenching the fist), and/or the pronator and supinator of the forearm, goes to the muscles of the upper arm, shoulders, neck, muscles of the face, the vocal cords, the abdominal wall, intercostal muscles (frequent sighs), and finally to the lower muscles of the back and the legs.

Please note the following:

Provided that there is tension of the patient's striated muscles, the proportion of autonomic and endocrine manifestations is low. and cognitive/perceptual disruptions are absent:

- The amount of spreading and storage of striated muscle tension gives an indication of the intensity of a patient's anxiety. If there is, for example, only tension of the muscles in the hand, the intensity is at its lowest. If the tension spreads itself from head to toe, then the intensity of the patient's anxiety is maximal.
- (Psycho) motor retardation could be considered as an indication that anxiety has already been spread and stored throughout the entire somatomotor system and that its intensity is maximal.
- Trembling can sometimes be observed after high tension of a group of striated muscles. In that case, of course, trembling is a discharge. Trembling needs to be differentiated from shivering, which is a sympathetic manifestation.

Assessment of b) manifestations of autonomic and endocrine patterns

Sympathetic reactions: dry mouth and throat, dry eyes, vaginal dryness, sweating in armpits, sweating of the palms, cold hands, blushing, acceleration of heart rate and force, shivering.

Parasympathetic reactions: light-headedness, drowsiness, dizziness, fainting, constipation, diarrhoea, urge to urinate, nausea, over-secretion of digestive hydrochloric acid in the stomach, wobbly legs.

Please note the following:

- Dry eyes: the cornea of patients wearing contact lenses would become irritated and it becomes painful to the patient to keep his lenses in. Sometimes such patients suddenly enter the practice wearing glasses and this could function as an extra indication that there had been a rise of the patient's anxiety.
- Particularly the vaginal complaints may be felt to be shameful. In an attempt to relieve themselves of these symptoms, some women may wash their vagina with soap, resulting in further damage to their vaginal flora and infection.

Assessment of c) manifestations of cognitive/perceptual patterns

- Disturbances in thought processes (incoherent, delayed, accelerated).
- Disturbances in thought content (disturbed orientation towards time/place/persons).
- Disturbances in perception (alterations in acuity of visual/auditory perception, tunnel vision, tinnitus, hallucinations, dissociation).

Assessment of the respective proportions of a), b), and c) patterns

The distribution of the respective a), b), and c) patterns gives us an indication of the nature and degree of a patient's ego-adaptive capacity as well as the patient's ability to regulate his anxiety for his own benefit.

A higher proportion of a) somatomotor manifestations over the proportion of b) sympathetic manifestations and absence of c) cognitive/perceptual disturbances is an indication that the patient is capable of managing his anxiety in a healthy way. The more we see the occurrence of parasympathetic manifestations and/or cognitive/perceptual disturbances, the more we get an indication of a patient's unhealthy regulation of anxiety. If the proportions of cognitive/perceptual disturbances and parasympathetic manifestations have outgrown the somatomotor and sympathetic manifestations, we know that the patient not only has a very unhealthy regulation of his anxiety, but he also has an extremely low ego-adaptive capacity.

Assessment of the velocity of rise, duration, and velocity of fall of the respective manifestations

Sometimes we meet patients whose anxiety manifestations rise and spread within seconds, and sometimes we meet patients whose rise and spread of anxiety manifestations take a relatively longer period. Mostly, with the patients of this second group, the fall of anxiety manifestations takes a shorter time than with the patients from the first group.

The higher the velocity of rise and spread of the respective manifestations of anxiety and the slower the velocity of fall, the more the person has difficulties in dealing with his anxiety.

The longer the duration of the respective manifestations of a patient's anxiety (the less fluctuation we see in the spread of the anxiety manifestations), the more that patient has difficulties in dealing with his anxiety.

Assessment of the patient's ability to adequately label his internal state as anxiety

Of all the patients entering an initial interview with anxiety on the forefront, it is an exception that we meet one who is actively oriented towards all manifestations of his specific anxiety pattern and is able to label them correctly.

Sometimes, at the time of an initial interview, we meet patients who make mistakes in labelling their specific anxiety manifestations (or don't label them at all), although they are passively aware of their internal state. More often, we meet patients who are unaware of their internal state and—as a consequence—they do not have the habit or motivation to label their specific anxiety manifestations.

Patients may make the following mistakes in their assessment of anxiety:

- The patient is only passively aware of part of his anxiety manifestations but labels these correctly. For example, when asked, a patient reports "some tension of the muscles in the neck, shoulder, and legs". Next to the fact that such a patient neglects the tension in the hands, arms, chest, back, and belly, he also ignores that he is tensed from head to toe, and that the intensity of his anxiety is fairly high. (See below the transcripts of patients 1 and 2).
- The patient is passively aware of part of his anxiety manifestations but labels these wrongly. For example, a patient recognizes his dry mouth and throat, but doesn't label this as an anxiety manifestation but, perhaps, as a consequence of smoking or as "being thirsty only" (see below the transcript of patient 3). Or, for example, the patient is aware of the pattern of striated muscle tension in his body but labels it as anger.
- The patient is completely unaware of his anxiety manifestations.

Although a patient may show anxiety manifestations, such a patient could report that he is nervous only, and at the same time, when asked, he would prove unable to process his internal state (correctly).

Due to the fact that most of our anxious patients are not used to (actively) processing their internal state, they make mistakes in distinguishing the three poles of the triangle of conflict. Furthermore, as another consequence, these patients have difficulty in perceiving the correct causal link between eliciting essential stimuli (the triangle of persons), aroused impulse, and/or feelings, anxiety, and defences (the triangle of conflict).

Assessment of the patient's specific way of preventing adequate processing of his anxiety

Defence mechanisms block the cognitive/perceptual processing of information, either at the level of the stimulus (e.g., denial of a painful situation) or at the level of the response (e.g., denial of physiological concomitants of an emotion). If a patient enters therapy with anxiety on the forefront, and if it is soon evident that he is (completely or partly) unaware of his anxiety manifestations, it will be because of his character defences of, for example, ignoring, neglecting or denying his internal state.

The pattern of a patient's anxiety, ego-adaptive capacity, and superego pathology

It may be clear from the above that a patient's specific pattern of anxiety-manifestations and his (in) ability to process his internal state gives an indication of the nature and degree of a patient's ego-adaptive capacity and of the degree of his superego pathology.

The higher the proportion of a patient's cognitive/perceptual disturbances and/or the higher a patient's autonomic manifestations over somatomotor manifestations of anxiety and the less a patient is adequately processing his internal state, the lower is his ego-adaptive capacity and the higher his superego pathology.

Physical problems concomitant to anxiety

Next to the abovementioned physical manifestations of unhealthy regulated anxiety other physical complaints can accompany the patient's anxiety.

Breathing disorders

Most of our chronically anxious patients have an unhealthy breathing pattern. Especially when a proportion of their anxiety is channelled via the somatomotor nervous system. Although it is relatively seldom that our patients will suffer from an acute hyperventilation syndrome, most colleagues will readily recognize this as such and will react appropriately. As, however, other forms of unhealthy breathing patterns are more difficult to assess, we want to direct the attention of the therapist towards their patient's breathing pattern. Do we notice a healthy breathing pattern with our anxious patients or not?

We are able to breathe because of our respiratory muscles. The principal striated respiratory muscles are the diaphragm, the external intercostal and the intercondral part of the internal intercostal muscles. The abdominal muscles assist in the breathing process.

The intercostal muscles are attached between each rib and they are important in manipulating the width of the thoracic cage.

The diaphragm is located below the lungs. It is a large dome-shaped striated muscle. The abdominal muscles (a group of six muscles) extend from various places on the ribs to various places on the pelvis. They provide postural support, movement and support to the trunk.

Upon inhalation the diaphragm contracts and flattens and the contracting external intercostal muscles lift the ribs. The effect is that because of enlarging the thoracic cavity the intrathoracic pressure is reduced and air is drawn into the lungs. By inhaling, oxygen is brought into the lungs and via the circulatory system the oxygen is transported all over the body to where it is needed.

In conjunction with the contraction of the innermost internal intercostal muscles, the abdominal wall muscles, and the relaxation of the diaphragm, we exhale and we release carbon dioxide out into the environment.

- Depth and frequency of our breaths is regulated by the neural system, primarily in order to maintain normal amounts of carbon dioxide but also to supply appropriate levels of oxygen to the body's tissues. The gases in the alveoli of the lungs are nearly in equilibrium with the gases in the blood.
- Deeper or quicker breaths (hyperventilation) exchange more of the alveolar gas with ambient air, resulting in low concentration of carbon dioxide (relative to the oxygen concentration) in the blood (hypocapnia).
- Since carbon dioxide is carried as carbonic acid in the blood, the hypocapnia on its turn results in the blood becoming alkaline (increase of blood pH). This is known as respiratory alkalosis.
- The increased pH level causes blood vessels to constrict.
- The cerebral vasoconstriction is responsible for light-headedness, paraesthesia, and fainting, which are often seen with hyperventilation.

Symptoms are:

- belching, bloating
- chest pain, confusion
- dizziness, dry mouth
- light-headedness
- muscle spasms in the hands and feet
- numbness and tingling in the arms or around the mouth
- palpitations
- shortness of breath
- sleep disturbances

The hyperventilation syndrome occurs in acute and chronic forms. Chronic forms of hyperventilation are often not recognized by clinicians. It is known that hypocapnia can be maintained if a patient exhibits frequent sighs interspersed with normal respirations.

In order to speak, it is necessary to breathe. Normal breathing occurs mainly through the nose. The nose moisturizes the air. Moist air is better tolerated by the lungs and leads to optimal oxygen exchange. Breathing through the mouth can lead to a chronically dry mouth. If we have a healthy breathing pattern while speaking, we inhale prior to starting our sentence, we exhale while uttering the vowels. Then we have a short speech pause during which we inhale, we continue our speech, exhale over the vowels, and so on.

With our anxious patients, we have come to witness two different unhealthy breathing patterns. These patterns often result in dizziness and light-headedness:

- A rapid and shallow breathing during galloping speech with many speech pauses.
  These patients mainly use their upper thorax while breathing. Their inhalation is shallow, therefore the air doesn't last long and maximum lung capacity is not established. As they have to inhale sooner, they increase their speech pace as well as the frequency of their speech pauses.
- A shallow or normal inhalation before starting to (galloping) speak, no exhalation during speaking, quick exhalation, and quick (deep) inhalation (with a kind of hissing noise) during speech pauses.

Sometimes a psychotherapist can be of help to their patient by drawing the patient's attention to his breathing pattern during speech, by inviting the patient to slow down his galloping way of speaking, or by helping the patient to use his full lung capacity and involve the diaphragm and abdominal muscles. Many patients with anxiety need to rehearse deep breathing techniques. The reality, however, will be that most therapists do not have that expertise. Therefore we would advise therapists to send their patients for proper breathing exercises to speech therapists or to singing lessons. In all cases, however, a therapist can help the patient to slow down his velocity of speech, and to take an upright posture, with a straightened spine and straightened shoulders. In taking such a position, the patient would enlarge the width of his thoracic cave.

Tension headache

According to the International Headache Society (IHS), tension headache can be episodic or chronic.

People with episodic tension headache have at least ten previous headache episodes lasting from thirty minutes to seven days and occurring fewer than one hundred and eighty times a year. The headache must have at least two of the following characteristics

- pressing/tightening (non-pulsating) quality, located on both sides of the head
- mild or moderate intensity
- not aggravated by routine physical activity
- no nausea or vomiting
- possible sensitivity to light or sound, but not both

People with chronic tension headache have an average headache frequency of fifteen days a month or one hundred and eighty days a year for six months and must also meet the criteria for episodic tension headache. In addition, people with chronic tension headache must not have another disorder as shown by physical and neurological examination.

There are no prodromal symptoms and the onset of pain is usually gradual. The pain may be on both sides of the head, or it may cause an aching or squeezing sensation located in the forehead, temples, or back of the head with radiation to the neck and shoulders.

The tension headache is thought not to be the result of sustained muscle contraction but a result of increased sensitivity of the nervous system and imbalances in neurotransmitters (serotonin, dopamine, noradrenaline, enkephalins).

When we had chronic anxious patients with episodic tension headache in our practice, a proportion of their anxiety was channelled via the somatomotor nervous system, the sympathetic nervous system, and sometimes with some parasympathetic manifestations.

Because of the increased healthy regulation of anxiety, thus along with a decrease in frequency, intensity, and duration of their anxiety, their tension headache disappeared.

Physical problems as a consequence of anxiety

Irritable bowel syndrome (IBS)

Englert (2004) refers to research indicating that when the hypothalamus-pituitary-adrenal axis is too active (e.g., under chronic strain) and levels of CRH in the brain are simultaneously too high, signals on the vagus nerve are blocked (the vagus nerve is a major thoroughfare of the autonomic nervous system and controls contractions of the stomach and digestive tract, and it sends nerve impulses to the heart and motor muscles).

During normal digestion, food moves from the stomach to the small intestine, where the nutrients are absorbed. By the time it gets to the large intestine (colon), only waste material remains. The colon absorbs water from the waste and passes the stool via muscle contractions to the rectum. Constipation occurs when waste material moves too slowly through the intestines and too much water is absorbed. The longer waste stays in the intestines, the more water is taken from it and reabsorbed into the body. Constipation may be acute or chronic and can be a symptom of irritable bowel syndrome.

Patients with IBS often experience alternating episodes of constipation and diarrhoea.

If a patient is suffering from constipation, we advise the therapist to check whether this constipation is perhaps a chronic one. Chronic constipation occurs gradually and may last for longer periods of time. When the patient's constipation lasts longer than three weeks, or involves abdominal pain or blood in the stool, then a physician should be notified. Many patients with the symptoms mentioned here below do not present to their physician, or they seek medical attention in a very late stage. Therefore, it is important to inquire about these symptoms.

At least three of the following symptoms should be present:

- patients have difficult defaecation
- patients complain of abdominal bloating or distention
- mucus is present in the stool
- there is increased stool frequency
- there is increased looseness of the stool at the onset of the abdominal pain.

Chronic constipation and/or IBS may be the consequence of lactose intolerance or of another disease However, it *may also* be the consequence of chronic anxiety and unhealthy emotion regulation. In these cases, one could expect that the patients' complaints should diminish the better the patient is capable of regulating anxiety and emotions in a healthy way.

In the meantime, the therapist may advise the patient to check with his physician about

- daily exercise (swimming, walking) to speed up the passage of food through the digestive system
- a high-fibre diet
- avoiding excessive fat and sugar
- eating meals on a regular schedule
- drinking plenty of fluids.

Migraine headache

According to the IHS primary headaches are classified as 1) tension-type headache, 2) migraine, 3) cluster headache and other trigeminal autonomic cephalalgias, and 4) other primary headaches.

According to the International Classification of Headache Disorders, the ICHD-II, there are two subtypes of migraine: migraine with and without aura.

The typical migraine headache is unilateral, throbbing, mostly aggravated by physical activity and lasting from 4 to 72 hours. Symptoms include nausea, increased sensitivity to light and sound. Migraine without aura is the commonest subtype of migraine and often it has a strict menstrual relationship.

About one third of migraine patients perceive an aura that precedes or accompanies the onset of migraine headache. Symptoms of an aura phase can include auditory or olfactory hallucinations, vertigo, tingling or numbness of the face and extremities, hypersensitivity to touch, disturbances of vision, paraesthesia of arm, face, lips, and tongue. The disturbances of vision (visual aura) may consist of flashes of white and black, or of multicoloured lights, or dazzling zigzag lines, or blurred, cloudy vision.

One distinguishes three phases: a prodromal, a pain, and a postdromal phase. The prodromal phase may be evidenced by irritability, depression or euphoria, fatigue, craving for food (chocolate), constipation or diarrhoea, increased urination, tension of the trapezoid muscles, restlessness.

The onset of the pain phase is mostly gradual. The pain may be unilateral or bilateral. Usually it alternates sides from one attack to the next. The pain may be accompanied by symptoms of aura, diarrhoea, sweating. There may be localized oedema of the scalp or face, stiffness of the neck, the extremities feel cold and moist. Postdromal phase: the patient may feel tired, or "hungover", may have cognitive difficulties, gastrointestinal symptoms, depression, or may feel refreshed, euphoric.

Migraine attacks may be triggered

- by menstrual cycle fluctuations, birth-control pills, hormone fluctuations during menopause
- by foods containing tyramine: (cheap) red wine, aged cheese, smoked fish, chicken livers, figs, and some beans
- other foods such as chocolate, nuts, peanut butter, avocado, banana, dairy products, fermented or pickled foods
- coffee, cigarette smoking
- after a period of stress when there is the possibility of relaxation. Migraine often occurs during the weekends, at the beginning of a holiday, after work in the evening.

Causes of migraine

Theories about the pathophysiology of migraine differ. Low levels of serotonin cause the blood vessels in parts of the brain as e.g., in the occipital area to constrict. Soon after, the blood vessels dilate which is thought to cause the headache. The exact cause of the drop in serotonin levels is not yet fully understood. Migraine was previously regarded as primarily vascular. Over the last decades migraine is primarily seen as a brain disorder, a form of neurovascular headache in which neural events result in dilatation of blood vessels aggravating the pain and resulting in further nerve activation. It involves dysfunction of brainstem pathways that normally modulate sensory input. The key pathway for the pain is the trigeminovascular input from the meningeal vessels. These nerves pass through the trigeminal ganglion and synapses on second-order neurons in the trigeminocervical complex, which then project through the quintothalamic tract and, after decussating in the brainstem, form synapses with neurons in the thalamus (Goadsby, Lipton & Ferrari, 2002).

Mistakes

Some therapists take migraine as a sign of anxiety. In our opinion, this is really a mistake.

First, there are women who suffer from migraine without aura. As mentioned above, this type of headache often has a strict menstrual relationship and headaches often occur during ovulation, and the day before and the first day of menstruation.

Second, apart from the menstrual-linked migraines, the periods of migraine often occur during relaxation after a period of stress, for example during weekends or holidays. In these cases—in our view—migraine can be seen as a consequence of unhealthy emotion regulation and/or anxiety but *certainly not* as a concomitant of anxiety.

In our experience, it may happen that during a therapy session the patient suddenly becomes a migraine headache. Mostly, this occurs in the phase of the breakthrough of the patient's sadistic impulse. The migraine headache can be understood as a projective identification, which was triggered by the patient's healthy guilt about aiming at the victim's head. The therapist should be aware that he obviously did not help the patient enough to bear the guilt that was triggered by the impulse. He could draw the patient's attention to the way the patient depicted the murderous impulse, to the inflicted pain on the victim's head, and to the way the patient turned the aggression onto himself.

Another possibility could be that the patient—as a consequence of the therapeutic process—starts to relax after a prolonged period of stress.

Whatever the ultimate origin of the migraine headache, clinical evidence suggests that the headache pain arises from alterations in blood supply of the head.

The application of biofeedback for control of vascular function could be of benefit to some migraine patients. Via an autogenic-biofeedback training programme, patients can be taught to increase the temperature of the fingers, thus redistributing vasomotor activity and presumably causing vasoconstriction of the extracranial arteries. It is relatively simple to supply a patient with a temperature trainer for home use and to teach him how to increase the temperature of fingers and head with the aid of autogenic training. The patient is required to keep record of home practice sessions, of headache incidence, duration, severity, and of medication used. In this way, patient and therapist could assess whether this temperature feedback has a positive influence on the patient's migraine. It is our experience that a patient can learn to increase the temperature of his fingers via temperature feedback and autogenic training within ten trials. If not, then it has no use to continue the temperature control with this patient.

Sleep problems

Sleep problems can occur as a consequence of a limited capacity to regulate anxiety and/or emotions in a healthy way, or it can be a symptom of a medical illness. Sometimes sleep deficit can even become a chronic problem resulting in circadian rhythm disorders. These persons will be tired during their waking hours, and they often have concentration and memory problems, headaches, or gastrointestinal distress. Their efficiencywith tasks deteriorates and, if the duration of the sleep deficit is long enough, performance in their work life is not only compromised, but accidents on the job will be more likely to happen. Especially with patients suffering from chronic anxiety and/or high superego pathology, we advise our colleagues to inform themselves about their patient's quality of sleep. These patients especially have the tendency not to perceive themselves as having a sleep problem.

Assessment of the patient's sleep pattern

- The length of time it takes to fall asleep (sleep latency). A sleep latency of more than thirty minutes is generally seen as a problem. Very often, such a long sleep latency is caused by a patient's ruminating about everything and nothing.
- Waking up a lot during the night and taking a long time to fall asleep again.
- Waking up too early and not being able to get back to sleep.
- Waking up feeling un-refreshed.

Some patients perpetuate their sleeping problem by drinking alcohol or by frequent napping during the day. Drinking some glasses of wine or other alcoholic beverages may help one to fall asleep, it also will interrupt the sleep some hours later.

Other patients, while worrying over their sleep problems will dread going to bed. This will result in an increase of sleep latency and/or the amount of time a patient spends awake in between sleep cycles. Please refer your patient to a sleep specialist if your patient finds it hard to stay awake at work or if your patient's daytime sleepiness interferes with normal functioning.

If a patient's sleep problems are the consequence of his unhealthy regulation of emotions and anxiety, then of course these must decrease the better the patient becomes capable of regulating his feelings and anxiety to his own benefit.

Since in sleep our unconscious has the upper hand, it may be that sleeping problems of a patient can be considered his defence against the experiencing of his complex transference feelings while dreaming/asleep. In these cases, the therapist may notice that the more his patient has experienced his impulse, guilt, grief, and (damaged) love about past experienced traumas, and the more patient has understood the links between his functioning in current interactions and those in the past, the better his patient will sleep during the night.

In the meantime, however, the therapist could teach his patient Jacobson's progressive muscle relaxation. This is recommended for patients having problems with sleep onset or maintenance.

In all cases, patients with sleep problems should avoid stimulants like coffee, tea, and nicotine near bedtime and upon awakening. These patients should not drink alcoholic beverages late in the evening. Advise your patients to minimizing noise, light, and temperature in the bedroom during night, to use their bed only for sleep (or sex), but to leave the bed and go to another room when having difficulty falling asleep again during awakenings, to return to their bed when feeling sleepy again (the bed should become a pleasant place again), and to wake up at the same time each morning (regardless of the amount of sleep that was obtained).

Transcripts of assessing the anxiety of five patients

The transcripts below are taken from the initial interviews with five different patients. Assessment of their anxiety will make clear that, relatively speaking, the first two patients have a better capacity to regulate their anxiety than the third, fourth, and fifth patient.

Processing of internal state and correct/incorrect/no labelling of anxiety manifestations

Although, with the first and second patient it soon becomes evident that they are not used to *actively* process their internal state, they are at least passively aware of some of their specific anxiety manifestations. Going the assessment it becomes evident that they label part of their specific anxiety manifestations correctly, part of their anxiety manifestations are not labelled as such.

The third patient is passively aware of a small part of her long-lasting anxiety manifestations (which have turned into somatic complaints), she makes lots of mistakes in labelling or she does not label at all. The fourth and fifth patient are practically unaware of their internal state.

Distribution of a) somatomotor, b) sympathetic and parasympathetic, c) cognitive/perceptual patterns of anxiety manifestations

All five patients have an immediate rise, spread, and storage of striated muscle tension (a) all five patients have sympathetic and parasympathetic manifestations, (b) but with patients 3, 4, and 5, they are more severe and long-lasting. Cognitive/perceptual disturbances (c): the tinnitus of patient 1 and the hazy view of patient 2 disappeared in the first 20 minutes during assessment. The dissociation of patient 2 and tinnitus of patient 4 did not occur during the session. Patient 5 has cognitive disturbances: incoherent, chaotic thinking.

Velocity of rise and spread of anxiety, duration, and velocity of fall

In the first 20 minutes of the interview, there is more fluctuation of the spread and intensity of anxiety in patients 1 and 2 than in the patients 3, 4, and 5.
The patients' specific way to prevent processing of their internal state:
All five patients "use" their defences of denying, ignoring, and neglecting to keep their cognitive/perceptual system away from processing their internal state (correctly).
The defences of ignoring, neglecting, and denying of the first two patients are less syntonic than those of patients 3, 4, and 5.

Patient 1

We enter the interview at 2 minutes from the start.

Vignette 1: (02.16–10.28 minutes)

Th Yes, tell me, what is your problem?
Pt Well this week I tried to write it down and …

As the patient is tensed from head till toe, as her breathing is shallow and as she speaks with a constricted voice, the therapist interrupts to check whether the patient is a) aware of her anxiety manifestations, b) aware of the fact that she neglects/ignores these manifestations.

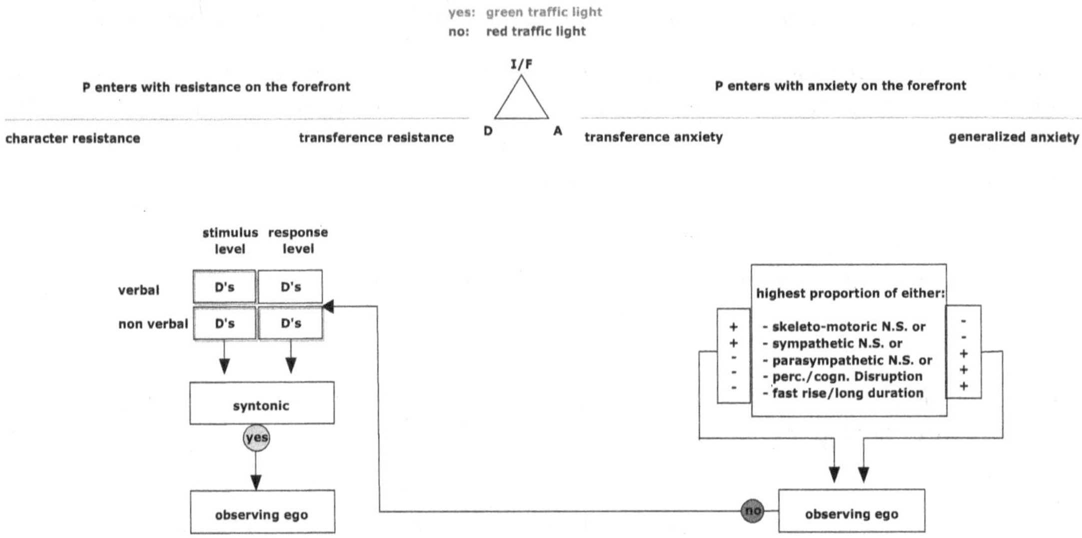

Figure 6. Anxious patient 1: road to the unconscious 1.

Th I will interrupt you.
Pt Yes.
Th I will do that often. Am I right and are you anxious?
Pt Yes.
Th How do you experience that anxiety physically?
Pt It feels … I feel all tensed.

The patient has an observing ego. Because of the fact that she is obviously used to ignoring/neglecting her anxiety, the probability is high that the patient and therapist will not be able to adequately assess all her anxiety manifestations. Therefore the therapist will confront the patient with her defences of ignoring/neglecting, identify and clarify them.

On the road to the patient's unconscious, we are at Figure 6, above.

Th Yes, that is what I see and at the same time I see that you ignore it. Are you accustomed to do so? (confrontation, identification)
Pt Yes.
Th And ignoring your anxiety and pushing yourself through this anxiety, so to speak, is that …
Pt I …
Th … pushing yourself through that anxiety.
Pt That I push myself through that anxiety.
Th That anxiety.
Pt Yes.
Th That is habitual to you. And do you understand me if I tell you that I think that self-neglecting and cruel towards yourself? (clarification of the function)

Pt (nods)

Th And obviously it is normal and habitual to you to ignore your anxiety, to push yourself through your anxiety and obviously it is also habitual to you to be self-neglecting. In any case, in relation to your anxiety, I think that you are nasty towards yourself. (confrontation, identification, clarification).

A patient's habit to "push her/himself through anxiety" serves often the function of "keeping a stiff upper lip", which is a defence, operating at the level of a stimulus. Thus a defence which is used as a cover-up in the relation with the therapist.

Pt Yes, because nasty sounds … (the patient is aware of her defences of ignoring, neglecting, but struggles to accept their self-defeating function)

Th It isn't nasty towards me, it is merciless towards yourself. Without empathy! How do you experience your anxiety physically?

With so many words the therapist invites the patient to drop her defence of stiff upper lip

Pt I have felt … let's say everywhere tension.

Th But at this moment … you are sitting here. How do you notice your anxiety physically? Tension? Muscle tension?

Pt Yes.

Th Where?

Pt It is … it is everywhere … and it feels somehow restless.

Th You say "It is everywhere and it feels restless". That is vague, not precise. Shall we do our assessment with care and precision? Where exactly is the muscle tension? Where does it start? (confrontation, identification)

Pt I have it here in my arms and here in the upper part of my legs.

As the patient acknowledges her habit of ignoring/neglecting her anxiety the therapist turns again to direct her attention to her anxiety. The patient is still looking at herself in a sloppy way and this is also an indication of the patient still struggling to accept the self-defeating function of her defences.

The therapist will continue by directing the patient's attention to all somatomotor manifestations of her anxiety and her dry mouth and throat.

On the road to the patient's unconscious we are at Figure 7, on the next page.

Th Yes and is there a connection between your arms and legs?

Pt There is.

Th In your body?

Pt I … What I feel is … I notice that my stomach and my intestines are tensed too. (the patient is starting to monitor her anxiety in a precise way)

Th Oh, jay, please do your legs next to each other.

Pt Yes.

Th Otherwise you lock yourself. So your hands, arms, shoulders, neck, the intercostal muscles, your belly, legs?

Pt Yes.

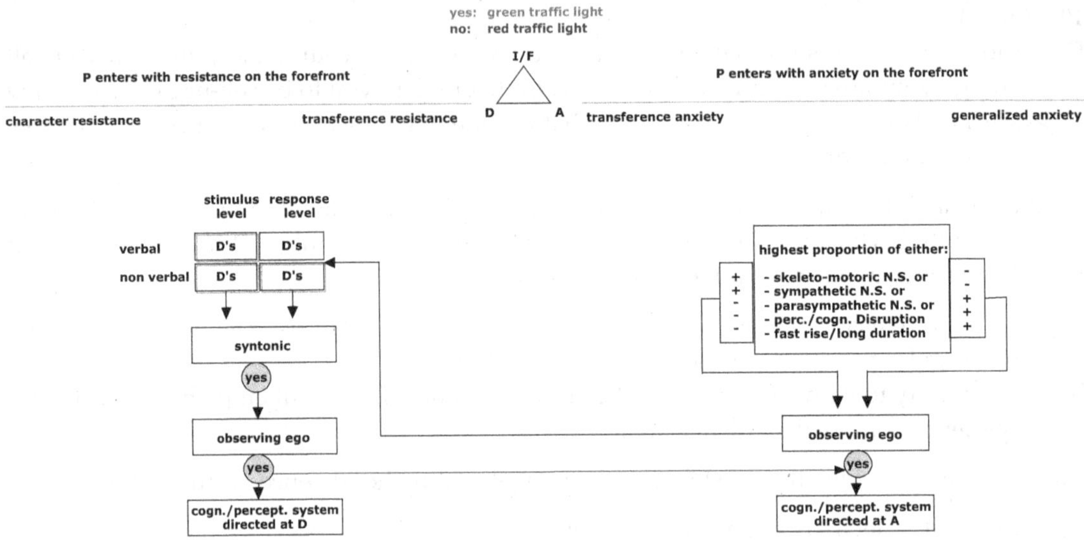

Figure 7. Anxious patient 1: road to the unconscious 2.

Th You have noticed that your breathing … thus these muscles are tensed … is shallow?
Pt Well I didn't notice, but I think that exactly is that oppressed feeling.

As the patient indicates a growing attentiveness towards her anxiety manifestations the therapist will go for a complete assessment of her anxiety.

Th Yes, and you have a dry mouth and a dry throat and if I draw your attention toward that …
Pt Yes.
Th Did you notice that (dry mouth and throat)?
Pt I hadn't noticed, but you are right.
Th And you tell me … your belly, the muscles of your belly, are tensed, but inside your belly too?
Pt Inside my belly, yes.
Th Inside. Do you often have diarrhoea or …?
Pt No, but it is … I have to visit the toilet often when I am tensed.
Th Pi-pi or poop?
Pt Both.
Th Both, thus your anxiety goes also via your bladder, urge for short pi-pi's?
Pt Yes.
Th And goes also via your intestines?
Pt Yes.
Th And then you have diarrhoea or is it creamy?
Pt Yes.
Th Nausea?
Pt No.

Th Ringing in your ears (tinnitus)?
Pt I shake a no, but I think a little bit.
Th Loss of vision, tunnel vision or do you see everything in a haze?
Pt (nods a no)
Th Cold or warm?
Pt My normal temperature.
Th It isn't that you get cold or sweaty when you get anxious?
Pt (nods a no)
Th Heart palpitations?
Pt No, I have … my heartbeat goes faster but that isn't palpitation.
Th You come here to give yourself and me insight into your problems. I see your anxiety rising sky high. At the same time I see that you ignore your anxiety symptoms. You recognize that, you recognize that you are accustomed to ignore your anxiety. And when you indicate that habit of yours, you indicate at the same time a self-negligent part. A part in you that is self-negligent, hard and ruthless towards yourself. But tell me, how do you think to deal with your anxiety if you maintain ignoring it? If you want to deal with me, then don't ignore me. If you want to deal with your anxiety, don't ignore it. Simple as that. You don't need to be a psychologist to understand that. How is your anxiety at this moment?
Pt Well the moment you focused on it, it diminished.
Th Yes.
Pt Things grow worse by hiding them.
Th Things, things, let's not speak in general terms. So your anxiety diminished and would that be the result of the fact that we focused our attention upon it?
Pt Yes.
Th That must be pleasant to you, because to me it seems unpleasant when you have to sit here all the time with such a high anxiety.
Pt Yes, but of course I am not continuously so highly anxious.
Th But I see that you still have much anxiety because I see tension up till here (intercostals muscles). I have interrupted you.
Pt Yes. (patient corrects her breathing and relaxes)

We are at Figure 8, on the next page.

Th You wanted to tell me about your problems.
Pt Yes … what I tried to tell you … I wrote some problems down and in doing so I realized that it all was about "hiding" and I think you noticed that issue immediately when focusing upon me hiding my anxiety. (the patient here acknowledges that part of her defences (pushing herself through the anxiety) was working at the level of the stimulus in the interaction with the therapist)

Pattern of the patient's anxiety manifestations

- There is an immediate rise, spread and storage of tension through out the patient's entire somatomotor system.
- Sympathetic manifestations: dry mouth and throat, acceleration of the heart rate.

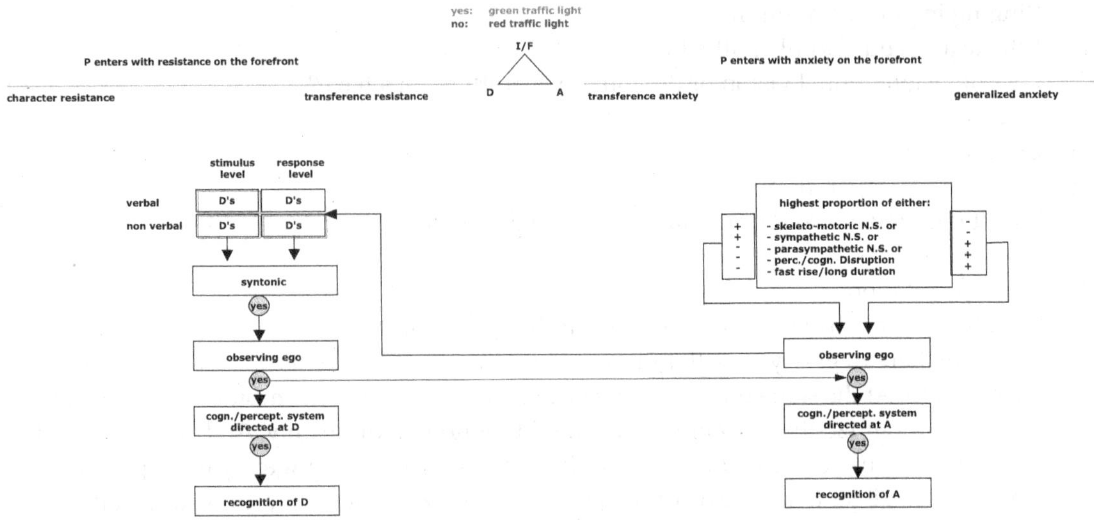

Figure 8. Anxious patient 1: road to the unconscious 3.

- Parasympathetic manifestations: diarrhoea, urge to urinate.
- Cognitive/perceptual disturbances: tinnitus (ringing in the ears).

At the beginning of the interview the patient is passively aware of a part of her anxiety manifestations. She has an observing ego that is awake. Only after the therapist's interventions she becomes aware of her shallow breathing and the tension of the muscles in her trunk and abdomen. It has become clear that the patient is not used to adequately processing her internal state. However, she labels her physical manifestations correctly as anxiety.

The patient's healthy anxiety regulation is partly blocked at the level of the stimulus and at the level of the response. Partly because there is still a weak observing ego operating at both levels.

Her syntonic defences of ignoring, neglecting are responsible for keeping her cognitive/perceptual system away from her internal state. So in this respect they are mainly functioning at the level of the response. The patient's defence of pushing herself through her anxiety/keeping a stiff upper lip functions at the level of the stimulus.

During the above described therapy process the patient's observing ego became more accurate, the patient's observing ego became more attentive (actively monitoring her internal state out of own initiative) and this resulted in a decrease of her anxiety manifestations.

Patient 2

We enter the interview at 1 minute from the start.

Vignette 2 (01.10–18.41 minutes)

Th Can you give me a concrete example of a situation where you encounter your problem?

Pt Well, last weekend I have been to Brussels together with my boy friend, and I had told him: I want you to show some more initiative for once. Then he booked a hotel in Brussels, and I never expected that he would do that. So I was already surprised about this action of his …

Th … I am going to interrupt you.

Pt Yes?

The therapist interrupts the patient because of the fact that she has a galloping breathless speech. There is a high probability that she will regularly feel lightheaded and she must have the habit to ignore/neglect these symptoms.

Th I often interrupt.

Pt Yes?

Th You will experience that.

Pt That's OK.

Th While you are telling me this, I have the impression that you are anxious. When I say so, can you recognize that?

Pt Yes.

Th And how does it feel physically, your anxiousness?

Pt Well, what I mostly feel, and right now as well, is that I just feel a kind of pressure. A kind of squeezed …

The patient is passively aware of a tight chest. She has an observing ego. Because of the patient's galloping and breathless speech, the therapist will function as a model in decreasing her own speech tempo. Therewith the therapist also has a part in regulating the patient's anxiety.

On the road to the patient's unconscious, we are at Figure 9, on the next page.

Th Where? Inside your body? In what part of your body?

Pt In particular in my chest.

Th In particular in your chest. That's where you notice your anxiety? In what other way do you notice your anxiety in your body?

Pt Yes my vision often becomes hazy. (the patient indicates perceptual disruption)

Th What do you experience now, while you are sitting here?

Pt I was very nervous.

Th Yes.

Pt It's also very difficult to me to start all over again.

Th Yes, but there is a lot of anxiousness, isn't it?

Pt Yes.

Th And then you get tears in your eyes. Are those … they look like tears of powerlessness to me, or are they tears of sadness?

Pt Well yes, I am fed up a bit that I … well, that I have to start all over again, well, all over … I mean … It's very difficult to …

Th Shall we first look into that anxiety, for it looks like a very unpleasant feeling to me …

Pt Yes, you know what, I just know so many things so well …

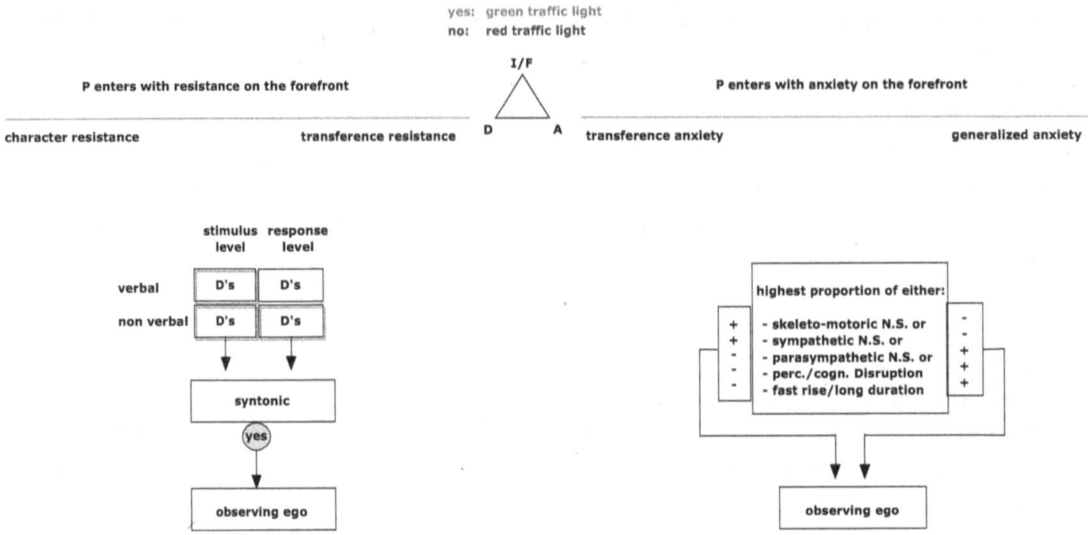

Figure 9. Anxious patient 2: road to the unconscious 1.

Th ... just hold it, just stop galloping.
Pt Hum?
Th Stop galloping, for you want to tell me everything at top speed. (confrontation, identification)
So there is anxiety and you notice it because of the pressure here. (confrontation, identification, clarification)
And in what other way do you notice it in your body?

Telling everything at top speed, so to speak, updating the therapist as quick as possible serves the function of giving the therapist priority. This is, of course, a defence that operates at the level of the stimulus. A defence that operates at the level of intimacy with the therapist.

Pt Well, that my vision gets hazy the moment that I give an example where I ...
Th Your vision gets hazy? (the therapist interrupts the patient's galloping, breathless way of speaking)
Pt Yes.
Th And in what other way do you notice it in your body?
Pt Well, that I get very stiff.
Th So there is muscle tension here, in your shoulders? If it is in your shoulders, is it also in your hands, in your arms, in your neck?
Pt Yes.
Th If I tell you so, can you recognize it? Or do you not take any notice?
Pt Well, I really feel in particular ... well, that I get totally stiff, that I am fully stuck ...
Th Stiff is muscle tension, isn't it?
Pt And in particular in the upper part of my body.

Th In particular in the upper part of your body.
Pt Yes.
Th There is also a dry throat, you have to clear your throat often. That is also a sign of anxiety. (confrontation, identification, clarification) These muscles are also tense, I see that you have to loosen them by sighing, isn't it? (confrontation, identification, clarification)
Pt Hum, hum.
Th Your legs are not too bad?
Pt No.
Th You say: I was very nervous.
Pt Yes.
Th And when did that nervousness start?
Pt In the car on my way to you
Th In the car. And apparently right away … as soon as there is anxiety, there is at the same time also powerlessness.
Pt Yes, right now there is.

As the patient is joining the therapist in assessing her anxiety manifestations and as she is acknowledging her defence of helplessness, the therapist decides to switch the focus to her other defences of galloping, ignoring/neglecting that keep her away from *precisely* monitoring her anxiety upon *her own initiative*.

Th I can say powerlessness, I can say helplessness. Then I say the same thing, What I see is: you enter this room and right away I see all signs of anxiety.
Pt Do you?
Th Yes, I do. And I see that you are ignoring it. You batter right through it, as it were. When I say so, do you understand it? (confrontation, identification)
Pt Yes, I understand.
Th I see that you are battering right through it and that you start galloping. (confrontation, identification)
Pt Yes, that's right.
Th So there is anxiety in your body, and at the same time you switch to the position of ignoring that anxiety, battering right through it and start galloping, like a bolting horse. Do you understand? (confrontation/identification and causality anxiety—defences)
Pt When I get anxious, I am often very hectic.
Th Yes that's what I call galloping, bolting.
Pt That's why I recognize what you are telling me.
Th Like terrified horses, they … .
Pt Can I get some more tea?
Th Do you have a dry mouth? (confrontation, identification)
Pt Yes.
Th That's a manifestation of anxiety (clarification). So muscle tension, what you call stiff, dry mouth and dry throat. Throat clearing, dry mouth, feeling thirsty. Hazy vision. Do you always have that when you are anxious, that hazy vision? (confrontation, identification, clarification)

Pt Only when there are explicit questions about it, then …
Th When I direct your attention towards your anxiety?
Pt Yes.
Th Then your vision gets hazy.
Pt And then it becomes worse …
Th Then it becomes worse and your vision gets hazy?
Pt Yes.
Th Do you experience that often?
Pt I am not encountering it very often during the daytime, for then I start galloping. Do you understand?
Th Then you switch to … bolting. So muscle tension, hazy vision, heart palpitations?
Pt Not those, but I feel pressure here.
Th Yes, but that's because of the muscle tension.
Pt But I don't have the feeling that my heart is racing.
Th Sweating or getting cold?
Pt Cold.
Th Cold. That's also a manifestation of anxiety. Ringing in the ears?
Pt Yes, a little bit, yes.
Th Diarrhoea or constipation?
Pt No, that in fact … yes, rather diarrhoea, but that doesn't happen very often.
Th Not very often.
Pt No.
Th But it does occur?
Pt Sometimes. I think if I would go the bathroom now, I would have diarrhoea. (the patient stops her defence of ignoring/neglecting of her internal state)
Th A bit creamy or fluid?
Pt Fluid, well …
Th Fluid stool that, whoosh, comes out like water?
Pt Well, not that fast, but I also was having flatulence for the past two days.
Th Flatulence?
Pt Yes.
Th Rubber legs or the feeling of your legs failing?
Pt No, but I often have the impression of not having proper contact with my legs.
Th Do you?
Pt That I do not feel them properly (dissociation).
Th Well, I think I have already mentioned a lot of manifestations of anxiety. Do you notice any manifestations that I have omitted?
Pt No, but I am rather considering the causes, but …
Th … just physically in your body? Did I omit some physical symptoms of anxiety?
Pt No, but I know that the moment it happens, that my eyes often start blinking, but that's also nervousness in that moment.
Th Yes, but nervousness is also anxiety, and that's also muscle tension, that's also … do you also have difficulty in keeping them open?

Pt Then it goes very much like this, you know? (the patient demonstrates the therapist blinking)
Th Yes. That's also muscle tension.
Pt And very often it's fully stuck here (points to neck).
Th Yes, but those are also muscles, isn't it?
Pt Yes, and I am really feeling that from here upwards.
Th From where?
Pt From here upwards.

The patient points to her belly and therewith she indicates that she is still monitoring her anxiety in a sloppy way. Would she have been precise she would have indicated that the somatomotor manifestations of her anxiety start round the eyes, hands, then spread to arms, shoulders, and from her neck downward to her feet.

The therapist decides to confront her again with her defences of ignoring/neglecting (at the level of the response), of galloping and giving the therapist priority (at the level of the stimulus) and to identify and clarify them again.

Th Yes, but the point is, what I notice is that you enter this room with a lot of anxiety. At the same time you ignore the manifestations of your anxiety, you batter right through them, and you start galloping. (confrontation, identification) and you want to explain everything to me.
Pt Yes.
Th I think it is in fact self-negligent. When I say so, do you understand? (clarification)
Pt Hum, hum. Of course I have already discussed that several times with my therapist.
Th So be it. I think that you often discussed that with her, but here we start all over again, for …
Pt … yes, it's difficult to me to forget all about that.
Th Of course there's no need for you to forget all about it, that's not the intention. So you say: yes, I recognize that, for I have already discussed it with my therapist. But I am pointing out to you: look, you enter this room with a high level of anxiety. Like an automaton, as if it's fully self-evident, you ignore it. You batter right through it and you start galloping, and the only thing you do is, how shall I say, giving me priority. You give me priority. You are willing to explain all and everything to me and, in the meantime, you neglect your own anxiety. As it were: oh it's unimportant that I am anxious, you, Josette, you are much more important, I'll just inform you zap-zap-zap very quickly. So that's what I mean, you give me, as it were, priority over your own anxiety. That's why I call it self-negligent. If I say so, do you understand? (confrontation, identification, clarification)

On the road to the unconscious, we are at Figure 10, on the next page.

Pt I recognize what you say.
Th But I ask whether you understand me?
Pt Yes. Yes, then I want to explain everything thoroughly, you see?

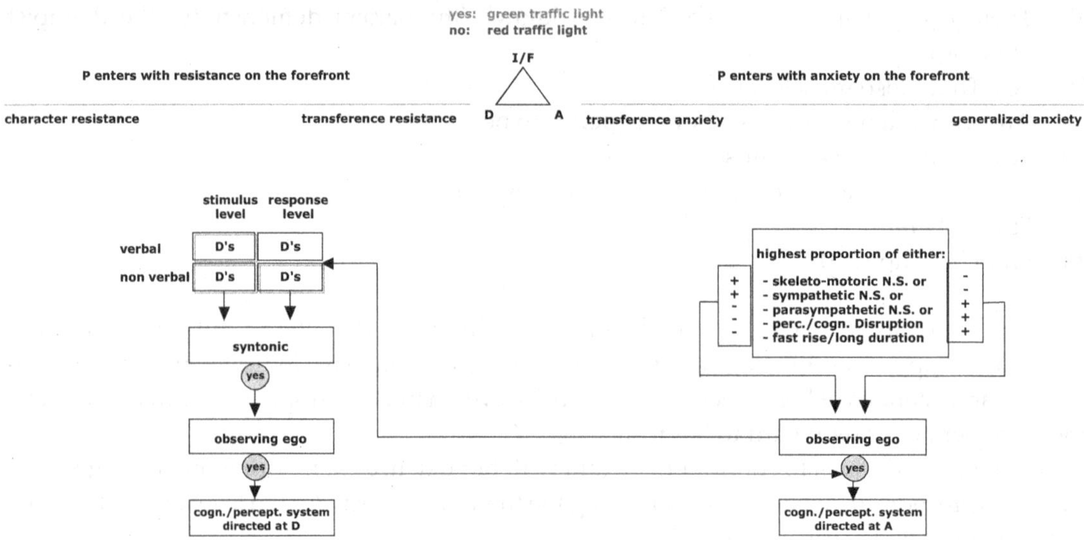

Figure 10. Anxious patient 2: road to the unconscious 2.

Th Yes, I see, you want to explain everything very well to me, so you ignore your anxiety, that's being shunted aside … that's not our concern for the time being, and to me you want to Hum, hum.

Th So yes, it doesn't matter that I am so anxious, as long as I inform you, Josette, quickly. (confrontation, identification)

Pt Yes, that's what I'm doing.

Th That's what you do. Then you behave self-negligently. I ask you whether you understand my language? (clarification)

Pt Yes, I do.

Th Yes, and that you neglect yourself in a way that's automatic, fully self-evident to yourself. To you that's perfectly normal. Oh, my anxiety is not so important. (confrontation, identification, clarification)

Pt Well, it rather has to disappear as soon as possible.

Th Well, if it would disappear, I wouldn't have said anything, but that ignoring and neglecting didn't make it disappear. (confrontation, identification, clarification)

Pt No.

Th By ignoring and neglecting, your anxiety didn't vanish. (confrontation, identification, clarification)

Pt No, that's correct.

Th You maintained your anxiety and it grew. And here it is only since I drew your attention to your anxiety that its intensity dropped. (confrontation, identification, clarification)

Th You see, you don't need to be a psychotherapist, but use your common sense. If you would ignore me, you wouldn't deal with me. The same principle goes for anxiety. If you ignore your anxiety, you don't deal with it. and that is what you are doing. In ignoring your anxiety, you don't deal with it. (confrontation, identification, clarification)

Pt No, because I think it scary (to look at my anxiety). (The patient still has not fully understood that in keeping her defences of galloping, ignoring/neglecting, giving others priority, helplessness she will not succeed in decreasing her anxiety.)

Th But what do you want?

Pt Yes, I want to say goodbye to my anxiety, that's what I told you before.

Th You want to say goodbye to your anxiety?

Pt In any case, I want to be less anxious the moment the focus is upon me, you know.

Th So you want your anxiety to diminish eighty per cent.

Pt I would love that, yes.

Th Yes, of course. Well the issue is that you do understand that it is completely impossible to get rid of your anxiety by ignoring it. How do you see that?

Pt Well, the only thing I can do is to try to deal with my anxiety, that is the only thing I can do.

Th If I were you, I would pay attention to my anxiety symptoms. You have noticed that you had less anxiety after my invitation to assess all of your anxiety symptoms. And of course, that is only logical. If you want to deal with your anxiety, then first meet your anxiety and assess it. And what I see you doing—and please tell me whenever you don't understand something, because I prefer explaining over you keeping up appearances (confrontation, identification, clarification) …

Pt No.

Th … and what I see is that immediately there is high anxiety in you and immediately you ignore that anxiety and immediately all your attention is with me and you give me priority instead of your anxiety. (confrontation, identification, clarification)

Pt Yes, I recognize that very clearly.

On the road to the unconscious, we are at Figure 11, on the next page.

Pattern of the patient's anxiety manifestations

- There is an immediate rise, spread and storage of tension through out the patient's entire somatomotor system, the patient has a galloping, breathless speech.
- Sympathetic manifestations: dry mouth and throat, cold.
- Parasympathetic manifestations: diarrhoea, flatulence.
- Cognitive/perceptual disturbances: hazy vision, tinnitus (ringing in the ears), dissociation (no contact with legs).

At the beginning of the interview the patient is passively aware of a part of her anxiety manifestations. She has an observing ego that has just woke up. Only after the therapist's interventions she becomes aware of her shallow breathing, the fact that she is tensed all over and of the pathway of her striated muscle tension. It has become clear that the patient is not used to adequately processing her internal state. The patient labels part of her physical

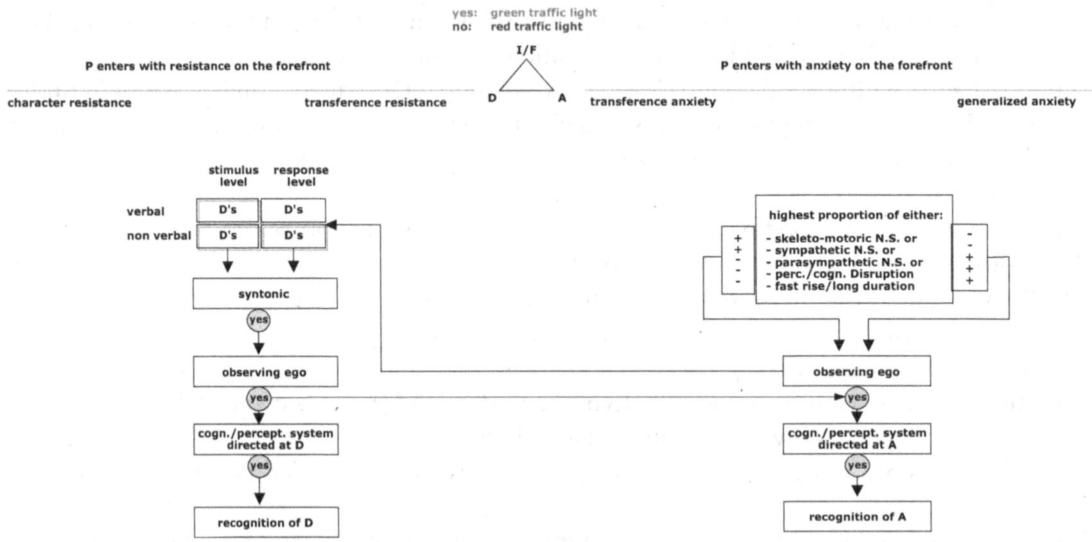

Figure 11. Anxious patient 2: road to the unconscious 3.

manifestations correctly as anxiety. She is not used to labelling her dry mouth and flatulence as anxiety manifestations.

The patient's healthy anxiety regulation is partly blocked at the level of the stimulus and at the level of the response. Partly because there is still a weak observing ego operating at both levels.

Her syntonic defences of ignoring, neglecting were responsible for keeping her cognitive/perceptual system away from her internal state. So, in this respect they are mainly functioning at the level of the response. Her syntonic defences of galloping and giving the therapist priority, both operating at the level of the stimulus.

During the above described therapy process the patient's observing ego became more accurate, the patient's observing ego became more attentive (actively monitoring her internal state out of own initiative) and this resulted in a decrease of her anxiety manifestations.

Patient 3

We enter the interview at 1 minute from the start.

Vignette 3 (00.53–13 minutes)

Th What is your problem because I think we have to use our time very effectively, because 3 or 4 hours isn't as much as it seems.

Pt Yes.

Th We have to work hard.

Pt OK, this is the first time for me.

Th Yes, yes.

Pt And I don't realize if I have a problem or not. (the defence of casting doubt on her own opinion/perception)

Th You don't realize ...

Pt I know that something is ... I know it is very nervous in me because I have physical symptoms, that maybe can be cured with therapy, I am not sure.

Th But you are feeling nervous.

Pt Uh, I am always stressed and anxious and, uh ... with no reason. (either the patient is used to rationalizing her anxiety away (operating at the level of the response) and/or she is used to bringing defences at the level of the stimulus in operation. This has the consequence of not being able to recognize any trigger for her feelings/anxiety)

Th And at this moment?

Pt Most of the time. (the defence of generalization, probably operating at stimulus and response)

Th At this moment?

Pt At this moment? No, it is OK, I mean I am a little bit nervous now (defence of minimization) but it is because ...

The patient has an observing ego, although still half asleep and which will not be very accurate because of her defences of casting doubt on her own opinion/perception, generalization, minimization. All operating on the level of stimulus and response. The therapist decides to check first the extent to which the patient's observing ego is asleep or awake and will be able to assess some of her anxiety manifestations.

Th So we are here to investigate your problems very carefully and with precision.

With so many words the therapist appeals to the conscious part of the patient that wants to establish a working alliance with the therapist.

Pt OK.

Th OK and a little bit nervous is also nervous, hum?

Pt Yes.

Th So when you say nervous, you say ...

Pt Restless.

Th When you say restless you say I am a little bit anxious.

Pt Right.

Th OK, so could you tell me the physical experience of your anxiety at this moment.

Pt Uh, it is always concentrated here. (the patient points to her belly) (always is a generalization)

Th Now at this moment too?

Pt Yes, also now.

Th What is here? (the therapist points to her belly)

Pt Well now, let's say, it's more here (the patient points to her stomach) but normally I am ... I have pain ...

Th Pain? Inside to outside? Pain, from inside to outside or from outside to inside?

If the pain is from inside to outside, then the therapist knows that the patient's smooth muscles are involved in the anxiety regulation.

Pt From inside to outside.
Th So, in the stomach.
Pt Yes.
Th And now you have here (therapist points to her chest), what?
Pt Now I am a little nervous. (minimization)
Th Tensed … so your muscles are tensed. (confrontation, identification)
Pt Yes, very.
Th Where?
Pt Here and here. (the patient points to her chest and shoulders)
Th And here (therapist points to her upper arms) too? (confrontation, identification)
Pt Yes.
Th And do you notice you have a dry mouth and throat? (confrontation, identification)
Pt I would because I smoke … probably.
Th No, but you have a dry mouth. (confrontation, identification)
Pt Yes I do.
Th You have to wet your lips regularly. (confrontation, identification)
Pt Exactly.
Th Yes, that's a sign of anxiety. (clarification)
Pt I see.
Th So …
Pt Probably. (the patient still does not label these manifestations as anxiety)
Th Not probably.
Pt Not probably? (patient laughs) … You see, I …
Th You didn't label it as anxiety?
Pt No, I never think about it. I know something is wrong but I am not sure what. (ignoring/neglecting and casting doubt).

As the patient's observing ego is hardly awake (so to speak) the therapist decides to switch the attention to the patient's defences in order to awaken her observing ego.

On the road to the patient's unconscious, we are at Figure 12, on the next page.

Th Yes, yes.
Th So you are suffering from anxiety.
Pt Most of the time and …
Th Most of the time but you're not investigating it precisely. (confrontation, identification)
Pt No, no, I …
Th So that's not so kind towards yourself, isn't it? (clarification)
Pt No, I guess not. (defence of staying in the middle)

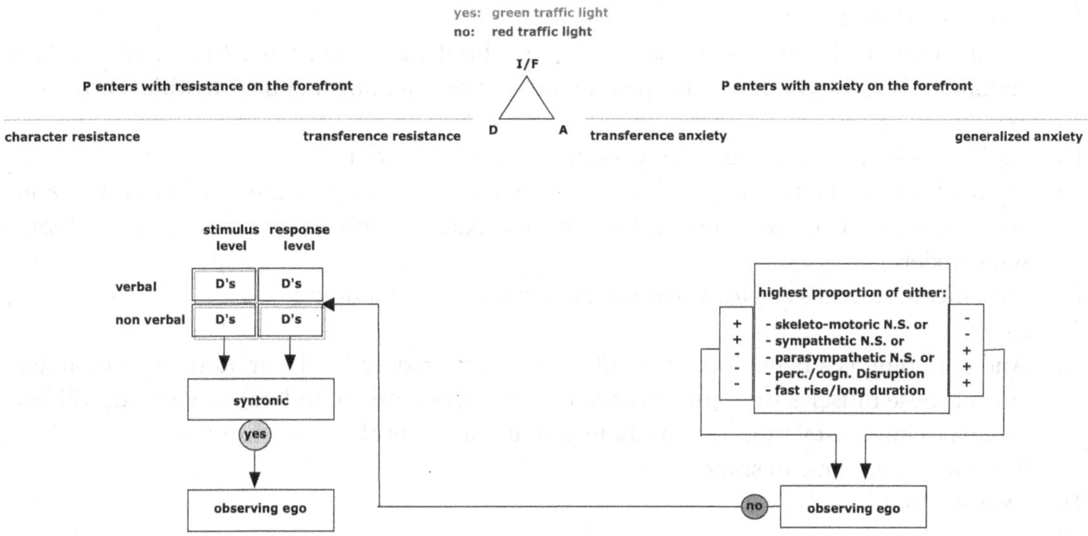

Figure 12. Anxious patient 3: road to the unconscious 1.

Th I guess not, or …? We are here to investigate your problems very honestly, hm, and very precisely (confrontation, identification, clarification and invitation to cooperate)

Pt It's not always easy to be precise when you don't know what is happening.

Th I mean … but I say it's not very kind to yourself if you ignore so much, so many … With one hand you tell me I suffer from anxiety and with the other hand you tell me I am also used to neglecting my anxiety or to ignoring my anxiety. (confrontation, identification, clarification)

Pt Yes.

Th I say that's not very nice towards yourself, it's hard, you take a hard position towards yourself. If I say so, do you understand me? (confrontation, identification, clarification)

Pt Yes, I do.

Th It's more or less cruel. (clarification)

Pt Yes.

Th I draw your attention to that fact because it isn't—to me—I wouldn't be happy when I would suffer from anxiety.

The therapist is functioning as an external constructive superego and with so many words is inviting the patient to drop her defences at the level of the stimulus, the interaction with the therapist. Subsequently, the therapist will alternately focus on the defences, operating at the level of the response and check whether assessment of anxiety manifestations is possible

Pt Hum.

Th And then ignoring it, then you take a very hard, nasty, ugly position towards yourself. (confrontation, identification, clarification)

Pt (nods affirmative)

Th So dry mouth, dry throat, tension of arms, shoulders, neck, here. (therapist points to abdomen) Mostly, you have also pain in the stomach. (confrontation, identification)

Pt Yes.

Th And how else do you experience your anxiety? (clarification)

Pt My restlessness. I am always … I want to go to the next step all the time. I don't, I rarely enjoy or appreciate the moment, I try to. (the patient confuses the defence of galloping with anxiety)

Th But I mean, so you say, you know yourself in a way as galloping.

Pt Right.

Th And galloping is a behaviour, it is not the same as anxiety. So dry mouth, dry throat, tension of these muscles (therapist points to arms, neck, and shoulders), anyway up till here (points to intercostal muscles), nasty feeling in the stomach, what else? Nausea?

Pt No, nausea, no, I mean sometimes.

Th Only seldom.

Pt Only seldom.

Th Only seldom.

Pt Yes, not very often.

Th Perspiration, feeling hot or cold?

Pt Cold most of the time.

Th Most of the time feeling cold.

Pt I am always very cold.

Th Yes, diarrhoea?

Pt No, unfortunately, it's the opposite.

Th Constipation, hum. Constipation can also be a signal of anxiety. Cold can be a signal of anxiety. Ear ringing (tinnitus)? (confrontation, identification, clarification)

Pt No.

Th No, no. Perception? You perceive me clearly or …

Pt Yes, yes, I do.

Th You don't get sometimes a hazy vision or that this part is falling out. (therapist mimics a tunnel vision)

Pt You mean a lack of concentration?

Th Tunnel vision.

Pt Hum?

Th Like a tunnel vision, that you only see this, and you don't see that. (therapist mimics tunnel vision)

Pt I don't have that

Th You don't have that symptom. So did we forget to mention some symptoms?

Pt No, the most … I mean, the real reason is that it's 25 years that I have been suffering from … (the patient points to her belly)

It becomes clear to the therapist that the patient has an experience of 25 years in denying and/or ignoring/neglecting/minimizing her internal state.

Th Constipation?
Pt Stomach problems.
Th Stomach problems.
Pt And they (medical doctors) told me … try to have treatment. There is absolutely nothing (wrong). They understand it's nervousness and maybe therapy would be good for you.
Th So you suffer 25 years.
Pt More than that, a little more than that.
Th From physical symptoms.
Pt Physical symptoms, yes.
Th You, yourself didn't relate these physical symptoms to anxiety.
Pt Maybe, I am not sure, I don't know. (Casting doubt on her own opinion/perception.)

Although the patient is able to monitor part of her anxiety manifestations she still is taking refuge in her array of defences. Therefore the therapist continues to confront the patient with her defences, to identify and clarify these.

Th That's what I am telling you. You, yourself didn't relate these symptoms to anxiety, hum, it is because of the fact that the doctor, or some expert told you: maybe these physical symptoms are caused by anxiety.
Pt Exactly … that it was probably nervousness.
Th Hum, but you know yourself as nervous. (boosting the patient's observing ego)
Pt Yes, I realize that I am, because also everybody tells me I am very nervous. I don't always realize that I am very nervous. (ignoring/neglect)
Th That's what I am telling you. For 26 years, you have these symptoms, it isn't nice.
Pt No.
Th No, absolutely not, no. You also know yourself as a nervous person but you cannot describe to me very well how you experience your anxiety. You tell me, I am used to ignore my anxiety.
Pt To take it lightly. (minimizing)

The patient, knowing her habit of minimizing and her self-neglect, indicates therewith a degree of satisfaction with these defences. The therapist continues to confront the patient with her defences, to identify and clarify them.

Th And I say that is the first problem we encounter, that is the problem of the self-negligent woman.
Pt Correct.
Th Correct. It is the first problem. Perhaps we have other … No matter what else we will discover, this is a major obstacle.
Pt Hum.
Th The problem of the woman, who is used to take a self-negligent position. You think it normal to ignore your feelings, ignore your painful anxiety symptoms, to minimize them. (confrontation, identification, clarification)
Pt Minimize them, yes.

Th I call that self-neglecting, I call that cruel, I call that very hard and this is the first problem and it is the problem of the woman, who takes a self-negligent position towards herself and it is normal, habitual ... How do you think we can solve your problems if you maintain that self-negligent position? (confrontation, identification, clarification)

On the road to the patient's unconscious, we are at Figure 13, below.

The therapist continues the interview by using a soft version of the head-on collision to further a conscious/unconscious working alliance with the therapist, to help the patient understanding that in maintaining her defences, she will not get any healthy grip on her emotions and anxiety.

Pattern of the patient's anxiety manifestations

- There is an immediate rise, spread, and storage of tension through out the patient's entire somatomotor system.
- Sympathetic manifestations: dry mouth and throat, feeling cold.
- Parasympathetic manifestations: constipation, stomach problems, nausea.
- Cognitive/perceptual disturbances: none.

At the beginning of the interview the patient is hardly aware of a part of her physical manifestations (stomach problem). The patient herself is not used to correctly label her physical manifestations as anxiety. Her observing ego is still half asleep. Only after the therapist's interventions, she becomes aware of her muscle tension, dry mouth and throat. It had become clear that the patient was not used to adequately processing her internal state. The patient is "only nervous", and she mistakes some of her defences (e.g., her restlessness, galloping) for anxiety.

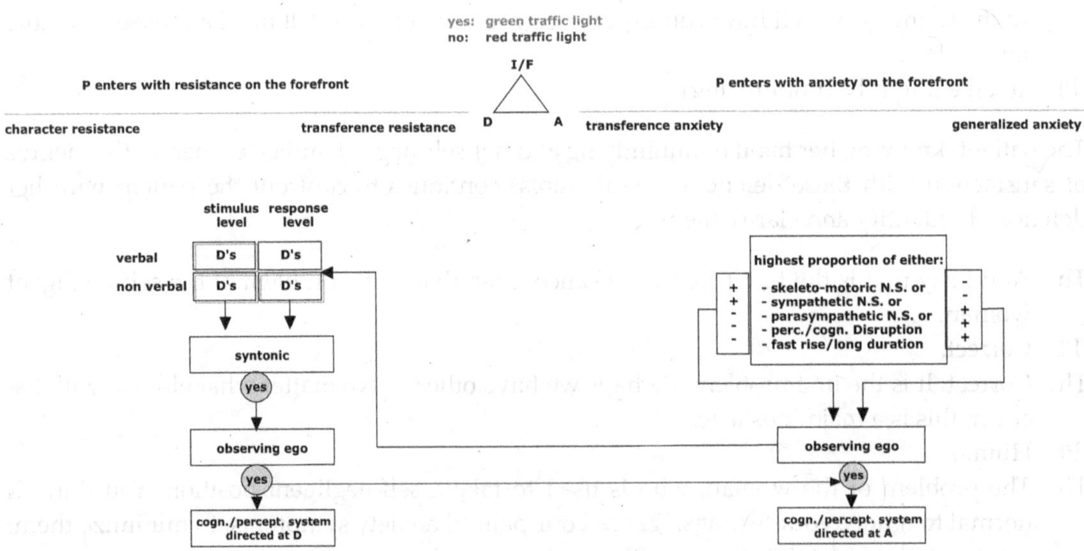

Figure 13. Anxious patient 3: road to the unconscious 2.

The patient's healthy anxiety regulation is partly blocked at the level of the stimulus and at the level of the response, partly because there is still some observing ego operating at both levels.

Her syntonic defences of denying, ignoring, neglecting, minimizing, generalization are responsible for keeping her cognitive/perceptual system away from her internal state. So, in this respect, they are mainly functioning at the level of the response. The patient's defences of minimizing/keeping a stiff upper lip and speaking in general terms function at the level of the stimulus.

During the above described therapy process the patient's observing ego becomes more awake, and this resulted in a fluctuation of her anxiety manifestations.

Patient 4

We enter the interview at 2 minutes from the start.

Vignette 4 (01.54–15.48 minutes)

Pt Uh, the problems that I have now, how do you call that, uh, is the fact ... at this moment I am in the process of a divorce, a divorce procedure, that the procedure, that contributes ...
Th Divorce, depressed.
Pt Yes, how do you call that, everything coming together.
Th Listen, I interrupt you, I think that you are very anxious, there is heavily sighing, you are trembling, am I right? (the patient is so heavily tensed that he is trembling, he is sighing and his voice is constricted)
Pt Yes, that's right.
Th Well, shall we first look how you feel your anxiety physically. How do you feel it physically?
Pt Uh, nervous, very nervous.
Th How do you feel that physically in your body?
Pt Trembling.

The patient has some observing ego but this is obviously not working on behalf of himself and his internal state.

Th You are trembling from head to foot, aren't you?
Pt Yes, nervousness, insecurity of course.
Th But I am asking you: how do you experience that in your body?
Pt Pressure, agitation from inside, and how do you call that, just oppressed, tight, a pressure.
Th I saw that you had to sigh very heavily.
Pt Hum, hum.
Th Are you aware of that?
Pt Uh, uh, yes.

The therapist doubts whether he is really aware of his sighing or that he is keeping up appearances. Therefore, the therapist mirrors the patient the tension of intercostals muscles.

Th So, then it is all tensed here. If I say so, can you recognize that?

Pt Yes, but it is more tensed here, according to me. (the patient points to his head)
(In pointing to his head, the patient has confirmed that he is not aware of the high tension of the intercostals muscles and that he is keeping up appearances. Let's say that his observing ego is still very sleepy.)

Th Well, what you indicate is that obviously you are not used to look at yourself in a careful and precise way. You know that you are very nervous but if I ask you how you feel that exactly in your body then you have problems telling me that precisely. (confrontation, identification of imprecise monitoring of his internal state)

Pt That's right.

Th So obviously we encounter here right away problem number one. Obviously it is habitual to you, very normal to treat yourself in a sloppy way. If I say so, can you recognize that?

Pt Yes.

Th To me it seems very uncomfortable to sit here all the time with such a high anxiety and then to ignore that anxiety and to push yourself through that anxiety. Because I notice that you are accustomed to do so. Am I right? (confrontation, identification, clarification of denying/ignoring/neglect (response) and of keeping up appearances and giving the therapist priority (pushing through his anxiety) (stimulus))

Pt Yes, that is right.

Th And that also is negligent, if I say so do you understand me? That you are negligent towards yourself, do you understand so or don't you? (clarification)

Pt Uh, negligent, yes, negligent, yes, the way I am and how I recently … or recent, how do you call that, how I am used to live recently.

Th Yes, but with negligence you don't solve your problems. (clarification)

Pt Hum, hum.

Th So that is the first problem we have to tackle and already in the first minutes this problem comes to the surface in full. So that is a major problem, an enormous problem.

The patient's observing ego is still half asleep. His defences of denying/ignoring/neglect at the level of the response and his keeping up appearances and giving the therapist priority (level of the stimulus) are still put into operation.

The therapist will continue the interview by appealing to the patient's ego and to his wish to cooperate with the therapist. Subsequently the therapist will focus again on the patient's anxiety.

On the road to the unconscious, we are at Figure 14, on the next page.

Pt Hum, hum.

Th I want to focus again on your anxiety. So I notice tension of your muscles in hands, arms, shoulders, neck and then via your back and front side, because your legs were tensed too and I notice that you are not used to direct your attention to that. (confrontation, identification, clarification of physical manifestations as anxiety and confrontation, identification and clarification of denial/ignoring/neglect)

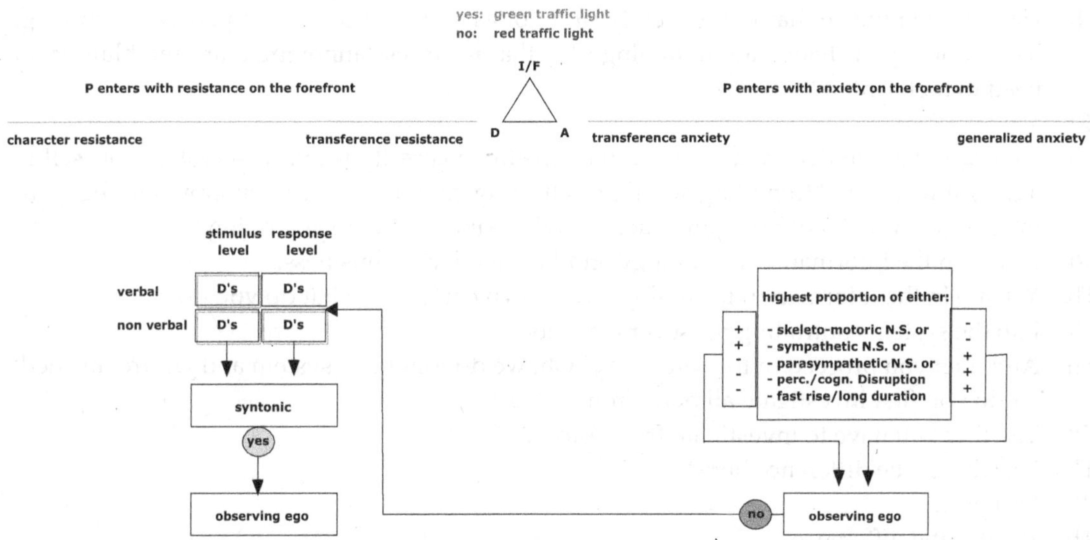

Figure 14. Anxious patient 4: road to the unconscious 1.

Pt No, that is right, because I, probably I don't think that important or I neglect that.

Th Yes, indeed, you neglect that and you could continue so but then we will be stuck immediately. Because if you neglect yourself, we will not be able to proceed. Do you understand that?

The therapist appeals again to the patient's ego part, to his wish to cooperate and clarifies again the function of his defences in the realm of the resistance against emotional closeness with the therapist.

Pt Yes.

Th Yes? So muscle tension and it was immediately there, wham, and so intense that you trembled all over, and also your voice was trembling. If I tell you so, can you recognize that? (confrontation, identification, clarification)

Pt Yes.

Th Dry throat, dry mouth, do you recognize these as symptoms of your anxiety? (confrontation, identification, clarification)

Pt Hum, to a lesser extent, usually it is nervousness, feeling awkward …
(the patient denies/ignores/neglects these anxiety manifestations and goes for minimization (nervous))

Th But nervous, that is vague, and you go again for sloppiness. (confrontation, identification, clarification)

Pt Yes, nervous, trembling.

As the patient sticks to his defences of vagueness and minimization the therapist continues the focus on the patient's defences.

Th How do you notice that in your body, and not as a broad outline but precise. Trembling: look, if only your hands are trembling then that is far less annoying than trembling from head to foot, isn't it?

Pt Yes.

Th So, if you want to deal with yourself then the first necessity is that you look at yourself in a careful way. And "trembling and that's all" is again that part of the sloppy self-negligent man, and that will not bring any success. What kind of job are you doing?

Pt I work in the information technology and I have my own business.

Th You are in the information technology, your own company, what do you do?

Pt I do the system controlling for several clients.

Th And then you proceed in the same way? Oh, we do roughly a system and we are finished. Or do you first investigate all parts from A to Z?

Pt Yes, first you have to investigate from A to Z.

Th So, what is the difference here?

Pt I think …

Th What is the difference?

Pt There is no difference, only I make a difference. (The patient has finally understood the self-defeating function of his defences. We will notice that his observing ego becomes more awake.)

Th That's what I tell you. You apply double standards.

Pt Hum.

Th Well, in your body there are different systems. And the first system is the system of anxiety: trembling from head to foot, a moment ago, hands, shoulders, neck, back, legs, mouth, your breathing becomes more shallow, short of breath. What other physical symptoms of anxiety do you know of yourself?

Pt My head becomes warm.

Th Warm head. Only your head?

Pt And mostly I get cold hands and feet in combination with that.

Th Warm head, cold hands and feet, yes.

Pt And how do you call that, I feel awkward, that is not physical.

Th No, that's not physical, that's right and what else … you didn't recognize a dry mouth and throat. Diarrhoea?

Pt Yes, sometimes, depending on the way I manage my life on that moment,

Th Pardon?

Pt Yes, when I live unhealthily then I have diarrhoea.

Th Oh, when you are negligent towards yourself then you suffer from that. In what way are you negligent?

Pt If something bothers me, yes, then I don't … that's again that sloppiness or self-negligence, then I cannot eat, I am closed off.

Th And then you can't eat?

Pt And that may take 5 days.

Th Oh, but that hasn't to do with sloppiness.

Pt Well …

Th That has to do with … if you are anxious, obviously you are sometimes in such a way anxious that your throat is choked and that your digestion is out of order. And that goes on for 5 days?

Pt That may go on for 5 days long.

Th And are your faeces like water or like cream?

Pt No, it can be like water.

Th Really like water?

Pt Yes.

Th Tinnitus?

Pt Sometimes.

Th The idea that your legs will not bear you?

Pt That too. When I climb the stairs, then I have the feeling that I will not reach the end, that halfway I collapse.

Th Man, that is a high anxiety. Are you used to label those symptoms as anxiety or are they so common to you that you don't label them as anxiety?

Pt No, these symptoms are so common to me that I don't label them as anxiety.

Th Is that important? To me it seems that anxiety is a feeling that one prefers not to suffer from, isn't it?

Pt That's right.

Th Yes, if you want to deal with your anxiety and you want to deal with it in order to manage your anxiety and to diminish it in successive steps, then of course, you must not ignore your anxiety. You don't need to be a psychologist to understand that. (clarification)

Pt Hum.

Th Well, the two of us are focusing at your anxiety and I don't know if I see it correctly, still your anxiety is fairly high, but not so high as in the beginning. Am I right? (confrontation, identification)

Pt Yes, that's right.

Th Guess how we got that result.

Pt That has to do with the conversation I had with F. (person who referred him). (Obviously, the patient has not understood that the decrease of his anxiety is the result of his taking himself more seriously and monitoring his internal state.)

Th But guess, guess, since we focus on your anxiety, your anxiety has diminished. How is that possible?

Pt Because I feel more at ease.

Th It is because you don't ignore your anxiety, because you acquaint yourself with it. Now that you don't ignore your anxiety as an unwanted stranger but deal with it as with a nasty acquaintance. So tinnitus, diarrhoea, warm head, cold hands and feet, elastic legs, immediate trembling from head to foot, tension in your muscles. Do you sometimes have a tunnel vision? (confrontation, identification, clarification)

Pt No, not that. Sweat outbursts.

Th Sweat outbursts and dizziness?

Pt Yes.

Th Dizziness, but your vision is …

Pt My vision is not influenced.
Th Not that you see everything hazy?
Pt No.

The patient's observing ego has become more awake. He is recognizing his anxiety manifestations as anxiety. He is more aware of his defences and their self-defeating function, but he still needs the therapist to recognize his defences.

On the road to the unconscious, we are at Figure 15, below.

Pattern of the patient's anxiety manifestations

- There is an immediate rise, spread and storage of tension through out the patient's entire somatomotor system, the patient is trembling and his voice is constricted.
- Sympathetic manifestations: dry mouth and throat, feeling warm, sweat outbursts, cold hands and feet.
- Parasympathetic manifestations: diarrhoea, nausea, not being able to eat (sometimes for five days), dizziness, the idea that his legs will not bear him.
- Cognitive/perceptual disturbances: tinnitus.

At the beginning of the interview the patient is passively aware of a small part of his anxiety manifestations. He has an observing ego that is still half asleep. Only after the therapist's interventions does he become aware of the fact that he is tensed all over, that he trembles, and of his sympathetic manifestations. Upon further investigation he describes parasympathetic manifestations and tinnitus but it becomes clear that he is not used to label these as anxiety manifestations. The patient is not used to processing his internal state. The patient's healthy

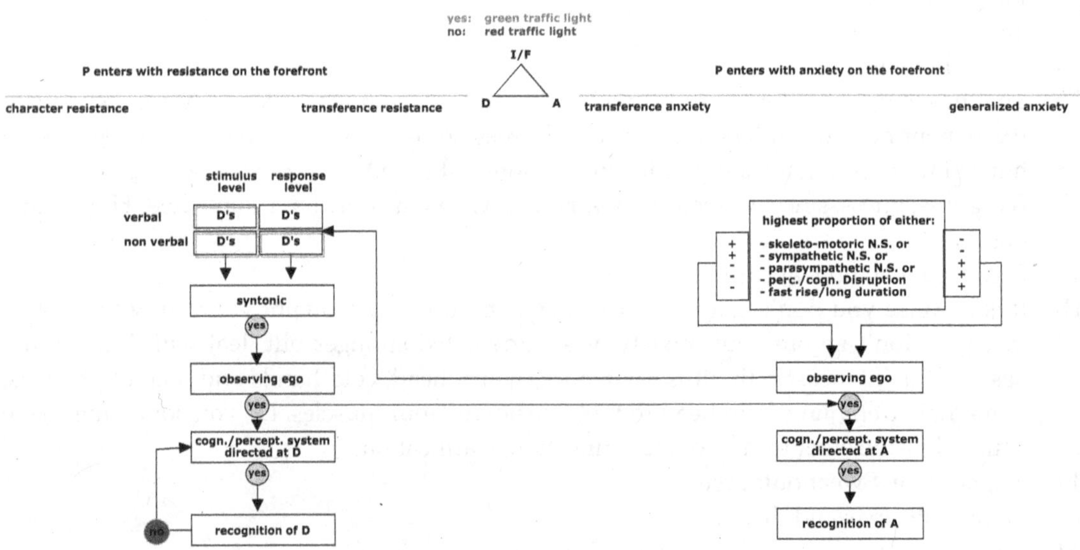

Figure 15. Anxious patient 4: road to the unconscious 2.

anxiety regulation is greatly blocked at the level of the stimulus and at the level of the response. "Greatly" because his observing ego is half asleep.

His syntonic defences of denying, ignoring, neglecting are responsible for keeping his cognitive/perceptual system away from his internal state. So in this respect they are mainly functioning at the level of the response. His syntonic defences of keeping up appearances and giving the therapist priority are both operating at the level of the stimulus.

Patient 5

We enter the interview at 2 minutes from the start.

Vignette 5 (02.03–12.14 minutes)

Pt Yes, I … how do I see my problems. I think I have little … I feel … I am not so happy with my life, I think. That is one issue. I have periods that I am able to work very hard and which makes me very happy.
(The patient is galloping with breathless staccato speech, she is tensed from head till toe)
Th I interrupt you Mary.
Pt Yes.
Th Is your anxiety rising?
Pt I think it does … very much. (the defence of casting doubt on her opinion/perception at the level of response)
Th Do you think so or is it rising?
Pt As a matter of fact … eh … I don't know if it is anxiety … or feeling … Anyway, it is very tearful. That's it, it's more tearful than anxiety. (because of her galloping, staccato, and breathless speech, it is difficult to hear what she is saying)
Th So it takes a fast rise?
Pt Yes.
Th Is that something you have noticed before?
Pt Not very often. (speaking in general terms)
Th Not very often?
Pt Not in this way, no.
Th When did you notice? You say not very often. When? Sometimes, when …
Pt Yes sometimes, in any case it is … it takes me by surprise. I had it once or twice with my therapist … it is because suddenly I have to think of it or something like that. (Because of her staccato breathless speech, it is difficult to understand the patient. She must be regularly dizzy. In a later part of the interview, this appears to be true.)

The therapist decreases her pace of speech and therewith regulates part of the patient's anxiety.

Th Suddenly you have to think of it?

As the patient tells the therapist in so many words that often her anxiety (response) takes her by surprise, she must also be totally unaware of the trigger (stimulus) for her physical manifestations. The therapist decides to check this.

Pt Yes, my God, what is the matter or what do I think is the matter, yes …

Th You don't notice that your anxiety has risen?

Pt Do I notice that I have caught anxiety?

Th Your anxiety has grown, don't you notice?

Pt Oh …? (obviously the patient didn't notice the increase of her anxiety)

Th Right from the start your anxiety was there and immediately there was tearfulness too, didn't you notice? (the tearfulness in this case is a parasympathetic manifestation of her anxiety)

Pt No (the patient is still denying her anxiety manifestations).

Th No, no, so you are not accustomed to paying attention to yourself?

Pt That has to come from very far. (with so many words the patient knows that she is ignoring/neglecting herself and she indicates a certain degree of satisfaction with that defence)

The patient's observing ego is fast asleep. The patient's defences of casting doubt, denying/ignoring/neglect at the level of the response and the patient keeping up appearances (?), operating at the level of the stimulus maintain the patient's unhealthy anxiety regulation. The patient is still extremely anxious.

At a slow pace, the therapist continues confronting the patient with her defences, identifying and clarifying them.

On the road to the unconscious, we are at Figure 16, below.

Th So you do know that you take a negligent position towards yourself? Because you are not accustomed to paying attention to yourself.

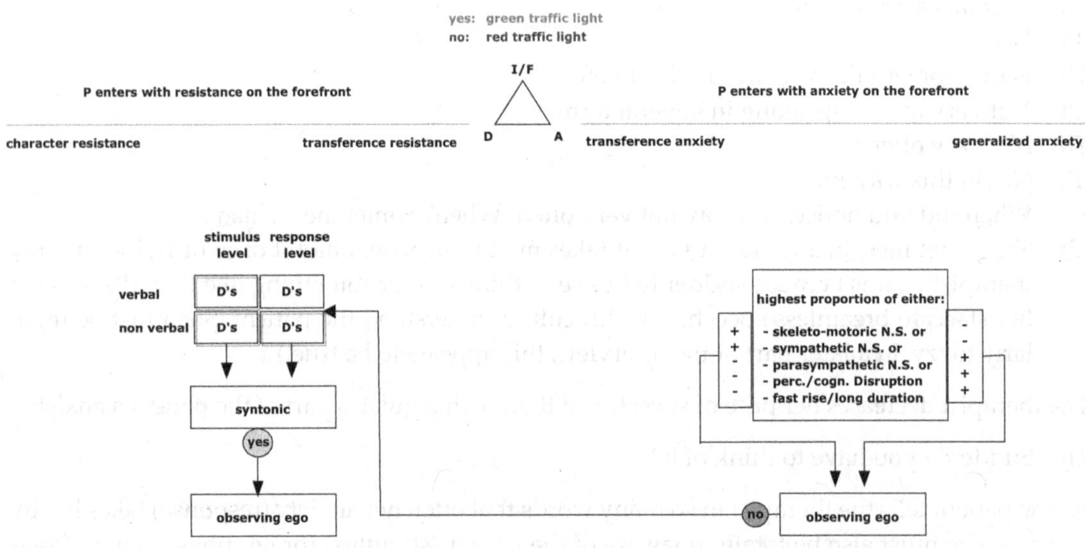

Figure 16. Anxious patient 5: road to the unconscious 1.

Pt I don't exclude eh … what … eh … you are saying, but … no, I don't think that I am really understanding what … I … uh …

Th But I ask you if you are accustomed to paying attention to yourself. Because you tell me that you have to think of your problems.

Pt Perhaps the nasty thing is … eh … about problems is … eh … I think of my problems, but perhaps I cannot feel so well … perhaps I think more than I feel or than I admit feelings. I think that I think a lot but that isn't the real admitting, I think that is one of the main issues.

As the patient is becoming incoherent, has increased her galloping and continues her breathless staccato way of speaking,, the therapist now proceeds at snail's pace.

Th Yes, but you didn't notice your anxiety? So at the moment you …

Pt No, it took me by surprise. I just don't feel the rise of my anxiety.

Th So the tearfulness took you by surprise?

Pt Yes, I hadn't thought that … (the patient starts to gallop again)

Th I will interrupt you often.

Pt Yes, no, that is …

Th What in your opinion is your problem?

Pt Well … I think it is … very clearly that I can admit my feelings …, the moment they are there and I am inclined to … perhaps I do recognize … lately with my therapist. I could recognize.
(the patient is incoherent and she has withdrawn from the eye contact with the therapist)

Th Woman, you have come here …

Pt Yes.

Th … to give yourself and me insight into your complaints and problems.

Pt Yes.

Th The moment you are here …

Pt No.

Th … you make contact with the curtains and you have to withdraw from the eye contact with me. If I am speaking, you look at me …

Pt Yes.

Th … but if you want to tell me something about yourself, then …

Pt Oh, then I look away.

Th Immediately you withdraw from the eye contact. Do you understand me and do you recognize it?

Pt Yes.

Th Yes, thus that is an automatism.

Pt It is something that occurs often, yes. (the defence of distancing, the patient doesn't take responsibility for the fact that it is she, who puts defences into operation)

Th Something that often occurs or something you often do. Because you are speaking about everything that happens to you, as though it takes you by surprise, but you are the one, that …

Pt … looks away again.

Th Looks away and you are the one that gets tearful.

Pt Is eh … …

Th You get anxious and tearful

Pt Yes, I think so too that I withdraw from the contact by looking at something else.

Th Obviously part of your problem is that it provokes anxiety to you to enter intimacy with yourself and with me and obviously it makes you anxious to give yourself and me insight into your thoughts and feelings and subsequently you withdraw from the eye contact. (confrontation, identification, clarification of defences at level of stimulus and response)

Pt Yes.

Th And you still didn't notice your anxiety? (drawing her attention to her anxiety)

Pt Did I notice my anxiety? … oh … I look away again … eh. I feel less anxious than some moments ago. (the patient starts to notice her defence of avoiding contact with the therapist and notices a decrease of her anxiety, less staccato speech, less confusion, yet there is still tension in the upper part of her body)

Th Yes, your anxiety is less, but don't you notice your anxiety in your body?

Pt No. (the patient is still ignoring/neglecting/denying her anxiety manifestations)

Th No? That seems awkward to me.

Pt Yes.

The patient's observing ego has become awake. She is noticing her defence of looking away (stimulus), her anxiety has decreased as is shown by less staccato breathless speech and less confusion.

On the road to the unconscious, we are at Figure 17, on the next page.

Th Isn't it?

Pt Yes.

Th Your muscles are tensed, you have a shallow breathing, a dry mouth and throat. Do you recognize that?

Pt Yes.

Th Do you have heart palpitations?

Pt No.

Th No, no, warm or cold?

Pt Very warm.

Th Very warm. Is your vision intact?

Pt Yes. There are tears but my vision is OK.

Th No problems with your visual perception?

Pt No.

Th Ringing in your ears? (tinnitus)

Pt No.

Th Do you sometimes have diarrhoea?

Pt No.

Th Constipation?

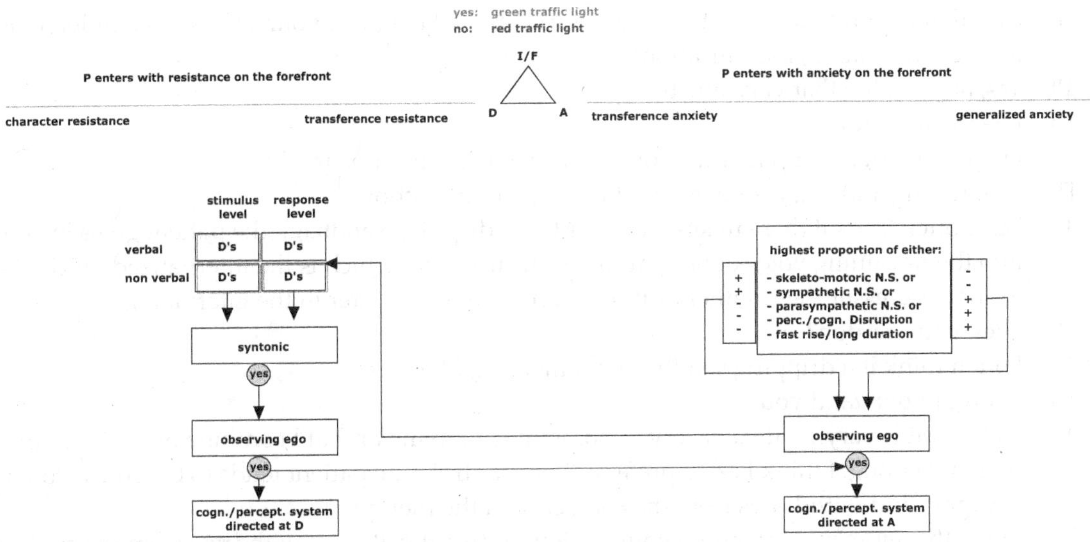

Figure 17. Anxious patient 5: road to the unconscious 2.

Pt No.

Th The idea that your legs will not bear you?

Pt Yes, sometimes, not often.

Th Nausea?

Pt Yes.

Th Also at this moment?

Pt No.

Th Which anxiety symptoms do you have at this moment if you inspect it carefully?

Pt I am nervous, but not ...

Th Nervous is an euphemism, a smooth-over word for anxiety. A second ago I mentioned your symptoms. Are your muscles tensed? (the patient is tensed in the upper part of her body)

Pt No, my muscles aren't tensed, I feel terribly hot.

Th Do you have shallow breathing?

Pt That is too ... yes, that's the only thing ... but ...

Th Your breathing is shallow but that isn't because of tension in your muscles?

Pt I didn't think of that.

Th In that case, these muscles are tensed and you have a dry mouth and throat. Well according to me anxiety isn't such a pleasant symptom.

Pt Yes.

Th And to me it is evident that you are not accustomed to pay attention to your feelings in a precise and careful way. I don't say you do so on purpose. (confrontation, identification)

Pt No.

Th I say that it is obvious to me that you are accustomed to ignore yourself. Do you understand me? (confrontation, identification)
Pt Yes, and I value that very much.
Th I beg your pardon?
Pt I value that (ignoring) in order for me to be able to continue my life.
Th So ignoring and neglecting yourself gives you satisfaction?
Pt Yes, I often think it (her anxiety) more or less a dripping sandbag. (the patient gives insight into the devaluing voice of her pathological superego, which is the internalized voice of a former aggressor (her mother as it will become evident, later in the interview)
Th I beg your pardon?
Pt I often think it a dripping sandbag or something like that.
Th I don't understand you.
Pt Not that it is very … always very … something extreme or that I continue or that my emotions are strong. I think I often prefer a sham control. (the patient tends to become incoherent again and withdraws from the contact with the therapist)
Th But at this moment you ignore your anxiety, automatically you withdraw from the contact with me.
Pt Yes.

The patient's observing ego has become awake. She has told the therapist that her denial/ignoring/neglect of her internal state is her defence against the internalized devaluating voice of her pathological superego part. Herewith the therapist knows that the patient's identification with her superego is becoming less solid, which will result in a growing observing ego.

On the road to the unconscious, we are at Figure 18, below.

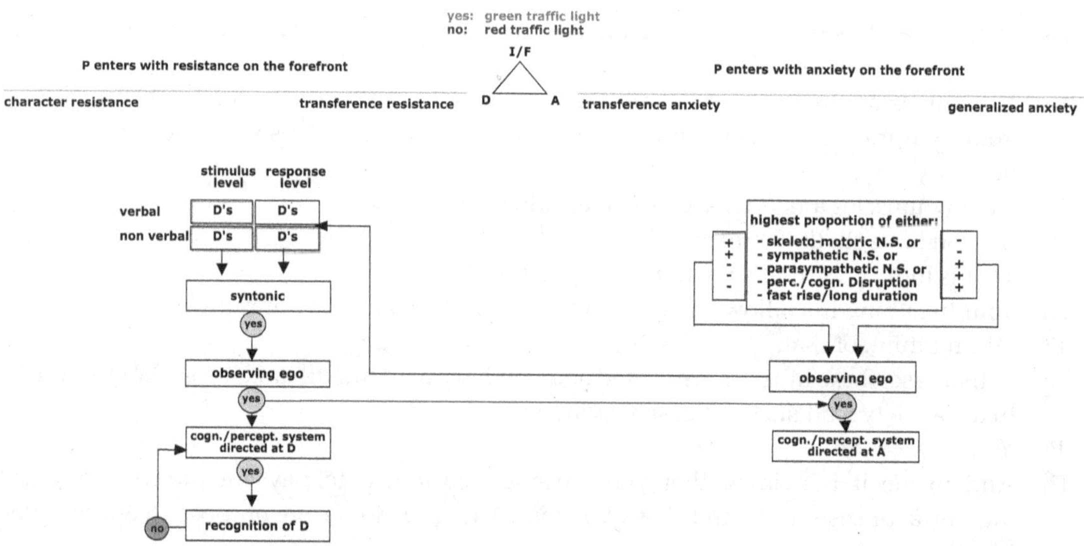

Figure 18. Anxious patient 5: road to the unconscious 3.

Pattern of the patient's anxiety manifestations

- There is an immediate rise, spread, and storage of tension throughout the patient's entire somatomotor system, breathless, staccato way of speaking.
- Sympathetic manifestations: dry mouth and throat, feeling warm.
- Parasympathetic: nausea, dizziness, the idea that her legs will not bear her, tearfulness.
- Cognitive/perceptual disturbances: incoherent, chaotic thinking.
- After drawing the patient's attention to her internal state, there is some fluctuation in the intensity of her anxiety.
- The patient is not adequately processing her internal state. Her cognitive/perceptual system is not at all directed at her inner state and thus not processing it. When confronted with her anxiety manifestations, she had not been aware of them. She didn't label her specific anxiety manifestations as anxiety. She is only "nervous".
- Her syntonic defences of denying, ignoring, neglecting are responsible for keeping her cognitive/perceptual system not directed at her internal state. Her incoherence and chaotic thinking inhibit a clear and precise look at her internal state.

Steps in the chapter

- Healthy and unhealthy anxiety regulation
- Importance of complete and correct anxiety assessment
- Complete/correct assessment should include
  - *the patient's way of preventing adequate processing of his anxiety*
  - *physical problems concomitant to anxiety*
  - *physical problems as a consequence of anxiety*
  - *mistakes*
- Transcripts of assessing anxiety of five patients

CHAPTER FIVE

Resistance, transference, ego-adaptive capacity, and multifoci core neurotic structure

Davanloo, as well as many ISTDP therapists, often speaks of transference, character resistance, transference resistance, superego resistance, and multifoci core neurotic structure.

However, in psychoanalytic and in the ISTDP literature, often the terms are used in a sloppy way. To give some examples: often terms such as defence and resistance or terms such as transference reactions and transference feelings are used interchangeably. Whenever terms can be used interchangeably, this would mean that the terms are completely synonymous (and that one of them could be considered as superfluous). However, terms such as defence and resistance, or transference reactions and transference feelings, are not synonymous. They refer to different descriptive statements, specifying different things. This lack of precision leads to confusion.

Confusion of the therapist is neither of advantage to the therapist nor to the patient, and will undoubtedly influence their working alliance in a negative way. So let us do our best to come to clear definitions of the concepts of character resistance, transference resistance, superego resistance transference, countertransference, and multifoci core neurotic structure.

Resistance

Apart from mentioning that resistance takes the form of a series of defences (which Davanloo classifies as obsessional, regressive, and tactical) and that defences are the ways in which the patient is defending himself against underlying feelings and anxiety, Davanloo is implicit in his operational definition.

We suggest (see also ten Have-de Labije, 1999) that for ISTDP purposes resistance could be conceptualized operationally as the set of defences, put into operation by the ego in interaction with the id and the superego to oppose:

- the rise of the complex of transference feelings and the experiencing of these
- the triggering mechanism for unlocking to become operative
- the process of unlocking the unconscious
- intimacy and the mobilization and development of the (unconscious) working alliance.

The relation between resistance and defences: the variable resistance

One definition of a variable is that it is a set of mutually exclusive properties. For instance, a hairstyle could be considered as a variable because blonde and brunette, curly and straight, long and short are mutually exclusive properties. No person can have predominantly blond, curly, long hair and at the same time predominantly dark, straight, and short hair. In fact, defences could be considered as the properties of the variable "resistance". However, we also can consider a defence a variable and when we do so, we quickly will discriminate a set of mutually exclusive properties. See, for example, the diagram below. No defence can be put automatically and at the same time non-automatically into operation. No defence can be put chronically and at the same time variably into operation, and no defence is at the same time put into operation with satisfaction and dissatisfaction.

Although the particular mechanism itself (e.g., chronic, variable) with which a defence is put into operation might occur in the patient's unconscious ego, it can be that the patient, with his observing and conscious ego, is aware of some other manifestations of that defence (e.g., the particular type of defence like "avoiding eye contact by looking away").

The more the patient brings his defences non-automatically into operation, variable and with dissatisfaction, the more these defences are "ego-alien", or dystonic. The more the patient brings his defences automatically into operation, chronic and with satisfaction, the more these defences are syntonic.

Assessment of the patient's defensive pattern

In assessing the defensive pattern of the patient, the therapist should not only examine the level on which they operate (at the level of the stimulus and/or response), and the *specific* kind of verbal (e.g., projection, intellectualization) and non-verbal (e.g., laughing, sighing) but he should also examine the degree to which they are automatic, chronic, satisfying (the degree of syntonicity) or non-automatic, variable, and dissatisfying (the degree of dystonicity). Next to the above, the greater the proportion of regressive defences and the more the patient's defences in the defensive pattern are syntonic, the lower patient's ego-adaptive capacity, the less the patient will be aware of their function. However, this does not imply that the patient will always be aware of their function when defences are dystonic. Thus with dystonic defences, the patient's awareness of their function (in *in vivo* or *in vitro* interactions: avoidance of pain, self-punishment, protection of the other against own anger/impulse) should also be assessed.

The more defences are automatic, chronic, and the more there is satisfaction with them, the more they are considered as syntonic and maladaptive. In these cases, the patient's reactions are the patient's habitual and representative reactions to *everybody*. As these reactions are so habitual and so non-specific to what the other person(s) does, says, or doesn't do or say, in the interaction, they have become rigid reactions to the world at large. Characteristics of former

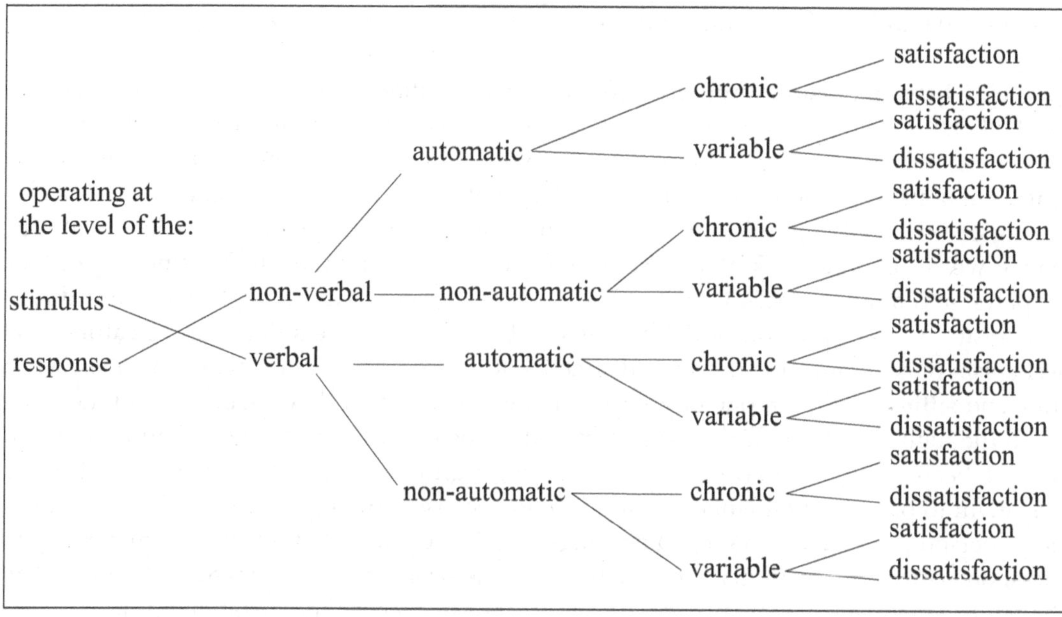

Figure 19. Properties of the variable defence.

(aggressor)-caretakers are constantly, chronically projected onto all persons in the present, the ego's discriminating function is absent and reality testing is poor. And the more they have become like this, the more we speak about the resistance as *a character* resistance and the higher the superego pathology. The latter implies also the higher the pathological influence of the superego in the interaction with the ego and the id. Davanloo speaks about a low, moderate and high degree of character resistance but no clear-cut criteria for the degree of character resistance are given.

When describing his Central Dynamic Sequence, Davanloo elaborates on his subsequent techniques with which the patient's "character resistance crystallizes into transference resistance" but nowhere he operationally defines his concept of transference resistance. What distinguishes transference resistance from character resistance is the fact that the resistance is *only now and then* brought into operation when in present interactions the person in the present is perceived conform aspects of former (aggressor)-caretakers. Thus the patient's defences can be considered to be in the realm of transference resistance when they reflect reactions that are derived from his experiences with important caretakers in his past and when the ego's reality testing and discriminating function is only *temporarily* lost.

In our view, the proportion and degree of syntonicity of character defences reflect the degree to which there is a static projection of characteristics of past (aggressor)-caretakers onto persons in the present interactions. Davanloo's sequential set of interdependent interventions is among other things on the level of this "generalization error" of patient's perception. His interventions are aimed at helping the patient to undo this generalization error and to clearly discriminate (again). The more the patient becomes aware of his perceptual generalization error and the more he starts to discriminate, the less he will allow his defensive battery to operate automatically (the more anxious he will become) and the more the character defences will crystallize in the transference.

You may have understood from the previous chapters that our perception of ourselves and that of others as well as the way we behave is greatly based on previous learning. The mechanisms of generalization and discrimination are involved in the way we perceive and give meaning to situations. Our mother may have told us that that funny, hairy creature, moustache, smelling of fish, walking and jumping with four paws, tail, colour grey is called a cat. The moment we see another look alike, also a funny, hairy creature, moustache, smelling of fish, four paws, and a tail, but this time a red one, we are taught that although the colour differs (mechanism of discrimination of the cat's distinctive features), we still call the creature a cat (mechanism of generalization of a cat's distinctive features). And do you also remember: when young and sitting in the car, one of your parents was driving, and you looked at all the other cars on the highway. But that one was a Mercedes, the other a Volkswagen. And how proud you have been when you had been discriminating rightly between these cars! You also had been taught to pay attention when crossing a road because moving cars can be dangerous. But when a person perceives a parked car as dangerous, it is evident that this person makes a generalization error and fails to discriminate between the properties of a parked and moving car. Behaviour then can become inappropriate on the basis of such a generalization error.

Defences are put into operation by the ego

Davanloo speaks sometimes of "superego resistance" (SER). In his many articles (see, for example, Davanloo, 1990), Davanloo suggests the SER to be maintained by the superego while at the same time he suggests the superego is only giving the directions to the ego to put resistance into operation. Already interactions within and between the systems of id, ego, and superego, and the unconscious and conscious system are complex, so the need to be as accurate as possible is of utmost necessity. The evocative stimulus, which triggers the resistance may originate in any of the psychological structures (id, ego, superego), but the perception of danger and the subsequent activity to avoid pain (defence) are both ego operations. As all resistance operates at least via the ego, it is at least the ego (and not the superego) that is maintaining or quitting the resistance.

The efficacy of ISTDP, i.e., the ego's increased capacity to experience and tolerate painful feelings in such a way and extent that there is only need for adaptive instead of maladaptive defences, is essentially reflecting a modification or restructuring of patient's underlying psychobiological state. This means that Davanloo's set of carefully designed sequential interdependent interventions and his therapy protocol have effectuated a restructuring within as well as across levels of many psychobiological systems or processes within the patient.

Superego resistance, resistance against emotional closeness, resistance against the experiencing of the impulse

As Davanloo speaks of superego resistance (SER), resistance against emotional closeness (REC), resistance against the experiencing of the impulse (REI), character and transference resistance, he suggests that these are to be classified as different types of resistance and that they should be differentiated from each other.

Drury (1990), referring to Davanloo, defines superego resistance as that form of resistance in psychotherapy in which the patient's need to sabotage his or her life outside the therapeutic encounter, as a result of punitive superego pathology, is regulated in the form of self-defeating defences in the transference.

Bleuler (1996), referring to Davanloo, defines the resistance against emotional closeness as a defence of every neurotic patient. This is a need to keep everybody out of one's innermost life, one's innermost thoughts and feelings, the need to prevent or destroy every warm, useful, and long-lasting relationship. It can be more or less pronounced and is often covered by other resistances. The source is a double unconscious anxiety.

Of course, the resistance against emotional closeness is not a concept, which is separate from the concept of superego resistance (nor from the concept of character resistance). What Davanloo calls "resistance against emotional closeness" (REC), "superego resistance" (SER) and "resistance against the experience of the impulse" (REI) are in fact facets of the character resistance. The question now is to which degree these facets of the character resistance are to be differentiated. The particular criteria of judgement when to assign a client's set of defences to which facet are left unspecified. Not allowing for intimacy, inside or outside the therapeutic setting is self-defeating, so here the definition of the REC falls within Drury's (and Davanloo's) definition of the SER. The same applies to the concepts of REI and the SER. Warding off the experience of emotions and impulses is self-defeating too. In this respect, the definition of the REI falls also within the definition of the SER. It seems to us that the "utility-status" of the concept of SER is questionable for the purposes of therapeutic decision-making (interventions).

Perhaps it is more clear not to speak of superego resistance but to speak of superego pathology and of character resistance and its two pillars: the pillar-resistance against emotional closeness (REC) and the pillar-resistance against the experience of the impulse/feelings (REI).

Transference

Each psychotherapist knows that the concept of transference owes its origin to Freud. Later in history other psychotherapists have developed this concept and the result is that there are not only differing opinions as to what transference really is but at the same time there is lots of confusion as to what the concept of transference really means.

Psychotherapists use several definitions of the transference. One definition of transference is "the inappropriate repetition in the present of a relationship that was important in a person's childhood". Other definitions are, for example, "The redirection of feelings and desires and especially of those unconsciously retained from childhood toward a new object". Or "a reproduction of emotions relating to repressed experiences, especially of childhood, and the substitution of another person for the original object of the repressed impulses".

According to others, the transference occurs when a person takes the perceptions and expectations of one person and projects them onto another person. They then interact with the other person as if the other person is that transferred pattern.

Another definition we found, is: "the process by which emotions and desires originally associated with one person, such as a parent or sibling, are unconsciously shifted to another person, especially to the analyst".

To be honest, we don't like the above mentioned definitions of the transference. "The redirection of feelings and desires … toward a new object" leaves anxiety and the defences out of the picture. A scientific book should not use websites for definitions-it opens a can of worms as to who is the author of the opinions.

There are colleagues who relate the transference only to the interaction patient–therapist. Of course, it can be that transference is merely uncovered and worked with by the therapist's interventions in his interactions with his patient, but this does not mean that transference only occurs in the interaction with the therapist and does not occur outside the therapist's office!

Definitions of transference may differ, however, in all cases, different schools and traditions fundamentally agree on the existence, dynamics, and pervasiveness of the transference, and in all cases transference refers to a conscious or unconscious process (or system) of several interacting components.

Thus the state of each component is dependent upon the state of the other components comprising the system. Of course, as each living system is an open system (it continually interacts with its internal and external environment of which it is a part), it means that the transference is both a system unto itself and simultaneously it is a subsystem of various larger systems of which it is a part. It follows that certain components may be shared by many different systems, and that a change to one component has a set of different effects on the functioning of the different systems that share this one component in common. From this perspective, one could investigate various component processes within a given level, as well as across different levels.

The first implication of the concept of a process or system is that no one component "equals" the whole process or system. It follows that in "controlling", by any means, certain components of the transference, the process will become altered, and this is exactly what the ISTDP therapist's interventions are aimed at doing.

Davanloo is not explicit in his definition of the transference but in his method of ISTDP the transference is used as a vehicle to gain direct access to the (multifoci) core neurotic structure, buried in the unconscious. Davanloo's interventions in the central dynamic sequence are designed to use the transference in order to overcome the resistance, to establish an unconscious working alliance, and to maximize the rise of the complex of mixed transference feelings to "threshold intensity" in order to trigger an unlocking of the unconscious. More specifically, at the level of the transference, Davanloo's set of sequential interventions is aimed at the different components comprising the transference, so as to influence both their functioning and their interactions.

We suggest that in ISTDP, the transference could be operationally defined as a process or system in which as a minimum the following interacting components comprise the transference:

- the patient's perception of a person in the present
- the representation of the introjected and repressed perception of an important person from the patient's past

- the repressed complex of the impulse and mixed feelings towards the representation of this important person from the past
- the anxiety, aroused by the repressed complex of the impulse and mixed feelings
- the set of defences, making up the resistance.

In the literature, we find different descriptions of the specific transference mechanism(s) with which the patient repeats his unresolved conflicts with earlier attachment figures. Some authors describe that the patient irrationally *repeats* stereotyped reaction patterns. Other authors describe that affects *are displaced* onto, or *transferred* to. And there are authors who describe that a patient *projects* characteristics of a former important person onto the therapist.

We prefer to speak of a patient *projecting* characteristics of former important persons onto persons in the present when we refer to *a static process*, as is the case when a person has character resistance and superego pathology, thus when the patient's observing ego is practically absent, when the patient makes generalization errors, and the discriminative function of his perception is lost, and when his reality testing is low.

We prefer to speak of a patient *transferring* characteristics of former important persons in the present when we refer to *a dynamic process*, as is the case when the patient has transference resistance, thus when the patient has an observing or attentive ego, when his reality testing and discriminative functions are temporarily low and can be corrected when focused upon.

An example of a patient's transference process

The particular patient is in ISTDP couples therapy. Half way into a breakthrough of her sadistic impulse towards her boss, the patient goes for passivity the moment her guilt had been mobilized. As challenging the patient to continue experiencing her rage didn't have the desired effect, the therapist investigates the patient's defences in the interaction with her husband and the therapist.

Th Please make it concrete: what will we think when witnessing your full rage?

F It is forbidden … and … you have to deal with that differently … so condemning me but also dictating me how to behave and restricting me again.

Th Let's look at this picture.

F Yes.

Th You want to investigate your rage, which is as you say the most filthy thing in your life, towards your boss.

F Yes.

Th Half way through your rage, you experience us as condemning you, as dictating you to quit it.

F Yes.

Th And to deal with it differently.

F Yes.

Th And then you suppress it.

F Yes, and that happens all the time.
Th And then you comply with us like you did …
F Here and now.
Th Yes and then you comply here with us. Is that clear to you?
F Yes.
Th (Th addresses husband) Is that also clear to you?
M Uhuh.
Th Well is it also conform the reality—I start with myself—that I will condemn you and prescribe to you that it's forbidden and that you'll have to act differently?
F Absolutely not, absolutely not, you've always encouraged me.
Th OK, you see the difference. I don't know if that's the same with Bob.
F That's different.
Th Towards Bob?
F And towards you (she addresses her husband). I feel ashamed: my God, what will come out in that rage, what else will happen, and then I feel ashamed and consequently I don't dare to show it to you.
Th So that's mainly towards Bob?
F Yes, particularly.
Th But does he react in a condemning way?
F No, no, absolutely not.
Th So that is also your perception: in reality, he doesn't react by condemning. Are you telling this out of compliance or do you really perceive Bob …
F No, I really perceive him like that. He never condemned me. I mean at this moment my rage is towards my boss but in the past it was often towards my father and Bob never said: Francis, you scare me if you … uh …
Th And neither did he say that you weren't allowed.
F No.
Th And if so, I don't want to deal with you.
F No.
Th And just do it another way.
F No.
Th He never said so about your rage?
F No.
Th So you see the difference with the reality. You see that the real Bob isn't like that and you see that you …
F Transfer that image onto him.
Th Onto him and consequently you comply with that transferred image.
F Yes, I do understand so.
Th That image.
F Yes, I do understand again.
Th What it is that you understand?
F Yes, now I understand. If you say that I am transferring that image then in fact it is again that image from the past, my father who was dealing with me like that, very restrictive towards

me, the slightest word of me that could be an expression of rage had to be suppressed, and I was an evil child and nothing was left of me when I asserted myself.

Etc. etc.

Th (The therapist addresses the wife) But if you perceive Bob to conform to the aspects of your father and immediately you move to complying, what is it then that you suppress?

F My true feelings. (The patient starts to cry.)

Th Yes. Is this sadness or helplessness?

F No this is merely sadness. Anger and sadness that I have to conclude: I am still doing it. Still I am scared to show the real me, to show my inner feelings, and it makes me very sad.

Th That you restrict yourself?

F Yes, and then I think …

Th Also in front of your beloved Bob?

F Yes and then I think: after some time I've ended the therapy and then again I will make a mess of it.

Th And you want to show your true self to Bob?

F I just want to show the real me, also to do myself a favour. I so much grant it myself to go only for honesty. I grant it myself and I grant it you, Bob, but mainly myself. Because each day I suffer as a consequence of making myself helpless. Life has become so restricted, little has been left to enjoy and that pain on my chest, me, that little bird in that very narrow cage, I don't want that anymore … and I think it very painful … I think I am not doing justice to you, the moment I transfer those images of my father onto you. Only it is often that I don't recognize it right away that I am doing so. And then there is another situation and although I understand so very well it is still happening to me, damn it. It scares me too because I know how the process works and I don't want that and still it happens. It makes me sad and I think how do I have to end this.

The therapist addresses the partner's silence, his rationalizations, and thereafter the marital collusion is made clear to the patients. The husband invites his wife to express her anger and rage.

Th And then what is your anger towards Bob?

F Yes that's my anger, that you shouldn't dare to stop me. That particularly you shouldn't … uh, I don't know. I have the tendency to push you away. I say don't meddle, this is damn it my anger. (The patient's impulse towards her husband is clearly mobilized.)

Th And how do you push him away, and only the force.

F Well, I push you away and I tell you; leave me alone!

Th But if you don't say anything and if you release the beast in you and you push him away?

The wife pushes her husband till he falls on the floor, kicks him in his belly, kicks his legs, kicks his whole body. Guilt and deep grief are mobilized, the patient is crying with heavy sighs.

F A regular cremation.

Th How? If you could choose, how do you cremate him?

F Well a regular cremation. A white coffin and, uh, many roses and beautiful music (cries).

Th And then? How do you cremate him? How do you cremate him in the white coffin and the roses?

F Well I just see that white coffin sink into the ground. That goes automatically.

Th And then?

F Then the ashes into the urn.

Th And where do you put the urn?

F In the living room. (The wife is still crying and she avoids the eye contact with her husband.)

Th Look at Bob. (Who, in his turn, has withdrawn from the eye contact with his wife and is silently crying.)

Th Bob, look at Francis.

F (Eye contact between the two partners is established.) Do you hate me now?

M No, rather myself.

F Why?

M Your rage doesn't come out of the blue. I think you've built it up in these 20 years. I have hurt you in the past. Yes, in fact I have taken my defiance towards my mother out on you. And that makes me very sad. I think you never deserved that.

F No.

M I have hurt you and also in the past I have told you so from the bottom of my heart and I apologized for that. You told me about your anger. But you never showed me before this rage and this extent.

F No, that is true, I've always suppressed this.

M I've hurt you, that you know and I am sorry. I also know where it comes from. It is my resistance against the treatment I got at home. Belittling. Devaluing me, being an outcast. And I repeated that in our relation … And that was the revenge on my mother.

F And my part has been that I have given my father almost all power over me and so I gave you all the power over me. There is bitterness about that, but I did it myself. I could have also said to you: damn it, get out of here. Who do you think you are to treat me in this way. I always allowed you to treat me like that. And also … often I ducked down.

M Yes.

The wife and the husband are holding hands, thereafter the therapist and the couple summarize the main issues of the session.

Countertransference

One of the first tasks of an ISTDP therapist is to establish a conscious/unconscious working alliance with his patient, and to help him taking an active position in joining the therapist to face and investigate his problems. Amongst others this implies that the therapist must be able to challenge the patient to quit his defences and to go for an unlocking of his unconscious, and for a conscious experiencing of his murderous rage, guilt, grief and damaged love. The demands on the ISTDP therapist are high. The therapist must not only be able to work—from moment to moment in a highly concentrated and focused way, he must be able to bear being the target of the patient's transference process: being the target of the patient's transference resistance, being the target of the patient's murderous rage, guilt, grief, damaged love, while still having empathy with the patient. The therapist must be able to maintain a high level of involvement with the patient. In other words: the ISTDP method and techniques require the ISTDP therapist to have a high capacity for entering and maintaining intimacy. In his teachings, Davanloo frequently pointed out that a therapist's complex transference feelings are easily evoked the moment a therapist is the target of a patient's transference process. Especially at such moments it is of extreme importance that the therapist is capable of dealing with his own countertransference in such a way that his anxiety and/or defences will not invalidate the therapeutic process. Let us not forget that also therapists have their neurotic problems.

We speak of countertransference in the therapy setting when the therapist responds to his patient as if he were an important person from the therapist's past. It is the transference process of that particular therapist. When the therapist is unable and/or unwilling to acknowledge the significance of his own behaviour that reflects his own transference process being put into operation, then—as a result—the working alliance and the therapy process will become lame. Let us not forget that therapists also have their neurotic problems. It is therefore recommended that therapists—during their ISTDP core group training—apply for ISTDP therapy themselves. It is important that the therapist acknowledges his neurotic conflicts that have not been resolved. Being aware of our own countertransference issues could also be used as a source of information about that particular patient we are interacting with in the session!

Some examples of countertransference

Many patients, especially those who have access to passivity, helplessness, compliance and pleasing endow the therapist with magical power and omnipotence. Often, when a therapist doesn't recognize his patients' defences of helplessness, passivity, compliance, the therapist and his supervisor should investigate whether this is of the therapist's wish to be all-knowing and powerful and taking responsibility for everybody else or that this is because of a lack of technical ability.

Of course, power struggles, arguing with the patient are also familiar examples of a therapist's countertransference. And what about difficulties in remembering what the patient has told when experiencing anger, or, for example, immediately understanding what a patient is reporting, notwithstanding the fact that the patient is vague and generalizes. Some therapists—mostly those who intellectualize themselves—take the intellectualizations of their patient as a manifestation of an observing ego.

Some therapists will experience anxiety while doing the therapy with a certain patient.

Another manifestation of countertransference is the therapist who restricts the investigation of his patient's transference reactions to interactions with current persons outside the therapy office and avoids to investigate these in the interaction with himself.

This brings us to those therapists who did invite their patient to investigate their transference process in the relation with the therapist him/herself. A therapist's discomfort with his patient's direct experience of anger and/or his sadistic rage may lead to the therapist becoming defensive. It is up to the therapist to recognize his/her specific ways of defending.

Ego-adaptive capacity

In Chapter One, we already mentioned that ego-adaptive capacity could be defined as the extent to which the ego mediates constructively between the external (the subjectively interpreted and/or objective demands of various persons in different situations) and internal demands (the instinctual demands of the id and the moral, punitive ones of the superego).

In Davanloo's ISTDP, the triangles of conflict and persons serve as a diagnostic tool, and as such they provide means for assessing the quality and degree of ego-adaptive capacity.

The state of the cognitive/perceptive system of the patient

It is the patient who has to observe and to assess his own problems in several *"in vivo"* or *"in vitro"* (thinking of a situation) interactions by using his cognitive/perceptive system.

So, in order for the therapist to assess his patient's ego-adaptive capacity, the therapist's first step is to investigate and to assess whether and to what degree the patient's cognitive/perceptive system is (mal) functioning for the sake of observing and assessing his own problems in several *in vivo* or *in vitro* interactions.

Emotions are elicited by essential stimuli from the outside world or from inside (thoughts). The essence of these stimuli is determined via cognitive/perceptive processes: the essential stimuli are analysed and interpreted in the context of earlier experience in order to establish their significance. It is well known that defences serve the function to weaken or inhibit emotional responses. Defence mechanisms block the above mentioned cognitive/perceptive processing of information, either at the level of the stimulus (e.g., denial) or at the level of the response (e.g., motoric retardation) (Frijda, 1993). Research on the psychophysiology of psychological defence mechanisms has led Schwartz (1982) to state that they may be employed to block symptoms of anxiety and pain from awareness.

There is common agreement among psychotherapists that character defences (which make up the character resistance) are habitual, rigidly fixed and usually ego syntonic. Often the patient even approves of his character defences and he isn't aware of the resistance function under scrutiny.

One could say that in the therapy situation the character defences serve the purpose of enabling the ego to resist taking an active cognizant and perceptive position towards the external and internal demands.

In other words, the character defences serve among other things the function of keeping the ego's cognitive/perceptive system dormant. Thus assessment of degree of character resistance gives an indication of the sleeping or awakened state of the cognitive/perceptive system.

Having determined that the cognitive/perceptive system is dormant is not the same as assessing the abilities of the cognitive/perceptive system or what is left of these abilities.

The triangles of conflict and persons can be used as a tool for diagnosis and assessment of which abilities of a patient's cognitive/perceptive system are still in operation. It may be clear that this is impossible as long as (massive) character resistance is in position and the cognitive/perceptive system is dormant.

This is one of the reasons why Davanloo developed the technique of head-on collision with the character resistance in order to awaken the cognitive/perceptive system as a necessary prerequisite step to assess what is left of its abilities.

Keeping the operational definition of ego-adaptive capacity (the use of the two triangles) in mind, it follows logically that with high ego-adaptive capacity, the patient's cognitive/perceptive system must be able:

Triangle of persons

1. to detect eliciting essential stimuli from the external world (current persons), to analyse them and to
2. interpret this information in the context of earlier experience (past, transference) in order to estimate the significance of the eliciting stimuli

Triangle of conflict

3. to detect, analyse, and interpret aroused feelings as, for example, anger, guilt, sadness, happiness, and to establish their causal link with the preceding essential stimuli
4. to detect, analyse, and interpret anxiety and its causal link with the preceding aroused other feelings
5. to detect, analyse, and interpret defences and their causal link with preceding anxiety, anxiety-laden feelings, and perception of essential stimuli
6. to detect, analyse, and interpret this whole dynamic process in order for the patient to determine whether he is fulfilling with this process what he really needs or wants.

The more a patient's cognitive/perceptive system is malfunctioning on the above mentioned points, the lower the patient's ego-adaptive functioning is.

Or … in other words: a patient's ego-adaptive capacity is lower, the more

1. a patient is not able to correctly label the concomitant physiological manifestations of a particular feeling (triangle of conflict)
2. a patient is not able to make a correct causal link with the preceding essential stimuli (triangle of persons: e.g., which exact words of the other person triggered the patient's feeling)
3. a patient is not able to correctly label the concomitant physiological manifestations of his anxiety

   It may be clear that when a patient is not able to correctly label the concomitant physiological manifestations of a particular feeling, he will easily confuse:
   - feelings with anxiety or with defences
   - anxiety with defences

4. a patient is not able to make a correct causal link with the preceding feeling or impulse
5. a patient is not able to make a correct causal link between anxiety and defences
6. a patient's anxiety is unhealthily regulated (higher proportions of parasympathetic manifestations, cognitive/perceptual disturbances and high velocity, rise, and spread of the anxiety manifestations)
7. a patient has regressive defences (e.g., projection, identification, idealization, splitting, etc.) in his repertoire.

Some examples

Confusion of a feeling with anxiety and with a defence:

Th You say you feel angry. How do you notice your anger in your body?
Pt I feel warm and tensed (confuses anger with anxiety)

Or:

Pt I become very calm and immobile (confuses anger with defence)

Causality mistakes:

Pt Authoritarian persons make me anxious (instead of: authoritarian persons make me angry/sad)

Or:

Pt When I comply, I become anxious (instead of: when I am anxious, I comply)

Not labelling correctly:

Pt Yes I am anxious, but I have a dry mouth because I am thirsty/because I smoke.

Or:

Pt Yes, always before an exam I have diarrhoea, but that is not of anxiety. It is because I have sensitive bowels.

Multifoci core neurotic structure

It is already mentioned that the first part of Davanloo's set of interventions is designed in order to trigger an unlocking of the unconscious so as to have a direct view of the multifoci core neurotic structure, which Davanloo considers responsible for patient's symptoms as well as character disturbances. Most ISTDP authors conceptualize this structure as consisting of mixed feelings such as guilt, grief and repressed sadistic and sexual impulses toward important object relationships from childhood. First, our question is why love is so often omitted in the list of mixed feelings. As far as we understand it is out of love, grief and guilt about the impulses that the patient has come to put a set of defences into operation. Also, it is after the resolution of the early traumatic experiences that the patient is free to experience again to the full extent his love towards important persons from his past. Second, the above conceptualization of core neurotic structure is ambiguous in the sense that it is not clear whether the representation of perception of traumatic experiences with important persons from childhood is included or not. This is a pity, because it seems evident that the many ISTDP authors never had the intention to exclude it.

The authors suggest the following definition of the concept: the unconscious (multifoci) core neurotic structure consists of the coupling of

- the representation(s) of the perception of traumatic experiences with important persons in childhood, with
- the representation(s) of a complex of mixed feelings such as love, guilt, grief, and sadistic and sexual impulses towards these persons.

Steps in the chapter

- Resistance
- Character resistance
- Generalization and discrimination
- Transference resistance
- Projection
- Transference
- Countertransference
- Multifoci core neurotic structure

CHAPTER SIX

Observational learning and teaching our patients to overcome their problems

Whatever the conceptualization of a psychotherapy school, all schools have the common goal of helping their patients to overcome their problems and live a (as-much-as-possible) happy life. So does ISTDP. Although Davanloo based his ISTDP largely on psychoanalytic theory, his therapy method and techniques are structured. The method and techniques have the aim *to teach* the patient to recognize self-defeating patterns of overt and covert behaviour, to quit these self-defeating patterns, and to replace them by constructive patterns of overt and covert behaviour, thus enabling the patient to access and experience impulses and feelings related to past traumatic experiences, and to express feelings, opinions, and behaviour in a constructive way. One cannot teach patients new ways of looking and expressing themselves, new ways of interacting with themselves and with other persons, by ignoring basic principles of learning theory. Therefore, this chapter will focus on theory and practice of observational or vicarious learning. Why? Because virtually all of our learning occurs on a vicarious basis!

Albert Bandura's social learning theory and observational learning

Psychological theories of learning, traditionally assumed that learning occurred only through performing responses and experiencing their effects. In 1941, it had been Miller and Dollard who explained how animals and humans model observed behaviours, which then became learned through environmental reinforcements. Miller and Dollard's work stimulated a flood of research and theories, and over time cognitive and behavioural principles were incorporated in theories of social learning. It became clear that virtually all learning, resulting from direct experience occurs on a vicarious basis by observing other people's behaviour and by observing the consequences of these behaviours for those other people. The capacity to learn by observation enables us to acquire rules and integrated patterns of behaviour without the need to form them by trial and error. If our learning would only take place via the consequences of our trial-and-error actions, we would not live very long! We can easily understand how we would have made fatal accidents if we would have learned to cross a road during rush hour by trial and error. Or learning to do surgery by trial and error! And what about learning to do psychotherapy by trial and error?

Albert Bandura (1977, 1982, 1985) was the first to incorporate the notion of modelling, or vicarious learning, as a form of social learning. In addition, he introduced a model of dynamic, triadic, and reciprocal interaction between the person and his environment. In this model of reciprocal determinism, 1) behaviour, 2) cognitive and other personal factors, and 3) environmental influences all operate as interlocking determinants that affect each other bidirectionally. The relative influence of these three interlocking subsystems/determinants will vary for different activities, different individuals, and different circumstances. In Bandura's view, behaviour is largely regulated antecedently through cognitive processes. Response consequences of a behaviour are used to build expectations of behavioural outcomes. Because of our ability to form these expectations we can predict the outcome of our behaviour before the behaviour is performed.

In the social learning view, observational learning is governed by four component processes: 1) attentional processes, 2) retention processes, 3) behavioural production processes, 4) motivational processes.

1. The process of attention determines what of the modelled event is selectively observed and which information is extracted. An observer will look for some aspects over others. The observer's expectations will channel what to look for, and will partly affect which features are extracted from these observations and how the observer will interpret what he hears or sees. Once discriminated, input is soon lost if not stored and saved in durable form.
2. Retention involves an active process of transforming and restructuring information about events. Observational learning relies upon imaginative and verbal mediators. Modelled events elicit visual images of serial acts and context stimuli. Likewise, observers encode modelled input into verbal symbols. These symbolic transformations (the imaginative and verbal representational systems) of external information function as guides for subsequent action. Cognitive rehearsal also serves as a memory aid.
3. The symbolic representations guide the behavioural production process. Feedback from action is compared against the model. Corrective feedback can further refine new skills.
4. Motivation and incentive processes will determine whether or not acquired competence will be expressed and performed. Thus a distinction is made between acquisition and performance. A person will be more likely to exhibit a modelled behaviour if it results in a valued outcome. A person will rarely perform a behaviour if he faces unfavourable incentive conditions or if he expects unrewarding or punishing effects.

In addition, Bandura's social learning theory assigns a central role to self-regulatory functions and to self-percepts of efficacy. Self-regulation can occur when the individual has his own ideas about what is appropriate or inappropriate behaviour and can choose his actions accordingly. It allows the gradual substitution of internal controls for external controls of behaviour. Self-efficacy is a type of self-reflective thought that effects one's behaviour. A person's judgement of personal efficacy will partly determine how much effort a person will invest in an activity and how long to persevere in the face of disappointing results. Thus, self-efficacy is a major determinant of self-regulation.

In the literature, the terms vicarious learning, observational learning, imitation learning, and learning by imitation are often used interchangeably.

The mirror neuron system and its involvement in observational learning

Vicarious or observational learning is considered one of the most basic mechanisms by which we learn. Recent findings from neuroscience research on the mirror neuron system begin to provide us with some partial insight into the neural bases of learning by observation and imitation.

The discovery of mirror neurons dates back to the early 1990s and stems from single neuron recordings with monkeys. A mirror neuron is a neuron which fires both when an animal acts and when the animal observes the same action performed by another animal. This is more likely when the observed animal is one of the same species.

For the first time, a neural system had been identified that allowed a direct matching between a visual observation of an action and its execution. Mirror neurons have been directly observed in primates. Studies using transcranial magnetic stimulation or brain-imaging techniques have demonstrated that a mirror neuron system also exists in the human brain. Several studies have demonstrated that a mirror neuron system matching perception of an action and executing that action exists in the human brain (Gallese, Keysers & Rizzolatti, 2004). During observation of an action, there is a strong activation of premotor and posterior parietal areas. The mirror neuron system seems to be involved in the encoding how an action leads to achievement of its goal, and in understanding and inferring the intention of an action (Rizzolatti & Craighero, 2004; Rizzolatti, 2005).

The mirror neuron system of an observer is activated in the relationship to another person or persons. Catalysts might be the observed motor actions or facial expressions such as disgust, joy, fear of another person (Gallese, 2005; Rizzolatti & Arbib, 1998). Thus, mirror neurons might be involved in our capacity to empathize. Perceiving another person, expressing a given emotion, will activate the same brain regions as when we would subjectively experience the same emotion. Similar direct matching mechanisms have been described for the perception of pain and touch (Gallese, Keysers & Rizzolatti, 2004; Gallese, 2006). Activation of mirror neurons is linked to social and cognitive mechanisms, to attachment, attunement, and empathy (Gallese, 2005; Gallese & Goldman, 1998; Schore, 1994).

The mirror neuron system: introjection, identification, imitation

The discovery of the mirror neurons has contributed to the understanding of perceptual systems, the virtual recreation of the external world in our brain, and the role of mirror neurons in our capacity to identify and imitate. As the biology and functioning of the mirror neuron system is only partially understood, the relationships between mirror neurons and psychological processes must be considered as hypothetical. First, we think it important to give definitions of the concepts of introjection, identification, imitation, and of sharing/empathy.

In his article "Identification: Psychoanalytic and Biological Perspectives", Olds (2006) refers to several definitions of the concept of internalization. One of them is Schafer's (1968) "introjection is the taking in of the object as a kind of fantasy and retaining that object in a virtual inner space such that one can have dialogue with it". This may more accurately be described as internalizing the object relationship, in the form of a virtual dyad. We ourselves would like to rephrase this definition of introjection as the taking in of distinctive features of another person as a kind of fantasy and retaining the specific features of this other person in a virtual inner space such that one can have a dialogue with this introjected other person. In this virtual inner space, there is a difference between oneself and the introjected other person.

Imitation describes the acquisition of new behaviours, attitudes, based on the observation of a model. Imitation requires that sensory input is converted into motor output in order to re-enact what was perceived. It involves attentional, retentional, behavioural production, and motivational processes.

Observation of the distinctive features of a model may lead to imitation, but does not necessarily do so.

Identification as adopting the identity and perspective of another person, could be defined as a process that consists of increasing loss of self-awareness and its replacement with the perspective of another person. For an interaction to occur, one *needs* to retain his self-identity and interact with the other person, thereby maintaining at least a social distance. When identifying, one lacks an awareness of the self, and therefore, the distinction between self and the other—necessary for interaction—is missing.

Understanding another person via empathy or sharing requires an activation of one's own psychological schemata, and hence to be self-aware, whereas identification does not foster any judgements that require treating another person as external to the self. Having empathy/sharing the perspective of another person, sharing the feelings of that other person is *not* the same as identifying with that other person. According to Freud, much of our psychological functioning is based on the dynamic interactions between ego, superego, and id. In Freud's view, the superego develops after successful resolution of the Oedipal conflict. Davanloo, however, believes the superego to be formed in the first few months of a person's life.

To the extent that there are neural subsystems that correspond to the concepts of ego, superego, and id, and their interactions, we could understand these neural subsystems as mirroring each other. These interacting subsystems together could then be conceived of as a system in which the constituent subsystems are dynamically interacting and mirroring.

In Chapter One, we already pointed out that it is in the interaction with our caretakers that we learn how to look at ourselves, to look at other people, to understand our own longings, feelings, behaviours, and those of others. The principles of Bandura's learning via observation have contributed to our understanding how we learn to see ourselves and the outside world through the eyes of important attachment figures.

Through the eyes of these attachment figures, a child learns

- how to look and understand himself
- how to look at the attachment figure
- how the attachment figure is looking at that child
- how to look at other persons in the outside world
- how other persons are looking at that child.

A child who has learned from his caretaker(s) that it is important to understand his own feelings, longings, opinions, and to give words to them, will probably also have learned from the same caretaker(s) that it is OK if these feelings, longings, opinions are different from those of his caretaker(s). In these cases, the child's capability to label his emotions correctly and to express them via words is a great deal formed by observation and imitation of repetitive modelling of his loving and empathic caretaker(s). Such a child's caretaker will also have taught his pupil that it is OK to feel that it wants to kick a sibling or the caretaker him/herself, but that it is certainly not OK to do so. Such a caretaker would have the mental flexibility to adopt the subjective perspective of his pupil, and such a caretaker must have a reasonably healthy regulation of his own emotions. Otherwise, such a caretaker would not have been able to tell his pupil that he is obviously angry and would not have had the capability to model how his pupil could express his anger in a constructive way.

In all these cases, the child will have internalized the distinctive features of the perceived sensory input, stemming from the observed caretaker in such a way that an internal dialogue with the introjected distinctive features of this caretaker is formed. In the child's virtual inner space, there is a difference between the self and the introjected other person, the caretaker. Because of the reinforcement of the caretaker(s), the acquired competence will be performed by the child and under guidance of corrective feedback this competence will be improved, self-efficacy will increase, external controls of behaviour (by the modelling caretaker) will gradually transfer into internal control. However, the psychotherapist colleagues undoubtedly will agree that it is highly improbable to see a patient who has had an upbringing as above described. During the course of life, there are more important persons in an individual's life: family members, teachers, peers, movie stars, cartoon figures, pets. They all can function as models, and our virtual inner space may be filled with many interactions and dialogues with important others. A person's inner space, which consists of many dialogues with constructive and empathic internalized others, may function as an antidote to learning by imitation of aggressive models.

Most patients who come to our practice are located on the right half of Davanloo's spectrum of structural neurosis. Most of them have high superego and high character pathology.

The higher a patient's superego and character pathology, the more a patient's ego has identified with its pathological superego. Most patients located at the extreme right of Davanloo's spectrum of structural neurosis are about a hundred per cent identified with their internalized former aggressors, and their observing ego is in a state of coma. To say it in other words, the self-identity is absent, there is no awareness of the self, there is no distinction between the self and the internalized other persons (the former aggressors). During the course of the patient's life, the process of internalization has led to a total loss of self-identity and self-awareness, which has been progressively replaced by the internalized aggressor's perspective and dictates how our patient had to look at himself, and at the world. Mostly, such patients have been severely mentally and/or physically abused by at least one overtly aggressive caretaker while the other one(s) were passively witnessing.

The virtual inner space of such a patient must consist of more than the sum of all successive identifications of those earlier unhappy years when the child was forced to become exactly that identity that his aggressors wanted him to be. These patients' superegos are formed by multiple former aggressors, they have invaded the patient's ego. These were the people the child depended upon. And of course, it is always the passive witness, helpless and/or ignoring and/or denying, who takes care that the overt aggressor can prolong his detrimental cruel behaviour. Especially these internalized aggressors, who occupy the patient's virtual inner space, called superego, took care that the traumas remain trapped in the virtual prison of the patient's inner world. If such patients experience feelings at all, they will experience feelings that result from the interaction with the people they depended upon which are mostly anxiety and unhealthy guilt. Their attentional capabilities are asleep, the patient's judgement of self-efficacy will be low, and self-regulation will be unhealthy. And when speaking about the mirror neuron system: these patients will have a mirror neuron system that can be understood as a mirror neuron prison (Neborsky & Peluso, 2008, 2009).

Implications for therapy

During the initial interview, one of the first tasks of the therapist will be to help the patient in recognizing his self-defeating pattern and to help him to quit this self-destructive behaviour. The therapist's techniques of confronting, identification, and clarification (see the next chapter) are aimed at weakening these self-defeating responses and helping the patient to perceive the negative consequences, while giving the patient more functional and constructive alternatives. In doing so, the therapist will function as an empathic model (or external constructive superego), reinforcing the patient to observe, internalize, and acquire the behaviour which is identical with the empathic position of the therapist.

As our patients are not accustomed to look at themselves with love, precision, and care, the therapist will have to repeat this many times together with the patient.

Many therapists will certainly have experienced that, although their patient grasps the specific features of his self-defeating pattern, he still continues to keeping this pattern upright.

Did the therapist address his patient's judgement of low self-efficacy? Probably not. Did the therapist address his patient's acceptance of low self-esteem, low self-efficacy, did the therapist address that the patient has given up hope? Probably not.

On the road to the patient's unconscious, there comes the moment when it is safe to help the patient with experiencing and expressing emotions. This is a great opportunity for the therapist to model what the patient could say to that other person with whom he is angry. In giving words to the patient's anger, the therapist functions as a model. Observing the therapist giving words to anger will reduce some of the patient's anxiety. In reversing the roles, active rehearsal, inviting the patient to express the anger, corrective feedback, anxiety will first increase but thereafter will take a further decrease, and the patient's self-efficacy and self-regulation will increase.

Steps in the chapter

- Bandura's observational learning
  - *model of reciprocal determinism*
  - *attentional, retention, behavioural production, motivational processes*
  - *mirror neuron system and observational learning*
- Introjection, identification, imitation
- Implications for therapy

CHAPTER SEVEN

The road to the patient's unconscious and the working alliance

The initial interview and its twofold task

In psychotherapy, one of the initial concerns of therapist and patient is to understand the nature of the patient's problems in order to resolve them.

This is specifically true for Davanloo's trial-therapy model of the initial assessment which he considers the only reliable method to determine if the patient is likely to respond to ISTDP. However, in achieving this twofold task (understanding the nature of patient's problems and testing patient's responses), it is at the same time the therapist's aim to implement Davanloo's theory to this particular patient and to relate his observations back to the particular theoretical constructs that provided Davanloo's framework for interpreting data and generating predictions.

This means that in order to assess and understand the patient's psychodynamics, character structure, ego-defensive organization and (last but not least) genetically structured core-neurotic conflict, the therapist has to implement Davanloo's set of interventions, which he refers to as the central dynamic sequence (CDS). This CDS can be considered as the treatment protocol for trial therapy.

In implementing the therapy protocol, the therapist also should predict where, when and how the patient is to respond. This means that the therapist should be able—at each moment—to observe the patient's responses, to recognize, and to understand them. If he is not able to do so, errors and even omissions of observation are likely to result, and consequently the implementation of the treatment protocol will be faulty.

Behaviour and its determinants are both complex. The therapist's need to unravel complexity (observing and recognizing patient's data, deciding on the interventions, the process of making predictions, testing them as right or wrong) has a fundamental implication. The therapist must be able to take a scientific attitude. In the Netherlands, in the postgraduate training of behaviour therapy, trainees are encouraged to conduct their behaviour therapies as single-case experimental designs. Although the single-case methodology is often associated with behaviour therapy, it is of course theory-free. The approach advocated here is to utilize the single-case methodology for (at least) the initial interview. One of the essentials of single-case methodology is that it requires clear specification of the independent and dependent variables.

A position, generally taken in psychology and psychotherapy is that behaviour is a manifestation which permits inferences to be drawn about unobservable inner psychological processes. Thus, by observing the behaviour of the patient, the therapist can draw his inferences about the inner processes that prompted the behaviour. The basic procedure followed in psychological experimentation is to manipulate a condition or factor outside the organism, the independent variable (e.g., the intervention of the therapist), that may have an effect upon a psychological process of the organism, the dependent variable (e.g., the specific patient variable), and then to observe the behavioural manifestations of these effects. The therapist, however, cannot come to know what effect was produced until he has observed the behaviour and analysed the measures he obtained. Clear measures are needed to attest to the fact that change has actually occurred.

As there is still a certain amount of confusion about the exact meaning of the concepts, which are used as the dependent variables (specific patient variables) in ISTDP, and about how they should be assessed, we have elaborated on them in Chapters Three, Four, and Five).

Clear definitions should not be restricted to distinctions (what the concept is and what it is not), but should also include dependencies (is the concept/particular patient variable a function of a more basic concept) and relations (how is the concept related to other concepts?, how is the particular patient variable related to other patient variables?).

Davanloo's central dynamic sequence

Davanloo's set of interventions, aimed at unlocking of the unconscious, which he refers to as the central dynamic sequence (CDS), can be considered as the treatment protocol for "trial therapy" with all patients located on the spectrum of structural neurosis. The initial interview with the patient is also called "trial therapy" because of its dual function: the diagnostic and the therapeutic function. On the basis of the findings of such a trial therapy, a decision can be made whether ISTDP is the appropriate therapy indication for this particular patient. Is the patient best helped with this kind of therapy? Or would, for example, behaviour therapy, or Gestalt therapy, better serve the needs of the patient? Is the setting of individual therapy the best one? Or should the therapist discuss with the patient that couples therapy or group therapy would be more suitable? It could even be that the therapist does not think himself capable and experienced enough to do the ISTDP with that particular patient. And in that case, the therapist would undoubtedly refer this patient to another more experienced ISTDP therapist.

In the initial interview or trial therapy, once there is an overview of the symptomatic difficulties of the patient, the therapist is almost immediately faced with the complex task of detailed assessment of the various aspects of the patient's psychopathology. This detailed assessment will be the basis upon which the therapist has to decide which aspect of the patient's psychopathology will be the first target of his intervention in order to establish a working alliance with his patient. The patient's response to this intervention will determine the therapist's second intervention, and so on.

Thus at each moment, on the basis of patient's variables, decisions have to be made as to which technique, with what timing and duration, has to be used in order to influence these variables in such a way that, in cooperation with the patient, the road to the patient's unconscious can be taken without accidents.

Not only during the initial interview, but also during all therapy sessions, a continuous assessment of the patient's (in session and in between session) response to the therapist's intervention or, in other words, a continuous assessment of the momentary status quo of a patient's psychopathology is a *must*.

This exactly is what makes this type of psychotherapy so difficult to master. But achieving mastery can be a rewarding challenge!

Incomplete and/or incorrect assessment of the patient's psychopathology (the dependent variables) and/or faulty application of techniques (the independent variables) by therapists and/or application of the wrong techniques don't help the patient and can even be damaging to the patient.

The road to the unconscious: red and green traffic lights

Needless to say, the road to the unconscious is within the patient and his particular variables determine the timing, duration, and sequence of the specific interventions/techniques in order to influence these variables in such a way that the full road can be taken, access to the unconscious core neurotic conflicts is achieved and that the patient's ego is capable of bearing his complex transference feelings. Taking the full road and reaching the goal without accidents requires an optimal working alliance between therapist and patient. So, at the moment of the first encounter, the moment of the initial interview, the first aim is to establish an optimal working alliance. Some of patient's variables will function as forces against such an establishment and could be considered as red traffic lights while some other variables will function as forces in favour of the working alliance to be established and these could be seen as green traffic lights.

There is common agreement among psychotherapists that the nature and degree of patient's character resistance and superego pathology can be considered as a measure of the severity of traumatic experiences to which the patient was formerly exposed in interactions with important persons and in the course of which he originally took refuge in his defences. The degree to which these patterns of character defences are promptly, automatically, and indiscriminately erected by the patient, irrespective of how closely later persons in his life resemble his original "aggressors", determine the degree of maladaptiveness of these defences. In the common undertaking of the initial interview, nature and degree of character defences function as red traffic lights and determine the selection and order of the therapist's (less or more powerful) techniques as well as the time it takes before defences become more dystonic and traffic lights will signal green.

At the level of superego pathology and resistance we could say that a patient enters therapy somewhere in between transference resistance and character resistance. Mostly, the patient's resistance takes the form of an intermingling of character and transference resistance (see also Chapter Five).

In the "worst case" for the working alliance to be established and developed, the patient has high superego pathology and massive character resistance at the onset of the therapeutic encounter.

According to Davanloo a self-constructive functioning of the patient's ego has become paralysed under the harsh and punitive mandate of the superego. Part (at least) of the ego has identified with the superego and the automatism, vigour, and tenacity with which the syntonic defences are put into operation is at its utmost and the patient's underlying anxiety ranges from vast to overwhelming. The indispensable ally of the therapist, that is, the patient's observing ego is so to speak asleep or even in coma. At least this observing ego is needed for the patient to become aware that he is automatically putting these and those defences into operation, with which he sabotages here and now the investigation of his problems and the cooperation with the therapist. Also, the resolution of the transference conflict depends on the patient being able to see the distinction between the therapist and the early object of his over-generalized feelings.

However, a patient may for example correctly recognize his transference distortions or unresolved self-punitive mechanisms, and may come to see the need for changing his behaviour without being able to do so. An observing but otherwise lamed ego still is no ally to win a case or to win the battle against the sadistic superego.

The minimal prerequisites for therapeutic change imply that a patient is not only aware of his particular psychodynamic "outfit" but also that he will be able to alter his maladaptive covert and overt behavioural pattern in order to experience painful feelings and to relive past traumatic experiences. Much therapeutic power would be gained if the therapist could cooperate with a patient's ego, capable of observing, of relinquishing his defences and capable of experiencing impulses, feelings, and anxiety. In pursuing the development and establishment of an optimal working alliance, Davanloo's interventions are first aimed at the awakening and gradual improvement of the patient's perceptual clarity and acuity. Second, the therapist and the patient's observing ego working together provides some inside information about the nature and degree of patient's ego-adaptive capacity and degree of superego pathology and careful monitoring of moment-to-moment responses allows—if necessary—for a restructuring of the patient's ego-adaptive capacity in such a way that the patient, on the basis of his intrinsic motivation, turns against the mandate of the superego, relinquishes his defences, and is capable to bear his impulses, feelings, and anxiety.

When there is anxiety at the onset of the therapeutic encounter, we could say that the patient's anxiety is somewhere on the continuum between anxiety as a transference reaction and anxiety as a sign of generalized anxiety. The patient's anxiety must be considered as a red traffic light if the proportion of autonomic symptoms is higher than musculoskeletal symptoms, if there is cognitive and/or perceptual dysfunctioning and/or if the rise and spread of physiological symptoms is fast and hardly no fluctuation is established. In these cases, these physiological symptoms evidence that the patient's ego is less or not capable of regulating his anxiety for his own sake. If there is a preponderance of the proportion of musculoskeletal symptoms over autonomic symptoms and the perceptual/cognitive system is largely unaffected, and if the rise and spread of symptoms is fluctuating, then anxiety could be considered as a green traffic light. Firstly, in these cases, it means that the patient's ego is reasonably capable of managing his anxiety (see also Chapter Four). Secondly, in these cases, anxiety, and especially growing anxiety, can be taken as a signal for the rise of the unconscious complex transference feelings.

As the therapist takes pains to help the patient to make his complex transference feelings conscious and to bear and contain them it follows that successful cooperation depends heavily on the functioning of the patient's ego-adaptive capacity. It is therefore very important for the therapist to test this capacity repeatedly. Some patients are unable to recognize the causal link between eliciting stimuli, aroused feelings, anxiety, and defences, nor can they distinguish between the different aroused feelings (e.g., anger, guilt, sadness, happiness), anxiety, and defences. The more a patient's cognitive/perceptual system is malfunctioning on these points, then the lower is the patient's ego-adaptive capacity and the more these signs must be taken as red traffic lights. The traffic lights will turn green the moment the patient is able to see the correct causal connection between eliciting stimuli, aroused feelings, anxiety, and defences and is able to differentiate between them.

A start on the road to change and to the unconscious core neurotic conflicts can be made from somewhere between the pole of resistance and the pole of anxiety.

Davanloo devised his CDS in such a way that the patient's red traffic lights will signal green in growing cooperation with the patient:

1. his observing ego is awakened
2. his perceptual clarity and acuity are improved
3. his syntonic defences become more and more dystonic (of course, syntonic defences have only changed into truly ego-dystonic, the moment the patient feels sadness or anger about having used them, about their self-destructive function, and the moment he is highly motivated to get rid of them)
4. that character resistance crystallizes into transference resistance
5. while rising anxiety can be managed, and
6. ego-adaptive capacity—if needed—is restructured
7. that there is a rise of the unconscious complex transference feelings, and
8. that the patient relinquishes his defences out of intrinsic motivation in order for
9. the complex transference feelings to be unlocked, experienced, and contained and
10. access to the core neurotic conflicts is achieved.

Figure 20 (between pages 126 and 127) presents the different traffic lights on the road to the unconscious core neurotic conflicts, and it can be used (as we will see in the next chapters) as a decision-tree for the timing, selection, and order of the therapist's techniques.

The concept of the working alliance in ISTDP

Psychotherapy is not a situation in which only the therapist is hard working and taking the sole responsibility for the therapeutic process. Neither is the opposite true. As each individual psychotherapy concerns an ordinary working situation between two individuals, both therapist and patient will be equally responsible in the undertaking of his tasks to fulfil their common work. It will not be difficult to understand that it is also the quality of the (conscious/unconscious) working alliance which will influence the quality of the therapeutic process and of the therapy results. A therapist's *conscious* ally, that is, a patient who is motivated and capable of dropping his defences and facing his repressed complex of impulse and transference feelings is the necessary condition to establish with the patient also the *unconscious* part of the working alliance.

Of course, no psychotherapy method, nor array of techniques is effective in the absence of a therapeutic or working alliance with a patient. Therefore, it is not surprising that presence and quality of a therapeutic or working alliance is a strong predictor of outcome in (individual) psychotherapy across diverse psychotherapy schools.

The construct of therapeutic alliance or working alliance refers to the cooperative aspect of the patient–therapist relationship in psychotherapy. As each individual psychotherapy is in fact a continuous interaction between two hard-working individuals, one in need of help, the other offering the help, but both equally responsible in the undertaking of his tasks to fulfil their common work, we prefer the term "working alliance" over "therapeutic alliance".

The specific ways in which a working alliance with a patient will be established and maintained are of course dependent on the particular psychotherapy school, its particular theoretical view on the patient's problems, its particular emphasis on certain aspects of the patient's problems, its particular view on specific curative elements and last but not least its particular method and techniques to "tackle" and solve the patient's problems.

Davanloo (1990), the creator of ISTDP, refers to the variables within the patient that influence the establishment and quality of a working alliance as forces operating against the therapeutic process and those operating in favour of the therapeutic process. The sadistic superego which demands suffering and the patient's (conscious and unconscious) resistance operate against the therapeutic process, while the repressed impulses and feelings (seeking an outlet and expression) and the patient's conscious willingness to cooperate with the therapist, to face the truth, to drop defences, and to face disturbing feelings operate in favour of the therapeutic process.

With regard to the concept of working alliance and the patient's part in it, he therewith distinguishes two components: a conscious and an unconscious component. "The conscious component consists of the patient's conscious will to get well, to cooperate with the therapist, to face the truth no matter how painful, to drop his defences, to face disturbing feelings. The unconscious component consists basically of the repressed impulses and feelings (the lower corner of the triangle of conflict) which are pressing for expression and are therefore on the patient's side" (Davanloo, 1990).

But what about the therapist's part in the working alliance?

As most of our patients come to the initial interview with high superego pathology, they will defeat any intimate relationship to a certain degree. Thus, it is mainly up to the therapist, who is supposed to have the necessary relational and technical skills, to establish a working alliance with his patient. Therefore, the therapist's skills in at least establishing such an alliance are central. Once such an alliance is established, both patient's and therapist's contributions to the alliance are equally responsible for safeguarding and maintaining the working alliance while steadily increasing its quality.

Successful ISTDP therapists tend to be those who are capable of establishing and maintaining a working alliance with the widest range of patients, located on Davanloo's spectra of structural neuroses and of fragility.
Given the centrality of a therapist's skills in—at least—establishing a working alliance, we think that a therapist's working alliance skills are worth a primary focus.

The conceptualization of the alliance that has been most prominent in psychotherapy, proposed by Bordin in 1979, includes three components:

1. the emotional bond, developed between therapist and patient, that allows the patient to make therapeutic progress
2. an agreement between therapist and patient about the goals of treatment
3. an agreement about the therapy tasks needed to accomplish these goals.

Mostly, when patients come to therapy, they do so because they are unhappy and they articulate their suffering in terms of complaints. For example, a patient may have a psychological complaint such as anxiety ("I am so anxious all the time, and mainly in new situations") or as depression ("although I have a nice life, I seldom enjoy it, I withdraw from social situations and I have problems falling asleep"), or as a lack of confidence ("I postpone most of my oral exams at the university, I always think I am not good enough, I have no confidence whatsoever in my intellectual capacities").

Of course, in articulating his complaint a patient only expresses one or more external manifestations of his internal problem. It is only seldom that a patient realizes that the complaints, he experiences in interpersonal relationships refer to one or more elements/aspects of an intrapsychic problem. And even if a patient does realize it, this does not necessarily mean that going the investigation patient and therapist will have the same vision on certain elements/aspects of the patient's problems. For example, the patient may think that he has access to his feelings, and may think that he is expressing them in a constructive way. Whereas, during the initial interview, it becomes evident that what the patient would call his anger, the therapist would label as anxiety. And when asked for a specific example of expressing his anger, it appears that the patient equates his defence of blaming with a constructive expression of his anger.

We therefore suggest adding a fourth component to be included in the concept of the working alliance: the therapist and patient should have the same vision of the patient's problems and the same definitions of the several elements/aspects that make up the patient's intrapsychic problem.

In this way, we conceptualize the working alliance as consisting of four components:

1. the emotional bond, developed between therapist and patient, that allows the patient to make therapeutic progress
2. the therapist and patient have the same vision of the patient's problems and the same definition of its constituting elements/aspects
3. an agreement between therapist and patient about (intermittent) goals of treatment
4. an agreement about the division of therapy tasks to accomplish these goals.

From the above, it follows logically that the therapist's understanding of the concept of the working alliance is crucial in the process, leading to a success or failure of psychotherapy. This makes it important to do our best not to keep this concept abstract, but to make it as concrete as possible for ISTDP purposes.

Ad 1: the emotional bond developed between therapist and patient

Since Rogers (1959), many therapists agree with him that a therapist's ability to empathize with the patient is of clinical importance and essential for establishing and maintaining a working alliance.

Rogers defined empathy as the ability "to perceive the internal frame of reference of another with accuracy and with emotional components and meanings as if one were the person" (pp. 210–211). Nowadays, there are theoretical distinctions as to the manner in which the therapist's empathy can be expressed. Emphasis is frequently placed on the patient's experience of the therapist as supportive, caring, trustworthy, fair, reliable, knowledgeable, helpful, understanding, and genuinely interested in the patient. We, however, doubt whether there exists any therapist In this world, who fulfils all of these criteria, and during the whole time each therapy lasts? No such ideal person exists in our view! Let us not forget that in ISTDP the working alliance is based on the real relationship between the patient and therapist, and the reality is that no ideal patient nor ideal therapist exists. However, this does not mean that a therapist should not give his best. There is no dispute that empathy—the capacity to share and understand emotions and emotional states of others in reference to oneself—plays an essential role in healthy interpersonal engagement. Many of our patients—in their upbringing—had to grow up without receiving empathy for their longings and feelings, or they had to grow up in interactions with their caretakers, where empathy was used for hurtful purposes. We like the view of Decety & Moriguchi on the concept of empathy (2007). In their opinion, empathy is a kind of induction process that can be understood as the result of four intertwined and dynamically interacting components:

1. affective sharing between the self and the other
   The meaning of a given object, action, or social situation may be common to several people and may activate corresponding distributed patterns of neural activation in their respective brains. This (automatic) sharing would explain how we come to understand each other
2. self-awareness (note: sharing emotion without self-awareness takes of course the form of identification without discriminating between one's feelings and those of the other)
3. mental flexibility to adopt the subjective perspective of the other
   Understanding others is greatly based on using one's own embodied cognition and using one's own beliefs, opinions, attitudes, feelings. Errors in taking the perspective of others are rooted in a person's failure to recognize the degree to which he projects the self-perspective onto others, and therewith the person fails to recognize that what is of importance to one person may differ that of another.
4. regulatory processes that modulate the subjective feelings

> Emotion regulation refers to the processes by which individuals influence which emotions they have, when they have them, how they experience and express them.
>
> The therapist's perception of his patient's emotional state will evoke emotions and generate emotion regulatory processes in the therapist. Without being aware of the emotional state of the patient, and/or the own evoked emotions, and/or without a degree of healthy emotion regulation, a therapist is in big trouble. Without self-awareness, mental flexibility, and emotion-regulation processing, it will become difficult or even impossible to intentionally/consciously have and express empathy.

The patient's decision to consider psychotherapy for his problems will induce within the patient an expectancy regarding the therapist. This expectancy will be based in large part on his previously learned perceptions about earlier important caretakers. It follows logically that these perceptions play a crucial role in the nature and degree of his (non-) receptivity (the nature and degree of his superego pathology and resistances) to the therapist's interventions. In the "worst case" for the working alliance to be established and developed, the patient has high superego pathology and massive character resistance at the onset of the therapeutic encounter. According to Davanloo, a self-constructive functioning of the patient's ego has become paralysed under the harsh and punitive mandate of the superego. Part (at least) of the ego has identified with the superego, and the automatism, vigour, and tenacity with which the syntonic defences are put into operation is at its utmost and the patient's underlying anxiety ranges from vast to overwhelming.

Although this patient's pathologically harsh and sadistic superego, originally arose out of the patient's guilt and grief-laden reactive rage, the need to maintain attachment (read: illusion of attachment) to the original caretakers, and the atrocities of childhood being past, the tragedy is that the patient himself has become the originator and maintainer of repeated self-injury while destroying each new and yet potentially unbiased relationship with his instantaneous, automatic, and indiscriminate pattern of maladaptive character defences. These (character) defences are put into operation by the patient's ego under the mandate of his pathological harsh/punitive superego.

Obviously, in establishing a working alliance, it is the healthy part of the therapist that seeks cooperation with the healthy part of his patient. It had been on the basis of this healthy part (sometimes almost non-existent), his longing to make ends with his suffering, that the patient had come to therapy and sought help. The patient's unhealthy part is, of course, that part which is responsible for perpetuating (self-) destructive processes and suffering.

With regard to empathy, this means that the therapist will invite his patient's healthy part, to have—together with the therapist—empathy for the patient not being aware of how normal and habitual his self-defeating processes have become and how (in what exact ways) the patient has grown accustomed to looking at himself as *not important* or even sometimes as *barely existent*, looking at himself as not important enough even to have the right to decide for himself. Not important enough to be understood with love, precision and care. Not important enough to understand his longings, feelings, norms and values, opinion, behaviours. Not important enough to understand the processes he puts into operation, that are responsible for generating and perpetuating his problems.

When witnessing a child playing with matches and trying to burn the curtains, one hopefully will immediately react and stop the child in his dangerous and (self) -destructive play. There will be an immediate recognition of the dangerous and hurtful consequences of the child's playing and experimenting with matches (affective sharing and self-awareness)! It will be clear to the witness that the child in being engrossed in the fascination of making fire is not aware how nearly he had hurt himself (and others) (mental flexibility). Most probably, the witness will be aware of his own anxiety regarding the hurtful consequences if the child's behaviour is not stopped (emotion regulation of witness).

The witness will have empathy with the child that was so unaware of the (self-) defeating behaviour while playing with the matches. He will intervene to stop the child playing with the matches and subsequently will explain to the child that this behaviour only results in burning and hurting himself, burning and destroying the house, and endangering the lives of other family members and pets.

In fact, at the early stages of an initial interview, when the therapist starts his task to establish a working alliance, he will arouse in himself a similar process into operation.

When witnessing the patient automatically devaluing himself ("in fact my problems are very stupid and when coming to you, I wondered whether they were important enough to go for psychotherapy. In fact, there are people with far more serious problems"), the therapist, hopefully, will immediately react and stop the patient in his automatic process of self-devaluing.

There will be an immediate recognition of the (self-) defeating consequences of the patient's habit of self-devaluing (affective sharing and self-awareness)! It will be clear to the therapist that the patient is not aware that and how he is self-defeating (mental flexibility). Most probably, the therapist will be aware of his own feelings regarding the consequences for the working alliance and the therapy process if the patient's behaviour is not stopped (emotion regulation of therapist).

The therapist will have empathy with the patient who was so unaware of the (self-) defeating behaviour while automatically going for self-devaluing. He will intervene to stop the patient, to direct his attention to his self-devaluing (confrontation and identification with his defences), and subsequently will explain to the patient that this behaviour only results in keeping himself unimportant, giving other people priority, and preventing therewith to understand his longings, feelings, opinions, behaviour, resulting in a continuation of his problems (clarification of the function of these self-defeating defences).

The therapist will have no sympathy for the dictates of the patient's pathological superego, but will have empathy for that part of the patient that automatically obeys the voice of his superego, the devaluing voice of his internalized former aggressors.

In taking an empathic position towards the patient's ego part, having no sympathy whatsoever with the patient's pathological superego part, the therapist functions, so to speak, as an external constructive superego to the patient. The therapist will at least continue to do so until the patient has internalized the empathic "modelling" of the therapist. After all, as long as the patient refrains from empathy with himself, the therapist will have no ally but also there will be a hundred per cent guarantee that each step forward in the therapeutic process will be followed by two steps backward. In the process of establishing a working alliance, the patient's grief (or constructive anger) about his self-defeating mechanisms that were responsible for the continuation of his suffering is one sign for the therapist to infer that the patient has joined the therapist in taking an empathic position.

As the working alliance is not restricted to the therapy session in the therapist's office, but is supposed to be maintained during the whole therapy, in and outside the therapist's office, in-between therapy sessions, during therapy sessions, it is of utmost importance that the patient be capable of taking an empathic position toward himself. Without this the patient's intrinsic motivation to understand his own processes with love, precision and care, to take himself seriously, to take the work with his therapist seriously, to take the therapist seriously and to "enjoy" his own efforts and those of the therapist in the common enterprise to reach constructive control over his own life and goals, any constructive progress in the therapy process will be of short duration. It is up to the therapist as well as to the patient to check whether the empathic position still is blossoming and when (if not) to investigate what caused the patient's decrease of motivation for understanding himself with love, care, and precision. After having done so, it is up to therapist and patient to each resume the empathic position.

Ad 2: the therapist and patient have the same view on the patient's problems and the same definition of its constituting elements/aspects

ISTDP techniques to establish a working alliance with a patient in order to cooperate taking the road to the patient's unconscious are largely based on an understanding of intrapsychic functioning as illustrated by the triangles of conflict and persons. As the processes of the inner interactions of id, ego and superego cannot be observed directly, Malan (1979), in following Menninger's triangle of insight (1958), operationalized the experience of the patient's intrapsychic conflict within the interpersonal context by means of the linkage of two concepts: i.e., the linking of the triangle of conflict and the triangle of persons.

As most of us know, the triangle of conflict represents three interacting subsystems, which are involved in the generation and perpetuation of the process of intrapsychic conflict: impulses and feelings (I/F: the lower corner of the triangle of conflict) arouse anxiety (A: the upper right corner) and defences (D: the upper left corner). It is hypothesized that the impulses/feelings that were evoked in the interaction with past harmful caretakers, have aroused anxiety and defences in order to maintain the relationship with these attachment figures. The patient's tendency to repeat the process of defending against anxiety provoking impulses/feelings in interactions with current figures and therapist is represented in the triangle of persons (P: important persons in the past, the lower corner of the triangle of persons); (T: the therapist, the upper left corner); (C: the persons in the current, the upper right corner).

Taking the road to the patient's unconscious, while establishing a working alliance with the patient, it must become progressively clear to the patient to look at his problem in terms of the two triangles.

It must become clear to the patient that in each interaction (in vivo: e.g., a face-to-face contact or *in vitro*: e.g., thinking of an interaction):

- he puts the same process into operation, notwithstanding the fact that the constituent elements of this process can be different
- therefore the patient should at all times take care to precisely assess and define in one concrete situation (past or present, *in vivo* or *in vitro*)

what the precise eliciting essential stimuli in the verbal and/or non-verbal behaviour of the other person(s) in the interaction with the patient had been/are
- whether he has/had access to his impulse (murderous rage) and/or feelings (guilt, grief, love, anger)
- whether he experienced his particular manifestations of anxiety
- which array of what specific defences he has put into operation

The working alliance with the patient is only then established when the patient understands that:

- his problems on the interpersonal axis are the consequence of his intrapsychic problems
- he—like the therapist—will understand and assess at each moment his problems in terms of the triangles of conflict and persons
- not only during the therapy session, together with the therapist but—most important—at all times outside the therapy office, in between the sessions.

Of course, going the process of establishing the working alliance it is up to the therapist to help the patient understanding his problems in terms of the two triangles, to define precisely the constituent elements and to check whether the patient and therapist agree on their vision of the patient's problems and the definition of the constituent elements.

Mostly, in the very beginning of an initial interview or of a therapy, the therapist will investigate the patient's problems in the direct interaction with the therapist (realistic relationship with the therapist). In this way, the therapist enables himself to rely on his own eyes in assessing the several constructive and/or self-defeating verbal and non-verbal mechanisms that are put into operation by his patient. At the same time the therapist enables himself to assess whether the patient is conscious of the particular mechanisms that the therapist will bring under scrutiny. And—very important—the therapist, while working in the realistic relationship with the therapist (T), will be able to help his patient becoming aware of the particular mechanism and its constructive/self-destructive function. The more the therapy process is advancing, the more the therapist will also work in the current interactions (C) outside the therapy office, in the past interactions with important persons (P) and in the transference (T). As the therapist herewith has to rely on the patient's eyes, it is extremely important that the therapist can be certain that he shares the same definitions of the elements that constitute the patient's problems and that the patient's cognitive/perceptual system is accurately processing and correctly labelling these.

Going the process of maintaining the working alliance it is up to the therapist to help the patient to assess and understand C-P-T-links. And help the patient to recognize and understand the causal link of his transferred reactions of past interactions to interactions in the currency. Thereafter, it is also up to the patient to understand the when-how-and-what of his transference mechanisms.

Ad 3: an agreement between therapist and patient about (intermediate) goals of treatment

Not only should therapist and patient share the same vision of the patient's problems, they also should agree on what a desirable intermediate goal might be in terms of changed behaviour,

decrease of anxiety, grasp on feelings, as well as the road and means in getting there. To both patient and therapist, the connection should be clear between the agreed-upon intermediate goals and the focus of the sessions. This implies that the therapist at all times is clear about the what, why, and how of the specific focus of the common therapeutic investigation. Each session, the therapist should have a concrete therapy plan. It is all too often that a session is wasted because of the therapist complying to his patient's momentary (self-defeating) preoccupations rather than focusing on the patient's main presenting problems.
Imagine the following situation in the very early phase of a therapy:

A female patient has entered the therapy with a very unhealthy regulated anxiety (e.g., a high proportion of cognitive/perceptive disruption, parasympathetic symptoms, a few sympathetic symptoms, and some striated muscles tension). Suppose it had become clear that the patient is used to ignoring and denying these physical anxiety manifestations, resulting in low performance in the working environment, with the risk of being fired from a job she loves so much and which keeps her away from social isolation.

An intermediate agreed-upon goal could be for the patient 1) to stop ignoring and denying her physical anxiety manifestations, 2) to take responsibility for her anxiety regulation.

Means for the patient to achieve this could be, for example, assessing her anxiety manifestations each hour during the day, assessing any increase of manifestations and relating them to what happened precisely in that momentary situation.

Suppose the patient enters the session, ruminating about whether or not to take two weeks off after Christmas.

The establishment/maintaining of a working alliance would become seriously stagnated if the therapist would comply with the patient's preoccupations rather than:

1. keeping the focus upon the mutual agreed-upon goal of stopping ignoring and denial of anxiety manifestations, and
2. checking whether the patient had taken responsibility for ending her self-defeating mechanisms of ignoring, denying,
3. checking whether the patient had taken responsibility for regulating her anxiety in a constructive way,
4. and/or what made the patient to "forget" this agreed-upon intermittent goal,
5. and—last but not least—checking the function of the patient's preoccupation in relation with continuing the self-defeating process of ignoring, denying her anxiety.

Ad 4: an agreement about the division of therapy tasks to accomplish these goals

Once a working alliance is established, it is the patient's task:

- to be honest towards himself and the therapist, and especially when a) there is something the patient does not understand, and/or b) anger or impulse towards the therapist is mobilized.
- to assess and monitor in all of his interactions (including the ones with the therapist), the yes/no and- how-what-where occurrence of his problems, by means of working with the two triangles.

This implies that the patient is intrinsically motivated to take responsibility for his own processes and is capable of:

- describing a moment-situation in concrete terms
- describing the observed verbal and non-verbal behaviour of the other person(s) that functioned as stimulus
- assessing the occurrence of physical manifestations and labelling them correctly as the appropriate feeling or anxiety
- assessing all of his defences (and not only two or three when he uses ten)
- taking constructive action regarding his anxiety (according to what was agreed upon with the therapist)
- taking constructive action to get access to his feelings and/or impulses, and if he does not succeed, taking the decision to bring this forward in the next therapy session
- taking constructive action to make C-P-T links and, if he does not succeed, taking the decision to bring this forward in the next therapy session.

It is the therapist's task:

- to check the quality of patient's and own contributions (along the above-mentioned four aspects) to the maintaining of the working alliance
- to make stagnated working alliance discussable, to check for impulse and painful feelings of patient towards therapist, to check for countertransference
- to do in each session his moment-to-moment assessment of patient variables correctly, to use his techniques in a proper way while each time taking care that the patient's impulses and feelings are brought into conscious experience in accordance with the nature and degree of the patient's momentary ego-adaptive capacity.

Problems in establishing (and maintaining) the conscious/unconscious working alliance with the patient: the process of learning and the patient's defences of passivity, hopelessness/helplessness

Learning (in general, but also to do ISTDP as a therapist and as a patient) requires amongst other things that the patient will be able to construct a conceptual framework that allows him to organize and integrate new knowledge into a coherent structure. Thus, in order for stimulating real and deep learning, it first will be necessary that we help our patients to build an intellectual curiosity out of intrinsic motivation (or attentive ego). Having accomplished that, we have created the possibility for shedding earlier ways of thinking and expression, for relating older with newer knowledge, understanding constituents of new conceptual structures, integrating them into these new conceptual structures, and the ability to place these conceptual structures into larger and meaningful patterns.

To many of our patients, when in the course of such a learning process, failure only represents disaster. Most of them had caretakers in their life who hid their neglectful caretaking behaviour by demanding excelling school results. By demanding performance, and still more if the performance was there, it had been never good enough. The process of achieving or not achieving these results, the joy of comprehending, the disappointment of failure, the joy of looking and looking again and finally grasping and understanding new concepts—this process had not been of interest to these caretakers, and many of our patients have struggled their way through a lonely phase of life.

To these people, failure has become such a great tragedy that they stopped to learn. They have become victims of their own minds. In accepting the position that it is only performance that counts, and in accepting their view on their failures, they have said goodbye to their intellectual curiosity and enthusiasm. The focus on performance solely leaves no space for intellectual curiosity. Many of them took refuge into the defences of passivity and/or of hopelessness/helplessness.

Intellectual curiosity can make us look for improving and perfectioning our ways of dealing with problems, looking for new methods and techniques, mastering these. The effort to understand new concepts, to look or to listen in another way than one is used to, can be great fun. Especially when this process can be shared with others.

Failure is a normal part of the process of learning. The possibility of failure is inherent in all learning, and the further one has progressed in a process of learning, the greater the risk of failure can become. An intellectual curiosity, while taking pleasure in a search for perfection (and being fully aware that perfection never can be accomplished) is at the base of real deep understanding. Because of the fact that perfection never can be reached, failure is a normal and realistic part of this enthusiastic strive of perfection, and, as such, it could be used to increase and deepen our understanding of why a particular step/path did not lead us to a desired outcome, it could be used to feed our intellectual curiosity.

Some of our patients enter therapy with a profound sense of inadequacy and worthlessness. They suffer from an inability to experience themselves as an active, lovable, and capable person. The judgement, or the so-called love and/or understanding by the other, has become paramount whatever the cost of personal self-destruction.

These patients have lost their future, their hope, and their longings. They perceive a lost future either because that had been taken away and/or because they have given up. Accumulation of traumatizing experiences has led them to the giving up of hope, to giving up being themselves, able to fulfil their own longings and giving direction to their future. Mostly, their longings have become a longing for the peace of being dead. Or a longing for the peace of emptiness while adapting to the needs of other people, whatever the cost. Their resolution is self-destruction and their cost is that of the Living Dead.

Therapy may offer these patients the conditions of hope. But this hope will only be satisfied on the basis of the therapist being able to help a patient to have faith again in his own capacity to love, to understand his own un-met longings. To have faith in being capable of bearing their rage, guilt, grief, damaged love that were consequent on abuse, and frustration/humiliation when hope and longing to be loved, to be understood, and accepted was not fulfilled. When this rage and the painful feelings were converted into anxiety, and/or into somatic symptoms, and turned against the self, it becomes impossible to have faith again in one's own achievements, in being important enough to take one's own longings and feelings seriously, to give direction to one's own future. To establish a successful conscious/unconscious working alliance with a patient, it is absolutely essential that the therapist is able to help his patient cease the defences of passivity, helplessness/hopelessness.

Mistakes that are often made by ISTDP therapists and that have a negative impact on the conscious/unconscious working alliance with the patient

The mistakes we encountered have been mostly the consequence of the fact that the concept had remained a) too abstract to the therapist, b) on the basis of insufficient theoretical and technical expertise, or c) on the basis of the therapist's own pathology.

Some examples:

Mistakes in unmasking the precise identity of a patient's sadistic superego

Most colleagues do not have difficulty in assessing the superego pathology of the perpetrator of overt physical violence or that of its victim (e.g., the husband who beats his wife, or the superego pathology of his wife, who doubles the inflicted harm with her self-torture of masochism and therewith reinforces her husband's physical abuse).

It is, however, our experience in supervision that many (young) colleagues fail to correctly assess the superego pathology of the perpetrator of mental/emotional neglect as well as that of its victim who has identified with this form of mental/emotional abuse and has become his own perpetrator.

In particular, it is the extent and the severity of this kind of superego pathology that is underestimated. Often, the supervisees/young colleagues fail to see and identify the ignoring, neglectful, or minimizing eyes and voice of their patient's pathological superego. Is it because of the fact that emotional and mental neglect has grown so normal? Also to the therapist? Creating a child, feeding and clothing it, sending it to school, and refraining from physical violence doesn't make one a father or a mother. Any human being, who, as a child, was more or less chronically in an interaction where the primary caregiver was mentally and emotionally absent (be it because the caregiver was depressed, had to work all the time and was tired after work, was passive, or controlling, devaluing or anxious, helpless or suffering from X, Y, Z) will have suffered (at least to some degree) ignoring, neglect, minimizing, and/or denial of its own needs, longings, feelings, and will have learned that the meaning of "being loved" is a rather empty one-sided concept. Being loved isn't a reality that has the patient as it's subject. Being loved has become a mandate that has the child's caregiver as it's one and only subject.

These are our patients who have become experts in looking at themselves with the ignoring, neglectful, minimizing, or even denying eyes of their parent(s) and/or punishing/scolding/devaluing themselves with their parent's tongue whenever they have "the courage" to listen for one second to their own needs/longings. These are our patients who function on their automatic pilot and who give—*per* definition—others priority. Just like they were verbally and non-verbally told to do so.

The development of a predominantly healthy, constructive, loving superego is—according to the authors—only possible if the child has been in an interaction with at least one caregiver that was involved, curious in getting to know her/his child's needs, longings, being present to set limits to his/her child's (self-) destructive behaviour, or to destructive behaviour of secondary and tertiary caregivers, or siblings, helping the child to understand and contain its feelings, its norms, values, opinions, to bear and contain frustration, to be respectful to constructive feelings, norms and values of others, helping the child to be curious and to discover the world. In such a case, that caregiver would at least to a certain extent compensate the harm done by other primary, secondary or tertiary ignoring/neglectful caregivers. In our practice, it is an exception that we meet a patient whose healthy, constructive superego is far more dominant than his pathological superego. Mostly, we meet those patients whose pathological superego is dominant. And in those cases, the therapist must be able to function as an external constructive superego that the patient's ego can internalize and use in his battle to say farewell to his pathological superego part.

Functioning as an external constructive superego does not only mean that the therapist should be in constructive control of his own painful feelings and impulses, and/or of his own countertransference reactions It does not only mean that the therapist should be patient or be in possession of all kinds of positive characteristics. Amongst others, it includes setting limits to the patient's self-defeating mechanisms in the interaction with himself, with the therapist, and with other persons. It also includes the willingness to invite the patient to unlock and investigate his impulse/feelings in the transference. Firmly setting limits to the patient's self-destructive behaviour and/or investigating the patient's impulses and feelings in the transference is what many therapists avoid (with or without finding some justification for their avoidance) to do. The tragedy is that to their patients these therapists have become an external neglectful superego. Often, these therapists don't realize how their own pathological superego is in a collusion with the patient's pathological superego. To these therapists, it is perhaps helpful to realize that their patients weren't so lucky to have another caregiver that could compensate to a certain extent for harm and abuse. How often these patients have been in interactions with caregivers that were "partners in crime". One caregiver by his behaviour (e.g., controlling, devaluing behaviour) being ignoring/neglectful of their child's needs and the other one being submissive, passive, helpless. Instead of setting limits to the partner's ignoring/neglectful abuse (and therewith conveying the message to the child that it is at least important enough to be cared for) the latter becomes a partner in crime. Because it is with this passivity, submissiveness and helplessness that he/she is of course maintaining and reinforcing the ignoring, neglectful abuse of the other caregiver. The message that this submissive, passive partner is conveying to their child is that caregiver #1 is right and should be obeyed. If and when the eyes/voice of these caregivers-partners-in-crime are introjected, and if and when the patient identifies with these eyes and voice, then of course the therapist should keep in mind that the introjected passive, submissive eyes and voice maintain the ignoring/neglectful eyes of the introjected primary caregiver. The *in vitro* interaction patterns being the representation of the *in vivo* interaction patterns!

One practical consequence of this principle is that if the therapist and such a patient would go for a breakthrough of impulse, guilt, grief, love towards caregiver #1, they should immediately have this followed by a breakthrough of impulse, guilt, grief towards the caregiver, who with passivity and submissiveness reinforced and maintained the harm done by his partner. If the therapist and his patient wouldn't go for these two breakthroughs in the same session, and restrict themselves to the breakthrough of impulse, guilt, grief towards caregiver #1, then the most important part (the face and voice of the passive partner in crime, who is in fact responsible for the maintaining of the patient's superego pathology) of the patient's pathological superego is still in command and the risk is of course that the patient will come next session again in total obedience to the two voices of his pathological superego parts.

Davanloo (1990, page 193) describes "that the higher the superego pathology (the higher the degree of punishment and sadism of the superego) the more the superego appears to have invaded and taken over the patient's ego, to have paralysed its functioning, and to have replaced the normal search for satisfaction and fulfilment with an ever-presented need for suffering." Or, in other words: the higher a patient's superego pathology the more the patient's ego part is identified with his superego part. When there is a hundred per cent identification, the patient's ego part has become totally paralysed, the observing ego is totally absent while—so to speak—in coma. The degree of a patient's identification with his superego part determines the degree of absence/presence of the patient's observing ego. The range in which the observing ego is absent to present may vary from coma (vast and totally absent) to fast asleep—sleeping—nearly awake, just awake but still in bed—awake but in need of coffee, awake and ready for the day. At this point (awake and ready for the day), the patient's observing ego has won in acuity and alertness and is ready to become an attentive ego or active investigator to his own benefit. A patient with an attentive ego is curious to learn from his therapist; curious and eager to investigate the conscious/unconscious processes he puts into operation that form and maintain his problems; curious and eager to investigate his own unlocked feelings, impulses, longings, norms, values; curious and eager to learn how to deal with these in a constructive way. Such a patient, once he has understood what the therapist taught him, will take the initiative to do his part in the common undertaking of a therapy session.

From the above, it may be clear that as long as a patient's ego part is totally or highly identified with his superego part, no working alliance will be possible, even not a conscious one. To establish a conscious working alliance with a patient, the therapist needs the patient's observing ego as a partner. To establish a conscious *and* unconscious working alliance the therapist needs the patient's attentive ego as a partner. However, in order for the therapist and patient to win their battle against the patient's pathological, sadistic superego, the patient also needs to be strong enough to quit the self-defeating processes he puts into operation and to bear and contain his impulses and painful feelings. Therefore—at first—as soon as the therapist has the patient's attentive ego as an ally, the conscious/unconscious working alliance should be focused on restructuring the patient's ego-adaptive capacity.

As stated above it isn't always easy to assess the precise identity of a patient's pathological superego, the extent to which the patient's ego part is identified with the abusive faces and voices of his introjected caregivers, the degree to which the patient's observing ego is still in operation and the degree and quality of a patient's ego-adaptive capacity. It occurs regularly that the therapist makes mistakes in his assessment of these patient variables. Mostly, the pathology of the patient's superego is underestimated and therefore the presence and quality of a patient's observing ego and quality of ego-adaptive capacity is overestimated. The consequence is that the therapist mistakenly assumes that a conscious/unconscious working alliance is established, that the patient's character resistance has crystallized into the transference resistance and that the patient's ego-adaptive capacity is strong enough to put pressure onto a patient's feelings and to go for an unlocking of the patient's impulses, guilt, grief, love. It is not difficult to understand that at least a misalliance and a patient doubling the intensity of his retreat into his self-defeating defences is the predictable result.

Mistakes in taking an empathic position

Yes, but to whom? To the patient's part that suffers under the burden of his superego pathology? Or to the eyes and voice of the superego? Mostly, mistakes are made on the basis of the therapist making an incorrect assessment and taking a patient's unhealthy reaction for a healthy one. Below are some examples where the therapist's empathic position is directed towards the patient's superego:

Colluding with the patient's superego

The therapist does not dare to interrupt and complies to the patient's superego part. Very often, e.g., because of the fact that a therapist does not dare to interrupt a patient's defiance, and complies to it, it is not clear to the therapist that he is colluding with the patient's superego and therewith he has set here the first step for a misalliance to occur.

Vignette

Suppose a patient enters a session with high anxiety (tensed from head to toes, dry mouth and throat, superficial breathing pattern, concentration problems).

Mistake of the therapist:

Th Do you notice that you are anxious?
Pt Yes, that is true, but that is not so important and I prefer to tell you about the conflict I had with X.
Th OK, then tell me about this conflict.

It would have been better:

Th Do you notice that you are anxious?
Pt Yes, that is true, but it is not so important and I prefer to tell you about the conflict I had with X
Th We will certainly investigate your conflict with X, but first I would draw your attention to the fact that you don't think this high amount of anxiety important. You are tensed from head to toe, you have a dry mouth and throat, you have a superficial breathing pattern, and I notice you have some concentration problems. These are manifestations of a high anxiety, but obviously you are used to these anxiety manifestations, and obviously you have accepted them. Do you understand me?
Pt Yes, that is true, I am so used to my anxiety that I have accepted it … the conflict I had with X …
Th So you recognize that you have accepted your high level of anxiety. This tells me that there is a part in you that looks at yourself as unimportant. Too unimportant to take care of your anxiety, of your suffering.

Or it may be that a therapist fails to assess his patient's compliance as such and takes it for the patient actively understanding the therapist. (Of course, if and when a therapist has failed to assess his patient's compliance, then we may safely assume that he also missed the patient's defence of projection, which serves as a preceding stimulus for the patient's subsequent compliance.)

Vignette

Mistake of the therapist:

Pt Do you want an example of my problems in the interaction with my friends or with my husband?

Th Well, I suppose your problems in the interaction with your husband are the most painful ones, so let us focus on the interaction with your husband.

The therapist took the patient's compliance for an active cooperation and missed the patient's preceding projection: giving priority to the therapist's opinion. The therapist did not realize his empathy was towards the patient's pathological superego, did not realize he was ignoring/belittling the patient's healthy ego part, and therewith repeating the patient's tragedy.

It would have been better:

Pt Do you want an example of my problems in the interaction with my friends or with my husband?

Th Do you realize that in asking me this, you give priority to my opinion, and it seems to me that this is a habit of yours. Making other people's opinion far more important than your own. Do you recognize this?

Mistakes in the assessment of the degree of syntonicity/dystonicity of the patient's defences. Another frequent mistake is the therapist taking the patient's cognitive understanding of the self-defeating function of one or more of his defences as a sign that the working alliance has been established and fails to see that his patient still considers the particular defence mechanisms with a certain degree of satisfaction. Failing to unmask a defence and its syntonicity will have a negative impact on the establishment and deepening of the conscious/unconscious working alliance with a patient. It is our experience that young colleagues often underestimate the malignancy and syntonicity of the following patient's defences: vagueness, speaking in general terms, passivity, helplessness/hopelessness.

Vignette

Vagueness

Mistake of the therapist:

Th Still you are vague in describing to me what your wife did or didn't do or said that evoked your anger.

Pt Yes, you are completely right, but if I have to remember everything what displeases me in the behaviour of the other … I think it was something she said about not trusting me that I would keep my promise and that made me angry.

Th And did you express your anger?

Here the therapist failed to assess 1) his *patient's satisfaction* regarding his vague recollection of his wife's utterances, 2) his *patient's vagueness* in describing the evocative stimuli (something she said …).

It would have been better:

Th Still you are vague in describing to me what your wife did or didn't do or said that evoked your anger.

Pt Yes, you are completely right, but if I have to remember everything what displeases me in the behaviour of the other … I think it was something she said about not trusting me that I would keep my promise and that made me angry.

Th You know, you have come here on the basis of your healthy part: your longing to understand your thoughts, opinions, norms, feelings, problems with love, care, and precision. Am I right?

Pt Yes.

Th But you seem satisfied with your habit of not being able to define for yourself what the other person precisely did or did not do that evoked your anger. Are you really telling me that you don't take your own perception, your own eyes and ears, your own memory, seriously? Are you really telling me that you are happy with this sloppy, negligent understanding of yourself?

Vignette

Speaking in general terms

Mistake of the therapist:

Pt Mostly, I have these kinds of problems in the interaction with my superiors.

Th Do you notice, you describe your problem in general terms: "mostly" and that will prevent us from understanding you in a precise way.

Pt Yes, I know, you told me so before. I suppose it is something typical of me that I have these problems mainly in the interaction with my superiors. (Although the therapist has confronted, identified, and clarified this defence of "speaking in general" before, the patient still has some satisfaction in keeping this defence.)

Th Sure, but we want to understand you in a precise way, so please give me one concrete situation in which you experienced your problem in the interaction with your superiors.

Pt As usual, it is on staff meetings, where my superiors start interrogating me in a devaluing way. I cannot stand devaluation and that has to do with my father.

The patient still speaks in general terms "usual", "interrogating me in a devaluing way", "I cannot stand devaluation". As we will see, the therapist fails to assess that his patient is 1) still using this defence of speaking in general terms and 2) its syntonicity: the automatic, habitual way in which the defence is put into operation.

Th So they resemble your father, and what do you feel?

It would have been better:

Pt Mostly, I have these kinds of problems in the interaction with my superiors.

Th	Do you notice, you describe your problem in general terms: "mostly", and that will prevent us from understanding you in a precise way.
Pt	Yes, I know, you told me so before. I suppose it is something typical of me that I have these problems mainly in the interaction with my superiors. (Although the therapist has confronted, identified, and clarified this defence of "speaking in general" before, the patient still has some satisfaction in keeping this defence.)
Th	Sure, but we want to understand you in a precise way, so please give me one concrete situation in which you experienced your problem in the interaction with your superiors.
Pt	As usual, it is on staff meetings, where my superiors start interrogating me in a devaluing way. I cannot stand devaluation and that has to do with my father.
Th	You keep on telling me that you mostly have these problems in the interaction with your superiors, that that is very typical of you and that—as usual—it is on staff meetings. I am sure that when you tell me all this, you think you are giving me a concrete and clear account of your problem in the interaction with your superiors, whom you experience as devaluing you. What you are doing is giving yourself and me some general rule, and this is not the same as looking in a very precise way at your interaction with your superiors in one situation, for example one situation of last week.

Passivity and helplessness/hopelessness

Of course, no working alliance will be established nor grow as long as the patient maintains a passive position towards his own feelings, longings, opinions, anxiety, and/or defences. It is not difficult to understand that the defenses of passivity and helplessness/hopelessness are highly malignant and preventing any working alliance from being established.

Hope, self-esteem, care for oneself and for the other go hand in hand. Hope points to the future, and according to us, hope can be considered as a continuous, lifelong process, fostering longings and re-appraisal of longings. Consequently, the achievement of realistic longings will feed maintenance and growth of self-esteem, self-assertion, self-care, care and empathy for the other, will feed new hope, new longings, re-appraisal, and so on.

In order for therapeutic success, it is absolutely essential 1) to assess a patient's access to the defences of passivity and hopelessness/helplessness, 2) to help the patient to understand that passivity, hopelessness/helplessness, and lack of self-esteem go hand in hand, 3) to acknowledge own achievements in order to cease these defences.

Vignette

Passivity and helplessness/hopelessness
Mistake of the therapist:

Th	And then? You go for passivity, like your mother did? Here, the process is as follows: you come here being unhappy, depressed, etc. Then I help you to make contact with your feelings and you are vivacious and attentive.
Pt	Yes.
Th	Then, in between our sessions, you fall back to passivity, you don't care about your looks or your feelings. Isn't it?
Pt	Yes.
Th	Isn't it time you say goodbye to this passivity?

Pt Yes, but I don't know how.
Th Here we go again, you go for passivity again, and in this way you will remain a very unhappy woman.
Etc etc.

Although the therapist confronts, identifies, and clarifies the patient's passivity, this will not lead to any real success because the therapist fails to confront, identify, and clarify that the patient's passivity is a consequence of mistakenly looking at herself as a very unimportant person, a woman who has no right to decide for herself, a psychic cripple, a helpless and hopeless person, who has deprived herself not only of self-esteem, longings, and capacities, but also of a future.

It would have been better:

Th And then? You go for passivity, like your mother did? Here the process is as follows: you come here being unhappy, depressed, etc. Then I help you to make contact with your feelings and you are vivacious and attentive.
Pt Yes.
Th Then, in between our sessions, you fall back to passivity, you don't care about your looks or your feelings. Isn't it?
Pt Yes.
Th But do you realize that only a woman who doesn't think highly of herself and who has accepted that will remain passive. Do you understand me? Why would I listen to my longings? It will have no use! Yes, that was the reality of your past, and now you are an adult and competent young woman. Capable of making ends with your problems, isn't it? On that basis, you came to therapy isn't it? That part in you that knows you are important enough to understand your longings and problems with love, precision, and care. That part in you that knows you are the only person who is the empress of her feelings and longings, and you are the only person who decides what is important to you, isn't it? A woman who wants to fight for realizing her longings, who sees herself as totally capable of realizing them, a woman who wants to live the coming fifty years as a happy woman, capable of containing painful and happy emotions, or not?
Pt Yes.
Th (continues to confront/identify/clarify with mistakenly looking at herself as unimportant, psychic cripple instead of competent, interesting woman with a future)

The sequence of projection-passivity-hopelessness/helplessness-compliance-defiance

When a patient enters an initial interview (and the sessions thereafter) with the character defences of passivity and/or compliance, it is not only important to realize that the patient is identified with a superego, but it is also extremely important to realize: 1) that the patient's chronic and habitual defence of projection is already there as a chronic trigger to put 2) other front-door defences like passivity and compliance into operation.

Vignette

Projection as a trigger for passivity and compliance

Th For which problems do you want my help?
Pt I have problems in relationships with my partner, with friends and colleagues, and I am depressed.

Th Could you give me a concrete example of the problems you experience in your relationships?

Pt What do you think is the best? Do you want me to give an example of a situation with my partner, or ...? (the patient goes for compliance/pleasing)

Th All examples are OK ... you may choose.

Pt Yes, but what do you prefer, you want an example of my interaction with my partner or with my friends or colleagues? (the patient sticks to compliance/pleasing)

Th If I understand you correctly, you have come here because of the problems you experience in relationships and because you are depressed, isn't it? And what I notice is that right away you want to be nice to me, you give me priority: "Which problem in what relationship I want to hear first". You make me far more important than I am (projection) and you, obviously, deprive yourself of the right to decide which problem of yours will be the first to investigate (identification with the dictate of the superego). It is very important that you understand me.

Pt Yes, I do understand you. Perhaps (!!!) I make other people far more important than myself. I did not realize that I did that also here with you.

Th So you look at yourself as unimportant (identification with the superego). Other people, including me your therapist, are far more important than you (projection). And you tell me this is normal, habitual, this is how it is: I am not important enough to understand myself with love, care, and precision. Not important enough to make my own choices and decisions. Not important enough to trust my own opinion. Perhaps it is true that I make other people far more important, etc.

Now that we understand that a patient's projection is the prerequisite for his character defences of passivity-compliance-helplessness/hopelessness, you may also understand that no defiance exists without prior projection and compliance. Defiance is only possible after having given the other person more power than he has. Thus, if a patient has access to a syntonic defence of compliance, we know:

- the patient projects
- the patient complies
- sooner or later, the patient will go for defiance
- and thereafter
- will go for passivity and the whole sequence will be repeated.

Having understood the above, we also understand that when a patient comes to an initial interview or to the sessions thereafter with a (front-door) character defence of defiance, that this is not only a response to a chronic projection, but sooner or later the patient will resort to the defences of compliance and passivity.

Mistakes due to not having the same view of the problem and its constituent elements

The therapist fails to assess that the patient brings his problems as solely occurring on the interpersonal axis instead of understanding that the problems on the interpersonal axis are the consequence of his intrapsychic problems.

Vignette

Mistake of the therapist:
(Suppose this is the tenth session.)

Pt Yesterday, I saw my friend Mary again, we had agreed to go for shopping because I need a dress for that party I told you about. To make a long story short, we didn't shop for my dress, we went looking for her jeans, and that is because I didn't assert myself.

The patient continues and describes the interaction with her friend in a precise and concrete way.

Th Do we agree that complying to your friend Mary is part of your problem?
Pt Oh yes, I don't want to lose her as a friend, that is why I comply.
Th Or help her, or understand her, or giving her priority. Always seeing the other as the most important one, the one who has to be pleased … and you … you look at yourself as the unimportant one. The same as you have experienced your mother, who had been so frequently ill. You don't need another person in order to comply … you already do that as an automatism because you consider yourself as unimportant.
Pt Yes, you are right. But what could I have said to my friend without being offensive? Because, you know, I hate to make arguments with my friends.

The patient has ignored the therapist's references to her intrapsychic problem, the problem the patient has with her internalized neglectful and frequently ill mother (part of her pathological superego). As long as the therapist has not made it clear to the patient that her problems on the interpersonal axis are the consequence of her problems on the intrapsychological axis, the patient will continue her superego pathology, the duration of therapy will be negatively influenced, and therapy results will be minimal.

Th Well, let us first look at your anger … because you speak about yes or no being offensive.

The therapist prematurely goes for investigation of the patient's anger and fails to assess that the patient does not enter the origin of her interpersonal problems: i.e., the patient's intrapsychic problem, the automatic, habitual way in which she sees herself as not important enough to give priority to own longings, in which she sees others conform the aspects of her helpless, frequently ill mother.
It would have been better:

Pt Yesterday, I saw my friend Mary again, we had agreed to go for shopping because I need a dress for that party I told you about. To make a long story short, we didn't shop for my dress, we went looking for her jeans and that is because I didn't assert myself.

The patient continues and describes the interaction with her friend in a precise and concrete way.

Th Do we agree that complying to your friend Mary is part of your problem?
Pt Oh yes, I don't want to lose her as a friend, that is why I comply.
Th Or help her, or understand her, or giving her priority. Always seeing the other as the most important one, the one who has to be pleased … and you … you look at yourself as the unimportant one. This view on yourself and on other people is exactly the same as you had in the interaction with your mother, who had been so frequently ill. Your mother, who told you repeatedly not to bother her with your emotions, wishes. Who told you to be silent, do the household tasks, the shopping. You don't need another person in order to comply … you already do that as an automatism because you consider yourself as unimportant. Your only importance is to forget yourself and to help, please, and understand other people.

Pt Yes, you are right. But what could I have said to my friend without being offensive? Because, you know, I hate to make arguments with my friends.

Th I don't say you do that on purpose, but do you notice that although you agree with me, you dismiss what I explain to you?

Pt What do you mean?

Th Already in the first session we assessed that you automatically gave me priority, you wanted to explain to me all the ins and outs of your problem while ignoring your own anxiety. We discussed that this habit of yours: giving the opinion or wishes or feelings of other people priority, started in the interaction with your mother, who had to be pleased, helped etc. otherwise she got another attack of migraine and then it was your fault, as your mother made that verbally and non-verbally clear to you. So, although you are now thirty-eight years of age, you still obey your mother's dictate that is in your head. The first problem you have is the problem you have with the mother in your head. You still listen, obey to the dictate of your mother ... as an automaton. So the first problem is between you and you. And all the problems on the interpersonal axis are the consequence of the intrapsychological problem you have with the mother in your head. Do you understand this?

Pt Yes.

Th OK, that is great. But let us check whether I have been clear enough and whether you have understood me. Could you repeat in your own words what I explained to you?

Pt (The patient gives an accurate account.)

Th Then you do understand that focusing on the consequence of your problem—the compliance to your friend—will be ineffective if we forget to focus first on one of the sources of your problems: the automaticity with which you still react on your mother's dictate: Child, don't look at your own longings and feelings, that is egoistic, I, your mother, already have problems enough ... etc.

Mistakes due to incorrect assessment of the patient's ego-adaptive capacity

The therapist fails to assess that the patient still does not differentiate adequately between the corners of the triangle of conflict, and fails also to assess that his patient makes causality mistakes.

Vignette

Not differentiating between anger and a defence
Mistake of the therapist:

Th And how do you notice your anger?

Pt I become very calm and I think "you filthy bastard".

Th And then, if we stay with "you filthy bastard", what is it you want to do with that person ... make a mental image.

The therapist fails to assess whether and/or how the patient experiences the physical manifestations of his anger, and whether the patient labels his physical manifestations correctly as the concomitants of anger. Also, the therapist fails to clarify to the patient that calling someone a filthy bastard (the defence of calling names) is not the same as having access to his anger. The fact that the patient equates his defence of calling names with his feeling of anger is already a sign of a low ego-adaptive capacity.

Therefore, the therapist's pressure on the patient's impulse is premature and risky. We only want to go for a breakthrough of a patient's impulse, guilt, grief, and love when we are sure that the patient's ego-adaptive capacity is sufficiently restructured. Safety first please!

It would have been better:

Th And how do you notice your anger?
Pt I become very calm and I think "you filthy bastard".
Th What do you mean with: I become very calm?
Pt My body becomes immobile in a way.
Th Making your body immobile is not a manifestation of anger. Making your body immobile is making the manifestations of anger disappear. Immobile! No movement in my body! How do you recognize when a person is angry?
Pt (The patient describes such a person, speaking with a loud voice and making gestures.)
Th So is there movement and power in a person's body when being angry? So anger is movement and power, and with immobility you undo yourself of movement and power. Do you understand me?
Pt Yes.
Th Do me a favour, let's check whether I explained it clear enough ... tell me in your own words what you understood.
Pt (Patient gives an accurate account.)
Th And you told me "you filthy bastard". Giving names doesn't tell us anything about your anger. It is evident that you don't think highly of that person in that moment, but that is all. Giving names is a way of not looking in a precise way at your anger, etc.

Or the therapist fails to assess that the patient doesn't differentiate between the physical manifestations of anxiety and anger.

Vignette

Not differentiating between anger and anxiety

Mistake of the therapist:

Th And how do you notice your anger?
Pt Because I don't like what she said.
Th Yes, but how do you notice your anger physically?
Pt In my body? I notice it because I become hot and tensed.
Th Do you notice that your jaw gets tensed?
Pt Yes, that is often when I get angry.
Th Yes, and you move your hands ... what is it that you want to do with her if you follow the tension of your jaw and hands?

The therapist fails to assess that the patient labels the physical manifestations of his anxiety (his muscular tension, warmth) as the physical concomitants of anger. Without correcting this, each other intervention of the therapist will be premature.

It would have been better:

Th And how do you notice your anger?
Pt Because I don't like what she said.

Th Yes, but how do you notice your anger physically?
Pt In my body? I notice it because I become hot and tensed.
Th Do you notice that your jaw gets tensed?
Pt Yes, that is often when I get angry.
Th But do you remember, we have assessed your anxiety, isn't it?
Pt Yes.
Th And which are your anxiety manifestations?
Pt Tension from head to toe, dry mouth and throat, warm.
Th So tension is a manifestation of anxiety and not of anger. Probably you confuse the manifestations of anger with those of anxiety because you are angry and anxious at the same moment. Do you understand that it is important to differentiate? Because you want to get rid of your anxiety but not of your anger.

Sometimes the therapist has problems in helping a patient to differentiate between sadness, anxiety, and the defence of helplessness.

Vignette

Not differentiating between sadness and helplessness

Mistake of the therapist:

The patient has tears in his eyes and he is tensed from head to toe.

Th What do you feel?
Pt I don't know.
Th But you have tears in your eyes, and you look very unhappy … are you sad?
Pt Yes, I suppose so.

If there would have been a mobilization of sadness, the patient's anxiety wouldn't have been spread and stored through his whole body and … . the patient would have known that he was sad. Moreover, a patient who has good access to his sadness will always be able to tell what his sadness is about. If a patient isn't able to do so, his tears are mostly a sign of helplessness.

It would have been better:

Th I see that you have tears in your eyes and at the same time you are tensed from head to toe, do you notice that too?
Pt Yes, I feel anxious.
Th And those tears in your eyes, are those tears of helplessness or of sadness?
Pt I don't know.
Th You don't know what your tears are about? Then I suppose you have tears of helplessness, do you recognize that?
Pt Yes, I feel very powerless.
Th You feel anxiety, but you don't *feel* powerless, you *do* powerless. You go for a powerless position, you see yourself as powerless. It is important that you understand me.

Many patients (as well as therapists) make a causality mistake: they attribute their anxiety to an externally perceived behaviour of another person instead of attributing their anxiety to a preceding emotion.

Vignette

Causality mistake

Mistake of the therapist:

Th How do you perceive me?

Pt Although I know you don't judge me, I experience you as judgemental and being judged makes me always anxious.

Th Oh, I understand. Surely you must have some nasty experiences with being judged.

Here the therapist fails to make the patient clear that when she wouldn't have a neurotic problem, being judged would evoke anger and/or sadness, but certainly not anxiety. Thus when the patient is faced with something painful/unpleasant: the sequence is feeling–anxiety–escape/suppress the feeling. Because of her long expertise in suppressing feelings that evoke anxiety, it is understandable that she links unpleasantness with anxiety. But this mistake has to be corrected!

It would have been better:

Th How do you perceive me?

Pt Although I know you don't judge me, I experience you as judgemental and being judged makes me always anxious.

Th Oh, good, so it is totally clear to you that I did not judge you and that I only asked for your opinion?

Pt Yes.

Th Now could you give me a clear example of what I would do or say or think in order for you to experience me as judgemental?

Pt You would say that I behave ridiculous and exaggerated.

Th But do you realize that persons who don't have a problem like yours, they would be angry and/or sad when being judged, isn't it?

Pt Yes, they would assert themselves.

Th Yes, but you, obviously, with your longstanding habit of suppressing anger and sadness, you only have access to anxiety, isn't it? And therefore we can understand that you make a mistake in causality. Judgemental persons don't make me anxious, persons make me angry and/or sad, and right away my anger and/or sadness make me anxious.

The therapist fails to make the patient understand that his problems can be understood in terms of the triangle of conflict and persons

Mistakes in checking whether the patient understands his problem in terms of the triangles of conflict and persons.

Most therapists, at the end of an initial interview or of a session, summarize the steps that were taken in the interview or session. However, some young colleagues underestimate the function of superego pathology, and they forget to check whether it is clear to the patient that he should look at his problems in terms of the triangles of conflict and persons. For example, the therapist could summarize the steps that were taken in the initial interview and in all other sessions the therapist could invite the patient to give a summary:

Vignette

At the end of the initial interview, instead of forgetting, the therapist could have an interaction with his patient as described below:

Th Isn't it? We did establish: anger, anxiety, and a range of flight techniques. Sadness, anxiety, and a range of flight techniques. And you said, gosh, now I understand, it is an eye-opener to me.
Pt Yes.
Th And you've said I certainly do so in all kinds of situations. So obviously there must be something in your feelings which frightens you so much that you have to escape from your feelings. And you gave other examples, and there we saw the same sequence: feeling—anxiety—flight And we saw that this sequence was fully automatized. It was fully normal to you to be a stranger of yourself, to ignore your own feelings, opinions, longings. And automatized is the same as unconscious. And as long as a process, a sequence is unconscious, we cannot influence it in a conscious way. Is that clear to you?
Pt Yes, I escape from myself, from my feelings, I see that now.
Th Yes, you see it?
Pt In fact, it is so obvious, but ...
Th Now you see it.
Pt To me, it wasn't obvious.
Th So now you say, gosh, an eye-opener?
Pt Yes.
Th Do you understand that that is only possible with strict honesty?
Pt Yes.
Th And strict involvement?
Pt Yes.
Th And looking at your problems under the microscope?
Pt I rid myself from my own power and I want to stop doing so.
Th So of what do you dispose, do you rid yourself?
Pt I rid myself of my own power.
Th Right.
Pt And that is exactly the feeling I have.
Th And is it clear to you, that your main problem is the problem you have with yourself. No matter with whom you interact, we see the same sequence: feeling—anxiety—escape mechanisms.
Th So we assessed that you put an array of mechanisms into operation, which is self-invalidating. And those mechanisms have at any way the function of undoing the power of your anger, the vulnerability of your sadness, and of your love which obviously frighten you. So it is important you understand that you monitor in each single interaction how you put the same sequence into operation. You give me each time a concrete description of an interaction. One at a time. You monitor whether a feeling is mobilized. If so: what are the physical manifestations? What is the feeling about? Give words to that feeling. You also monitor the physical manifestations of your anxiety, and you stop going for your escape routes. Do you still know your specific anxiety manifestations? And which escape routes we assessed? etc.

Mistakes due to absence of agreed-upon (intermediate) goals

The therapist fails to discuss in concrete terms which intermediate goals are essential to be attained in order for aiming to reach the subsequent therapy goals. Mostly, this is omitted because of the fact that the therapist has no therapy plan (neither for the session nor for the subsequent phases in the therapy process). For instance, with a fragile patient, an intermediate goal could be to attain that the patient's anxiety is as much as possible regulated via the somatomotoric and sympathetic nervous systems.

The therapist underestimates the importance of maintaining a high quality working alliance in between sessions (see also below under agreed-upon division of tasks) and fails to link the focus of the session to these intermediate goals. We advise to using the last 15 minutes of each session by inviting the patient to summarize the therapy process and to highlight what had been important to the patient. We also advise to using the first 5 minutes of the subsequent session inviting the patient to report in what way he had continued the work that had been done during last session.

Mistakes due to lacking agreed-upon division of tasks

Because of the fact that therapists do not realize that the most essential part of the working alliance is operating in-between sessions (and is thus not restricted to the therapy sessions themselves) they fail to assess e.g., the passivity, psychic helplessness, dependency of their patient and they take it as normal that their patient did not continue the work which was done with the therapist during the sessions.

Videotaping of sessions

It is only seldom that a therapist knows exactly why the session he just ended did not work out as he had thought it could have worked out. Mostly, the therapy process with a patient is stuck because of everything (verbal and non-verbal) the therapist did not see, did not hear, was unaware of. Checking our own therapeutic work, peer-supervision, and supervision is the most effective when based on the videotaped sessions with a patient. It goes without saying that the therapist needs the written (and videotaped) consent of the patient to audiovisually record his session.

Length of each session

Generally speaking, the initial interview lasts 3 to 5 hours. Thereafter, normally, in the Netherlands at least, the duration of an individual therapy session as set by government regulations takes 45 minutes. For ISTDP purposes, this is far too short. See alone the first 5 minutes (check of the working alliance) and the last 15 minutes (summary of the session), which would leave therapist and patient with only 25 minutes to unlock the patient's unconscious in accordance with his momentary state of ego-adaptive capacity. In other countries, duration of an individual session is mostly 60 minutes. We advise, however, to have a 90-minute duration of each session. In the Netherlands, this is agreed upon with the health care organizations and insurance companies. In other countries, as we came to know, this is not always possible. In such cases, a possibility could be to do 90-minute sessions once a fortnight. If this is not possible either, then ISTDP will become a masochistic enterprise (both to patient and therapist), and in those cases, we advise our colleagues to investigate which other psychotherapy method could be of help to their patient.

Forms: assessment of patient's variables after initial interview and each time after ten sessions

In the Appendix, you can find assessment forms, which may help you to keep an overview of the particular patient's variables, and of your therapy process.

Steps in the chapter

- The dual purpose of the initial interview
- Moment-to-moment assessment of patient's variables as red or green traffic lights
- The CDS: changing red traffic lights into green on the road to the patient's unconscious
- Diagram of red and green traffic lights (the dependent or patient's variables)
- Working alliance, establishment and maintenance, responsibility of patient, of therapist
- Definition of working alliance, four components
- Empathy, agreed-upon view of the problem, (intermediate) goals and means to reach them, division of tasks
- Easy to make mistakes
- Videotaping
- Length of ISTDP sessions
- Forms: assessment of the patient's variables—initial interview/after each ten sessions

CHAPTER EIGHT

The independent variables: ISTDP techniques to change red traffic lights into green

ISTDP techniques: target, selection, timing, duration, dosage

Although Davanloo's intensive short-term dynamic psychotherapy is theoretically based on the psychoanalytic reference realm, his techniques are derived from structured psychotherapy methods such as behaviour therapy or cognitive-behaviour therapy.

The term "structured" refers to the fact that the therapist takes an active and directive stance. It is the therapist who—at each time in the therapeutic process—determines the focus of investigation. Especially in the early phase of the therapeutic process, the therapist also may take the position of a teacher, teaching the patient how to look and to understand his problems.

At each time in the therapeutic process the timing and selection of the specific technique, the dosage of that technique, and its duration are dependent on the momentary state of the patient's variables and the patient's reaction to the interventions.

However, a therapist's clinical judgement can never be fully manualized and, although the therapist's use of the techniques is prescribed by the therapeutic method, in this case by the ISTDP method, we advise our colleagues not to forget to use their common sense and to apply their interventions with flexibility and creativity.

The road to the unconscious is of course in the patient, and the specific patient's variables are in fact at each moment the in-session conditions with which the therapist and patient have to work. This calls for the therapist's selection (and recognition of) in-session consequences that are welcomed and that are taken as indicating therapeutic change and a growing (conscious and unconscious) working alliance. The question now is: which operations/techniques of the therapist and what conditions will be instrumental in achieving these in-session consequences?

Table 4. Davanloo's techniques aimed at which targets to effect which in-session consequences.

Working in **C, P, or T** ↓ / **Target** →	**I/F (complex transference feelings)**	**A**	**D**
Techniques:			
Confrontation	Pt's cogn/percept. system is directed at I/F	Pt's cogn/percept. system is directed at A	Pt's cogn/percept. system is directed at D
Identification	Recognition of I/F	Recognition of A	Recognition of specific D
Clarification	Recognition of I/F Recognition of causality with antecedent perception of C/P/T Recognition of causality with A/D	Recognition of A Recognition of causality with antecedents Recognition of causality with D	Recognition of specific D Recognition of causality with antecedents Recognition of function (neg. & pos. consequences)
Separating ego/superego (1) confrontation/identification/clarification of defences, (2) confrontation, identification of longing to understand with love/care/precision/honesty, (3) decision of healthy part	Rise of I/F Intrapsychic crisis	Recognition of anxiety by observing/attentive ego	Recognition of defences as obedience to dictate internalized aggressors Observing/attentive ego Assessment of internalized aggressors Intrapsychic crisis
Biofeedback (describing the physiol. sympt. of the I/F and directing Pt's attention to it (=confrontation/identification/clarification)	Separating I and/or F from A and/or D Recognition of I/F Furthered experiencing/containment of I/F	Separating A from I/F and/or D Recognition of A Furthered experiencing/containment of A	–

(*Continued*)

Table 4. (*Continued*).

Anxiety regulation (biofeedback and shift from T–C)	–	Shift in balance between auton./ skeletomot. and cogn./percept. Symptoms	–
Challenge	–	–	Motivated ego to quit D Rise of I/F, of A, of D Crystallization of char. res. into transf resistance
Pressure	Motivated ego to quit D Rise of I/F, of A, of D Crystallization of char. res. into transf. resistance	–	Motivated ego to quit D Rise of I/F, of A, of D Crystallization of char. res. into transf. resistance
HOC	–	–	Motivated ego to quit D Rise of I/F, of A, of D Crystallization of char. res. into transf. resistance Grief over self-destruct defences and lost chances If no grief: self-compassion Experiencing/containing I/F
Role play: - Modelling - Role reversal	Mobilization of anger (with patients using the defence mechanism of instant repression) Separating anger from defences	–	Separation of anger and defences
Portraying I	Furthered containment of I Reduced A Recognition of causality I/guilt/ sadness/A/D Furthered discrimination between containment and acting out Unlocked core neurotic conflicts	–	–
Work through	Deepened experiencing/ containment of I/painful emotions Resolution of I/F (complex transf. feelings) Enhancement of positive F Enhancement of intimacy (recept./express)	Reduced A Healthy regulation of A	Transferred perceptual distortions eliminated Acknowledgement of origin of defensive pattern Acknowledgement of own responsib. in maintaining D Recognition of C-P-T links and triangle of conflict Elimination of maladaptive D

In his many books and articles, Davanloo elaborated extensively on the when, how, and why of his structured techniques, guided by the triangles of conflict and persons, and he did so with patients situated at different loci on the spectrum of structural neurosis.

Psychoanalytic techniques such as identification, clarification, working through, are used in a structured, systematic, and repetitive way. Techniques that are often used in cognitive-behavioural therapies, such as pressure, challenge, biofeedback, reality testing, or even portraying the impulse, are integrated by Davanloo with modifications into the psychoanalytical framework. With regard to the portraying of the impulse, Feather & Rhoads (1972) illustrated with some patients their desensitization to drive-related imagery and, in doing so, they are among the first proponents for integrating the behavioural and psychodynamic paradigms.

A summary of ISTDP techniques, aimed at which targets or patient variables in order to achieve which in-session consequences, is presented in the table below. And to facilitate students' mastering these techniques, extra attention will be given to the "do's and don'ts".

Working with the triangle of persons

All ISTDP techniques can be applied in the realistic and/or transference relationship with the therapist (T), in the realistic and/or transference relationship with persons in the current (C), or in the relationship with important persons from the past (P). Although this seems obvious and simple, it is very easy to mistakenly work in the C, T, or P.

Misunderstanding when working in the T

Some colleagues think that working in the relationship with the therapist equals working in the transference. This is of course a grave mistake! Working in the relationship with the therapist can mean working in a) the realistic relationship with the therapist or b) working in the transference with the therapist. As most of our patients are located on the right half of the spectrum of structural neurosis they all come with a large repertoire of syntonic character defences. We have noticed that the colleagues, who mistakenly equal working in the T with working in the transference, first correctly assess their patient's massive defence repertoire as highly syntonic thus as character defences, and they correctly decide to work in the relationship with the therapist. However, as soon as they do so these colleagues suddenly forget that they have assessed the massive syntonic defence repertoire of their patient as defences in the realm of character resistance and subsequently they state that they are "working in the transference". What a confusion! As long as a patient has massive character resistance, one does not work "in the transference", one—hopefully—works in the realistic relationship with the therapist, and one helps the patient to get access to his observing ego. In this way, the therapist could help the patient to discriminate between his static projection and his perception of the realistic therapist. It is only after the patient's observing/attentive ego is functioning and after his defences have become dystonic (after a patient has had grief or constructive anger about his self-defeating defence mechanisms) that one can work in the transference. Thus, the more the character resistance has crystallized into the transference resistance, working in the transference becomes possible.

We want to emphasize here that resolution of the patient's process of transference and resolution of his multifoci core neurotic structure depends largely on the patient being able a) to see the distinction between the therapist and earlier important persons and b) to function at an adult level of cooperation. The patient may idealize the therapist, but the therapist should counteract these regressive urges of the patient. The therapist must therefore do his part to be a "real person" to the patient in order to help see the link between his emotional response that he brings from his past and applies to new individuals in his present life.

Some colleagues mistakenly believe that their patients only have access to their system of transference in the relationship with their therapist. The consequence is that they ignore that and how their patients transfer their perception of former important persons onto persons in the Current situation, that and how these patients subsequently have a rise in transference feelings, which they suppress with their defence repertoire. The consequence is that insufficient links between transference, current and past (T-C-P links) are made. Making T-C-P links, or interpretation of the triangle of conflict in the transference and then making the link with the same pattern in current and past interactions/relationships is of eminent importance. The therapist will also use the interpretation of these C-P-T links to assess and weaken residual resistance. And, of course, if insufficient T-C-P links are made together with the patient, the patient will only have a superficial understanding of his problems and results will not last.

Some other colleagues mistakenly believe that it is not necessary to go for the direct experience of transference feelings toward the therapist. They mistakenly believe that it is sufficient to go for the direct experience of transference feelings toward persons in the current situation. These therapists deprive themselves of acknowledgement of their own countertransference processes. Also, these therapists deprive their patients of the intimacy and experience with a therapist, who is determined to help and who will not retaliate when the therapist is the target of his patient's murderous rage, guilt, grief, love. The consequence will be that unlocked impulses and feelings will not be experienced with that high intensity as it would have been if the patient would have had the experience of unlocked transference feelings towards the therapist.

Some young colleagues make it very difficult for themselves (and their patient) to go for a correct and efficient assessment of their patient's problems by working in the C when they should have worked in the T.

As the majority of patients that come to the ISTDP initial interview are located on the right half of the spectrum of structural neurosis, we can safely assume that their observing ego is either malfunctioning or even absent. In those cases, one may understand that starting the interview by working in the C (outside the therapist's office and thus outside the interaction of patient and therapist) would be very unwise. The therapist cannot rely on the patient's presentation of his own functioning and that of others in his current interactions outside the therapist's office. Besides, the therapist still has to assess whether his patient is in the habit of using projections and their precise nature.

It may be evident that the start on the road to the patient's unconscious is preferably made in the interaction with the therapist. Thus although the therapist may ask the patient to give a concrete example of his problem (which is asking for the patient's view on his problems in the C), the therapist then should switch to working in the interaction patient–therapist, the T, by monitoring his patient's verbal and non-verbal behaviour when giving such an example.

Using the C to go for the T

A patient may come to the initial interview with defences or with anxiety on the forefront.

Vignette

Suppose a patient enters with defences on the forefront:
For example:

Th "You tell me—in a very humouristic and entertaining way (T)—that you had this terrible accident (C). Yet you lost one of your legs, you lost your job, you lost your partner (C). This must be all very painful to you. And yet, I notice that you use your sense of humour and your verbal talents as cover-ups (T). And because, evidently, this is a habit of yours, you must be doing this outside this office (C) but you do it also here in the interaction with me (T).

Do you understand me and can you recognize this, or not?"

Maintaining the work in the T will enable the therapist to help the patient to recognize which defences he puts into operation, to recognize the self-defeating function of these syntonic defences. During this process, with the growing dystonicity of the patient's defences, (more) anxiety will come to the forefront and the therapist will be able to help the patient assessing his own anxiety. If the patient's anxiety appears to be regulated in a relatively healthy way, we can safely assume that in the meantime—by the therapist's interventions—the patient's observing ego has gained in acuity. If so, then it is time that the therapist could invite the patient to give more examples of his problems in the C, and the therapist and patient could stick for a while working in4 C.

Vignette

Suppose a patient enters with anxiety on the forefront:
For example:

Th "You want to give me insight into your problems (C) but right away I notice your anxiety is sky high. You are tensed from head to toes, you have a dry mouth, you are sweating, and you seem to have some concentration problems. Do you also notice that in telling me about your problems you are anxious? (T)".

"Yes, I am a little bit nervous. How do you recognize that yourself? I have sweaty palms and I have a pressure here (points to chest). And further? No that is all".

Here the patient evidences that she is severely neglecting/ignoring/denying her bodily manifestations. Of course, in using these defence mechanisms, the patient will refrain from observing the physical manifestations of her anxiety.

The therapist now has to point out that the patient's reaction to him (T) reveals that the patient is used to neglect/ignore/deny his physical manifestations of anxiety and in this way the patient will never be able to get grasp of his anxiety. Only if and when the patient understands the importance of quitting his defences, the therapist will be able to help the patient to assess his anxiety and to take responsibility for dealing with his anxiety. From that moment on, the therapist could ask again for examples of the patient's problems (C). The patient's reactions on this invitation, and the (verbal and non-verbal) way he is giving insight will enable the therapist to acquaint the patient with other defences (T) and with increase and decrease of his anxiety manifestations (T). During this process, assuming that the therapist's interventions are properly timed and chosen, the patient's observing ego will have increased in acuity and it is time to go for working in the C and sticking there for a while.

Working in the C

If working in the C is properly timed by the therapist, it has some advantages:

a. Working in the C could then help the patient understand that he puts the same intrapsychic process (feeling-anxiety-defences) into operation, notwithstanding the fact that he is interacting *in vivo* or *in vitro* with different persons (therapist, persons in his current life, important persons in his past) in different situations. This could also help the patient to get an attentive ego and to relinquish his defences out of intrinsic motivation.
b. Working in the C could help the therapist to properly assess nature and degree of his patient's ego-adaptive capacity, and would enable the therapist to restructure the patient's ego-adaptive capacity in such a way that it is safe to help the patient to unlock and contain his feelings.

Working in the transference with the therapist and with persons in the currenct life

Working in the transference (this can be transference onto the therapist and/or transference onto persons in the current life of the patient) and/or in the relationships with important persons from the past (P) will occur mostly after 1) the patient's ego part has been separated from his superego part, 2) the patient's ego part has become observant/attentive and his discriminative capacities as well as his reality testing are present, and 3) after he has had a breakthrough of grief (or constructive anger) because of his taking refuge into his maladaptive defences. In other words, when the patient's character resistance has crystallized into the transference resistance.

The techniques of confrontation, identification, and clarification

Target: anxiety, defences

Some therapists mistakenly use the term "confrontation" for "challenge". This is really an inappropriate use of the term "confrontation", and herewith the students confusion is only increased.

Confrontation means that the therapist directs the patient's cognitive-perceptual system to some aspect of his intrapsychic problem. As the therapist will immediately follow this up by identifying this particular aspect to the patient, this means that the techniques of confrontation and of identification are inseparable. Whenever a therapist directs his patient's cognitive-perceptual system to a certain target (confrontation), he will immediately identify this target, followed by clarifying its meaning or significance.

Some examples:

Target: anxiety

Do you notice (confrontation) that you are tensed from head to toe (identification)? Muscle tension is one manifestation of anxiety (clarification). Were you aware of this tension, which is a sign of anxiety and do you understand me? (repeating confrontation, identification, clarification and check whether these interventions resulted in a desired response yes/no.

Desired response of patient: yes/no. If yes, to what degree?

If the patient would confirm his anxiety, the therapist still has to assess to what degree his patient's cognitive-perceptual system is directed at his anxiety and whether the patient is accurately and correctly labelling his concomitant physical manifestations as anxiety.

Suppose we would have the following patient–therapist interaction:

Vignette

Pt Yes, you are right. I am anxious. But merely because I don't know you yet.

This is not a desired response because the patient's cognitive-perceptual system is not directed towards his/her physical manifestations of anxiety. The therapist will repeat his defences of confrontation, identification, and clarification.

Th Yes it is true that we didn't know each other before but I asked you whether you noticed that you are tensed from head to toe. Being tensed all over doesn't seem so nice to me. Are you aware that muscular tension is a sign of anxiety?

Pt Yes, I have some tension, mainly in the upper part of my body and I always have that when anxious but mostly I try not to pay attention to my anxiety.

This is still not a desired response. Although the patient admits having tension (meaning that the patient's cognitive-perceptual system must be directed to these physical manifestations), he/she is only aware of "some tension in the upper part of his/her body" (meaning that he/she is observing in a sloppy, incomplete way). The patient also indicates that he/she is habitually neglecting/ignoring his/her physical manifestations of anxiety.

As the patient's syntonic defence of neglecting is preventing the patient from accurately directing his cognitive-perceptual system at the physical manifestations of anxiety, the therapist has to switch his target of investigation and to direct the patient's attention to his/her defence of neglect.

Vignette

Target: syntonic defence of neglect

Th So, shall we assess that not paying attention to your anxiety (confrontation, identification), neglecting the fact that you are tensed from head to toe (confrontation, identification), at least now, here with me (confrontation, identification) did not result in any decrease of your anxiety, didn't it? (clarification). And if I understand you correctly, you seem more or less satisfied with your strategy of neglecting, ignoring your anxiety manifestations (confrontation, identification). Do you realize, do you understand that neglecting your anxiety only results in maintaining your anxiety (clarification) and is that really what you want? Do you understand me?

Pt Yes, I understand you, but I must admit that I never looked at this, this way

Is this a desired response or is the patient complying? The therapist has to check.

Th What do you mean "I never looked at this, this way?"

Pt It is only now that you explain that I realize that not attending to my anxiety only resulted in an increase of my anxiety. Most of the time I am anxious, in fact in each interaction with other people. And when I enter a new situation, e.g., when I meet new people, my anxiety is at its utmost.

The patient evidences being aware of the maladaptive function of the defence of neglecting/ignoring. This is a welcomed response. The therapist repeats the interventions of confrontation, identification, clarification, and checks again whether the patient is really understanding or paying lip-service.

Th Ok, so you are beginning to understand that continuing to neglect your anxiety (confrontation, identification), the physical manifestations of your anxiety (confrontation, identification), like neglecting, ignoring your muscular tension (confrontation, identification), is in fact very cruel towards yourself (clarification). Or am I wrong?

Pt No, you are absolutely right. I now see that this neglecting of my anxiety is in fact really harmful, I didn't do myself justice. No if I would act like this toward my son I would be ashamed of myself.

The patient has understood that he/she is neglecting/ignoring and that continuation of this defence is maladaptive. As this is a desired response, and as the patient's cognitive-perceptual system will now be directed towards his/her physical manifestations, the therapist can switch the focus of attention again to the patient's anxiety. The therapist will continue the techniques of confrontation, identification and clarification. Target: all the concomitant physical manifestations of the patient's anxiety.

When properly applied, the techniques of confrontation, identification and clarification promote a new awareness with the patient. The patient's existing mis- or non-understanding of the particular target under scrutiny is offered new possibilities to understand this particular aspect of his intrapsychic problem. As therewith the base is laid for enhancement of the patient's autonomy, the therapist should not underestimate the importance of a proper application of these techniques.

If a therapist uses the techniques of confrontation and identification but omits to follow by the technique of clarification, he must not be amazed when this results in more defended responses from his patient.

Confrontation, identification without a subsequent clarification lays the base for misalliance.

It may be evident that the techniques of confrontation, identification and clarification, targeted at a patient's anxiety and/or defences are mainly used at the start of the road to the patient's unconscious.

Confrontation, identification without clarification: mistakes of the therapist

Vignette

Target: defence

Th What in your opinion is your problem?
Pt I am not sure, I don't know whether my problems are normal or not
Th Do you notice that you are questioning what precisely your problems are and ruminating whether your problems are normal or not (confrontation/identification).
Pt I am only explaining … you asked me, isn't it?!

It would have been better:

Th What in your opinion is your problem?
Pt I am not sure, I don't know whether my problems are normal or not.
Th Let me interrupt you: Do you notice that you are questioning what precisely your problems are and you are ruminating whether your problems are normal or not Confrontation/identification). Obviously there is a part in you, that doesn't think your opinion important enough to be trusted and immediately you have to find prove whether your problems are normal or not. So the first problem we encounter is the problem of the man, who doesn't think highly of his own opinion. (clarification) Do you understand me and if yes, do you agree or not?

Confrontation, identification, clarification, and pressure to feelings

Target: feelings

Somewhat further on this road the techniques of confrontation, identification and clarification will be aimed at the patient's feelings.

Specifically when the patient's cognitive-perceptual system has increased its acuity, when the patient—out of his growing intrinsic motivation—is actively directing his attention to his manifestations of anxiety, and to his automatism with which he brings his defences into operation.

Vignette

The patient's observing ego has turned into an attentive ego.

Pt Yes, especially when my boss humiliates me, as he did last week (the patient reaches for a glass of water) …. Oh, I actually get a dry mouth, I have tension in the upper part of my body, I am really anxious now and I must make an effort to keeping eye contact with you … Out of her own initiative the patient gives insight into the fact that she is monitoring her physical anxiety manifestations upon her own initiative, that she is labelling them correctly and that she wanted to quit her defence of avoiding eye contact with the therapist. The patient's observing ego turns into an attentive ego.

Thus when the therapist's interventions have resulted in 1) installing an attentive ego, in 2) the patient monitoring his own anxiety manifestations, and 3) a growing dystonicity of the patient's defences there will be opportunity to investigate the patient's nature and degree of ego-adaptive capacity, and his capacity to regulate and experience his feelings. Mostly, in this phase, the techniques of confrontation, identification, clarification will be alternated by using the technique of pressure to a feeling.

Let us look at the following therapist–patient interaction:

Vignette

Th You tell me you felt anger in that meeting, when your boss humiliated you by calling you lazy and incompetent. How did you notice your anger physically?

The therapist draws the patient's attention to the physical manifestations of her anger to check the patient's regulation/dysregulation of her anger. Did she appropriately register her physical manifestations of anger?

Pt I don't know, I was just angry. I think I felt tensed and powerless because it is so unfair.

The patient does not give the therapist a desired response. She evidently did not register her concomitant physical manifestations and as a result of this not attending to these important cues, she fails to differentiate between manifestations of anger and anxiety. This particular aspect of dysregulation of anxiety and anger, i.e. this failure to differentiate refers also to a low ego-adaptive capacity. The therapist will continue by differentiating between anger and anxiety and by putting pressure on the patient's anger.

Th You say you felt anger, but at the beginning of this session we assessed that tension is a sign of anxiety, not of anger. Obviously you confuse these physical manifestations of anger and anxiety because they occur at the same time (confrontation, identification, clarification). If you take yourself seriously, what would you tell your boss in your anger. Let's look at it, here with me (pressure to the feeling of anger).

Pt I would tell him that I don't deserve this reaction. I worked hard to find out where the mistake was in the corporate balance sheets. He is only venting off his frustration onto me and I don't want to be used for that.

Th I notice that your voice grows louder, you are sitting upright, your right arm is making this vertical movement, obviously your head is clear, because you are wording very precisely what your anger is about (confrontation, identification and clarification). Do you notice that too?

Pt Yes, and it feels great. I notice this power, that originates here (points to belly), and yes, when I am anxious and feeling tension, then it experiences more like a downward movement.

The patient gives a desired response. Her attention is actively directed to her concomitant physical manifestations, resulting in correctly labelling the manifestations of anger and anxiety and in a restructuring of ego-adaptive capacity.

The importance of confrontation, identification, and clarification

Proper use of these techniques:

- will help the patient to undo his identification with his pathological superego and
- at the same time, will help the patient to undo the "sleeping state" of his observing ego or to actively use his observing ego in a proper way.
- This prepares for the installment of an attentive ego (the patient is out of intrinsic motivation curious to monitor the several aspects of his problem on the intrapsychic and interpersonal axes).
- will help the patient to make his syntonic defences dystonic.
- will help the patient to restore biofeedback loops between body and brain and within the brain.

And last but not least these techniques offer the patient new explanations and prepare the patient, further along the road to his unconscious, for linking various issues from the past to the present.

Confrontation, identification, clarification, and undoing the identification with the pathological superego/separating the patient's ego and pathological superego parts

Target: observing and attentive ego

A patient's pathological superego originated out of the need to preserve attachment with the aggressive/hurtful care taker(s) and its development, according to Davanloo, may be understood to involve identification with the(se) aggressor(s) in the context of these attachment bonds. Thus the nature, degree and chronicity of the damage, caused by the caretaker(s) and the patient's subsequent reactive murderous rage, guilt, grief and damaged love will determine the extent to which the patient's ego part is identified with his harsh punitive superego. The patient's defences, put into operation by the patient's ego under the dictate of his superego will serve the function of staying alienated from longings, impulses, feelings, own opinions, norms and values. The nature and degree of syntonicity of the patient's defences will reflect the superego's dictate to the patient's ego how to understand and to look at the self and others.

If the patient's identification with his harsh, pathological superego is not undone, the patient will never be able to

a. consciously experience these painful feelings and impulses which are related to these past traumatic experiences,
b. understand why and how the impulses, guilt, grief, love resulted from damaged longings and trust in important relationships,
c. understand why and how he suppressed his longings, impulses, guilt, grief and love with anxiety and defences and kept them buried in his unconscious,
d. understand why and how he sentenced himself and kept on functioning as a convicted prisoner, to

e. understand why and how he repeated his malfunctioning in his many interactions in the present and
f. see the link with his past interactions with important others.

Undoing the patient's identification with his superego is thus crucial and an important part of each ISTDP therapy is thus aimed at helping the patient to separate his ego and superego parts.

Confrontation, identification, and clarification of the patient's syntonic defences will have resulted in an increasingly active observing ego. In most cases, the therapist will continue by using a more powerful technique like challenging to stimulate the patient to quit his defences. Although this will result in a rise of the patient's complex transference feelings, mostly the patient will still continue his submissiveness to his superego's dictate. *It is at this moment* that the therapist will go for explicitly separating ego and superego parts, clarifying the function of the patient's submissiveness, and challenging the patient to stop his self-defeat and to give priority to his healthy part.

Vignette

Th Well, don't suppress three quarter of your sadness …. Is it that normal and habitual to you that your sadness and your feelings are unimportant? You come here on the basis of a small healthy part, on the basis of your longing to understand yourself with love, with precision and care, and to give yourself and me insight accordingly, but the moment you're here you go for a "good joke". And yet, you are telling me about very painful experiences. With joking, you neglect and devalue your painful experiences. I call that self-destructive. With joking and keeping up appearances, you also prevent that I can understand what painful processes are exactly inside you.
Pt Yes.
Th Ha, ha, ha, stiff upper lip, keep up appearances.
Pt Yes, that's right.
Th Well, I call that … "that's right, that's right", makes it far worse!
Pt Well I know that I am keeping up appearances and that doing so isn't right.
Th Well right or wrong: it is nasty, it is neglecting, it is cruel.
Pt Hmm (nods) (cries)
Th Well, this isn't all your sadness, isn't it?
Pt (the patient now continues her sadness and cries with deep heavy sighs)

Or another example of separating ego and superego:

Th I already told you: you are laughing whereas I don't think it funny at all what you tell me.
Pt Mhmm.
Th Often you utilize "perhaps". Is it "perhaps" or is it "for sure"? And then you tell me about a situation with your child in a way which is distanced, not involved with yourself. Is it really such a trivial situation with your child? I wouldn't know if it really is. If such a situation regularly occurs …
Pt It's more … uh …
Th Why do you have to shrug it off as trivial? Oh, trivial situation—I'm exaggerating now—oh, how trivial, this is not the way to take yourself seriously. It is very important that you understand me, because I think this is the first problem, all the different ways in which you are not involved with yourself. You come here on the basis of your healthy side. The side that wants to understand herself with precision, honesty, and love …

Pt Mhmm.

Th And the very moment you are here you go to a self-destructive part, you go for keeping up appearances and you are laughing and pleasing, but it is not me who is the most important person here, it is you who is the important one, and when I ask you for an example you tell me: I have some trivial situations with my daughter. But obviously these situations with your daughter are very important to you. And I thought you wanted to understand yourself with love, precision, and care. Do you understand me?

Pt Yes.

Th What is happening now?

Pt Now I have to cry.

Th Then cry ... I wait ... just cry

Pt (The patient cries with deep heavy sighs.)

Confrontation, identification, clarification, and the therapist as a provider of biofeedback

Target: impulse/feelings, anxiety

At least since the sixties we know that it is the existence of feedback loops, both within the brain and between the brain and (the peripheral organs of) the body that makes it possible to have a self-regulating (and therefore self-correcting) care for one's own health. Disruptions in biofeedback loops can lead to physical and psychological disorders (Schwartz, psychobiological foundations in *Handbook of Psychotherapy and Behavior Change*). Restoration of biofeedback loops, or creation of new biofeedback loops between the body and the brain and within the brain, can help the patient to modify his psychobiological state for the sake of his physical and mental health (see also Chapter Two).

Already for a long time, the application of biofeedback has been used as an active intervention in behavioural therapies. In a narrow sense, biofeedback could, for example, be given to a patient via a blood pressure monitoring system in order for the patient to use this feedback to lower his blood pressure. In a broader sense, if the therapist monitors a patient's psychobiological state, and if he focuses the patient's attention (confrontation, identification) e.g., on his heightened muscle tension and subsequently labels it as a symptom of anxiety instead of anger (clarification) then the therapist functions as a provider of biofeedback using this as a means of helping the patient to distinguish e.g., between the physical symptoms of anger and anxiety. In the long run, this will restore feedback loops between peripheral organs and the brain as well as some feedback loops within the brain, and will enable the patient to regulate his anger and his anxiety for the sake of his own health.

Role play, modelling, and role reversal

Target: anger

Many patients—especially those with access to the defence mechanisms of instant repression and all those patients with a low ego-adaptive capacity—don't discriminate between the poles of the triangle of conflict. There are patients who, during the therapy session, tell their therapist they feel anger and when the therapist invites them for expressing it, we see a combination of some physical mobilization of anger and the verbal defence of blaming or the defence of "giving behavioural instructions" to the other person in the interaction.

An example:

The patient shows some physical manifestations of anger: he sits upright, his left arm is outstretched and moving as if underlining his words, his voice is louder.

Pt I am very angry at you , when you always forget what you promise, you are very cruel to me and untrustworthy too. You should know better than that and you shouldn't behave like this. I think you should do what you promise or otherwise you shouldn't promise things at all!

It is perhaps not so difficult to understand that it is rather easy to mistakenly take this as a constructive manifestation of anger. However, if we read and listen carefully, we would notice that the patient's reaction is a) mainly externally oriented (*you* forget, *you* promise, *you* are cruel, *you* etc.); b) is blaming the other for faulty behaviour (forgetting promises is cruel); and c) is instructing what would be a better behaviour (you *should do* what you promise, etc.). The patient is vague, and is speaking in general (you *always*). And, most important: reference to the action tendency of anger—setting limits to the behaviour of the other person in the interaction while wanting to continue the relationship with that person—is lacking!

Let us first look at what exactly is missing in the patient's verbalization:

- there is no exact description of the evocative stimulus (what did the other do/say or not do/ say in that particular moment-situation
- therefore there is no exact description of *causality* between the evocative stimulus and response anger
- there is no exact description of *the resulting inner process* of patient's anger including his wish to continue the relationship (in a more constructive way).

In intimate relationships, it is only seldom that a person's anger or disagreement is about the verbal contents of what another person is saying. Disagreement with verbal contents is mostly restricted to issues where there are rules that are internationally agreed upon. For example:

- No, Paris isn't the capital of Germany, Paris is the capital of France. Or
- No 1 + 1 doesn't equal 3, 1 + 1 equals 2.
- Mostly, the anger/disagreement concerns the *relative positions* of the interaction e.g., a disagreement concerns variations of an up-position
- I tell you that you must do it now and not tomorrow (behavioural instruction, command)
- You should have known that this really isn't done (moralistic)
- When you still don't understand this (devaluation)
- This is really nonsense, let's look at ... (dismissive)
- (after another person has expressed a personal experience). I had a similar and even more pronounced experience (taking over, competitive) etc.

Or a disagreement concerns variations of a down-position

- I don't know, I do what you like (helplessness and compliance)
- I cannot remember these things (helplessness, selective memory loss)
- it is difficult to look at you (helplessness)
- it is difficult to monitor my anxiety (helplessness).

Or a disagreement concerns an up-via-down position

- you have to tell X … because I have a headache (command via helplessness)
- I cannot remember this so you must not forget … (command via helplessness), etc.

In all these cases, the disagreement consists of the fact that one doesn't want to accept the *complementary* position. Thus, when there is disagreement with a perceived up-position, one doesn't accept the complementary down-position. When there is disagreement with the perceived down-position, one doesn't accept the up-position, and when one disagrees with the perceived up-via-down position, one doesn't accept to be blackmailed to take an up-position. A constructive expression of a person's anger should contain the following elements

- a concrete description of the evocative stimulus (what is the other saying/doing/not saying/doing
- a concrete description of the perceived position the other person is taking (the particular up, down or up-via-down variant)
- a concrete description of the unwanted complementary position
- a concrete description of the desired positions.

An example:

A patient tells that her husband and she had discussed their holiday plans and had agreed upon Spain as their holiday destination. The husband had promised to book their holidays and it appeared that he has booked for Iceland instead. Upon the patient's reaction that that wasn't what they had agreed upon, the husband had answered that the patient reacted hysterically. The patient had felt angry, anxious, and had withdrawn. When reporting this, the therapist noticed some mobilization of the patient's anger. Upon this observation, the therapist invited the patient to give words to her anger. The patient went for blaming, but took this for an expression of her anger. The therapist confronted, identified, and clarified the patient's defence of blaming and has directed patient's attention to the causality stimulus-anger-anxiety-blaming. After that, the therapist invited the patient again to express her anger, the patient's anger was again mobilized, and the patient went again for blaming.

Via role play (modelling and role reversal), the therapist could help the patient to give words to constructive anger.

Steps are:

- The therapist models expression of anger while taking care that all elements are given words

- The therapist draws the patient's attention to these elements and checks whether the patient has understood the importance of these elements in giving constructive insight in anger
- The therapist invites the patient to imitate the therapist
- The therapist and patient check whether all elements are expressed
- The therapist now invites the patient to express anger in own words
- The last step is repeated until the physical mobilization of the patient's anger is clearly experienced by the patient, while expressing uncontaminated (without noticeable anxiety and without defences) anger and—of course—with a clear head.

Vignette

Patient's wording of her anger could be:

- You didn't book our holidays in Spain, instead you booked in Iceland and when you tell me
- I react hysterically when I say this wasn't what we agreed upon (concrete description of evocative stimulus)
- I become very angry (causality evocative stimulus—emotional response anger)
- I think you are very dismissive of me and I don't accept that (disagreement with perceived
- position of the other person in the interaction)
- I don't like to be dealt with as a person who exaggerates or is hysterical when I disagree with you (concrete description of unwanted position)
- I see myself of equal importance to you and I like to be taken seriously. I cannot force you to be open to my criticism and when you continue to dismiss me you will hear my criticism again and again. I do hope, however, that you will listen to my criticism and take it seriously (concrete description of desired positions).

Mostly—during the several trials in the role play—the patient resorts intermittently to the following sequence of other defences, an increase of anxiety, some mobilization of anger, more increase of anxiety, more mobilization of anger, decrease of anxiety, full mobilization of constructive anger.

The trials of modelling and role reversal should be repeated until

- the patient is able to express her anger constructively (all elements are present) without
- "having to think", thus when the words come fluently
- the patient has a clear head
- when the physical manifestations of anger are present and properly described by the patient
- when the somatomotoric channelling of the patient's anxiety is not further than the intercostal muscles and when there are some slight sympathetic manifestations.

Sometimes when therapist and patient are from different countries, their spoken language will be English. As speaking in the native language while giving insight into painful feelings will induce more anxiety, we advise that the last 2 or 3 trials of role-reversal should be done in the patient's native language. After each trial, the therapist has to invite the patient to translate the spoken words in English. This is done to check whether the patient has resorted again to some of his/her defences.

Target: sadness

An example:

Sometimes, during a patient's first couple of breakthroughs of his murderous rage, guilt, and grief, it may happen that a patient fuses his grief with, for example, helplessness, denial, or another defence, in order for escaping the full extent of his pain. Here we remind our colleagues to the action tendency of sadness and grief: the acknowledgement that history/reality cannot be undone and thus have to be faced.

A constructive expression of a person's sadness should contain the following elements:

- a concrete description of the evocative stimulus (what is the other saying/doing /not saying/ doing and causality with sadness
- a concrete description of the perceived behaviour of the other person
- acknowledgement of the particular meaning of the other person's behaviour and the implications for oneself
- a concrete description of acceptance of this acknowledgement.

Vignette

A patient had a major unlocking of her murderous rage, guilt, grief towards her father, who had physically and sexually abused her. There had been unlocking of past traumatic events, in which the patient's mother chronically had been a passive witness. The patient's murderous rage towards her mother had been mobilized, the patient portrayed her rage, resulting in the murdering of her mother. There had been guilt. In the portrayal, the patient is sitting on the floor, she holds the murdered body of her mother in her arms, she is crying, there are some deep sighs, and the patient stops her crying. The therapist asks the patient what went on inside her while she cried.

Pt I am sad that she never protected me. She paralysed and watched how my father beat me up or she escaped into the kitchen. But I don't believe she would have acted that way when she would have known that my father came to me during the night. (the patient denies)

Th I thought that during 5 years your father came about 3 times a week to your bedroom in order for sexually harassing you. You also told me that the apartment had only three rooms: one living room, one bedroom for your parents, one for you.

Pt Yes but I want to believe that she didn't know … (the patient continues her denial)

Th The therapist goes for modelling:
I am so sad that you sacrificed me (acknowledgement of perceived evocative stimulus and its meaning/right causality)

I would have wished that you would have had the courage to defend me but you hadn't, you haven't, and you will never defend. I have to accept that. (reference to the action tendency of sadness/grief)
Now you say this in your own words unless you want to continue your denial and to protract your suffering

Pt I wish you would have thought me more important than your own anxiety, in fact you prostituted me and it hurts me awfully to acknowledge that … (the patient bursts out in sadness …

Anxiety regulation

Target: anxiety

Restoring biofeedback loops

We have already explained that the therapist can function as a provider of biofeedback when using the techniques of confrontation, identification, clarification. The patient has to be helped to take responsibility for a healthy regulation of her anxiety. The patient could do so by regularly monitoring his physical manifestations of anxiety, and understanding it's mobilization in the context of the triangles of conflict and persons.

Relaxation exercises

In some cases, a patient could be helped by learning the progressive relaxation technique of Jacobson. Jacobson's progressive relaxation technique is focused on the anxiety regulation via tension of the striated muscles and progressive relaxation of the specific groups of striated muscles. If a therapist has no experience in working with Jacobson's progressive relaxation technique, he could ask a behaviour therapist colleague to teach him how to apply this technique.

Also patients could be helped to relax by learning to breathe properly. As we cannot be knowledgeable in all and everything it isn't a sin if a psychotherapist has no expertise in teaching his patients how to breathe properly. Most of our patients, however, have an unhealthy breathing pattern *when speaking*. In those cases, a patient is not helped that much by teaching him to relax or breathe properly. As the problem occurs when speaking, one helps the patient the best in referring him to a (good) speech therapist or to a professional song-pedagogue. Singers have an optimal breathing pattern.

We do not advise therapists to teach their patients an autogenic relaxation technique. This is really contraindicated when the patient's anxiety is mainly regulated via the parasympathetic system and when there is cognitive/perceptual disruption. Jacobson's relaxation training is focused on the anxiety regulation via the striated muscles, whereas most autogenic training focuses on the anxiety regulation via mental and parasympathetic processes.

In case a patient gets dizzy, the therapist could help the patient by inviting him to stretch the arms (like when one does when wakening up). This temporarily stretching causes the blood pressure temporarily to increase, which will undo the dizziness/light-headedness.

The therapist switching from working in the T to working in the C

The therapist could decide for this technique when a patient's anxiety is mainly regulated via parasympathetic manifestations and cognitive/perceptual disruption.

Vignette	
Imagine the following therapist–patient interaction:	
The therapist has asked the patient to give an example of an argument with her partner:	
Pt	Now I have difficulty hearing you. What did you say?
Th	So your anxiety increases. Can you still see me clearly?
Pt	I see you somehow in a haze, I have difficulty to focus
Th	Your anxiety is too high at this moment, we don't want that. Let's back off for a moment. You told me you loved to watch birds Did you do that last Sunday again?
Pt	Oh, yes … the patient tells about the bird watching …
Th	How is your anxiety now?
Pt	I can hear and see you well. I have some tension in my arms and neck.
Th	Ok, you wanted to tell me about the argument with your partner.

Challenge Target: the patient's defences

The technique of challenging, originally used in structured therapies like cognitive therapy or cognitive-behavioural therapy, is implemented by Davanloo as a technique to motivate patients to quit defences, resulting in a rise of the patient's complex of transference feelings and therewith promoting a crystallization of character resistance into transference resistance.

In cognitive therapy, the patient is challenged to replace his distorted thoughts and irrational beliefs with more effective thinking. In cognitive therapy, this challenging is only effective when the patient is fully aware of his specific ways of distorted thinking (e.g., catastrophizing, dichotomous thinking, minimalization), and when the patient understands how these ways of distorted thinking and irrational beliefs influence his low self-esteem and maladaptive functioning.

The same reasoning goes of course for ISTDP. For example, as long as a patient does not understand that not attending to his physical manifestations of anxiety by continuing his defence of neglecting/ignoring these manifestations, the application of challenge is premature. Thus only if and when a patient (as a result of the therapist's appropriate use of confrontation, identification and clarification) at least cognitively understands that a) he is neglecting the manifestations of his anxiety and that b) he is therewith maintaining his anxiety, which is not to his own benefit, then and only then a therapist could decide to apply the technique of challenge.

See, for an example, the following therapist–patient interaction:

Vignette

The therapist decided to challenge the patient to quit his defence of neglecting/ignoring.

Th Five minutes ago you understood how self-defeating it is to continue neglecting your anxiety. Yet, you do as if you don't have any alternative, as if you don't have the right to decide: I will stop neglecting my anxiety. I will stop harming myself. I will use my perception for my own benefit and I will monitor my physical anxiety reactions.

Pt Yes, I am trying but it is not so easy. I did this all of my life, so I cannot stop neglecting right away.

Of course, this is not the desired response the therapist has hoped for. However, the therapist does understand that challenging the patient to quit defence #1, will result in the patient bringing defence #2 into operation. The therapist will challenge all subsequent defences.

Th Now you are doing injustice to yourself because obviously you see yourself as helpless, as not having the capacity to take yourself seriously and direct your perception to your physical manifestations and label them. This is unskilled labor you know. You don't need to go to school or to the university to focus on your own bodily reactions. Do you understand me or not?

Pt I realize that I was raised like that. Never mind your physical pain, or your anxiety, don't be a Sissy! In fact, it makes me sad that I still comply with what my parents taught me. It didn't help me.

The patient's response can be considered as a desired consequence of the therapist's technique of challenging. If the therapist is wise, he would continue by using the technique of separating superego and ego parts, followed by putting pressure on the patient's feeling of sadness.

Head-on collision Target: defences

The techniques Davanloo uses in his CDS are, of course, not new ones. An exception can be made for Davanloo's head-on collision (HOC), which contains elements from psychoanalytic and cognitive-behavioural techniques, and it can be considered as a powerful technique.

The head-on collision is a very powerful technique and should be applied *after having used* the techniques of confrontation, identification, clarification, and challenge. It must be clear to the therapist that the patient has cognitively understood that he brings his particular array of maladaptive defences into operation, but nevertheless continues to use them The patient must cognitively understand that in this way he is defeating the therapeutic process. The head-on collision can be used at the level of the patient's character resistance or at the level of the patient's transference resistance. As the dosage of power of the technique of head-on collision is maximal (compared to the technique of challenge or of pressure), it is—out of necessity—always applied with patient's suffering from extreme high character resistance and superego pathology. In those cases, it might even be necessary to apply the HOC more than once in the initial interview or in a following session.

When properly used the HOC both mobilizes the patient to become effectively involved in the therapeutic task, and increases the complex transference feelings. It is essentially addressed to the unconscious part of the working alliance, with the aim of mobilizing this against the resistance (Davanloo 1987a, 1988b; Kalpin, 1994).

The HOC consists of the following components:

- outlining of the therapeutic task and appeal to the unconscious working alliance
- clarification of the key defences, their malignancy, often with special emphasis on the a) resistance to emotional closeness with the therapist and b) the parallel with resistance to emotional closeness with other persons in the current
- emphasizing the free will of the patient and his decision to be a partner in the working alliance
- undoing the patient's tendency to imagine the therapist as omnipotent
- putting pressure on the patient to quit his defences
- repetition of the components.

The dosage of the HOC can be varied by the number of repetitions of the components and by the therapist's tone of voice. A low dosage HOC contains practically no repetitions of the components and is spoken with a "conversational" tone of voice. The higher the dosage of the HOC, the more the therapist repeats synonymous contents of the components with a challenging tone of voice.

Vignette

Imagine the following therapist–(female)patient interaction:

During the initial interview, the patient has understood that she goes for vagueness, laughing, distancing, helplessness, rationalizing as strategies to keep herself amputated from her feelings and to avoid intimacy with other people and the therapist. Although subsequent challenging the patient to quit these defences resulted in a rise of her anxiety, evidencing a rise of her complex transference feelings, the patient continues to bring her array of defences into operation. As the patient's anxiety is mainly regulated via the sympathetic and striated muscle systems, the therapist thinks it time to start a head-on collision.

Outlining the therapeutic task:

Th Look, you have come here on the basis of your healthy part: your longing to understand your problem with love, precision and care. You came here on your own volition and you wanted my help in understanding the processes that constitute your problem, the processes that you put into operation. Am I right or wrong?

Pt Yes, you are right, but it is extremely difficult to stay with my sadness.

Outlining the therapeutic task and appealing to the patient's unconscious:

Th The tears and sadness you had 10 seconds ago, isn't it? Now you and I are here together to assess the precise nature of your problems.

Clarification of the malignancy of key defences:

Th Do you notice, this is the sequence: a painful feeling, sadness has been mobilized. But it has to be cut off immediately with laughing, and subsequently with vagueness. Automatically. And this is the first problem with which we are confronted, notwithstanding all the other problems you are going to tell me. The first problem is the problem of the woman who does not take herself seriously, who treats herself without care, who obviously does not think herself worthwhile. The woman who thinks it very normal to eliminate feelings and thoughts with vagueness, with distancing, with helplessness, with rationalizing.

Clarification of malignancy of defences with special emphasis on the a) resistance to emotional closeness with the therapist and b) the parallel with resistance to emotional closeness with other persons in the current life.

Th And you can tell me also that you are an expert of avoiding intimacy with your partner. I believe you immediately. You do the same here with avoiding eye contact, with laughing, with vagueness. I cannot force you to drop those defences, but you must understand that as long as you avoid the intimacy here with me, as you also do in your other interactions, I will not be able to help you.

Undoing omnipotence and clarification of malignant defences to avoid intimacy with the therapist:

Th And immediately, we are faced with a major problem, because it is useless to idealize me. How can I help you when you cover your opinion, feelings, norms with drab veils. You put me outside. We are both in contact with all your drab veils instead of with each other. As soon as there is the slightest intimacy between us and sadness is mobilized, you go for your cover-ups.

Emphasizing the free will of the patient and his decision to be a partner in the working alliance:

Th But that is not what you want, is it? I suppose you have come here out of your own will and desire to understand yourself with love, care, precision, and honesty. And you wanted to take the responsibility for the processes you put into operation and that make up for your problems, isn't it?

Undoing omnipotence, challenge to quit defences, pressure to feeling:

Th I only can repeat that: if you keep yourself unimportant and if you automatically continue to go for your cover-ups, then I will not be able to help you. I will not be able. The issue is not that I don't want to. The issue is that I will not be able. I am not a magician. You will have to give me insight if you want me to be of help. You have to think yourself important enough.
What is your sadness about?

Pt That I think myself unimportant.
etc.

The patient becomes intensely sad and cries without holding back.

Portraying the impulse, guilt, grief, love, and working through

A therapist only goes for bringing the patient's murderous rage, guilt, grief in the conscious experience of his patient, when he is sure

1. that the patient's ego-adaptive capacity is restructured enough;
2. that there is an optimal conscious/unconscious working alliance with the patient;
3. that he is capable of assessing that his patient's murderous rage is close to breakthrough;
4. that he is capable of monitoring his patient's anxiety from second to second;

5. that he is capable of properly assessing the somatic pathways of impulse, guilt, grief;
6. that he is capable of making C-P-T links directly afterwards.

Example of portraying the patient's impulse, guilt, grief, love

Visualization and portraying are terms for a class of cognitive processes which involve quasi-sensory conscious experiences in the absence of particular external stimuli and absence of actual, overt, physical movements.

Of course, portrayal of a murderous impulse, guilt, grief, and love is of little value when the patient keeps his portrayal vague, isn't aware of his action tendency, and escapes from the results of his murderous impulse.

Vignette

Suppose a therapist is sure that he has accomplished the above-mentioned six requirements. The therapist has invited his patient to bring his impulse, guilt, grief, and love into the conscious experience.

Pt I see my mother sitting in the kitchen, as always at the kitchen table. I feel strong, I enter the kitchen and I pull her out of the chair.
Th How?
Pt My both hands are around her neck, I look straight into her eyes, I hold her for a moment and then I push her against the wall, hard, very hard, her head bounces against the wall, I push and pull and push and pull and I hear that her skull cracks .... I see blood on the wall.
Etc. etc.

The patient is very concrete in the description of his action tendency, the results of his aggressive acts on his victim.

After kicking his mother in her belly, breaking the arms and legs, he has strangled his victim. The patient gives a concrete and precise description of the posture of his dead victim and of the inflicted damage. The eyes of his mother are closed.

Th And if you look through her closed eyes, what do you see?
Pt I see her blue eyes, they look astonished and sad ...
(The patient is silent and concentrated upon his inner process.)
I feel guilty ... this hasn't solved anything ... besides ... I love her ...
Th If we make a picture of your guilt and love, what do you do?
Pt I kneel down, and take her in my arms ... like this ...
(The patient is silent ...)
I kiss her on her forehead ... I have her cheek against my cheek.
(The patient is silent ... cries ... waves of deep heavy sighs ...)
Th What is your sadness about?
Pt That we love each other, but in fact we are strangers ... she wasn't able to deal with her own anger, nor with my anger, she withdrew. I started to comply and to please, but even that didn't result in

her coming out of her depression. I longed for her being happy, playing with me, asking me for my experiences at school, my friends, my study.
Etc.

Th Where do you bury her?

Pt (The patient is silent … after a while …)
At sea, the Mediterranean, Majorca, we once spent a holiday there. She was relaxed … it was the only time that I have seen her laughing.

Th OK … we travel to Majorca and when we are there, where do we go?

Pt It is on the Northern part of Majorca. I have put her in a white sheet …
(The patient is silent.) …
We are at the beach … I look for a boat ….
I put her in the boat, it is a sailing boat. I sail and on open sea I give her to the sea.
(The patient cries … waves of deep heavy sighs …)

Th What do you say as a final goodbye?

Pt I would have wished that I could have made you happy, I would have wished that you would have cuddled me, would have seen me, would have stimulated me. I would have wished we would have talked. I always thought it was me who was at fault. I didn't realize it was you who had so many problems. I hope you will find peace.
Etc., etc.

Pt Still if my friends or my partner withdraw … I immediately think I have done something wrong and I immediately start to please and to comply. The same as in the interaction with my mother.
Etc.

Steps in the chapter

- ISTDP techniques and their target
- Moment-to-moment assessment of the desired consequence
- Confrontation, identification, clarification, and their importance
- Confrontation, identification, clarification, and separating ego parts from superego parts
- Role play, modelling, and role reversal
- Biofeedback
- Anxiety regulation
- Challenge
- Pressure
- Head-on collision and the constituent components
- Preconditions for application of portraying I/F and working through
- Example of portrayal of I/F

CHAPTER NINE

An initial interview with a transport-phobic patient

The DSM-IV classifies phobias as agoraphobia (with and without panic attacks), as social phobia and as specific phobia.

Agoraphobic persons have an irrational fear of activities outside of the home. They often have anticipatory anxiety of becoming physically unwell/ill. Or they are afraid they will go fainting, thus losing control and thereby causing public disturbance/nuisance. In addition, agoraphobics misapprehend causal antecedents of painful feelings and they develop their symptoms in a climate of notable interpersonal conflict (Goldstein & Chambless, 1978).

Social phobia, or social anxiety disorder, is characterized by extreme anxiety in social and performance situations. A social phobic person is mostly preoccupied with doing something inappropriate and being devalued, judged, or blamed because of that or because others will notice their anxiety symptoms (blushing, sweating, shaking).

A specific phobia is an extreme fear of a specific object or situation that is not in proportion with actual danger or threat. Mostly, five types of specific phobias are defined:

- animal type (fears of animals such as dogs, cats, rodents, spiders, snakes, etc.)
- national environment type (fears of heights, storms, water, etc.)
- blood-injection-injury type (seeing blood, needles, watching medical procedures, receiving injections, etc.)
- situational types (fear of driving, flying, elevators, enclosed places, etc.)
- other types (other specific fears, e.g., fear of choking, of loud sounds, etc.)

In our therapeutic experience with fifty Dutch fear of flying patients, thirty had other situational phobias, such as avoiding other forms of transport (train, tram, passenger in a car, being the driver of a car), avoiding elevators, avoiding cinemas, avoiding heights. They all (with the exception of driving the car and avoiding heights) experienced themselves as being trapped in the specific phobic situation. As being surrendered or turned over to unreliability of persons (pilot, air traffic control) and material. They all had an external locus of control, they all had problems with intimacy and had different degrees of unhealthy regulation of emotions and anxiety. They all misapprehended causal antecedents of painful feelings and the link with the development of their fear of flying.

In fact, it is not only the agoraphobic and fear of flying patients that misapprehend causal antecedents of their phobic complaints. In fact, all phobic patients do. Also, all phobic patients take a passive to sometimes paralysed position toward their anxiety and feelings.

The phobic patient often presents a problem for the ISTDP therapist. Shouldn't I refer the phobic patient to a behaviour or to a cognitive-behaviour therapy? Wouldn't that be a more effective treatment for this patient? Well, this should be discussed with the patient. Many phobic patients benefit from behavioural and cognitive-behavioural treatment programmes that are explicitly focused on helping the patient to overcome his specific phobic complaint.

On the basis of his research, Davanloo locates phobic patients somewhat left from the middle of the spectrum of structural neurosis. We cannot confirm that finding. Having seen hundreds of different types of phobic patients during decennia as coordinator of a big department of cognitive-behaviour therapy in the Netherlands, we have witnessed severe superego pathology and low to very low ego-adaptive capacity with these patients.

Apart from the fact that most of these patients have no access to their feelings, or confuse feelings with defences, and apart from the fact that mostly their anxiety is very unhealthy regulated, they allow their phobia to lead them to a progressively restricted and isolated life. In addition, often their phobic problems (especially the social phobic problems) are co-morbid with depression. Most of these patients had developed their problems in the interaction with one overtly emotional harmful parent, while the other was a passive or helpless witness. Parents of agoraphobic patients often depict the outside world as dangerous and they convey the message to their child that it will not be able to cope with these dangers without their protection (Guidano & Liotti, 1985). Parental abuse may wear a mask of protection! Other examples are the rationalizations of a parent to justify cruel and devaluing remarks: "I am only helping you become a better person." "It is a hard world and I am helping you to cope with it." The tragical end result we encounter in our therapeutic practice is that the parental saying " you are …." has become the "I am …." of our patients.

It is only in the minority of cases that we would locate a phobic patient left from the middle of Davanloo's spectrum of structural neurosis. Mostly, we would locate them right from the middle!

We don't need to explain here that the complaints and/or problems for which patients seek help are no discrete/independent entities. These complaints/problems have functional and causal relationships with other problem areas of the patient. They are part of a complex of interacting systems/processes that are reciprocally influencing (and maintaining) each other.

The patient's expectations of the purpose of an initial interview and of the therapeutic process will influence the patient's involvement in the subsequent sessions It is therefore important to be clear and concrete about what is expected of the patient (and what is expected of the therapist), what is the purpose of the working alliance, what is the patient's task, what of the therapist. The nature of the therapeutic process during the initial interview will set the stage for the coming therapy sessions.

In taking a phobic situation as a starting point for further investigation, the therapist could draw his patient's attention to how his particular defences reflect his perception of himself and his perception of others. Thereafter, the therapist could extend this investigation to other interactions of the patient in the relation with the therapist and in the relationship with current persons and persons from the past.

For instance, after a micro-analysis of a patient's agoraphobic complaints, the therapist could reformulate the patient's problem as follows:

We have investigated the physical manifestations of your anxiety and you have described to me that you don't dare to leave your house all on your own. You don't dare to enter supermarkets or big stores without the company of your partner, you don't dare to make use of the public transport without company. You avoid those situations because—as you have told me—you are afraid that you will lose control on yourself, you are afraid that you will faint, will make yourself ridiculous. But do you realize that you describe yourself at the same time as helpless and incapable to deal with your anxiety. You have to depend upon another person in order to enter those situations. You cannot trust yourself. Do you understand me? So obviously you are used to see yourself as a helpless person. Do you have this perception of yourself also in other interactions?

The following transcript of a 3 hour initial interview with a transport phobic patient will illustrate how micro analysis of a phobic situation can be used to make the patient conscious of his superego pathology. Makes the patient conscious of the several ways he keeps himself unimportant and amputated from longings, feelings, opinions. Makes him conscious of how he perpetuates his problems and defeats solution.

Initial interview (0–18 minutes)

The patient is referred by his therapist because no real progress was made. Neither had the patient profited from prior therapy. Because of his phobias, the patient was severely restricted in his professional life. He never had successful intimate relationships.

After getting acquainted and the therapist having explained the common task of assessment and definition of patient's problems in order to come to a therapy indication and therapy plan, the patient is asked to give a concrete example of his problem. The patient reports that he experiences his problems daily, and he has a concrete example because soon he has to travel to Austria by train. As he has a fear of flying, he avoids travelling by plane. He has no car because driving a car makes him anxious too. The idea of having to travel by train makes him panic. The patient thinks that over the years, his anxiety has generalized.

In telling this, he withdraws from the eye contact and the therapist confronts him with this defence. The patient is well aware of his withdrawing from the eye contact, and he thinks it is his automatic reaction upon the despair he feels when anticipating on this journey. He explains that normally when feeling anxiety, he will freeze and will make himself immobile. As that, however, is impossible in the presence of the therapist, he withdraws from the eye contact (defence at the level of the stimulus). The therapist clarifies that automatically he has to withdraw from the intimacy with the therapist. The patient answers that he is used to hide himself in all kinds of interactions as he is also used to avoid all painful issues. As no exploration of patient's problems can be done as long as these syntonic defences (at the level of the stimulus) are put in operation, and as the patient is recognizing his defences, the therapist challenges the patient's healthy part to stop his defence of automatically withdrawing. The patient then immediately moves to helplessness and he is asking the therapist whether she could imagine that he wouldn't know how else to behave (helplessness at the level of the stimulus). The therapist confronts him with the fact that his former therapies ended with failure, clarifies and challenges his defence of psychic crippledness with reference to his superego pathology and to the intimacy with the therapist. The therapist goes on by inviting the patient to give concrete insight in his problems concerning the train journey. The patient's anxiety is immediately mobilized via tension in the striated muscles, getting warm, and heart palpitations.

We enter the interview at 18 minutes.

Vignette 1 (18.40–25.05 minutes)

Th So you have to go to Austria?

Pt Yes.

Th And in anticipation of that … go ahead.

Pt First I think it not a problem. The more the moment comes near or if there is a sudden change to which I wasn't prepared … in fact it makes no difference … being prepared to me means not to think about it, that is the best.

Th Escaping?

Pt Yes. Because the moment I think about it … a story builds up inside my head. I imagine that it is terrible to sit for four hours in that train.

Th That is what you imagine?

Pt Yes.

Th And what is that terrible imagination?

Pt Starting to hyperventilate enormously, that's what I am afraid of. That the situation which I could suppress until that moment, i.e., I have to leave that train. I have to leave, that I can't suppress that anymore. That I will pull the emergency brakes. That I have to think of everything that might happen and have to think about all the solutions at such a moment.

Th So, if I understand you correctly, then you are afraid of the anxiety, you'll have in the train.

Pt Yes.

Th And subsequently you are afraid of loss of control?

Pt Yes.

Th And you are afraid that you make a kind of fool out of yourself, is that what you say, by pulling the emergency brakes …

Pt Well, making a fool of myself, that isn't what bothers me … but what will happen next … and then my anxiety increases.

Th And what will happen next? You pull the emergency brakes …

Pt The train stops in the middle of nowhere, somewhere in a meadow in Germany or Austria, and I think: I have to leave that train. And then, and then, I am lost and I am standing there. Although I know that it will not happen.

Th But what you tell me is that you have an anticipation anxiety for the anxiety in the train, and that subsequently you have to move towards invalidity, you lost control of yourself. You move to the position of psychic crippledness. As a chicken or turkey in panic, you have to pull the emergency brakes. As a chicken or turkey in panic, you rush to the meadow and there you are: totally desperate in the meadow.

Pt Yes, and that is often the moment …

Th But may I draw your attention to the fact that to you, obviously, it is totally normal to use anxiety as a signal to move immediately to a psychic crippled position.(confrontation of and identification with the causality anxiety and helplessness (defence at level of response).

Pt Yes.

Th Well, it is important to assess this. To you, obviously, it is very normal, as soon as there is anxiety, it is very normal to you, very habitual to you to move to the position of a crippled chicken. You only know yourself like that. You've lost the control of yourself and that is a normal condition to you. I want to assess that here. You gave me more examples. You are hardly in this session, and I ask you for a concrete example of your problem and immediately your eyes wandered away. I confronted you with that and you answered: yes, I know, I am aware of that. But obviously, you also think that normal.

Pt But isn't that exactly the problem?

The patient, being well aware of his helplessness, avoiding eye contact and still maintaining these defences, indicates herewith his satisfaction and high degree of syntonicity. His defence of helplessness also supports his avoiding of eye contact and functions thus also on the level of the stimulus.

Th And you tell me, yes, that is a custom of mine, because when the anxiety is mobilized I immediately become desperate. Usually I will freeze like a mouse and I don't move and I am not there anymore. But here in your presence I can't do so. So I take refuge in other ways of escapism. But in telling me all that you refer to yourself, you talk about yourself as if you are a psychic cripple. That is what I want to assess here together with you. And I want to assess that you think that very normal, you don't know better. (confrontation, identification: causality anxiety—helplessness at level of stimulus and response).

Pt Well, the last, I don't think it normal, but …

Th Not normal, OK, but automatically you move to all positions of psychic crippledness. Obviously you have a low opinion of yourself. (confrontation, identification, clarification at the level of response)

Pt That is true.

The patient—also as a result of his prior therapy—is passively aware of his anxiety manifestations and labels them correctly (striated muscle tension, warm, acceleration of the heart beat, dry mouth and throat, acute hyperventilation, freezing). His observing ego, however, is not at all directed towards his defences.

After 25 minutes on the road to the unconscious, we are at Figure 21, on the next page.

The therapist goes on to confront the patient that apparently he thinks it normal to see himself as crippled and helpless, that apparently he thinks it normal that he has no control of

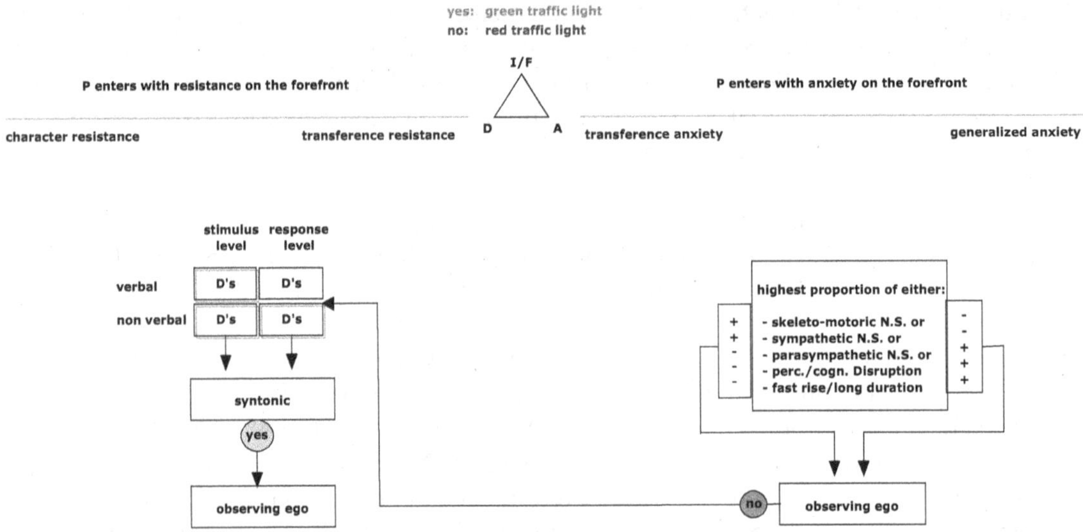

Figure 21. Transport-phobic patient: road to the unconscious 1.

himself and that apparently he thinks it also normal to engage himself in controlling the outside world, all of which is self-defeating. The patient interrupts the therapist by explaining that that is exactly the reason that his problems increased instead of diminished. As patient's anxiety is mainly channelled via the striated muscles, as the patient is well aware of his battery of defences but, in the meantime, is vigorously maintaining them, the therapist decides to start a powerful challenging of his defences to further an intrapsychic crisis, to mobilize at least a conscious working alliance, and to separate the patient's ego and superego parts.

We enter the interview 2 minutes later, at 27 minutes.

Vignette 2 (27.00–33.05 minutes)

Th But you are an intelligent man, because you immediately understand it? (boosting the ego part)

Pt Yes.

Th And subsequently you tell me, almost satisfied, with a certain amount of satisfaction: yes, dear therapist, I think this is the reason that my anxiety has spread out like an ink spot. Do you see how self-destructively you manage your life? Against better knowledge and understanding, you degrade yourself to a psychic idiot. As soon as there is anxiety, I move to the position of psychic crippledness. In the meantime, I control the outside world. Although I know long since that in controlling the outside world, I don't solve my problems and that I maintain my anxiety. But nevertheless, I will continue doing so. And, oh gosh, through the years my anxiety has only augmented. And while telling me that you nod with satisfaction, yes, this is how it went. Distanced. You are totally distanced from yourself. Self-negligent. Non-involved towards yourself. Do you understand me if I tell you so? Do you see what you do to yourself? You take a totally non-involved position towards yourself. Non-involved, self-negligent, self-destructive. You strip yourself of your own intelligence and are even satisfied about that. Self-destructive.

Pt Well, it is a kind of untrue satisfaction because … well, it is very ambivalent. It has become a kind of survival and at last it turned out to be the wrong one because nothing has been solved.

Th But now you defend yourself to me.

Pt Yes, I sit here … that satisfaction bothers me because I am dissatisfied, and …

Th But you point the ambivalence out to me … and we had the intention to investigate in strict honesty and you decided to take the implications of your own words seriously.

The therapist is pointing out that there is still some satisfaction and appeal to the working alliance.

Pt Yes.

Th So there is a part which is satisfied and there is a part which is possibly not satisfied. But the part that is satisfied is here and now on the foreground. The non-involvement, your intellectualizing, distanced intellectualizing. Seeing the ins and outs of your problem and, in the meantime, it is habitual to you to use anxiety as a signal to go for psychic crippledness. And in the meantime, you are accustomed to ignore your problems and to go for controlling the outside world. And you told me also something about your fear of flying. Don't tell me about fear of flying. There also you only occupy yourself in trying to control the situation. Isn't the sound of the aircraft engine different, aren't we flying at too much of an angle, isn't this a strange movement of the aircraft? You do everything except paying attention to yourself. And you are here in order to pay attention to yourself. I point that out to you. I don't say that you do it on purpose. Mind my words. But I point out to you that it is very habitual to you, very normal not to take yourself seriously. You don't pay attention to yourself, you don't take your own words seriously, you don't take your own intelligence seriously. That seems to me problem number one. That is a major problem. Do you understand me?

Pt Yes.

The therapist continues asking the patient what went through him when acknowledging the words of the therapist.

Immediately the patient hides in vagueness, which is challenged by the therapist. The patient puts his thumb in his mouth, spills the coffee, followed by taking refuge in merely stating that he is accustomed to hide for years. The therapist challenges the self-defeating function of his defences and asks the patient whether he wants to cooperate as an equal partner. The patient opts for an equal relationship with the therapist.

We enter the interview 1 minute later, at 34 minutes.

Vignette 3 (34.10–35.05 minutes)

Th But you are doing it. Whether you do it on purpose or not, the effect is the same. Do you understand me? What went on inside you, that moment? Or have you lost it?

Pt No, that I don't take myself seriously. I don't take my intellectual capabilities seriously. I don't take my own words seriously. Yes, that's right. How is it possible and indeed I take it for granted. I always take a step aside whenever something concerns me or whenever a conflicting situation threatens. Either I take a step backwards or a step aside. I will never do a step forward. I will never take a firm stand. Neither on behalf of others nor on behalf of myself. In fact, it is the other way round: neither on behalf of myself, and therefore neither on behalf of others.

The patient, however, sticks to distancing, and the therapist continues heavy challenging of the patient's defences with reference to his superego pathology and with reference to the working alliance with the therapist. The patient keeps on moving to psychic crippledness and rationalizations. Then sadness is mobilized and immediately the patient moves to his helplessness and rationalizations. The therapist starts a head-on collision.

We are 9 minutes later, and we enter the interview at 44 minutes.

Vignette 4 (44.10–58.50 minutes)

Th You are lonely and except from yourself you have distanced yourself from other people. As an expert. And as an expert you enter this session. Distanced, totally distanced. A man who takes that for granted, self-negligent. A man, who comes for help, but who takes it for granted that he has restricted himself and that he is hiding himself behind all kinds of walls. Who takes it for granted to show himself as a psychic cripple. Piling one failure onto another. A man, who has to look back on the rubble heaps of failure. And now there is sadness. And are you going to programme yourself on a failure of these three hours by showing only half of your sadness? Did you come for that?

Clarification of main defences, emphasis on intimacy with the therapist, pressure to quit defences as part of the HOC.

Pt No.

Th But also you suppress your sadness physically. As an automaton. You make it immobile. Yes, and immediately your eyes avoid me. Erecting a wall, like you're used to? And wasn't your sadness exactly about that? About all those failures and loneliness, caused by these walls. Against better knowledge, here and now, you build walls between you and me. It is your last chance. You already have ended a therapy where you didn't reach the results you'd wished. And now you continue your crippledness and distancing and all other kinds of hiding manoeuvres. And the fact is that your sadness was about exactly that. Do you want involvement with yourself?

Appeal to conscious/unconscious working alliance, emphasis on intimacy with the therapist, pressure to quit defences as part of the HOC.

Pt Yes. That is to say. The sadness is about having spoilt the last ten years of my life. Spoilt by myself and my incapacity to deal with it. Yes, I don't know how bad or well I know myself. I don't know how well other people know themselves. When I am confronted with some difficulty and I don't succeed, and I still don't succeed a second time, then I quit. And now I am mainly speaking about situations in which I experience anxiety.

Th But what is your feeling now? Is it sadness or anger? Or is it sadness and anger?

Pt There is very much sadness.

Th But I don't see it. Do you want me to be of help to you with care or with sloppiness?

Pt With care. The reason that I suppress it is mainly because there is a fighting spirit in it. But I use this fighting spirit in the wrong way.

Th Now you start to rationalize and you keep stuck in mere statements. With expertise you move to your rationalizations. Can we look at your sadness?

Pt Yes.

Th Can you use your fighting spirit in favour of your sadness. I cannot help a man who isn't involved with himself. Not because I cannot do so. No therapist can do so. So make your choice, because we are close to your sadness and the two of us want to understand you for hundred percent, isn't it? About what loneliness were you speaking?

Outlining the therapeutic task, appeal to conscious/unconscious working alliance, undoing omnipotence therapist as part of the HOC.

Pt Emotional loneliness. It isn't that there are no people around me. I myself am not capable to give something essential to the people around me. If somebody comes to me with problems or with something else, I only can think rationally. I can't give, I can't ask.

Th And this is all normal to you or do you have sadness about that?

Pt No, this is my sadness.

Th But I don't see it.

Pt Even, if …

Th I don't see your tears. Obviously, it is anxious and shameful to show me all your tears. And you think: why should I admit this stranger into my life? But this is the stranger that is supposed to help you. Obviously, it is anxious and shameful to show me all your tears. I cannot force you to give me insight into all your tears. It has to be your choice. But there are tears. About being damaged … about being lonely … about failure.

End of head-on collision.

Pt (crying)

Th Just cry, just cry. Don't suppress. Don't suppress. Follow all the grief. There is a lot of grief.

Pt So much has been shoveled under. I want to confront it but I can't. I can't get hold of it.

Th There is grief now. And immediately you declare yourself a psychic cripple. Immediately you deny yourself. There is grief, which is emotion, and immediately you move to the crippled position. At this very moment. But there is grief about loneliness and being hurt and failure upon failure. And about anxiety, spreading itself like an ink spot. And about withdrawal from yourself and from others. Who has hurt you so much that you had to find this solution?

Pt I see what I do to myself and what I don't do. I don't admit anybody, not even myself.

Th Who has hurt you so much that you decided to see people as untrustworthy strangers. So that you have to go for cover-ups and for distancing. Because this is a pattern of yours that you know since long. That's what you told me in your grief. How long do you know this pattern of yours?

Pt Almost as long as I live.

Th Almost as long as you live.

Pt I think since high school, perhaps since primary school.

Th High school, perhaps primary school. How old are you?

Pt 42.

Th 42, primary, high school.

Pt 12 or 13 years.

Th 30 years you know yourself as somebody who isn't interested in himself. Somebody distancing from himself. Not admitting other people into his emotional life.

Pt Yes.

Th You say, of course I couldn't tell anybody of my inner life. Of course I had to hide that. But to me that is not so normal. I don't take it for granted that you should hide your inner life. And I ask you again: who has hurt you so much that you decided unconsciously, preconsciously: never and never again I will show my painful feelings. Who is the person that did so much damage to you? Strict honesty. Otherwise we will not succeed. From whom you had to hide your inner life?

After 58 minutes on the road to the unconscious, we are at Figure 22, on the next page.

As we have seen, the working alliance is mobilized against patient's resistance, there has been a breakthrough of grief about he himself having disposed of his feelings, having moved to a non-involved position towards himself and the outside world for at least 30 years. The patient then vividly remembers a painful and shameful situation with his mother in the car. He gives the therapist concrete insight in this situation. The patient then concludes that, obviously, it was already at an early age that he must have taken a decision not to be involved with himself and to keep up appearances towards his mother. The therapist asks the patient how he experienced his mother and the patient starts to rationalize. The therapist goes for a head-on collision.

We are 7 minutes later, and we enter the interview at 65 minutes.

Vignette 5 (65.06–78.26 minutes)

Pt No, it was very shameful.

Th So how did you perceive your mother if it was so shameful? That side in you that said don't do it, don't tell her, how did you perceive your mother from that side? Or do you move to the non-involved position again, and thereafter denial and moving to not taking yourself seriously? You could go on like this during the whole session. But then we will not make any headway. You can also make the choice to take yourself seriously and to listen very carefully to the impact of your own words. One side wanted to tell your mother. The other side didn't want to tell her. What do you want? Continue your endless rationalizing?

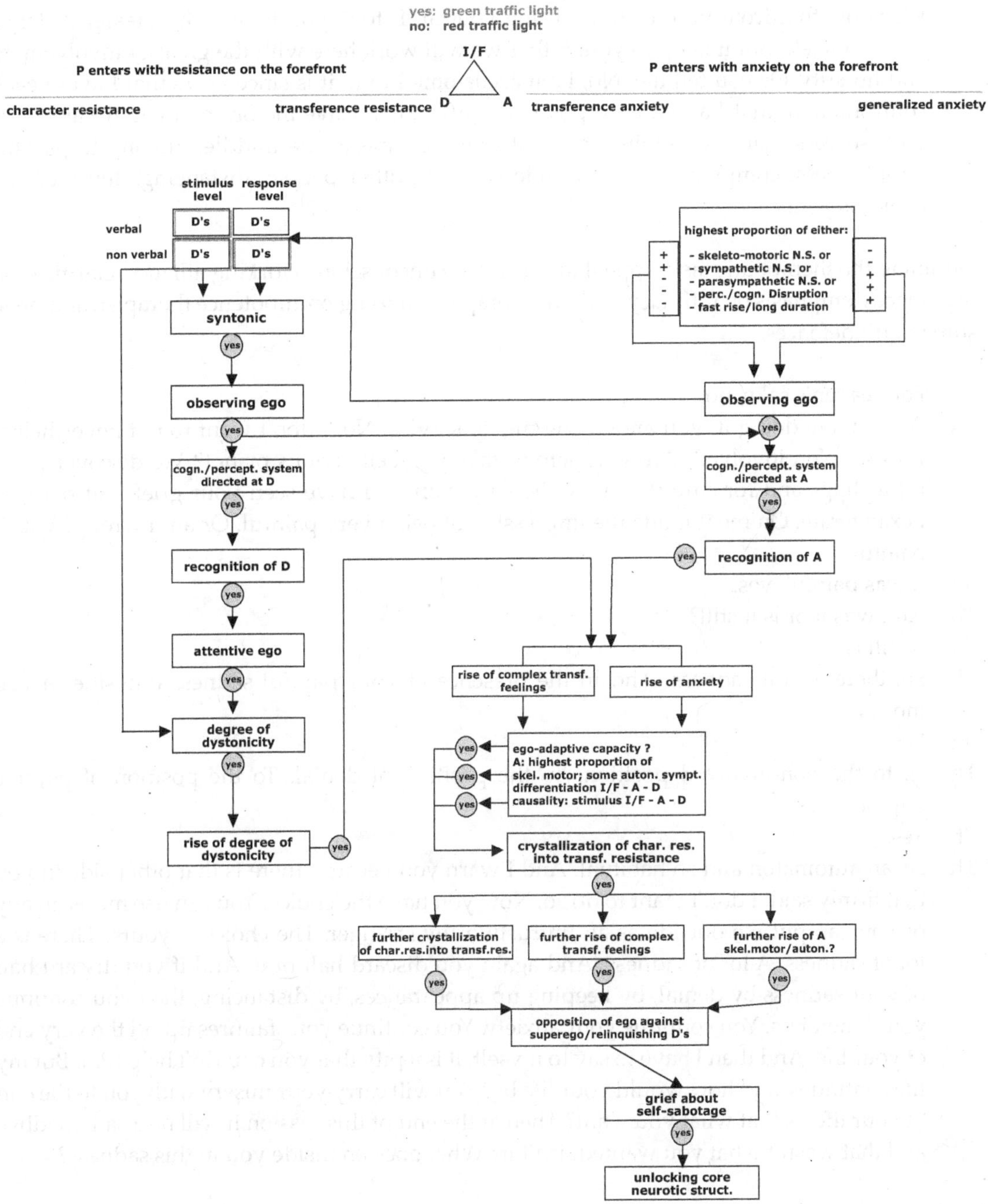

Figure 22. Transport-phobic patient: road to the unconscious 2.

We know that from you. It didn't bring you far. It took you to an even greater distance from yourself. But it is up to you. Either we will work here with the greatest involvement and honesty. Or you tell me: No, I am accustomed to it, it is since years that I avoid each confrontation, that I avoid each possible conflict, just leave me on my own. Because it is with success that I cope while rationalizing, keeping in the middle, moving to psychic crippledness, complying, always understanding other people, distancing. Tell me. The choice is yours.

Outlining the therapeutic task, appeal to conscious/unconscious working alliance, clarification of defences, emphasis on intimacy with the therapist, undoing omnipotence therapist, and pressure to quit defences.

Pt For heaven's sake, no.

Th But you are doing it, you are paying me lip-service. No, I don't want to but nevertheless I do so. Non-involved. Are you here to take yourself serious or not? We discover painful feelings and for sure they must be very painful. I have seen your grief. But perhaps I exaggerate. On me it made the impression of being very painful. Or am I wrong? Was it painful?

Pt It was painful, yes.

Th And was it or is it still?

Pt It still is.

Th So, there is still sadness. And in the presence of your painful sadness one side in you moves …

Pt Yes.

Th … to the non-involved position. To the position of denial. To the position of psychic crippledness.

Pt Yes.

Th As an automaton and so habitual. And I warn you because there is that other side in you that firmly said: I don't want to do so. Now you have the choice. You can use me as an ally or you can put me outside as an untrustworthy stranger. The choice is yours. There is a lot of sadness. A lot of sadness. And again you discard half of it. And if you discard half of your sadness by denial, by keeping up appearances, by distancing, then you continue your loneliness. You continue your anxiety. You continue your failures up till the very end of your life. And then I have to say to myself: it is a pity that you couldn't help him. But my life continues, and how would your life be? You will carry your misery with you to the end of your life. Is that what you want? Then at the end of this session it will be a sad goodbye and that wasn't what you wanted, isn't it? What goes on inside you in this sadness?

Repeating a head-on collision.

Pt It is very deep.

Th It is very deep. It is grief. Deep and old grief. And immediately moving to the crippled position. Not taking yourself seriously, escaping the pain. What is going on inside you, because you say it is very deep. That is only a statement. Let me help you. Unless you say: stay outside, stranger. What is going on inside you?

Pt Again the failure on failure on failure.

Th Failure on failure on failure. An accumulation of failures. While at the same time you are longing for friendship, partnership, emotional closeness. And in spite of that, also here, whenever painful feelings are mobilized, repeatedly you move to denial, to rationalizations. Self-destructive. Do you notice? Do you notice?

Pt Yes, I do see it.

The therapist's head-on collision has mobilized again patient's grief, and its intensity makes the patient realize to what extent he has distanced himself from his feelings. The therapist points out to the patient that if he wants to take the implication of his grief, he has to take himself seriously.

We are 6 minutes later and we enter the interview at 84 minutes.

Vignette 6 (84.30–91.22 minutes)

Pt OK, the honesty towards my mother was one of deception, because I never had played it openly. The game was keeping up appearances. That's what I played. Jokes, also many jokes, and I didn't want to disturb all those jokes.

Th Keeping up appearances towards your mother, and you didn't want to spoil that, but obviously you …

Pt Yes, I have been, I don't know if I am right, but I always had the idea that I was her favourite.

Th By keeping up appearances, yes.

Pt And I didn't want to endanger that.

Th By keeping up appearances, yes. So you bought your favourite position with jokes and keeping up appearances.

Pt Yes.

Th That's what you tell me.

Pt Yes. Because evidently there was a very essential element in my life that I didn't wish to share with her.

Th Yes, and you bought your favourite position.

Pt Yes.

Th How did she hurt you because you had to buy her love?

Pt Well, she is a very strong woman. Often dominant. Automatically it gave me the feeling: I have to have her on my side. I don't want her as an adversary. Yes, it is a powerful position she is in.

Th So, already as a child you thought: I cannot afford to have her against me.

Pt I cannot afford to have her against me, oh no.

Th That must have made quite an impression if you had to think: I cannot afford to have her against me. How did she hurt you with her oppressing and dominating? How did she act dominating? Because you said you preferred her on your side. Obviously you had seen some scenes.

Pt Well, she could make some scenes, yes. An arbitrary example that I remember very well is, that especially at night, when I was in bed—on the attic we had our wardrobe, and sometimes we had made a mess of it—then I heard her messing around and then she became angry because of all our mess. And then, how shall I express it, she became so angry. Everybody was ordered out of their beds and we were obliged to tidy away our clothes. And it was, let me guess, 11:30 hrs in the evening. And of course, it isn't unreasonable that one should tidy away his clothes.

Th Are you starting to rationalize again?

Pt No.

Th So you tell me that you …

Pt No, but what struck me, and what I was afraid of later on, was that it had to be done at that very moment, with yelling, when it suited her.

Th She became hysterical, she yelled, and then everybody had to bow to her hysterical tantrum?

Pt Standing at attention, yes.

Th OK.

Pt And I was thinking: I'll make sure that it doesn't happen again.

Th OK., we are one and a half hour in the session, I propose a 15 minutes break.

In this last vignette, the patient told us that his mother's tantrums, and especially her throwing at night all his clothes out of the wardrobe had made him decide to have his mother on his side instead of having her against him, and that this decision was at the origin of disposing of his feelings and his moving to non-involvement. Before having the 15-minute break, the therapist recapitulates that the patient felt grief about maintaining this self-negligent and non-involved position, which was only self-defeating because it resulted in loneliness, in being a stranger to himself, and in a generalization of his anxiety. After summarizing the automatism in which the patient regularly moves to psychic crippledness, passivity, rationalizations, and distancing, there is a break of 15 minutes.

After the break, the patient tells that he is still sad but he has lost the full contact with it. Subsequently, the patient takes a passive position followed by rationalizations. The therapist reminds him of his decision to take himself seriously, and the patient keeps on being passive. The therapist challenges his defences with regard to his superego pathology, the working alliance, and the intimacy with the therapist. The patient tells that he wants to hide his insecurity by keeping up appearances and the therapist draws the parallel with patient's interaction with his mother. As the patient sticks to his passivity, helplessness, and rationalizations, the therapist decides for a head-on collision resulting in patient's decision to investigate his painful feelings towards his mother.

We are now 32 minutes after the break, and we enter the interview at 122 minutes.

Vignette 7 (122–128.12 minutes)

Pt And that was the moment I was in my bed. I was in a very safe place. And then I heard that messing around from downstairs, and I thought: oh gosh, there we go again, there we go again. At that moment.

Th You are sloppy, you start with your sloppiness. You start with your sloppiness and distancing. What's the use of looking in a sloppy way to that picture, which is deeply engraved in your soul. That messing around. Whose? Whose?

Pt My mother's.

Th You distance and you don't mention the person in question. That messing around. That messing around of my mother's. Tell me what you want.

Pt Yes.

Th Sloppy or precise.

Pt Detailed, yes, and precise.

Th OK, I wait. So you were in your bed, and then? Can we look precisely at that picture which is engraved in your soul?

Pt When my mother comes upstairs, then she is the same woman from whom I want love and care. But at that moment she is ranting and raving so much that she is completely unreachable to me.

Th How is that ranting and raving?

Pt Like a fury she threw all the clothes out of the wardrobe and nobody could stop her and I wasn't allowed to speak to her.

Th She screamed as well?

Pt Yes.

Th Because you say that she acted like a fury. What did she scream?

Pt Who has put this here. Who made all this mess. John, come here!

Th So you were called like a dog. And in the meantime, she threw all the clothes out of the cupboard?

Pt Yes, and then I became angry. I thought: Jayh, woman, does it have to be right now. It is already a week like that. So, why now, suddenly because it is all in your head, because you have to get rid of it now, we all have to dance to your tune.

Th And do you feel this anger. Because now, there is anger, isn't it? How do you feel it physically?

Pt I feel strong and frustrated. I feel … I want to do something.

Th Physically. You say: I feel strong now.

Pt Yes.

Th And how do you feel this strength in your body?

Pt My hands, they want to grab something. Power in the upper part of my arms. Fists.

Th Fists. So upward, forward force. Is that different from anxiety? Does it feel different from anxiety?

Differentiating anger from anxiety.

Pt Yes, this feels much more powerful.

Th Does it feel as an upward, forward force?

Pt Yes.

Th And how does anxiety feel?

Pt Anxiety feels …

Th Physically.

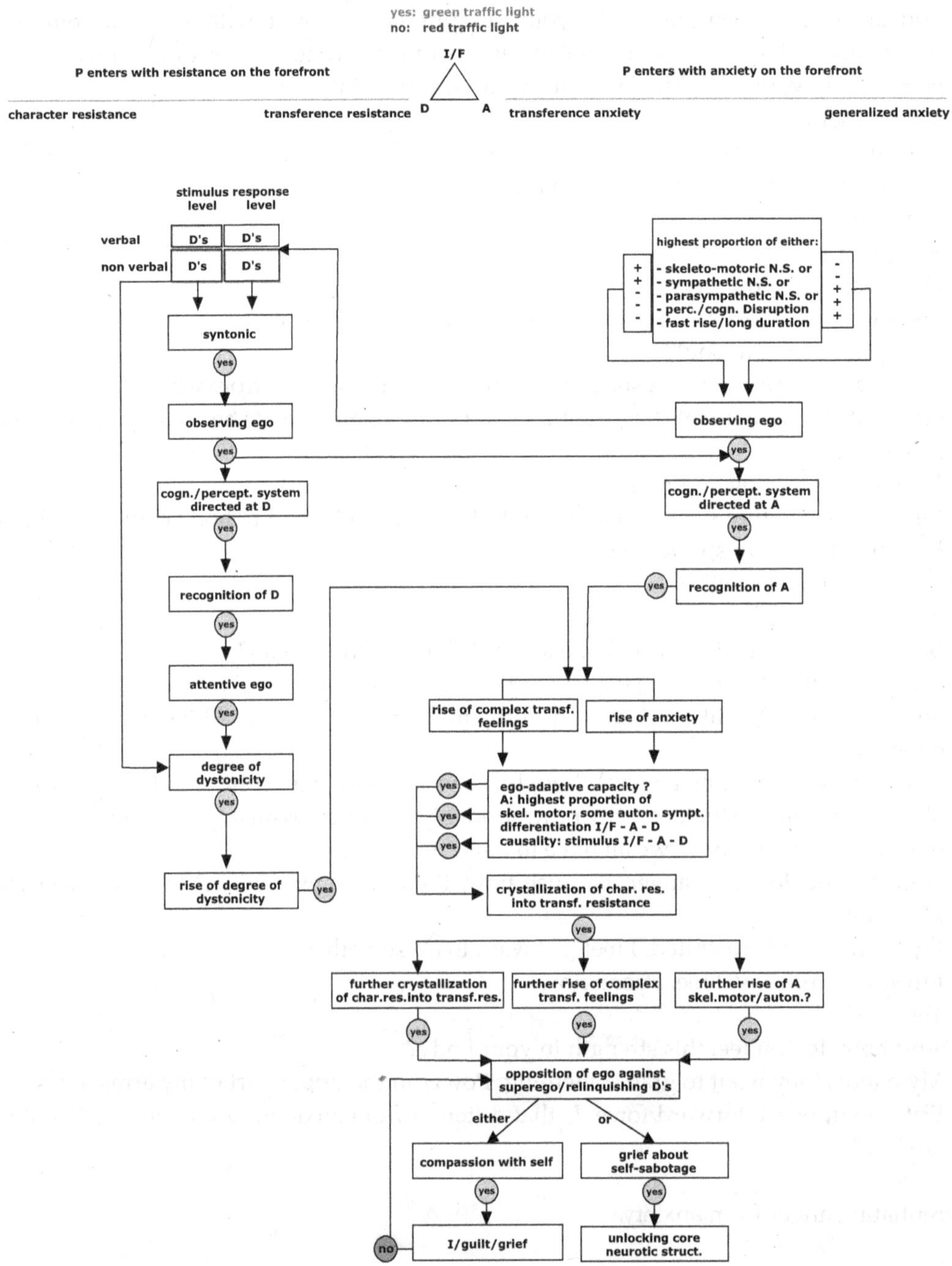

Figure 23. Transport-phobic patient: road to the unconscious 3.

Pt As tensed muscles, only costing energy.
Th Discarding energy.
Pt Yes.
Th So you do know the difference between anger and anxiety?
Pt Yes, anxiety … Anger, I think a very positive emotion. It feels nice to me.
Th But you manipulate yourself in such a way that you never feel that positive, nice power because you prefer anxiety. The same with that sadness. How felt that grief? Of course it was painful. But did it give some relief?
Pt Yes, I thought: hurray. I didn't let myself go totally crazy, I haven't lost all my feelings.
Th So you thought: hurray.

As we saw the working alliance has won over the forces of resistance, the patient is highly involved, he is experiencing anger towards his mother and he is able to differentiate between the experience of anger and anxiety. Subsequently the therapist draws patient's attention to the dynamics of his inner problem in terms of the triangle of conflict.

After 125 minutes on the road to the unconscious, we are at Figure 23, on the previous page.

We are 5 minutes later, and we enter the interview at 130 minutes.

Vignette 8 (130–133.30 minutes)

Th Already in the beginning of this session we assessed that by erecting all these walls you yourself took care to become estranged from your feelings. So grief, anxiety, wall and then you have only access to your walls and not to that grief, which evokes anxiety. And not to the anger, which evokes anxiety. It is very important that you understand this. That is why I explicitly point this out to you.
Pt Yes.
Th So what you see is that you have an internal problem. That is what we have assessed. What we have discovered is the following: he moment there is a painful feeling e.g., sadness or e.g., anger, then you start up an automatic process. Immediately you turn that feeling into anxiety. Immediately anger and anxiety or sadness and anxiety are turned into a repertoire of walls. Tak tak tak, one wall after the other. It is important that you understand this. Anger, anxiety, helplessness. Anger, anxiety, rationalizing. Anger, anxiety, coming with arguments. Anger, anxiety, complying. Anger, anxiety, distancing. Anger, anxiety, understanding the other person instead of yourself.
Pt Yes, and I can add one. (the patient is highly involved, his observing ego has turned into an attentive ego).
Th Which one?
Pt Amorous, anxiety, distancing.
Th So, that is the internal problem. As soon as a feeling has been mobilized, e.g., being amorous, e.g., anger, e.g., sadness, then immediately anxiety is evoked.
Pt Yes.

Th And immediately you use anxiety as a trigger to go for all kinds of crippledness. In fact, all walls are forms of crippledness. Complying, defiance, distancing doubting, forgetting, immobile, empty head, keeping up appearances, debating, rationalizations. OK?

Pt Yes, I do understand.

Th It is very important that you understand. Being amorous, anxiety, wall. Anger, anxiety, wall. Sadness, anxiety, wall. And the problem is that it is an automatic process. It isn't even a conscious choice. Do you understand me.

Pt Yes. Perhaps it has been, once upon a time, a conscious choice, but I've become such an expert that ...

The therapist continues to recapitulate the causality between mobilization of patient's feelings, anxiety, and defences in order to achieve full insight his inner dynamic process, the patient is highly involved and, in so many words, he adds the defence of repression to the list. The therapist points out that although they discovered the causality between anger and anxiety in the patient, they still didn't understand why experiencing anger should evoke his anxiety. Upon the therapist's suggestion that they could go for such an understanding, but that in that case the patient has to take the decision to quit all his defences, the patient decides to go for experiencing the full extent of his anger. However, at first the patient moves to helplessness and after the therapist challenges his defence, the patient tells that his mother treats him like a dog and that he feels like a tormented animal.

We are 28 minutes later, and we enter the interview at 161 minutes.

Vignette 9 (161–163.07 minutes)

Pt She is yelling and I get more and more angry and ...

Th How do you grasp her.

Pt I push her against her side. I don't push her against her chest, I don't push against her back.

Th Against her side.

Pt The way she stands there in front of my wardrobe, that's how I push her. I give her a shove towards the staircase. And she has to go downstairs. At any rate she has to go downstairs.

Th How, keep that picture in front of you, how does she go downstairs?

Pt Whether she is standing or sitting, I keep on pushing. I keep on pushing.

Th How does she go downstairs. We don't investigate your rage without looking at its effects.

Pt She falls downstairs.

Th And then. What is the tormented animal inside you doing next?

Pt Jeez, that tormented animal is immediately enormously scared.

Th And if you don't let yourself be taken away by this fright?

Pt Downstairs, downstairs and out of sight, out of sight.

As the therapist draws patient's attention to face the wounds he inflicted upon his mother the patient moves again to helplessness. After the therapist challenges his helplessness, the patient tells that he doesn't want to hurt his mother, and the therapist confronts the patient that in refusing to face the full extent of his rage, which obviously also implies his intent of hurting her, the patient decides not to take refuge any more in defences.

We are 8 minutes later, and we enter at 171 minutes of the interview.

Vignette 10 (171.07–186.55 minutes)

Pt Yes, but when pushing her downstairs my anger diminishes.

Th How is she lying below the staircase? What damage does she have?

Pt Bruises.

Th Bruises, and what else do you see?

Pt She must have cut herself.

Th She must have—do you see that or not?

Pt Yes, I see her lying below the staircase.

Th What do you see exactly?

Pt A damaged head.

Th A damaged head. What kind of damage do you see on her head?

Pt I see … I see bruises on her face, I see blood, coming from under her hair, the skin of her skull is torn.

Th You see blood. How is that blood running?

Pt Alongside her eyebrows.

Th And if you keep on looking at that picture of your mother. Lying there with bruises and blood on her face. Then what is going on inside you?

Pt Then I am scared to death.

Th You are scared to death. What's going on inside you?

Pt Oh God, I went much too far.

Th God, I went much too far. So then fright and guilt are coming.

Pt Oh yes.

Th And if we make a mental image regarding your fright and guilt: oh God, I went much too far. What do you do, if we make a picture from that?

Pt Then I see my longing for her love, which I don't …

Th If you don't distance yourself, what do you do? Seeing her lying there, seeing the damage, inflicted by you and you went much too far. What do you picture yourself doing?

Pt Quick as lightning I am going to help her.

Th How do you help her? Do you lift her? Do you kiss her? What do you do?

Pt I take her in my arms.

Th How? Show me.

Pt At her shoulders, and her head here.

Th And then?

Pt Then I press her firmly against me.

Th You press her firmly against you. Don't erase that picture. And then? Investigate your feelings.

Pt Then I press her against me and I want to be very close to her.

Th You want to be very close to her and then there is sadness. You've positive feelings and sadness. Don't suppress. And then? Don't erase. Investigate.

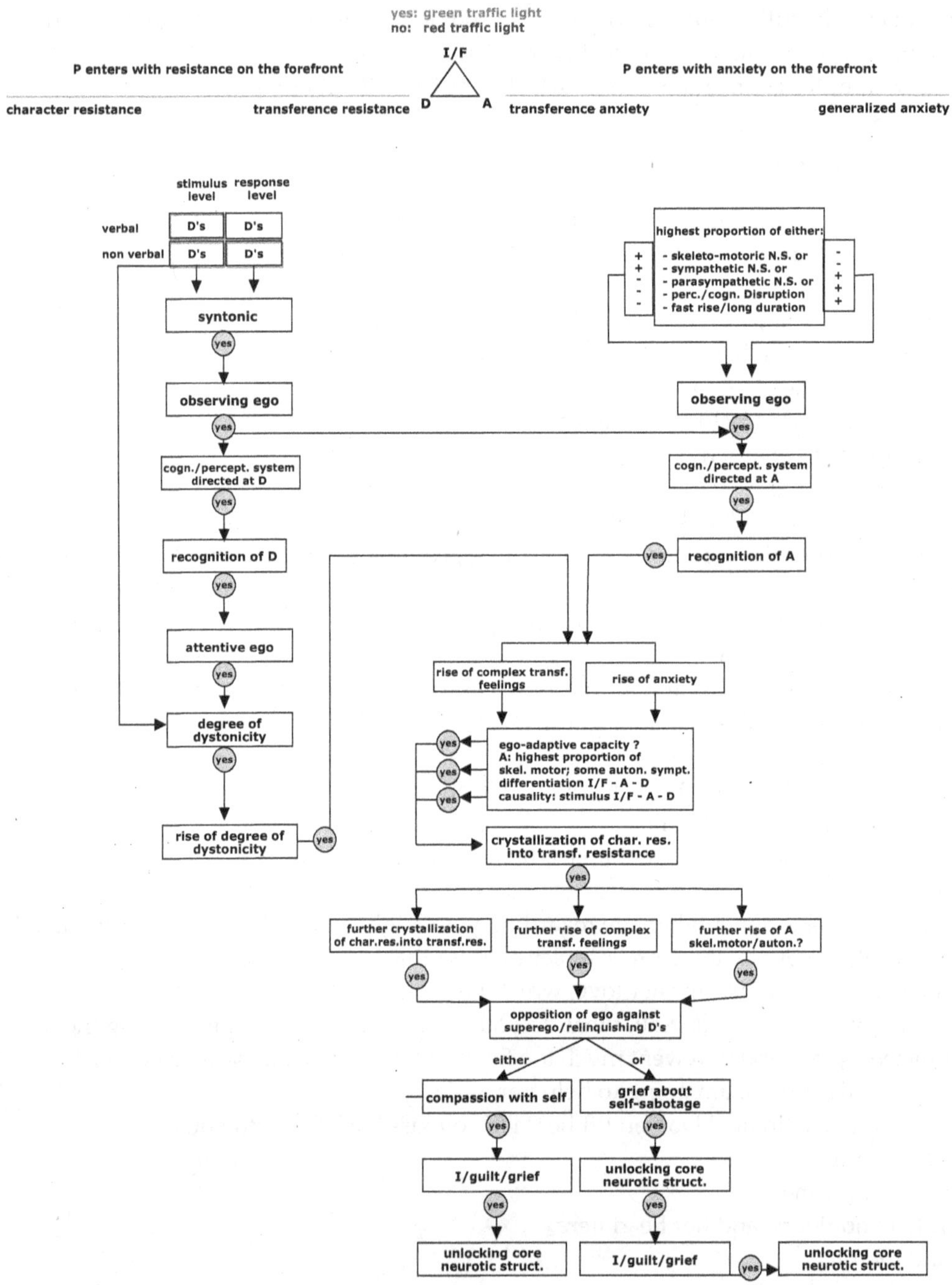

Figure 24. Transport-phobic patient: road to the unconscious 4.

Pt I press her against me.

Th And then? What do you say to your mother?

Pt That I want to be very close to her again and that I ... that I ... in everything want to feel safe with her.

Th Is your sadness about not feeling safe?

Pt My sadness is about having these feelings inside me, but I don't share these feelings with her. She doesn't know my feelings and I don't know her feelings.

Th What is your sadness about at this very moment? Because there is sadness but you keep away from it.

Pt It concerns our distance.

Th Which the two of you made.

Pt That I ...

Th Because you hold your mother in your arms, but you threw her from the staircase. Because she torments you and she is dominating and hysterical. Because she tormented you.

Pt Yes, and it feels that she let me down.

Th Yes, and there are tears in your eyes. May I see them? May I see them?

Pt When she dies she will never have known that and how much I have loved her.

Th So your sadness is also about that you've distanced yourself from her?

Pt Yes, and that in the midst of all these series of jokes and the keeping up appearances I feel very lonely. And in fact she is the only person with whom I long to be close. Apart from dominating she is also ... she is fascinating. I mean ... I also want ...

Th Contact.

Pt I want to have contact, and we have so on other matters. But specifically where it is very essential, there she is repulsive to me.

After 170 minutes on the road to the unconscious, we are at Figure 24, on the previous page.

Th We have now ... I am looking with half an eye at the clock.

Pt Yes.

Th You enter this session as a walled-in fortress. I draw your attention to your walls, to the extremely non-involved, self-negligent and crippled position you take towards yourself and towards me. Then I say: make your choice. You can continue being non-involved with yourself and with me. You become sad and there is painful grief about at least thirty years of loneliness. About thirty years of having said goodbye to your loved ones and to you yourself. Grief about strict loneliness, about being a stranger to yourself. A stranger to your family. Then I say to you: once you must have taken a decision. And you relate that decision to your secret and to the situation in the car with your mother. And you describe two sides inside you. One side is longing to tell his mother, the other side says: don't do it, you cannot trust her. Then you tell me that long before that situation you had a silent agreement with your mother. And that agreement was: I prefer you on my side. I don't want you opposite me. And I buy you with keeping up appearances and with jokes. Then I ask you: what is that position opposite you? Then you give me an example.

That position is when your mother at 11.30 p.m. in the night is hysterically (those are not your words) screaming and yelling, throwing all your clothes out of your wardrobe. And she is tormenting you and she calls you like a dog and you are obliged to clean up the mess. Subsequently, I say to you that surely you must have painful feelings about that. And immediately you take refuge to all kinds of walls, psychic crippledness, non-involvement, rationalizing, and so on.

And we detect a new wall, that very important wall of split-second pictures in your mind and with a sharp drop the picture has gone. Then I say to you: if we take a honest look, we detect at the one hand that that rage, that animal inside you. And we make a mental image to give form to your rage. And that animal inside you wanted to push your mother and without sparing her you wanted to throw her from the staircase. And she was lying below the stairs with bruises on her face and blood running from under her hair. And at the other hand, say the loving side in you, when seeing that, you were scared to death and you felt guilty. And you took your mother in your arms. You say to me: I want to take my mother in my arms and I want her to press very close against me. And then there is sadness.

(Patient is crying.)

Don't suppress it. Then there is sadness about having lost each other. About how you have lost her. That's what we made you conscious of. With that rage, that feels that you want to mutilate her. And now we understand everything. Now we understand why it is that your feelings evoke anxiety inside you. And now we understand why you are frightened for loss of control. And now we understand that these walls have a protective function. Not only towards yourself but also towards other people. To spare them from your rage, which frightens you and which makes you feel guilty. And now we understand that banning your mother out of your heart was also a protective act. There is sadness and you tell me: I don't want these walls and I don't want these walls between me and other people. Neither do I want that rage. OK? I don't want the walls because I want to admit people into my intimate life. But because of the rage inside me I can't admit them.

Pt Yes.

After this summary, the division of therapeutic tasks is discussed.

It is clear to the patient that he has to take himself, his longings, thoughts, feelings, norms and values seriously. That he has to quit his defences, he has to monitor his anxiety. He has to be very precise in describing to himself what exactly another person in his interactions did/said that evokes which specific feeling. In himself, he has to give words to his feelings.

As there had been a waiting time of nine months, it had been agreed that the patient would have once a month a session with his referring therapist. During the waiting period, the patient had travelled by train to Austria. In order to arrive at the practice of the ISTDP therapist, the patient also had to travel by train (thirty minutes). In the first ISTDP session, the patient updated the therapist in what way he had been able to continue the therapy process of the initial interview. Therapist and patient elaborated on his perception of transport situations (train, aircraft, car): as unpredictably harmful and inescapable, the perception of himself in these situations (being trapped and incapable of dealing with his emotions and anxiety), his defence of helplessness, and the link with several interactions between the patient and his mother. On the third ISTDP session, the patient arrived in the car he had bought. The therapy ended because of the fact that the patient had increased access to his feelings, had constructive intimacy with himself, siblings, parents, friends, colleagues. Some months after ending the therapy, the patient made some flights.

Steps in the chapter

- DSM classification of phobias
  - *agoraphobia (with and without panic attacks)*
  - *social phobia*
  - *specific phobia*
- Analysis of the patient's phobic complaints reflect perception of himself and of others
- Transcript of an intial interview with a transport phobic patient

CHAPTER TEN

Steps on the roadmap to the unconscious and its application to patients suffering from depressive disorders

Depression is one of the most common disorders seen in clinical practice. Depression is a complex diagnostic construct that casts a large umbrella over diverse conditions. Some of the varieties of depression as defined by psychiatrists are summarized in Table 5. This chapter cannot do justice to the entire topic of depression, but it is designed to give the reader an organized method to assess whether a depressed patient is suitable for intensive short-term dynamic psychotherapy. Suffice it to say, just as in traditional approaches, all organic causes of depression (thyroid, endocrine, metabolic, drug withdrawal) must be ruled out before undertaking psychotherapy.

Classically depressive neurosis (dysthymia) was seen as responsive to dynamic psychotherapy, but recent research indicates ISTDP can address many forms of depression. The central symptoms of all depression are, of course, a depressed mood and loss of interest in life's activities. Table 6 illustrates the entire spectrum of depressive symptoms. In contrast to the

Table 5. Types of depression.

Bipolar (I and II)
Recurrent
Major depression
Atypical depression
Dysthymia
Adjustment reactions with depressed mood

Table 6. Depressive episode according to ICD-10 (similar to DSM-IV).

General criteria

- The depressive episode should last two weeks.
- No hypomanic or manic symptoms sufficient to meet the criteria for hypomanic or manic episode at any time in the individual's life.
- Not attributable to psychoactive substance use or to any organic mental disorder.

Typical symptoms

- Depressed mood to a degree that is definitely abnormal for the individual, present for most of the day and almost every day, largely unresponsive to circumstances, and sustained for at least two weeks.
- Loss of interest or pleasure in activities that are normally pleasurable.
- Decreased energy or increased fatigability.

Additional symptoms

- Loss of confidence or self-esteem.
- Unreasonable feelings of self-reproach or excessive and inappropriate guilt.
- Recurrent thoughts of death or suicide, or any suicidal behaviour.
- Complaints or evidence of diminished ability to think or concentrate, such as indecisiveness or vacillation.
- Bleak and pessimistic views of the future.
- Sleep disturbance of any type.
- Change in appetite (decrease or increase) with corresponding weight change.

normal emotional responses to unwanted and stressful events, depression is a mental disorder which, because of its severity, tends to recur and places a high cost on the individual as well as society. It is important to note that up until the present time, no common causes for depressive disorders are known which would allow for aetiological-based valid classification. Despite the current trend in ICD-10 and DSM-IV to pigeonhole depression according to timing and severity, there is little evidence to support that major depression is any more than a syndrome. It is most likely that major depression is a diagnostic construct which we impose upon a continuum of depressive symptoms.

Common presentations of depression

Depressed mood versus depressive episode—major depression

The symptom criteria for a major depressive episode according to ICD-10 are listed in Table 6. The typical symptoms are depressed mood and lack of interest pleasure energy. Depressed people may feel sad, anxious, empty, hopeless, helpless, worthless, guilty, irritable, or restless.

They may lose interest in activities that once were pleasurable, experience loss of appetite or overeating, or problems concentrating, remembering details, or making decisions; and may contemplate or attempt suicide. Insomnia, excessive sleeping, fatigue, loss of energy, or aches, pains, or digestive problems that are resistant to treatment may be present. They may also consider violence towards themselves and/or others. Tragically, not infrequently, they do act on these distorted feelings and perceptions.

Depressed mood is the hallmark of all depressions. It is a sustained emotional state that is characterized by sadness, poor motivation, misery, discouragement, hopelessness, emptiness, unhappiness, distress, pessimism; it cannot be delineated from emotional states universally

Table 7. Dysthymia according to ICD-10.

Criteria

- At least two years of constant or constantly recurring depressed mood.
- Intervening periods of normal mood rarely last for longer than a few weeks; no episodes of hypomania.
- None, or very few, of the individual episodes of depression within the two-year period should be sufficiently severe or long-lasting to meet the criteria for recurrent mild depressive disorder.
- During at least some of the periods of depression, at least three of the symptoms listed below should be present.

Symptoms

- Reduced energy or activity.
- Insomnia.
- Loss of self-confidence and feelings of inadequacy.
- Difficulty in concentrating.
- Frequent tearfulness.
- Loss of interest in or enjoyment of sex and other pleasurable activities.
- Feeling of hopelessness or despair.
- A perceived inability to cope with the routine responsibilities of everyday life.
- Social withdrawal.
- Reduced talkativeness.

Subtypes of depression (DE/MDE)

Some authorities see it as important to classify depression into severity subtypes. Melancholia refers to depression with somatic symptoms; depression is also classified if there are psychotic symptoms that are congruent or incongruent with the mood.

Other depressive types

Depression has been further classified as seasonal, subsyndromal, premenstrual, and postnatal.

experienced by human beings when confronted with life's adversities. The main way to distinguish depression from prolonged sadness is that the intensity and depth of the pain becomes so unbearable that the death wishes of a depressed individual become a comforting remedy. Even if it has been triggered by a life event, it evolves autonomously and doesn't change even with reasoning and encouragement. It is associated with cognitive and somatic symptoms (guilt, self-reproach, suicidal thoughts, and unpleasant bodily sensations).

The depressive state shows anhedonia, cognitive disturbances, psychomotor disturbances, vegetative symptoms, and frequently co-morbid anxiety symptoms.

Psychobiology of depression

The human brain may be divided into a variety of systems that influence cognitive, emotional, and perceptual functions. Three important systems are the prefrontal system, the limbic system, and the basal ganglia system. These functional systems are highly interdependent with one another and work interactively. Depression results when reward- and mood-regulation systems are damaged by overwhelming environmental stress (loss), intrapsychic conflict, and/or genetically based hormonal/neurotransmitter depletion.

The primary neurochemical systems

Supporting the functional and anatomical systems described above is an interlaced grouping of neurochemical systems. These neurochemical systems can be conceived of as the fuel that runs the communication network of the brain. Clearly, the basic fuel of the brain is glucose, and that brain cannot function without a continuous burning of this basic source of energy. But over and above that, neurons communicate with one another via certain basic neural transmitters. Below is a brief review of some of the major neurotransmitters implicated in depressive disorders and frequently therapeutically manipulated by use of psychiatric drugs.

- *The dopamine system*
  Dopamine is a catecholamine neurotransmitter. It is the first product synthesized from the essential amino acid, tyrosine. There are three subsystems within the brain that utilize dopamine as their primary neurotransmitter. These all arise in the ventral tegmental area. From there, they branch upwards into three tributaries: 1) the nigrostriatal pathway, 2) the mesocorticolimbic pathway, 3) the arcuate nucleus from the hypothalamus and pituitary. Dopamine functions as the "pleasure neurotransmitter" because this is the primary neurotransmitter in the brain reward system and is associated with adventuresome and exploratory behaviours. The importance of this neurotransmitter in the successful treatment of depression cannot be overemphasized.
- *The noradrenaline system*[1]
  Noradrenaline is also a catecholamine neurotransmitter. It also originates from the essential amino acid tyrosine. The enzyme dopamine beta hydroxylase converts dopamine to noradrenaline. The noradrenaline system arises from the locus coeruleus and is diffusely distributed throughout the brain.

The above two systems were first considered as causal in depression when the "catecolamine hypothesis" (Schildkraut, 1965, 1995) was first proposed. In short, this theory proposed that depletion of noradrenaline and dopamine caused depression. Later, it became apparent that serotonin was involved (below). The "serotonin permissive hypothesis" (Prange, 1974) evolved, which stated adequate levels of serotonin must be present in order for noradrenaline and dopamine to function, thus modern theory looks towards a balance of neurotransmitters. It is also noteworthy that pools of post-synaptic receptor sites expand in response to depletion of neurotransmitters and shrink when pre-synaptic levels return to normal.

- *The serotonin system*
  The serotonin system is non-catecholamine neurotransmitter. It originates from the essential amino acid called tryptophan. Tryptophan, also called 5-HTP is metabolized into the neurotransmitter, serotonin. The distribution of the serotonin is strikingly similar to that of the noradrenaline neurons. Serotonergic neurons originate in the Raphe nucleus of the midbrain. Serotonin plays a role in modulating mood, anxiety, and aggressive or violent behaviour. "The serotonin hypothesis" suggests that depression originates as a result of depletion of brain levels of serotonin. Serotonin is seen as an enabling neurotransmitter that allows noradrenaline and dopamine to stabilize mood. Evidence for this hypothesis comes from research which examined the brains of individuals who killed themselves because of depression. The levels of serotonin in the brains of these individuals were markedly depleted. An altered level of brain serotonin has also been associated with impulsive and violent behaviour.
- *The cholinergic system*
  Acetylcholine is the neurotransmitter of the cholinergic system. Similar to dopamine, acetylcholine has a relatively specific location in the human brain. The major nucleus of these

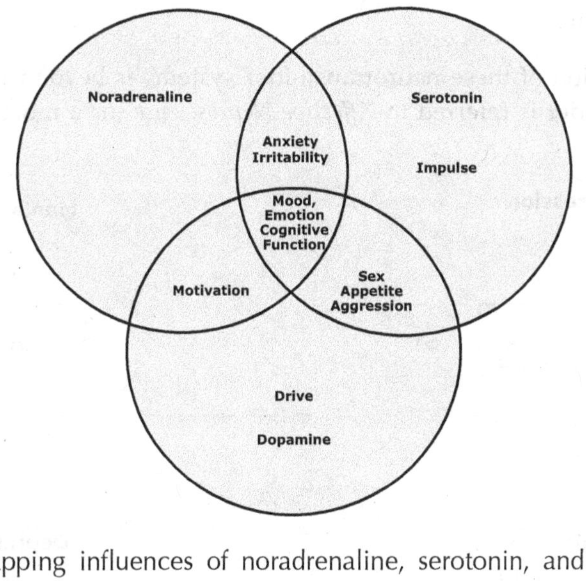

Figure 25. The overlapping influences of noradrenaline, serotonin, and dopamine on mood, emotion, drive, and cognition.

neurons reside in the nucleus basalis of Meynert, which lie in the ventral medial regions of the globus pallidus. From there, these neurons project throughout the cortex. A second group of acetylcholine neurons originate in the diagonal band of Broca and the septal nucleus projecting to the hippocampus and the cingulate gyrus. The third group resides within the basal ganglia. The system plays a major role in the encoding of memory, although the precise mechanisms are poorly understood. Patients suffering from Alzheimer's disease show deterioration of the acetylcholine levels in their brains. Current drug therapies which elevate levels of acetylcholine temporarily improve memory functioning in Alzheimer's patients (Fan, 2010).

Interestingly, the acetylcholine system seems to oppose the dopaminergic system within the basal ganglia and maybe implicated in disturbances of motor functioning, as well as in psychosis. Davis & Janowsky proposed the cholinergic hypothesis of depression and postulated that increased cholinergic tone was responsible for depressive symptoms in vulnerable populations. In any case, we are certain that the parasympathetic nervous system is largely mediated via the cholinergic system, and thus in the authors' eyes, the system must be considered a factor in depressive states (Janowsky, 1972).

Acetylcholine counterbalances noradrenaline, dopamine, and serotonin to sustain mood. Excess acetylcholine (relative) leads to depression, and excessive catecholamines lead to mania.

Other systems

- The GABA system
- The glutamate system
- The endorphin system
- The oxytocin system

An elaborate discussion of these neurotransmitter systems is beyond the scope of this book and an interested reader is referred to *Affective Neuroscience* for a more extensive discussion.

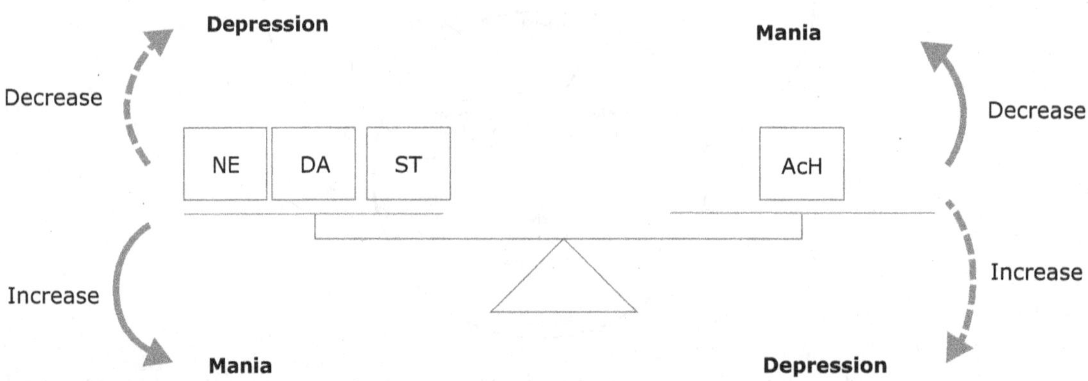

Figure 26. Janowsky & Davis cholinergic hypothesis for mania and depression.

Suffice it to say, that all benzodiazapines are GABA agonists and thus decrease anxiety. Glutamate is an activating amino acid and neurotransmitter which is involved with learning and memory. Its neurons are distributed throughout the hippocampus and the cortex. The endorphins mediate pain and alter mood when under stress. They also may be activated along with oxytocin when one falls in love. Oxytocin helps mothers to bond with infants and is thought to promote exclusive attachment and pair bonding.

Psychopharmacology versus dynamic therapy

Biological psychiatry is in a bit of disarray as this chapter goes to publication. A large seven-year National Institute of Mental Health (NIMH)-sponsored study of treatment of depressed patients called the Star*D study (Sequenced Treatment to Alleviate Depression study) showed disappointing results for both medication proponents and cognitive-behaviour therapy (CBT) proponents. The proposed seventy per cent response rate for depressed patients (Hamilton Depression Scale, HAM-D > 14) is now seriously called into question, and therapies like ISTDP now have a new promise in the therapeutic spectrum.

What the study showed was that two-thirds of patients in the STAR*D trial still had residual symptoms after their initial therapy (Trivedi, 2006).

The American Psychiatric Association Guidelines 2010 for treating depression state

> The overall goals of treatment of Major Depressive Disorder should focus on alleviating functional impairments and improving quality of life in addition to achieving symptom resolution and episode remission.
>
> (Section 6, *APA Guidelines*)

> The goal of acute phase treatment for major depressive disorder, insofar as possible, is to achieve remission and a return to full functioning and quality of life. Remission is defined as at least 3 weeks of the absence of both sad mood and reduced interest and no more than three remaining symptoms of the major depressive episode. However, it is not uncommon for patients to have substantial but incomplete symptom reduction or improvement in functioning during acute phase treatment. A number of studies have provided compelling evidence that even mild residual symptoms at the end of a depressive episode are associated with significant psychosocial disability, compared with asymptomatic remission; a more than three times faster relapse to a subsequent major depressive episode; and in first-episode patients, a more chronic future course.

The authors support this view of treating depression, and in our view, ISTDP has an important but underutilized value in treating this illness. However, monitoring the patient's response to the trial therapy is crucial to safe and effective treatment.

In clinical practice, one could make a case in using ISTDP trial therapy as a screening process for treatment of depression without using antidepressants. As the art of psychotherapy is currently clinically practised, many patients who come to therapy are already on antidepressants.

There are four basic categories of antidepressant drugs used today. These categories are 1) selective serotonin reuptake inhibitors, 2) noradrenaline/dopamine reuptake inhibitors, 3) selective noradrenaline, serotonin reuptake inhibitors, and 4) monoamine oxidase inhibitors. There are other drugs that are used in combination for response augmentation, particularly psychostimulant, thyroid hormone, lithium, and, most recently, atypical antipsychotic medications.

Antidepressant strategies are most frequently effective in patients who have severe vegetative symptoms of depression and who have severe anxiety and/or agitation. These medications can be safely used to stabilize patients prior to initiation of intensive short-term dynamic psychotherapy. Like all treatment interventions, these therapies come at a cost. In particular, drugs that elevate brain levels of serotonin can blunt affective experiencing. It is wise for psychotherapists who are treating patients with clinical depression to conduct unlocking of the unconscious of their patients while they are on medication as well as when medications are discontinued. In the author's experience this enhances access to the affect of unconscious guilt and allows further therapeutic dismantling of the punitive superego structure, which initiated the depression to begin with. Further, systematic researches into the protocols of treating depressed patients are underway in the Department of Psychiatry at Dalhousie University in Halifax, Nova Scotia (Abbass, 2002, 2006; Research Protocol Dalhousie School of Medicine Department of Psychiatry, 2011, -).

The dynamic point of view

Metapsychology of depression: depression as pathologic bereavement

Many practitioners have become disillusioned with the psychodynamic approach to depression. Aaron Beck (1979) -, a psychoanalyst, has rejected the dynamic model as an effective approach to depression and focused his attention on patients' disturbed thoughts. His observation was in fact correct, but the authors believe that the ineffectiveness of the dynamic model was a result of the passivity of the psychotherapists as opposed to the incorrectness of the psychodynamic model. Davanloo, Kalpin, Abbass, and others have successfully demonstrated that ISTDP is a successful and effective treatment for major depression.

In *Mourning and Melancholia*, Freud described in exquisite detail the dynamic mechanism of depression and its relationship to object loss. He writes that the aggression that the person feels towards the parent is re-directed by the superego against the ego (Figure 1). He states that when the object is lost and there has been a pre-existing ambivalence, the hate portion of the feeling is relieved by an identification of the ego with the lost person followed by a sadistic attack against that person as represented by the ego. Our understanding of this mechanism remains intact today; however, a great deal has changed in its application to the clinical situation. Davanloo's technique involves mobilizing the depressed person's ambivalence towards the loved person. Thus, we see depression as a form of pathological bereavement and the goal is converting pathological bereavement to acute grief.

The patient with depression by definition has pre-existing ego/superego pathology, as do so many other patients on the right half of the spectrum of structural neurosis. The patient has had an inadequate observing ego and thus has had not noticed and/or denied and ignored anxiety as well as other feelings during the prodromal phase of their illness. The superego in effect eventually imprisons the ego and deprives it of its observing capacities and punishes it for being "disobedient" or "bad".

ISTDP and depression

Research

There are a series of studies showing ISTDP as an effective treatment of depression. (Abbass, 2002, 2006; Driessen, 2010). These studies go counter to the traditional wisdom that psychotherapy helps mainly with social adjustment and relapse prevention and antidepressant drugs help with the melancholic and vegetative symptoms of sleep and appetite symptoms. It seems that ISTDP may have a unique effect on the core symptoms of depression. The explanation for this finding is controversial. During an ISTDP initial interview with the patient, the therapist assesses whether this therapy is the proper indication for this particular patient. (Fig. 1); see also Chapter Three). The authors have samples of severely depressed patients on waiting lists for electro-cortical shock therapy (ECT), who have responded favourably to ISTDP and have not needed this intervention post-therapy (Abbass, 2010; Neborsky, 1999; Psychiatry Grand Rounds University of Maryland). A large meta-analysis of 1,365 patients in 23 studies reveals a highly statistically significant effect size when compared to controls (Dreissen, 2010). The studies demonstrate that the effects last when measured one year after termination.

Antidepressant medication is synergistic with ISTDP, but benzodiazapine medications may mask the anxiety pathway and thus may hamper the clinician from observing the pathway of unconscious anxiety. It is wise to have patients off this category of medication before attempting a trial therapy.

The way, an optimal interview could go is illustrated in the case history transcribed below. At the beginning of the interview, the therapist helps the patient become aware of their ego-syntonic defences and the ego begins to differentiate itself from the superego. Healthy curiosity begins to emerge because of the therapist interventions and the patient wants to explore her inner processes. The patient will have an initial breakthrough of sadness for the ways in which has been mistreating himself. After his ego part is demarcated from his superego part by this experience of compassion, more systematic examination of the triangles of conflict and persons becomes possible. The examination gives the therapist the possibility to assess the flaws of the patient's ego-adaptive capacity and to restructure this at the same time. At this point in time, the techniques of challenge to quit use of habitual defences and pressure towards experience of feelings is utilized.

Clinical examples

Case 1

In any case, the goal of the initial interview is to shift the patient from a state of perceived hopelessness, into being disobedient to the dictates of the punitive superego, to a position of realistic hopefulness, that allied with the therapist to end the dictate of superego and to look in an honest way to former traumatic experiences with primary caretakers in order to resolve unfinished business with them so that they can restore happiness in relationships with their attachment figures and important persons in their present life. The transcript below shows ISTDP treatment of a patient who was referred by her psychopharmacologist for an ISTDP trial therapy for treatment of mixed anxiety and depression, non-responsive to pharmacotherapy.

The patient appears for the initial interview stylishly dressed and made positive contact with the interviewer. The patient complained that she cried each day, had a lowered mood, and could not concentrate on work, since the end of a serious love affair with a married man four months earlier. She reported sleep and appetite difficulties. The patient's depression improved slightly with antidepressants, but she was static at the time of the interview. She reported passive suicidal wishes that she would die or be killed accidentally. She suffered from daily ruminations and obsessions about her ex lover and her worthlessness. This was her first serious episode of depression, which lasted more than two weeks and required medical attention. Summary of the case: the above patient a forty-eight-year-old female presented with symptoms of severe anxiety and major depression.

Th I'm glad you could make it in so quickly.
Pt Thank you. Me too.

Begins the inquiry phase:

Th So I do like to review your problem and the help I you would like me to give you. If you could state the problem again, it would be really good.
Pt So I have been seeing Dr. Ki, not for a long time, but some and he has put me on 30 mg of Citlopram everyday and my problem, I'm 41, and my problem has always been around insecurity and relationships and my parents stayed together throughout their marriage and shouldn't have. You know, my Mum would beat on my Dad and my Dad—they just had a horrible marriage to the point where my Dad was ill and dying which is about six years ago, he actually asked me not to come to his funeral.
Th I appreciate what you're telling me and it's very relevant.
Pt But go to why I'm here, exactly now, right today.
Th Exactly.
Pt I can't do relationships. I've done dumb relationships my whole life. From the point where I started to be able to do relationships, which was very late, because I'm a geek, looked like a boy until she was about 20. And nobody was interested in me and then all of a sudden things kind of shifted but I picked very, very badly, including …
The patient is giving relevant history letting the therapist know about the know about a the dysfunctional marriage of her parents, and she gives insight into a history of low self-esteem and relationships with men in which she was abused.
Th So as far as your femininity, it was a late-blooming ….
Pt Very much so.
Th Kind of a delayed process for you.

Pt Yes, I was always the one, you know, in grade school, where they put her at the bottom of the list of most attractive in the class.
Th You kind of smiled when you said that. I was curious. Why did you think it was funny?

The therapist notes the first defence- a front door defence against emotional closeness with the therapist.

Pt It's not, it's awful. (laugh)
(Striated muscle anxiety increases.)
Th So do you notice anxiety, anxiety at all?

The therapist focuses her attention towards her anxiety as she is not observing her anxiety.

Pt Yes, I'm anxious about, you know where I am at in life because I've never really wanted to and so I have terrible allergies, I'm just getting used to this. I have terrible anxieties around the fact that I always was …
Pt Uh yeah, so I'm very anxious about the fact that I keep messing up my relationships.
Th Well, that's certain an explanation for why you're anxious, but I would like to examine the anxiety that you do have cause I see it right now and I want to make sure you're observing the same phenomena that I'm observing.

She moves into her intellectualizing and externalizing defence as she escapes the anxiety caused by her wish to enter intimacy with the therapist.

Pt Okay.

The therapist encourages the development of an observing ego.

Th So where do you notice the anxiety inside?
Pt Always right here. That's where I feel sad. Is that what you mean, physically, like I have, there's a weight on my chest all the time.
Th There's a weight on your chest, but is that anxiety to you, or is anxiety something else?

Anxiety, sadness, and ignoring (defence) are fused which indicates low ego-adaptive capacity.

Pt Umm
Th That's a good question.
Pt To me anxiety …
Th To me anxiety is a sense of danger.
Pt Fear.
Th A sense of danger.
Pt Yeah, fear, yeah, cause I don't have, but nobody does. You know, like I run a start-up company, it's on the brink of disaster every moment of its life.
Th That's external.

The defences exposed so far are ignoring, intellectualization, avoidance of closeness, and smiling.

Pt Yeah.
Th Okay. But anxiety's internal.

So, on the roadmap we are at Figure 27, below.

Pt Yeah, I'm anxious about that, I'm anxious about the fact that I'm 41 and I actually did want to have kids and that may not happen and I'm anxious about the fact that I don't want to be alone and I'm anxious about the fact that maybe I shouldn't even be here in L.A. and I'm anxious about ... yeah, I'm anxious about a lot of things.

The patient reveals her chronic extroversion and tendency towards rationalization and externalization.

Th Okay, so you have anxiety and you have a lot of mental activity which is consistent with, which you keep identifying is these sources of external threat. You mind just keeps going back and forth to what the perception of what the external dangers are for you, okay. But if I could focus your attention not only on the symptoms of anxiety, but you have also complained of depression.
Pt Somewhat, yes, 'cause I had a really bad go at the beginning of the year with depression, a situation, I believe, because I had a bad relationship moment and it certainly helped to keep me going.
Th Helped to keep you going in what sense? What do you mean as far as ...?
Pt I don't hope to be hit by a car every day. Not that I would ever do anything because it's horrible, suicide, but the idea of being hit by a car was quite appealing.

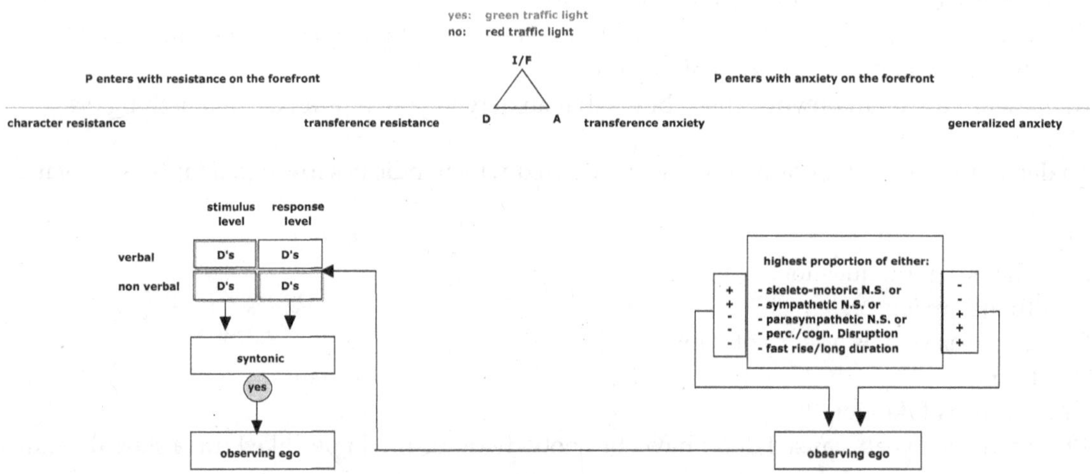

Figure 27. Depressed patient 1: road to the unconscious 1.

Therapist mentally notes the idea of a violent death and passive suicidal thoughts.

Th I see, so you were in a lot of distress, a lot of very strong emotions around a relationship at the beginning of the year and anxiety was one of those emotions. Correct, and the anxiety apparently hasn't abated or have you been anxious all your life?
Pt I'm just an anxious girl. I've always been anxious whether it was in 5th grade over a test, you know, I've always been an anxious girl.
Th Okay, so you have, what I would describe a mild to moderate case of generalized anxiety? You don't have agoraphobia or fears of this or that particular thing it's just a generalized feeling of anxiety?
Pt Hmm mm
Th And the depression got bad following the breakup of the relationship.
Pt I mean I've had depression, mostly around relationships—I go really far down when they end or I get rejected.
Th Okay, and reactive in a sense.
Pt Yes, very. It's always me and it's always, you know …
Th It's always you with …
Pt It's always my fault. If only I'd …

Defence of self-blame is added to the list.

Th You blame yourself? Okay.
Pt If I were prettier, if I were younger or if I were, whatever.

The patient gives us insight into her superego pathology with a devaluing attacking style.

Th Really? That's, you feel that's accurate feedback to yourself?
Pt No, intellectually I can probably come up with the rationale as to why it's not accurate, but it doesn't change the fact that you feel it.
Th But it's just so blaming.

This is the first attempt at making her defences dystonic to the commands of her pathologic superego.

Pt Uh huh.
Th You … I'm kind of big on you understanding defence mechanisms and to me blaming oneself in that way is a nasty defence, uhh, like cause relationships are complicated. It's not because of you being imperfect. That's what you seem to attack yourself for is, uh, uh, your imperfections or flaws.
Pt Um mm. Yeah.
Th Do you think of yourself as a perfectionist?
Pt Uhh, no. I mean I try really hard and …

Th So why do you take that stance against yourself to blame yourself when things don't go your way?

Pt Because it's mostly with relationships and the evidence is strongly in the favour of him.

Th But you said it's because you're not beautiful enough or you're not this enough or you're not …

Pt It's go to be something.

Th Or you're not young enough, or some other, you know, I mean, do you see cruelty any of, that's to me a defence, I mean it's like a, it's a way you inflict pain on yourself. You see, I'm trying to point out to you in my opinion, despite not knowing you very well, how important, I think, anxiety is in you and for you to start to pay attention to it in a different way, because you tend to rationalize and intellectualize, explain anxiety is all external and uhh, it isn't to me. Anxiety is about brain arousal and your brain has been on overdrive perhaps since childhood.

The therapist drew her attention to her additional defences of externalization, rationalization, intellectualization, and makes them dystonic by pointing out their self-defeating function.

Pt Umm mm

Th You know, we can go into why that is, I'm sure you probably already have some ideas about that.

Pt Umm mm

Th But it's important that you start to recognize that you're on overdrive.

Confrontation of patient's habitual self-neglect through compulsive achieving …

Pt Yeah, I am, I'm always on overdrive.

Th Yeah, you see that.

Pt Yeah.

Th Good. And cause you're showing me a smile again, what's coming up for you?

Defence against closeness with the therapist for the second time.

Pt Because in a weird sort of way always being on overdrive and always seeing it as my fault has also allowed me, that the word success is in my head even though I don't feel very successful right now cause I've got a very difficult situation with my company, but …

Th You're saying that …

Pt Cause I've decided that I was butt-ugly, so I needed to change that and I needed to get, you know, skinny and workout all the time and have people fix me, you know, I don't know, grow my hair or whatever it was.

Th Umm mm. Change your appearance?

Pt Yeah, and then I decided that if I was going to be ugly, then I'd better, you know, I went to Yale, I'm a lawyer, I worked in the Orient for years, I did all these things to make me …
Th To make you what?
Pt Less flawed, to make it less my fault.
Th Oh I see, to make yourself less flawed. These are in your mind, not educational treasures …
Pt To make myself no longer on the bottom of the list.
Th Yeah, they weren't educational treasures for you to enhance …
Pt No, they were as my lifeguard decisions.
Th Antidotes?
Pt Yeah. You're perfect on paper. I made myself perfect on paper.
Th Antidotes to this sense of yourself is defective and I think there's a list, isn't there, of defective defects you could …
Pt I probably could come up with a pretty good …
Th I mean in your mind, are you there? Do you get the sense of this being rather hard or impunitive, or do you think this is just a good thing? I'm not saying it hasn't paid off in certain …
Pt Yes, it paid off in certain respects. I suppose great cost as well, because here I sit and maybe if I had just been less anxious about being perfect, I would actually be happier, uglier and you know …
Th You know, you're very, very right. I can't tell whether you're just saying that cause you figured out that was what I was pointing out to you or you really mean that. I can't determine …
Pt I can't, I can't do it, so I'm not that bright because half of my problem right now is that …
Th No, I meant what you just said. Were you being sincere or were you just …
Pt Yeah.
Th … parroting or …
Pt No, I was being sincere.
Th Oh good.
Pt If I'd been, if I'd just chilled out and just been fat and ugly, maybe I'd be happier. It's ironic, but I can't do that now. I can't just go fat and ugly and mediocre anymore.
Th I can even, the way you're framing that, this extreme or that extreme, it's like you're describing like you're on compulsive trajectory.
Pt Hmmm
Th Like you, you don't have the ability to turn off the speed of the treadmill, right? I mean that's what you're …
Pt Hmm mm
Th I'm not telling you to be fat and ugly. I'm just pointing out to you that the way you're paying attention to yourself has a nasty edge to it.
Pt Hmm mm. Hmm mm, yeah.
Th You see …
Pt I think it's also based on fear because I don't want to go back to the bottom line.
Th Well, again that's what comes up right away, it's like a threat.

Pt Yeah.

Th Uhh, you're saying the next thing, if you turn down the speed of the treadmill, you're going to go backwards, not continue to go forward.

Pt And every time I have a relationship disaster I take on something else to make me more perfect, so now I'm, you know, looking at time and running marathons.

Th Okay, so let's, uh, for a minute go back to the anxiety then I'll respond to that. How is the anxiety doing? Has sit changed at all since you came in, has it modulated in any way?

Pt I've never really ever thought of myself as anxious. Depressed.

Th Um mm

Pt Coo coo *(crazy)*

Th Umm mm

Pt But not anxious, but I guess I am fearful.

Th Maybe your coo-coos, a devaluating word toward yourself?

Pt Truthful.

Th Anxious.

Pt Um mm.

Th And has it improved or is it the same, the sensations in your body?

Pt The same.

Th Okay then, let's take a more careful look at the anxiety. If you scan your body, do you have tension anywhere?

Pt Yeah, my nail is digging into my thumb.

Th And why are you doing that?

Pt Uh, I don't know.

Th Is it to inflict pain or …?

Pt I don't think so.

Th Just it's in tightness, okay. Anywhere else?

Pt In my chest.

Th Yeah, I can see. You have had a shallow breathing pattern that …

Pt Umm mm

Th Okay.

Pt It always hurts there when I get hurt.

Th Of course, that's your heart, right?

Pt Um mm

Th But the tension is the muscles wrapping around your body, tightening.

Pt Right.

Th Right. The tensing of, is a way of holding in.

Pt A pain or something.

Patient begins to move towards her anxiety (tension) and emotions. The working alliance is beginning to grab hold against her ignoring, denying, neglecting, externalizing, compulsive defences. Anxiety is now on the forefront and the therapist turns up the degree of the patient's attentiveness.

Summary

The patient appeared with a mixture of ego syntonic defences and skeletal muscle anxiety on the forefront. The defences were ignoring, smiling, blaming, devaluing, intellectualizing, rationalizing, and externalizing. Notice the box in the lower right of the roadmap where the cognitive perceptual apparatus is directed towards the physiologic and cognitive manifestations of anxiety. Soon the evaluator will move to the lower part of the chart, which is referred to as restructuring of the ego.

On the road to the unconscious we are at Figure 28, below.

Th Yeah, right, wrapping it up.
Pt Yeah.
Th Do you see any heartbeat, is the heart coming quickly or trying something else.
Pt No.
Th Okay, so sweating, flushing, any other symptoms.
Pt Tight.
Th Tight yeah. And gastro intestinal problems, you have any GI problems, you don't have that.
Pt (shakes head)
Th How about cognitive perceptual problems as far as attention, concentration, vision, being able to see clearly, blurred vision?
Pt Concentration's usually, sometimes it depends on how my mood is.
Th Hmm mm.
Pt You know, if I can focus, I'm pretty good at focusing when I get into something or you know, I go to a meeting or have to give a speech, you know, I cry.
Th Hmm mm
Pt But some days are just harder than others.

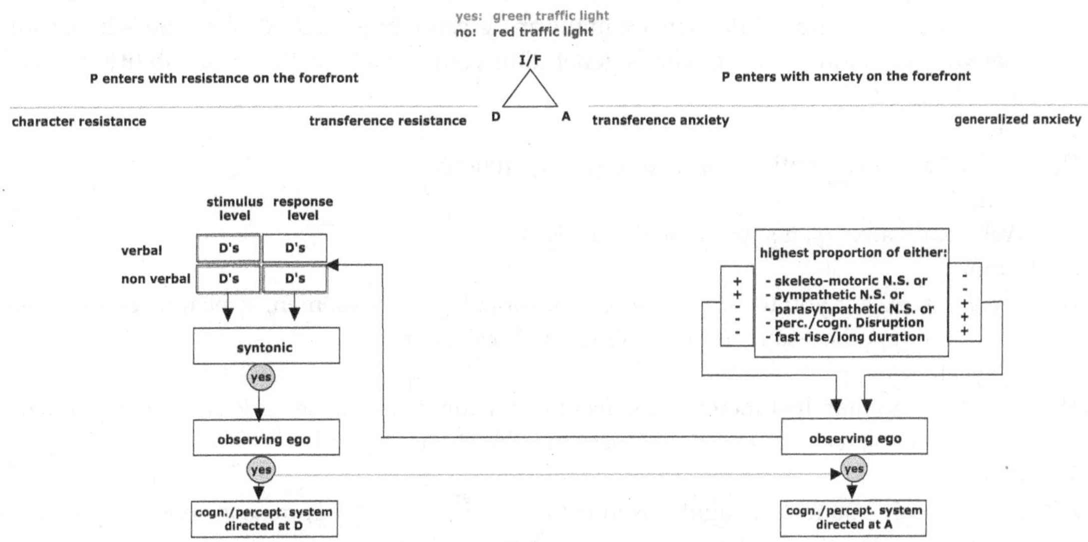

Figure 28. Depressed patient 1: road to the unconscious 2.

Th For sure.

Pt To get into stuff, but I think that's not abnormal for anybody.

Th Sure, sure. Okay.

Pt Sometimes it's hard.

Th So we mainly have as the symptoms of anxiety is a generalized sense of danger …

Pt Fear.

Th And some tension. Now I notice your legs are crossed and your hands are wrapped around. Could you sit more squarely and does that cause a change in the level of anxiety when you do that? Do you notice anything, any shifting at all of the anxiety inside?

Pt I don't think so.

Th Okay. You know you told me that there's a rela … okay if you could for just a moment because I want you to be able to observe the flow better to your body.

Pt Okay.

Th You told me that there's something that you notice in your heart that's happening and sore.

Pt In here.

Th And if you focus your attention on that, what happens to the anxiety?

Pt (big breath)

Th Increase, decrease, or stay the same?

Pt Stays the same right now.

Th A little bit of increase I thought. I thought there was a little bit of fumbling of your thumbs.

Pt Oh really?

Th Yeah. Do you see a little? You can kind of feel a little low degrees?

Pt Uh huh.

Th See, I'm trying to get you to see a dynamic here, that if you pay attention to the emotional part of you, there's a subtle increase in the anxiety, not huge, subtle, okay? So is it possible that your emotions are, uh, what's generating your anxiety, is that a possibility that you would consider?

Pt Sure.

Th And what is the emotion that you're sitting on here.

Pt Fear.

Th Well, fear's anxiety, it's the same thing, right?

Pt Umm.

Th See, I don't want you to go into these obsessions about boys, men, appearances, business. You can find a thousand and one things to obsess on, right?

Pt Oh yeah.

Th Yes, don't do that. Just focus on the feeling in your chest and see if you can identify what that is. Do you feel this wake of anxiety just then? That's good.

Pt Really?

Th I saw it yeah. You feel the tightness in your chest increase. It happens in split second, that's what I'm trying to … if I can show you on the brain where the area of your mind we're working on, so …

Pt So what is that, what is it, what do you mean?

Pt Yes.

Th You see, and I'm just trying you to open another door inside, another tool for yourself to use. Now you said this feeling in your chest is related to the event in January, is that …?

Pt Oh, probably this and other things.

Th Don't you think that's important?

Pt This and other things?

Th The fact that you have that feeling?

Pt Oh yeah.

Th You do?

Pt Yeah, good.

Th And you know that feeling and you know what it is.

Pt Um mm.

Th What is it?

Pt Well, I guess it's anxiety over being around.

Th Again, see I have a problem with that formulation. To me, that's just like recycling toxic waste. That's the message you tell yourself all the time. It's just not true. It's a way of deflecting your attention away from you. In other words, if you think about emotion (pause), you have all this emotion in your chest, okay, you're a very feeling person, okay? Emotion trying to push itself up into consciousness, but you're using anxiety as a way of distracting yourself from the emotion and then the obsessions occur, you know, so your attention goes outward and you're looking at the environment all the time, searching, searching, search for things you can fix cause it gives you a sense of control.

The therapist links the patient's anxiety with her obsessions and compulsive over achievement.

Pt Um mm.

Th And you keep upping the ante in yourself, there's more and more about yourself that you find wrong. There's more and more of this you have to fix. Now I'm trying to point out to you that it's self-destructive action.

Pt Um mm.

Th It's inefficient, it won't fix the problem that you've got, and the more energy you put in that direction, the more you're defeating yourself. If I say that to you, do you understand it?

Pt Absolutely.

Th Does it make any sense to you?

Pt Yes, because I've done a lot of that.

Th I know.

Pt I speak Chinese, because, you know, I figured if I spoke Chinese maybe that would fix it.

Th Did it?

Pt But it didn't.

Th But you've come here cause you've recognized with Dr. Ki's assistance that, you know, maybe there's a block inside of you that you're not paying attention to, and I'm kind of bringing that block to your attention.

Pt Okay.

Th Cause I think that it's not useful to sit here and listen to you describe all the things that are wrong with you.

Pt I cannot speak Japanese.

Th Well, you can eventually learn that too, but I'm not sure that's going to fix this part.

Pt Um mm

Th So do you have any inkling of what it is that you are experiencing inside? What the feeling is?

Pt (pause) The only word that's in my head is fear.

Th Fear. See, you're kind of just at the level of anxiety and the symptoms of fear are what's there. What are you feeling that you can identify as fear, one a sense of danger, you know that's … and what else?

Pt Do—wanting to …

Th Well, that's just putting a negative worst case on the danger.

Pt Yes, danger.

Th Negative forecast. But what's going on, look at your hands. You see, ignore yourself. Did you know that's a defence?

Pt What?

Th The ignoring. You ignore your physical self. Your attention doesn't go toward your physical being. It goes toward your environment. Do you see that?

Pt Yeah, I mean I've had somebody say that to me before where I was asked, you know, it was different, it was a girlfriend of mine said to me something to me. I asked her a question and she said, Oh, you know, I can't talk about that. I feel like my heart is beating really strong and that my stomach is … so let's not talk about that cause I feel like that. And I just didn't understand what she was talking about.

Th Yep. So you're blind to your own self, you see. (pause) Do you see that as a problem when I bring it to your attention? Do you see that as a problem that we should address?

Pt Probably.

Th Oh, you sound uncertain and uncommitted.

Pt Well, no, I'm not going to be uncommitted. I'm very committed to things when I'm in them. I'm desperate.

Th Yeah, but I don't want you to be uh, I mean …

Pt It doesn't work.

Th I don't want you to be nearly here if you're here. Do you follow? I like you here, but I want you to understand what I'm saying and as an equal form an opinion. I mean, you know more about the language that I know and I know about mental health than you know.

Pt So my question will be, so what?

Th You got it.

Pt So if I'm ignoring myself physically, what does that mean?
Th That means you're blind to your anxiety, you can't regulate it on your own behalf. You have no, you have no …
Pt So I don't realize when it's hitting.

It is obvious that the patient has low ego-adaptive capacity; despite the largest portion of her anxiety being skeletal motoric, she cannot differentiate the poles of the triangle of conflict, nor can she accurately observe stimulus feeling, anxiety, and defence. The therapist patiently takes her through each pole of experience.

Th And you don't understand its cause. You create faulty causality in your mind. You're, you're chasing sources that are all external to yourself. Again, you seem to have understood what I said before so let me say it again so make sure it gets through. Here's the emotions: (*The therapist holds a glass multi-coloured paper weight as an example.*) You said they're linked to a million different things and I believe you. They rise and give you anxiety and then instead of attending to, this is your attention, instead of attending to your anxiety and trying to get out what you're feeling, your attention turns to the outside world, to the next language, to the next challenge, the next task, the next defect that you can fix. That's compulsive behaviour.
Pt Okay.
Th It gets you nowhere. It's self-defeating because it doesn't address this. This is where the problem lies. Why else would you see a psychotherapist if you didn't want to address this.
Pt No, I do want to address that. It …
Th Good. So then the ignoring becomes a problem, you say.
Pt Okay
Th You see, ignoring yourself, self-ignoring is a problem. Not because I say so. I just want you to see the logic. Do you see the logic there?
Pt I see the logic.
Th And how does that effect you when you see the logic?
Pt (pause)
Th It's self-ignoring, it's self-neglecting, or the direct opposites of introspective psychotherapy. (long pause) So do you want to take a careful look at what's in the chest?
Pt Yes, definitely.
Th So describe what's the sensation of, not the tension part, but the feeling part? (short pause) You said there was … the minute you walked in, you said "I have an awful lot going on in my heart."
Pt Um mm. Well, it's just always really tight.
Th That's your tension.
Pt Right.
Th Remember, the tension is just the, just … you're just wrapping muscle around that part.
Pt Right.
Th That's all you're doing is tensing up around that heart, but it's not Chandra with what this is, what's there, what is that part?

Pt It's very sad.
Th Oh you're sad.
Pt Lonely, sad.
Th Could we see the sadness?
Pt Yeah.
Th How does it feel?
Pt Sad. (Shows the full pathway of grief)
Th It goes right to your eyes.
Pt Yeah.
Th And you want to cry.
Pt Yeah, cause it's sad.
Th Okay, I'm sure it is, but I need to know about your sadness and to understand it to get a more comprehensive look for you.
Pt Uhh (pause). I guess always being alone, like being, even when I'm with somebody, I always choose a person who is not going to love me for whatever reason, so just always just being alone. Even being up here in LA, it's very alone for me.
Th Uh huh.
Pt So it's alone wherever I am.
Th Okay, so you, you have a sadness. If I listen carefully and let me restate it in my language.
Pt Yep.
Th And if I don't get it right, feel free to correct me, okay?
Pt Yep.
Th You're sad cause you mistreat yourself. If your desire …
Pt I do mistreat myself.
Th If your desire is to have an attached relationship and you go out of your way to select people that have no interest in having attached relationships, then loneliness is the enviable consequence in that.
Pt Great, I totally, I know.
Th So you mistreat yourself.
Pt Yes.
Th And you're sad about doing this do yourself.
Pt Yes.
Th Or …
Th Do you realize the evidence is incontrovertible here, okay? You're a brave woman; look at the evidence, okay? You're cruel to yourself when you don't have to be, when you need kindness, you're cruel. When you need to be intelligent, you're dumb.
Pt Yeah.
Th Okay?
Pt Yeah.
Th When you have to satisfy your longings, you go out of your way to frustrate them and you ignore and you neglect yourself here. I mean there's obviously a lot going on that you are going to trust in you …
Pt Hmm

Th So I want to know, okay, who was your role model in this behaviour, I mean, obviously you didn't learn this on your own. Someone taught you how to be this way, okay? So if your two parents, for example, who was the one that taught you to ignore yourself and neglect yourself and to be cruel to yourself? Who was your prime instructor in this pattern of mistreatment?

Pt Umm (pause). I don't know. It's not as though I was beaten.

Th Um mm.

Pt Um, my dad was very stiff upper lip British. Whenever there was a problem, he'd just say, You're just a grain of sand on the beach, like it doesn't matter, just buck up.

Th Okay, you call that kind or cruel.

Pt But he was the kindest person on the planet.

Th You call that kind …?

Pt It was probably not the best thing to say.

Th Cause what did it make you feel?

Pt Like I didn't have a right to feel sad. He would always be really mad at me when I was down and you know, he had people for a cocktail party or something and couldn't come up because I was too sad and he'd be really mad at me and call me selfish.

Th So, again rather than getting kindness, you got speeches, lectures and you were criticized, called names, called selfish?

Pt Yeah.

Th It makes a lot of sense to me now.

Pt But he was a really nice person, that's the thing, he just couldn't deal with emotions and he was terribly abused in his own marriage by my Mum who was horrible to Dad.

Th So we have another side to take a look at, so your mother was cruel to you and horrible to you.

Pt Yeah, she, she's, she's just not, she's always, you know, very much into appearances and very much into that and she would say awful things to me.

Th Like, for example?

Pt You'll get back, you're a bitch, blah, blah, blah. She'd throw forks at me. About two weeks before my dad died, six years ago, I was sitting in the basement. I was living in London at the time when I was home and she came down and started like pounding on me and umm …

Th Physically pounding on you, physically, okay. So she assaulted you?

Pt Um mmm.

Th And you were doing what?

Pt A load of laundry.

Th But in her mind what were doing to provoke her, just breathing?

Pt Honestly, I was doing all of the laundry. She thought it wasn't appropriate that I would be doing a load of laundry.

Th Oh, I see, I see. So she was the one who addressed you as being imperfect and she took a punitive stance towards you.

Pt My brother put her in a car and sent her to her sister's.

Th Now tell me again, at what age did your mother start to define you as imperfect, when did she show that you were not her precious little jewel, her treasure?

Pt I don't know, I mean (pause), I don't know, I don't know, I just never, you know, I'm just the ugly duckling who liked physics. You know she was a model and she, you know, very into status and my dad was an accountant, you know. So everybody was imperfect. My mother was unhappy because dad didn't make enough money; I was ugly and my brother gay. I mean her life is a disaster as far as she's unconcerned. Now she's got an unmarried 41 year old daughter and a gay son.

Th So again, when you look at yourself through your mother's eyes …

Pt I'm a disaster.

Th I see. So now we understand why you're on the treadmill.

Pt Um mm.

Th You're nodding. Tell me why you're on the treadmill?

Pt Because I've always been trying to be perfect, prettier, smarter, more languages, richer boyfriends.

Th To meet her criteria.

Pt Um mm.

Th I see, so your mother put you on this planet to enhance her stature.

Pt Yes, very much so.

Th And if you didn't do that, you were what, shit?

Pt Pretty much. "We spent a lot of money on you, Sally, and you went to Yale."

Th Yep, you must have a lot of feelings about what we're discussing.

Pt Yeah, I'm angry at my Mum, but it doesn't, you know …

Th Know what?

Pt Umm.

Pt Yeah, but it's weird cause I don't like … my father was the nicest person on the planet. Like when he was diagnosed with cancer, he said to me, Sally, I've always done to others as I would have done unto myself, so if there's a God up there, he can come at me. Everybody loved him, he was hilarious, he was generous to a fault and you know he was a good, good person.

Th I'm sure, I'm sure he was.

Pt He just couldn't deal with emotions, like I never got hugged. Hugged, I was never hugged by my parents. And told that they loved me!

The patient communicated that she understood her problem in terms of the triangle of conflict, showed increased motivation to feel, and gave two strong specific examples of attachment trauma with both her mother and father. This turned a red light into a green light. This is now the right time to pressure towards experience.

On the road to the unconscious, we are at Figure 29, on the next page.

Th And when you tell me that, what do you notice inside, uhh, if your touching goes to you? What do you notice in your body there if you take a stance that you're not worthless?

Pt For what?

Th I guess. You don't know, what do you observe?

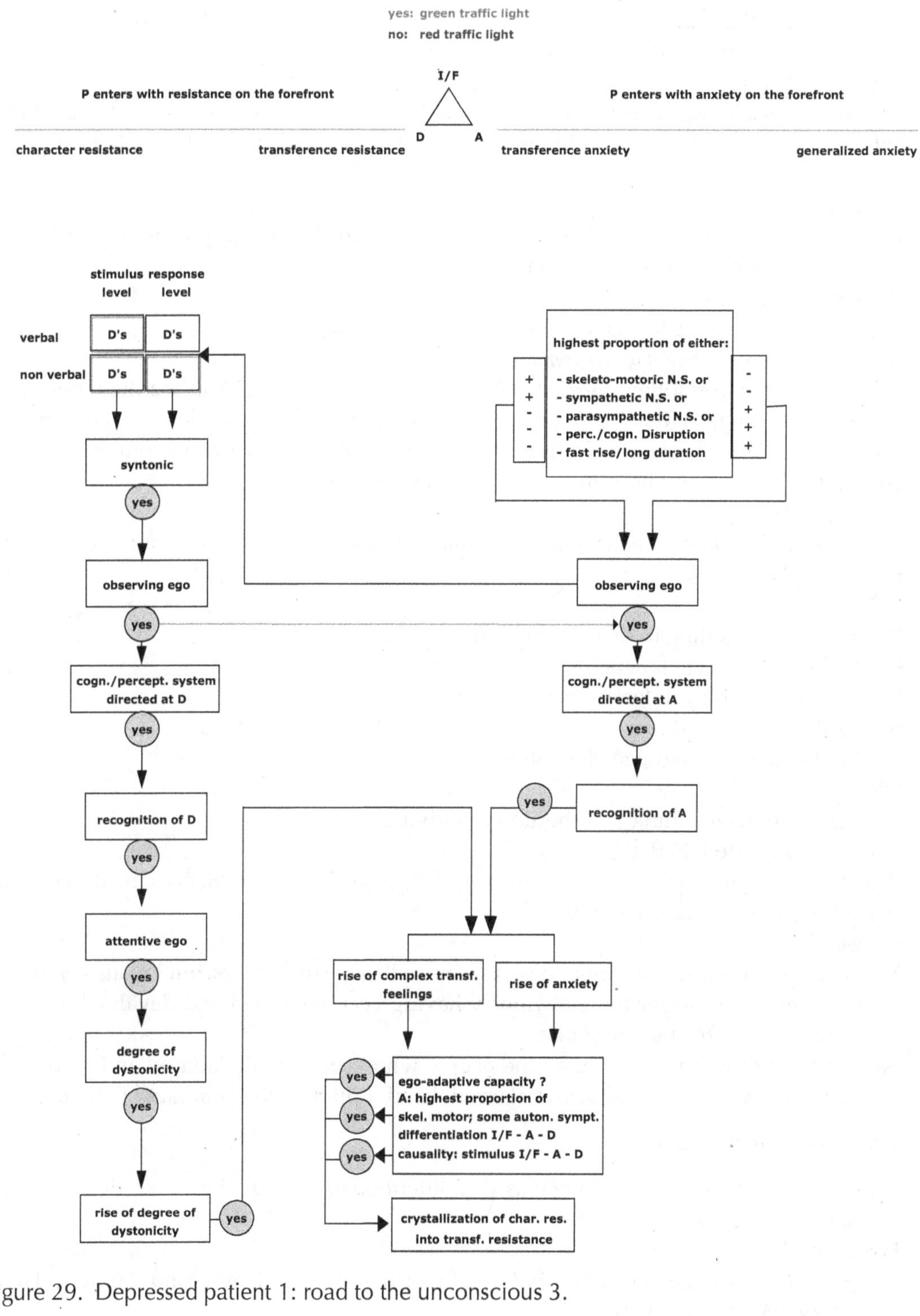

Figure 29. Depressed patient 1: road to the unconscious 3.

Pt Sadness of anything in my body and the sadness is always here, but I don't feel …

Th How do you know it's there? You do observe it.

Pt Yeah, I guess I do.

Th Of course, you do. But you see, what you don't do is place any value on it. It's as if I'm talking to a robot who follows the instructions that her mother and her father gave her to a tee.

Pt Um mm.

Th I'm not saying your father wasn't a wonderful man, but I'm telling you as an attachment figure for closeness and intimacy and emotional connectiveness …

Pt Yeah, he wasn't actually.

Th He doesn't get a very good grade, does he?

Pt No. (crying) [*breakthrough of self-compassion … grief #1*]

Th No. Why would you follow those flawed instructions to the tee? You see the ignoring is your way of being obedient to those instructions. That's where your defence mechanisms come from in order to comply to the faulty attachment instructions from your mother and your father. You weren't born this way, this is acquired pathology.

Pt You're right.

Th So why comply? Do you really agree with that, do you really agree that your emotions are that important?

Pt No. No.

Th You wouldn't be sitting in that chair if you agreed.

Pt No, I'd be out learning Japanese.

Th Right. So why don't you learn a new language?

Pt It doesn't seem to work.

Th No, I'm talking the language of emotions.

Pt Oh.

Th That's the language I think you should be studying.

Pt (pause) So how do I do that?

Th Well, tell me what you observe, like any other language. What are you noticing down there as a reaction to this conversation?

Pt (pauses)

Th You were saying earlier the emotion was sadness. It came up to tears, but I'm also wondering whether there's anger there obviously having been neglected and devalued by your mother and neglected by your father?

Pt (pause) Yes, but when I think of all the people who were sexually abused and who were beaten up and who were, you know, starved, I had it pretty good compared to that.

Rationalization, minimization.

Th You know, if I measured how long was your attention to yourself, how long do you think you say it was?

Pt Five seconds.

Th I think you're being generous. So you're not worth more than five seconds? (pause) How many billion people in the world?

Pt Lots, about six billion.
Th So that's a lot of attention that you pay to other people. And put you as the most unimportant grain of sand. That's your compliance to your father, you see.
Pt But isn't it unfair that I should be fucked up like this and I haven't had it as bad as everybody else, a lot of other people.

The patient is identified with her parents' devaluation; she received the message that she was ungrateful, that "other people have it worse than you", and that's what she did.

Th You clearly learned the messages and applied them brilliantly, but where have they gotten you?
Pt Nowhere.
Th You notice how hard you're fighting me to sustain those messages? (pause)
Pt It makes no sense.
Th Very well. (long pause)
Pt (crying) So instead … [*breakthough of self-compassion grief* #2]
Th I'm just letting you know what's going on inside. Please don't try to perform for me, I don't need that, I don't want that. I would just like to know and understand what is going on inside of you when you see what's going on between us. You do see it, you do understand.
Pt Well, I'll try not to cry all the time, but …
Th But now you're crying … for you
Pt And most of the time, I mean I'm not, most of the time, I mean, I can put myself into a good mood anytime, not anytime, but you know, if I think too much, then I'll just cry and then …
Th But what are you thinking about right now?
Pt I guess just how sad I am.
Th Why are you so sad?
Pt Because I don't like my life, I don't like … Let me just tell you why I'm so sad, is because I've been a very good daughter to my mother and I've been a very good daughter to my father but very bad to myself (sobbing). … [breakthough of grief over self-sabotage #1]

On the road to the unconscious, we are at Figure 30, on the next page.

Th It's a crisis in you.
Pt Yeah.
Pt Just how weird, you know I don't like my mother and my biggest fear is becoming her?
Th Well, you're wise, I think you are well on the way. The cruelty that you're showing me, the nastiness towards you, those are her messages towards you to a tee. You listen to those voices very long and before you know it, you're going to treat everybody else the way she treated you.
Pt Yeah.
Th Now is that your goal?
Pt No.

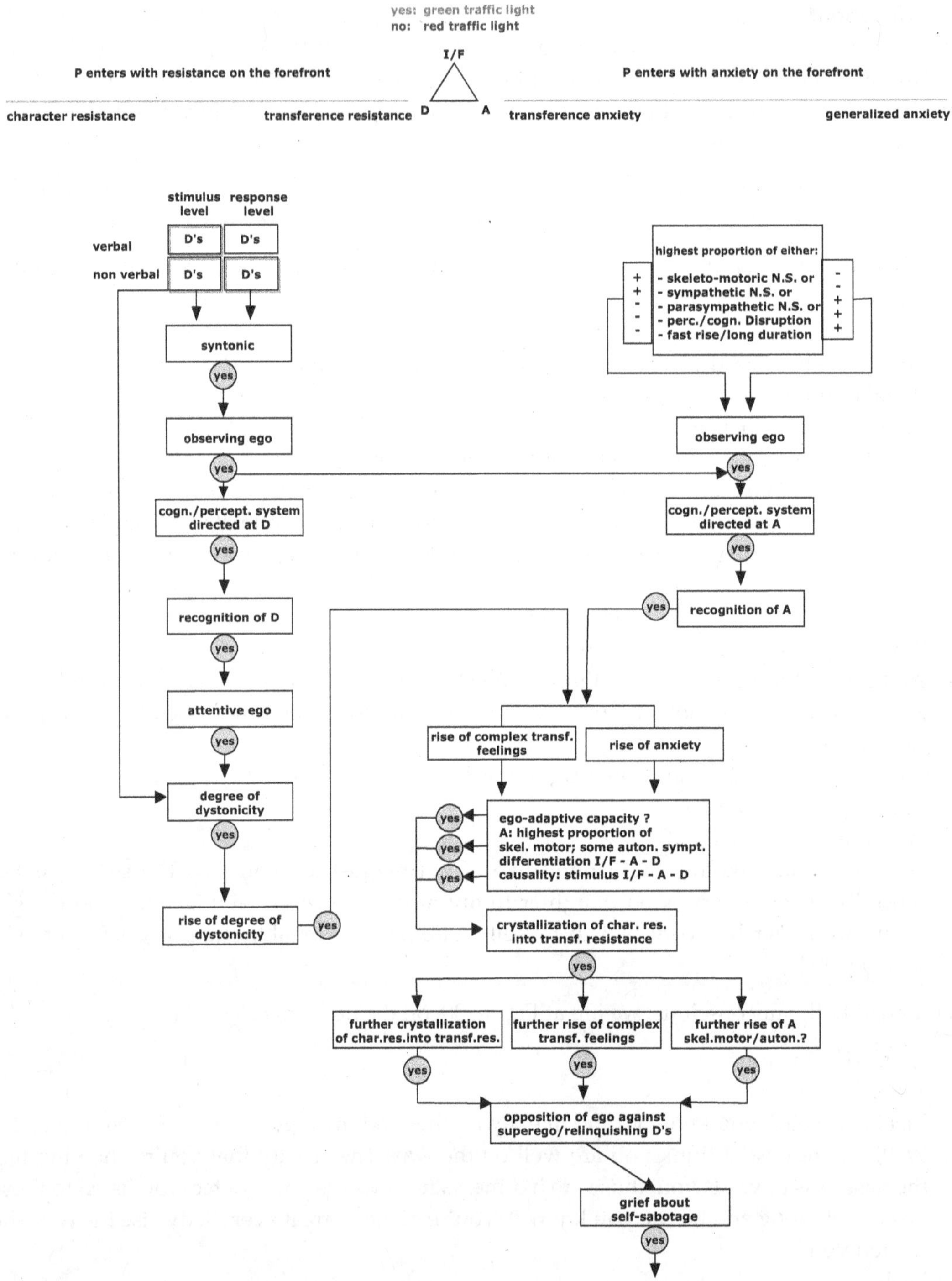

Figure 30. Depressed patient 1: road to the unconscious 4.

Th What s your goal? What do you want to model for?

Pt To not treat myself and not treat others the way she treated my dad, myself and my brother. My brother left … Yes. But I see in me too ironically the more decent people that I have dated, I feel myself turning into somebody who, I don't know, gets exasperated like my Mum, which maybe is why I end up with people who are mean to me, because they can be mean to me and I can't be mean to them.

Th They are your Mum.

Patient notices her identification with her pathological superego. Her mother the perpetrator and her father, the victim. With passive, nice guys she is the bitch (Mum) and with nasty mean guys she is the pleasing victim (Dad).

Pt Yeah.

Th You've just been dating your Mum, that's what you did, and you're compelled to imitate your father.

Pt And I found my dad in this last one that I dated except he was married. And so I couldn't have either of them really, neither Mum nor Dad.

Pt Umm, and then of course the next word that pops into my head is, "you're a looser".

Th Really? The nasty voice came in.

Pt Well, it hasn't been fixed in all these years.

Th The minute your mother gets worked up, you become passive and compliant like your father. So stand up for yourself, speak back.

Pt I'm very compliant, very, very compliant with bad men too. Do anything they want.

Th I understand. So take a first step here while your mother tries to sabotage your hope. Speak up for yourself. What would you like to say back?

Pt No, maybe this time it will work. I'm sure she …

Th Stop being so weak. You can't be weak with her. Stand up for yourself and tell her to back off. Speak up.

Pt But it's loud because she's saying how …

Th You get louder.

Pt … fix this.

Th I don't want to hear that crap. You get louder. Stop listening to the devaluing messages. Our relationship creates literally again five seconds of hope and then she comes in and squashes it. Kind or nasty?

Pt Nasty.

Th Yeah. How's that feel? Assert yourself here instead of being compliant.

Pt Well, in fact she doesn't know I asserted myself because she's not here.

Th Oh, well she's always here. Don't go back to denying. You think I'm just sitting here hallucinating. Do you think I haven't met your mother already.

Pt Yeah, cause she's in me I suppose.

Th Yeah. That's the mother that's the problem.

Pt Well, I think that I'm a nice person.

Th Okay.

Pt But sometimes when I'm with, like if I were dating a really nice person and he were weak or something, I get mean.

Th You become the …

Pt My Mum.

Th Yeah! So your Mum and Dad act out their dysfunction in you?

* * *

Th Be careful here, because you're going to create …

Pt Destructive.

Th And then the self-destructive part of yourself takes over, and then you go back to being compliant and loyal to the messages of your mother and your father. That's all that happens. You don't know how to conduct your life from the healthy place.

Pt Okay.

Th Cause there are ways you could remember. That means that the trauma was already in you.

Pt But it wasn't as if I was left lying in a crib.

Th How do you know?

Pt Well, maybe I was because I was born with dislocated hips and I was in a cast to here for like a year, but I mean how long I don't know.

Th I don't see any other way for you to get over this, put this behind you. How did you need to know everything there is to know about you. What wouldn't you want to know? See what I mean?

Pt I guess the old adage, what's done is done, and so just …

Th Uh uh uh. That's your father's voice. Speak better, Dad.

Pt My Dad, if I need to know in order to make myself better.

Th You were a very loving man, Dad, but you were very misguided when it came to the attachment needs of a young girl.

Pt You were very misguided when it came to the attachment needs of a young girl and your own attachment needs.

(At this point in the interview, when the grief subsided, the therapist elected to take a 15-minute break after 90 minutes.)

Th Before the break, we were trying to understand your anxiety and depression. As we began to explore the issues we found that your dad was a loving man but was avoidant of his and your emotions. Your Mum, it seems, was angry and envious and unhappy with him for his lack of money and you for your lack of beauty. You said that you identify with your Dad in relationships at times and with your mother at times. When we tried to address your feelings about your current relationships, we found a number of habits which interfere with your ability to address your feelings: intellectualizing, ignorning, minimizing, denying, repressing, joking, smiling, passivity, compliance, and defiance. In order to address your depression, we would have to overcome those mechanisms which you use to keep your feelings at bay. Am I clear?

The therapist summarizes the defences which the patient used in the first session:

Pt Yes.
Th So you mentioned earlier that the January break-up was particularly traumatic, so if we could practise these new skills. If we could look at you through these new eyes, could you tell me what it was that was so traumatic, what was so hurtful to you in January?
Pt Maybe I should go all the way back to certainly I did something that I shouldn't have done, which was get involved with a married man.
Th Okay.
Th So there was a certain degree of recklessness. I think you're describing lack of personal self-protection.
Pt Yeah, I should have never gotten involved.
Pt I umm (pause) (sigh) … he was just so loving to me and we had a lot in common because we were at Yale together and we didn't see each other for years and then my mentor passed away a year ago, my mentor, one of my best friends and somebody I was very very close with. He uh …
Th So there was a lot of positive energy in this relationship. How about the sexual part?
Pt Everything was absolutely beyond perfect.
Th Um mm. So you felt loved?
Pt More loved than I've ever felt in my whole life.
Th Did you feel attractive?
Pt Uh huh.
Th And you felt desirable?
Pt Everything.
Pt Except now, we don't speak.
Pt So, so we met in New York in January and just decided that the best thing to do was to just let it go because you can't do anything.
Th We decided or …
Pt Well, he decided. I had no say in the matter. I mean I would have wanted to … for himself and …
Th And what did you feel internally?
Pt Abandoned.
Th How does that mean, what do you mean?
Pt Well, I mean he let me go!
Th Yeah, is that abandoned or is that rejected?
Pt Rejected? Yes.
Th He chose her over you, or his family with the package deal.
Pt And it becomes very difficult because I got used to waking up every morning to, you know, with him and talking with him during the day and emailing before I went to sleep.
Th Yeah, you were in love.
Pt Very much so.
Th Yeah.
Pt Very, very, very much so, and it's been very, very, very, very difficult.

Th But may I point out to you. You seem, for whatever reason, reluctant to open the door as to how you felt.

Pt Well, I know how I felt. I was madly in love with him. I found the person that I wanted to be with for the rest of my life and … (crying) Oh, I'm not sure.

Th Oh well, it's a line, you know what I mean? But known how you feel to have loved and lost. I see anxiety. No, that's not how you feel. You shut down. You, you, that's a defence. You shut down your feelings. You shut them down.

Pt How?

Th With a defence. Empty. You can make yourself empty.

Pt I feel really sad.

Th I'll credit that.

Pt I felt really …

Th I think it was grief.

Pt Oh yeah, yeah, there was definitely grief.

Th Good. Then you cried?

Pt All the time.

Th Good. You know what tears are in that situation? Tears are the liquid of lost love.

Pt Yes

Th It's your body releasing the energy …

Pt Yeah

Th … of the love that you felt, and you're mourning the loss of the love.

Pt Yes

Th Cause this is really big for you. You're implying it was the first time you really felt love in a really complete head to toe kind of way.

Pt Yeah, and I did not feel like my Mum towards him, even though he was just a really nice guy—it could be because he was unavailable, you know, like I just, I don't think so.

Th I think you are evaluating something that doesn't sound worthy of devaluation. You took a risk and lost.

Pt Yeah. (still crying)

Th So I still believe you're shut down. You're not feeling what I call all of your feelings about the rupture in the relationship about the rejection. There had to be anger

Pt It's hard to be anger at him.

Th What makes it hard?

Pt I, I don't know. It's just hard to be angry at him. I mean he didn't …

Th What makes it hard?

Pt I think cause I love him so much and I think he's …

Th Who's the person who says loving is incompatible with anger. I mean you're talking to me as though these things are scientific facts and they're not.

Pt Yeah, I suppose that's true, so I could be angry at him.

Th Yeah. And for some reason or other you're shutting the anger down.

Pt Well, maybe I could be angry at my father too but I can't be angry at my father cause he …

Th He is very much like your father.

Pt He *is exactly* my father.

Th Yet, you've vaulted up the anger. "You've said I'm not allowed to feel angry." You've said, "I'm not allowed to feel angry towards my father."

Pt Well, okay, yeah.

Th Who says you're not allowed to feel angry towards your father? Who's the author of that commandment?

Pt Yeah.

Pt That he (the ex-lover) even sort of opened any kind of doors when he knew he couldn't follow through. I don't know who he thinks he is for ditching me the way he did and go back to his shit wife.

The patient has the first breakthrough of visible anger towards her ex lover/father.

Th Now you're so much more real now. Do you feel that anger as you were expressing it? Were you able to …?

Pt Yeah.

Th What did it feel like as you put it into words?

Pt It doesn't get through.

Th Cause remember what our goal is here is to teach you new principles of mental health that are tried and true, not these messages of vaulting it up.

Pt Um mm.

Th No, that's not the right way to do it. So what was it like to just express the anger just in the moment? Of course, it doesn't get him back, but just what's it feel like to just put your anger out there? Good, neutral or negative?

Pt It feels good, it feels good, but then you hear about forgiveness, she forgave in order to move on.

Her hedonic system (perhaps dopaminergic system) is being restored to health.

Th So did we get in touch with all of the anger or just the tip of the iceberg?

Pt I, I don't feel, I mean I'm angry, but I'm not, that's not the primary thing.

Th But how do you know, how do you know if you put the anger in a vault immediately, in a split second, if you just locked it up tight? Cause I saw you *seething* actually when you were putting your anger into words.

Pt Well, I'm probably seething at a lot of things that are on top of Roger and at least he's a person who has treated me in a weird sort of way better than anybody else.

The patient uses defence of minimization and diversification.

Th And not because if you seal it over, I would tell you you're seeing Dr. Ki and you're on the psychoactive medications because of this depression that surrounds these feelings.

The patient links repressed and suppressed grief, anger to depression.

Pt Hm mm

Th Correct?

Pt Yes.
Th So they've got to be big feelings.
Pt Yeah, I'm very sad and I'm very scared.
Th Okay, you want to talk about sad and what else do you want to talk about?
Pt Anger.
Th Do you have a right to anger or no?
Pt No, because I got myself into this pickle. My father would not speak to me if he knew what I was doing or what I have done.

The patient declares her loyalty to her pathologic superego.

Th I see.
Pt He would say it was reprehensible and wrong and I should be shamed of myself.
Th So if you want to punish yourself by banishing your right to have anger, you know what you're left with?
Pt Not much.
Th Yes, depression.

The therapist separates the ego from the pathologic control by the superego.

Pt Yeah.
Th So pick your poison, which do you want to do? Punish yourself or do you want to reclaim your right to have anger?
Pt (crying) Yeah, I could be very angry at Roger.
Th Could be or are? Look at the anxiety …
Pt Why I am, but it's …
Th You are but you're not important enough to acknowledge your anger? Pay attention to …
Pt Yeah, it's not about important enough, it's about …
Th What?
Pt The anger is somewhat tempered by, it's a lot tempered by the fact that I'm madly in love with him still so …
Pt I'm angry that he didn't …
Th I know why you're angry and how it feels. Do you notice where I keep directing your attention? This is what I want you to do every day of your existence, not just when you're sitting in this chair. How does it feel, your anger? Investigate it because it's important, it's an important part of you.
Pt I feel.
Th Yes, don't convert it into anxiety for goodness sakes. It'll just create more arousal, more stress hormones and that's the last thing in the world you need. And don't get compulsive and learn another language. Investigate the anger. You suppressed your anger, didn't you?
Th I can see you going into shock is the first thing I see on your face, like get a little drifty.
Pt Yeah, not shock cause I didn't expect anything else.
Th But the intensity of the emotion causes you to get shocky. You kind of look like a deer in the headlights on your face, that's the way you look.

Pt Yeah, cause I, I didn't know how I was going to keep going because of such a great loss.
Th What does that mean? Did you think of suicide?
Pt No, I wanted to hit by a bus which is different from suicide.
Th Well, what, why do you mean you want to be hit by a bus?
Pt I wouldn't have jumped in front of the bus, I was just hoping it would jump onto the sidewalk and hit me cause it would feel better not to feel anything.
Th But wouldn't that be a powerful force against you?
Pt What do you mean?
Th The bus.
Pt Yeah.
Th Powerful force against you. Now do you think of anger as a force in you?
Pt Yeah.
Th It's so common to do that because you didn't want to have to feel the force of your own anger. Now I suggest to you that you have a powerful anger.
Pt So what do I do with that? Feel it, but how do I feel it?
Th Well, well, if you just listen to what I said to you about the projection, is that helpful just to learn about that mental process? Remember I said if you learn about …
Pt Yeah.
Th Your mental processes, your values and your feelings, all your feelings, that's your mental process. It's like you have a very small container for your anger or your rage. You're not allowed to feel it for very long. The other place you send it is into a black hole, depression. Do you study physics? So you know about black holes, right? What do they consume?
Pt Everything.
Th Energy, yeah. Matter, energy. So your energy is being redirected away from God into the black hole.
Pt As opposed to?
Th At him.
Pt So make a mental picture. But why is it better to direct it at him?
Th Bear with me for you asked that question. You'll understand in a minute. Direct it towards him. What would happen if the bus went towards him?
Pt Well, I wouldn't want that.
Th Why not?
Pt Cause I don't want him just to die.

The patient uses the defence of negation.

Th Why not?
Pt Well, it would be easier if he died cause then I wouldn't have to think about him roaming about on the planet with his wife.
Th Of course. So you do want to think about him dying.
Pt Yeah, guess so. It would have been easier if he had died.
Th So what would he look like if he were run over by the bus?
Pt He wouldn't exist. He'd be crushed, wouldn't he?

Pt Yeah.
Th So picture him, not you. What would you do after the bus crushed him?
Pt Guess I would think about his funeral cause I wouldn't go.
Th Immediately though, when you look at him. Can you see as a corpse there?
Pt Yeah.
Th What would you do as the grieved party, what would you do with his corpse in the moment?
Pt I'd be sad.
Th And what would you do?
Pt I'd probably sit next to him or something.
Th Good. That's a beautiful image. And tell me what would be inside of your heart after he was destroyed by your rage?
Pt Oh, I feel guilty just I'd just killed him.
Th How does that feel?
Pt Not so good.
Th What does that mean, not so good? I mean physically. I'm always asking physical sensations. What do you notice with this? What do you feel after murdering your lover who rejected you? How does the guilty side feel?
Pt Don't feel anything.
Th You're kind of getting shocky?
Pt I guess so.
Pt Yeah, but I see myself trying to put him back together. (tears)
(pause)
Th If you accept that you can't put him back together, then where would you lay him to rest?
Pt I guess I'd probably take him to his favourite tree in the south of France and bury him there.
Th How would you bury him? Would you dig the hole yourself?
Pt Get a shovel and um bury him there.
Th Hm mm.
Pt (sigh) Put lots of lavender around it. He liked lavender. (crying)
Th Hm mm.
Pt And that's it.
Th How do you put him in the ground, do you put him in as best you can and if you see his corpse down there in the ground and you were to express your good-bye, how would you say good-bye?
Pt Well, I guess I want to say, Roger I'm sorry for killing you.
Th Well say it.
Pt I'm sorry for killing you because I over reacted. I think of him with his wife. I see her as the same bitch as my mother who didn't deserve my father.
(pause)
Th So tell him I killed you.
Pt I killed you ...

Th Because …

Pt He mistreated me. And he shouldn't have. You can't do a thing about his wife cause if I hadn't killed you, you would have lived in misery with her.

Th I can see in your heart and in your mind and in your eyes, that you still love him even though he's in the grave, so don't …

Pt I'll always still love him, I'll always love him.

Th Tell him in the grave.

Pt I'll always love you but you were really rotten to me, really rotten.

Th Because you …

Pt Because you took advantage of me and you knew that you didn't have the balls to stand up for yourself and leave somebody who mistreats you like my Mum mistreated my Dad, and …

Th And but I've come to understand the connection.

Pt And I've come to understand the connection …

Th Between you and my Dad.

Pt Between—I always understood the connection. But I know …

Th Tell him.

Pt That you are ruining your life like my father ruined his life. And I tried to rescue my father and I couldn't, and I tried to rescue you and couldn't, so I think I'll just run you over with a bus. It's easier.

Th And your understanding yourself …

Pt And I'm understanding myself …

Th And your need …

Pt And my need …

Th To rescue men who take a castrated position …

Pt To rescue men who take a castrated position …

Th And the futility …

Pt And the futility …

Th Of those efforts …

Pt Of those efforts.

Th And I will only end up …

Pt And I will only end up …

Th Destructive to me …

Pt Destructive to me.

Th So when I bury you …

Pt So when I bury you …

Th I'm also burying my depression …

Pt I'm also burying my depression …

Th Because I no longer have to protect …

Pt Because I no longer have to protect …

Th You, my father from my rage …

Pt But that doesn't do me any good with that.

Th Well, again if you get this out of your system, if you get the need to rescue castrated men from their misery that they impose on themselves, I think it would be worth it. That's the whole thing.

Pt Yeah, yeah, yeah. (crying) But Roger was really the only one I really loved besides my Dad.

Th See, you chastise yourself for the wrong reasons. You see, you accept impossible missions. You over estimate ability to make gold out of lead .... I hope you would give up that belief that your love can transform a man from being a wounded bird into being an eagle.

Pt But the eagles end up hurting me too.

The patient tells a story of being set up with by a matchmaker with a successful film-maker who devalued her for being perfect on paper but too old.

Pt Well, he considered himself to be, you know, a diva. He's ...

Th I don't give a shit what he considers himself to be. What does that statement mean?

Pt It means I don't know. It means ...

Th It's devaluation.

Pt Yeah, it is. So he totally devalued me. He totally knew I was perfect on paper and he ...

Th And you know what's wrong with you.

Pt And I said, I know, I spoke with Janet and she told me ...

Th You know what's wrong with you? You accept devaluation.

Pt But we've all been with people and not, you know, liked them for whatever reason.

Th You accept devaluation.

Pt So what should I say in that instance?

Th Okay, who's talking to you when they say that? Who is he enacting?

Pt My mother.

Th And what was your impulse?
(pause)

Pt To stab him with a large butcher knife in his throat and what his eyes bulges.

Th And then.

Pt Cut off his penis and testicles and put then in his throat.

Th Can you see the colour of his eyes?

Pt I think so.

Th Good.

Pt They're blue-grey, my mother's eyes. The same eyes that cut me to ribbons and made me feel like I was nothing. I remember wanting to kill her when she verbally demolished my dad. I loved him so much. Why wouldn't he stop her? I wanted to protect him. Am I so awful wanting to kill my mother because I loved him?

Pt (Sobbing.)

Th But we have two corpses, one of your Dad (Roger) as well as your mother. Perhaps you were rageful at him as well for his passivity and unavailability.

Pt Umm, my Dad ...
(pause)

Th He was a big disappointment to you.
Pt He was a big disappointment?
Th To you.
Pt To me? Yeah, probably.
Th And you never got over it. You see, the severe guilt is towards the rage for your father and the compulsion is towards self-punishment.
(pause)
Th Children that are ignored, it doesn't mean that they don't have emotions. They have high-octane emotions, so you're feeling unprotected by your father and rejected, yet you adored the man so you want to kill him because he's not protecting you, he's hanging you out to dry with your narcissistic mother and he's not even protecting himself from her so he's showing you the role model of a castrated uh, man. You have rage for him, you kill him …
Pt Hm mm.
Th You feel guilty …
Pt Hm mm.
Th Oh my God, I'm unworthy. All I deserve, you know, either the predator men or the castrated men, that's the only thing I'm going to bring into my life, is predators or castrated men and I'm going to go pretending to myself, okay? That's there's something wrong with me. That's my cover story that I'm not valuable enough, that I'm an nerd, that I'm this, that I'm that. You're none of those. You're just a guilty little girl who wants to be punished cause she's so angry at the dad that she loves so much. (sigh) How much of that can you repeat?
Pt Um. (pause) Uh (clears throat) … a nerd, ugly duckling, it's just a cover story because I go after predators or castrated men because that's self-punishing because of the anger I feel for my father who …
Th The guilt, remember that feeling, guilt.
Th You had the guilt when you were sitting next to a …
Pt But I didn't feel guilt, I just felt like I was sitting next to Roger.
Th You told me it was guilt. I tried to get you to focus on it, but you said see ya.
Pt Right, but I …
Th You think the guilt caused disassociation?
Pt So guilt is supposed to feel like my ankle hurts, or …
Th Yes, guilt is unbearable, intolerable.
Pt So how does it feel?
Th Painful.
Pt Like a physical pain?
Th If you go there, but you don't go there, you don't let yourself go that deep. You get anxious and just say, hey, cause guilt causes people to want to kill themselves. What did Oedipus do he discovered his crime of patricide and incest with his mother? What did he do?
Pt I don't know. I never read Sophocle's book.
Th You're off science?

Pt Uh huh. (laugh through crying)

Th Look it up.

Pt Okay.

Th He tore out his eyes.

Pt Hm.

Th And he gave up all of his wealth and power and wandered as a blind beggar cause it was unforgivable to him. Didn't matter to him that his father actually picked a fight and tried to kill him twice.
(pause)

Pt So if could actually feel physically the guilt?

Th Well, not just guilt, all your feelings, rage—it goes pain of trauma, you know, not being protected, pain of trauma, rage over not being protected or not being seen, neglected, guilt over the rage, grief about the loss of the attachment and it crystallizes into a complex and you go on a journey of self-punishment and self-abuse. You simply recruit players, you know, in this, you know, in this tragedy. Going from the role of your aggressive castrating mother to passive men or, in Roger's case, trying to rescue him from his aggressive wife in order to live happily ever after, or in the case of the filmmaker, being the castrated victim yourself of your aggressive mother.

Pt Maybe Roger or some other guy—I mean consciously have recruited a bad guy, could I?

Th No, it's random, but you pay selective inattention to the signal. Remember, when I said I was feeling really happy and really like liking you when you were telling what you should have said? That's you if you had recovered from the trauma of your childhood. That's the woman you would have been. You have read the signals and you would have said this guy looks good on paper, but, you know, he's a nightmare, he's a walking nightmare from my attachment matrix needs. He would be nothing but misery, he would be all appearance and no substance.

Pt Then why is it so hard for my head to accept that. Instead it wants to go to, Naw, he just wasn't into you, maybe ...?

Th Because that's the script is eternal rejection, eternal unfulfilled, seeking in order to undo the guilt over the rage against your loving but avoidant father. Your love for your mother is there as well but it is more deeply repressed. You're a creative young woman, you know. Your design for yourself is both brilliant and diabolical.

Pt Why?

Th Because of the need for self-punishment.

Pt Cause of the guilt over the anger I feel towards my father and cause of the guilt disappointing my mother if she's not ...

Th You know, you have complex feelings toward your mother too and you have guilt over your rage at her as well. We used to think it was other stuff now, but we kind of know that children who are guilty who are either abused or neglected, grow up feeling bad about their rage and they seek punishment rather than fulfilment. That's the take home message. You're seeking punishment, you're not seeking fulfilment.

Pt Because I'm somehow guilty.

Th You were abused and guilty as a child. Abuse causes rage, neglect causes rage. The child doesn't have the mind of a parent to say, Your rage is okay, so you ascribe guilt to it and then you seek punishment cause you're such a nasty child. And men are wonderful tools of self-punishment. They're more than happy to cooperate. You know that.

Pt I've seen it.

Th You know, a lot of men are not very nice to woman and if a woman doesn't insist on a man being nice, watch out.

Pt I've never been very insistent.

Th How could you? I'm just asking you to have empathy and understanding for what's been on your plate up to now.

Pt And how do I fix it?

Th That's what I do for a living.

Pt Is that helping to fix it, right now, talking? I know the answer's yes, but maybe I want …

Th I don't think talking means anything; understanding means everything. Talking is only a means to create understanding of self, right?

Pt Right.

Th Do you understanding yourself anymore than when you walked in?

Pt I guess the piece I don't understand is the guilt piece.

Th Cause you didn't let yourself feel it.

Pt I guess. I just don't see myself …

Th I must tell you, you portrayed the action tendency of guilt beautifully. You couldn't have, you said I would want to undo it. I would want to bring him back. I would want to put him back together.

Pt What do you mean?

Th Well, every emotion has a genetically programmed action to it.

Pt Okay.

Th So if you feel guilty, the genetic uh, the programmed action is to repair, to undo the harm. You can see it in nursery school when you hit a kid and one kid hits a kid and they then feel guilty about doing it and they come and make nice. They're undoing the guilt.

Pt But I ran Roger down with a bus.

Th That was your rage, couldn't put him back together, too much, destructive force. You know for a linguist, I really feel like I'm talking mentor in Chinese and you've never had a lesson. Remember I said I wanted you to start to study the language of the emotions?

Pt I guess, okay, so (pause) I guess I have to refrain what abuse means to me because I've never considered myself abused because I had, you know, went to great schools …

Th Neglect, denial, and minimization.

Pt I guess, and I guess cause my dad was so non-abusive …

Th Neglect, full dismissive, ignoring of and passive toward your mother.

Pt Yes and that qualifies as abuse even though I wasn't whipped, I wasn't sexually abused …

Th Neglect and abuse. It's a bad combo. He had dealt a bad hand.

Pt But where's the abuse?

Th Your mother.

Pt The nasty things she'd say?
Th The nasty looks on her face, the nasty attitudes, the retaliation.
Pt Okay. And I'm guilty because …
Th The power of your passion, your rage. How can you have passion without rage?
Pt So my guilt is because I feel this rage and I shouldn't because everybody says I had the best father ever.
Th That's the crazy making message, this is not coming from me.
Pt He (father) looked great on paper. (sobs)
Pt Okay.
Th You looked sad there for a second. When I said he looked great on paper, you looked very sad, very sad. The crying of ignoring your healthy side. See you couldn't tell me these things if you didn't know what he was doing was harmful. Dismissing, being publicly disparaged by your mother, and extolling the virtues of ignoring and suppressing your emotions. But you seem really connected to you right now.
Pt Well, what's next, what do I do now?
Th If you'd like, I'd book another appointment. I can get started in two weeks.
Pt Right, and then so *what's the road map* and what do I do between now and then?
Th It usually takes us about a half a year of work with you to get things turned around.
Pt Okay.
Pt Okay. And just keep paying attention to …
Th That's everything. That's what changes the game is where your attention goes.
Pt Hm mm.

At 2:45, the interview ends and the patient is hopeful, feels better, and is eager for more therapy. We have completed this pathway on the traffic lights (see Figure 31, on the next page).

Summary

In the trial therapy, we found two pathological superego systems, one devaluing and one dismissive. The father was the warmer parent but gave the child a model of victimization in love relations. She had no conscious awareness of anger towards her father until the unlocking occurred. The trauma with her mother was one of obvious perpetration with verbal, emotional and physical abuse. The patient used projective identification in her romantic relationships to re-enact the victim perpetrator paradigms. Her depression was precipitated by the break-up of a love affair with a married man who refused to be rescued by her from his allegedly aggressive wife. His rejection of her love mobilized rage, guilt, and grief that was greater than her ego-adaptive capacity could process, resulting in symptom formation. The ego used syntonic defences at stimulus as well as at response, devaluing, ignoring, denying, smiling, minimizing, repressing, intellectualizing, rationalizing, externalizing, defying, complying, projectively identifying, and acting out (affairs, overachieving). By the end of the initial interview, the ego was somewhat freed from the compulsion to repeat and had early autonomy from her punishing allegiance to the commands of her internalized father and mother.

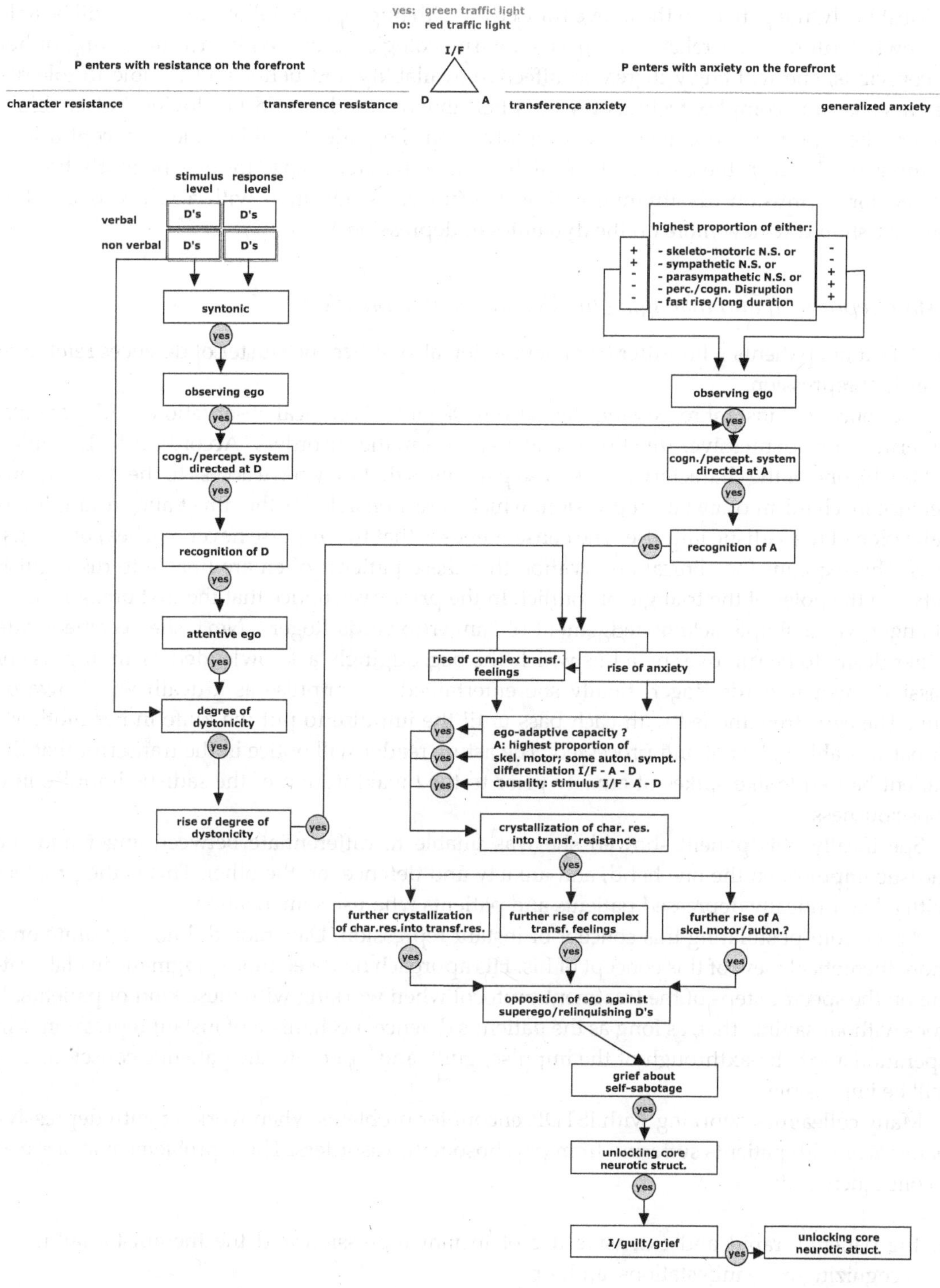

Figure 31. Depressed patient 1: road to the unconscious 5.

Most likely, the patient in the above transcript, with appropriate follow-through, will be able to slowly terminate her reliance on psychopharmocologic agents. With each unlocking of her unconscious, she will enjoy increased affective availablity and better will be able to tolerate her unconscious complex feelings towards her abusive mother and her loving but enabling father. The repetition compulsion will dissolve and the patient will be able to accept a love relationship. Later in the chapter, there will be an annotated transcript of a patient who was treated for depression (dysthymia) without concurrent medication with a full recovery. But next, we should review more on the dynamics of depression.

Instant repression and managing the dynamics of depression

By definition, patients who suffer from depression also utilize the cluster of defences refered to as instant repression.

The concept of instant repression stems from Davanloo's clinical observations with patients, suffering from depressive, functional and psychosomatic disorders. According to Davanloo (1987a, b), one of the characteristics of these patients is that they have access to the unconscious defence mechanism of instant repression, which is responsible for the direct and instant internalization of the sadistic impulse. The consequence is that the impulse never reaches consciousness. This explains the clinical observation that these patients often are unable to distinguish between the poles of the triangle of conflict. In the prior case, notice that the first breakthrough of anger was a simple acknowledgement of "anger towards Roger". Next, she became aware of her desire to be run over by a bus which she begrudgingly acknowlegded as an impulse of passive anger towards Roger; finally she entertained the impulse as a death wish towards him. The ego strengthened with each pass until the impulse to put the knife in her mother's throat was able to be felt and processed. The astute reader will notice in the transcript that the patient had knife like spikes of anxiety prior to the breakthrough of the sadistic impulse into consciousness.

Specifically, this patient showed she was unable to differentiate between anger and the sadistic impulse, on the one hand, and anxiety and defence, on the other. This is the problem with all neurotically depressed patients and patients who use somatization.

Apart from postulating this concept of instant repression, Davanloo did not elaborate on a more theoretical view of this concept of his. His approach has been more pragmatic in elaborating on the specific steps of the treatment protocol when working with these kind of patients. It goes without saying, that, as long as the patient's defence mechanism of instant repression is in operation a safe breakthrough of the impulse, guilt, and grief into the patient's consciousness will be impossible.

Many colleagues, working with ISTDP, encounter problems when working with depressive patients or with patients suffering from psychosomatic disorders. These problems may arise as a consequence of:

a. the patient's rapid and extensive use of instant repression and the therapist's failure of recognizing its manifestations, and/or
b. the therapist's failure in helping the patient undoing this defence mechanism.

In our view, a more elaborate understanding of the concept of instant repression may help the (I)STDP therapist to recognize it in a timely manner and to act accordingly upon it. Patients suffering from depressive, functional, and psychosomatic disorders often have severe superego and character pathology. We all know that the array of character defences, utilized by our patients, may interfere with the therapist's ability to conduct a trial therapy. This is because these defences are automatically put into operation and the degree of this automatism reflects the degree to which they are unconsciously put into operation. It goes without saying that, the more defences are syntonic, the more automatically and therefore the more unconsciously the patient puts his defences into operation. A patient who has access to the defence mechanisms of instant repression puts these syntonic defences already in the unconscious into operation, the moment feelings or impulses are triggered.

Second example of a depressed patient

The patient presented for ISTDP for symptoms of chronic low grade emptiness and unhappiness, particularly in his career as a physician. He worked at a large clinic and found himself feeling unhappy with the administration and thus found his patient care activities unrewarding. He was excited by the recent birth of two twin children and loved his wife. He wanted ISTDP to prevent himself from doing to his children what his mother did to him. He was the oldest of three children both of whom have had difficulty becoming independent adults. His father was described as warm and loving but his mother was described as harsh, controlling and demanding that her children be perfectly behaved and good little soldiers. His father took a secondary role, sustaining his mother's controlling and punitive stance. She used shaming as a parenting technique and she herself suffered from life-long depression. He discovered he was controlled by and terrified by his mother's judgement. During the therapy, the patient's mother suffered from a terminal illness and died. So the relationship between the patient's unconscious conflict and his bereavement was easily examined. Below is an excerpt of his twelfth psychotherapy session, which lasted ninety minutes. The core of his complex feelings towards his mother is exposed and worked through.

Clinical example: overcoming instant repression

Th OK, so tell me about, improvement, lack of improvement, the same, what's the assessment, for you?

Pt I felt last week's session was helpful, quite helpful?

Th How?

Pt Well, it was something about a realization about, we were talking about sometimes, bad is bad and black is black or and you know that um, that um calling a spade a spade, right. And I realized how waffley that I've been, because I feel guilty, you know there's this guilt and this thing about judgement and all this crap about. So, I thought about that a lot and I noticed that um, as I was trying to make decisions I was just making them quicker. On purpose, I was saying this is how I feel and this is what I'm going to do. And it seems …

Th See, what you've underestimated in your mind, is the importance of understanding what your values and what your beliefs are.

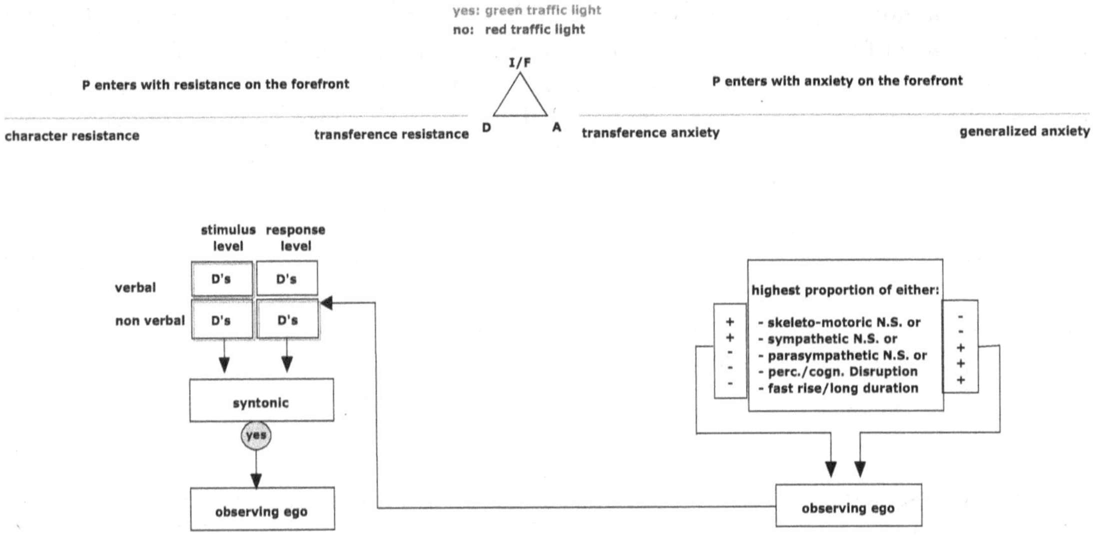

Figure 32. Depressed patient 2: road to the unconscious 1.

Pt That makes sense.

Th Because all decisions follow your values and beliefs. If you are unclear as to what you believe, what your values are, the decision-making process is onerous, it's like flipping a coin. So, yeah, of course.

Pt I don't really, it's not really clear to me, why is this all whishy whashy stuff, where that originated. But it's pretty clear that it's existed.

Th You know where it originated?

Pt Well, I'm not, I guess I'm not, I guess it's really not even that important anymore.

Th I think it's very important. You see if you go backwards to that, you're asking for trouble, because asking for the depression to come back and take over your mind again.

Pt Well, what happened was …

Th You understand what I mean?

Pt I do.

Th That's all you doing, is going back to denial and repression. (The therapist points out the defences that comprise instant repression.)

We are on the roadmap at Figure 32, above.

Pt But, I'm wondering whether, the reason why I say, I'm not sure how important it is because, it may be just as important or more or seeming, seemingly so, to just act. To just to see how it feels to make a decision and watch some stuff to come up and go, I don't care, you know.

Th But again, that's all fine and dandy, but what I'm seeing here is, you're wearing blinders again.

Pt I don't think I'm wearing blinders. (The patient is in denial of denial.)
Th So then, answer the question. Where did the problem start?
Pt Well, I came from, it came from this lineage of a sense of self that was poorly formed and, and poor.
Th That's psycho babble.
Pt Yeah, (Patient has a laughing expression and then proceeds to laugh at himself out loud), I know .... Um.
Th Who did it come from?
Pt It came from my mother. (expressed confidently)
Th There we go. And you have a wonderful look at that with clearer eyes and hold it there as abuse. You haven't wanted to see your mother's abuse as wrong.
Pt Correct.
Th And your dad helped you, in the sense of not wanting to see this as wrong either.
Pt Ah hum (nodding head)
Th So you had a doubt, you had a double whammy of it. Because in your mind, if your mother was abusive than she was bad. So you had to blur the lines between good and bad, to protect your mother from being labelled as bad.
Pt (Patient, head nodding in agreement) that's pretty concise. (patient laughing) Um.
Th But why is it so hard for you?
Pt It's not that it's hard ...
Th Yes it is, don't deny. Observe ...
Pt It's less hard than it was.
Th Less is not enough.
Pt But where ...
Th Why is it still? What are defending against inside? (Pause) What comes up if just look at it as bad? What your mother did to you was bad. It wasn't good, what she did to your siblings, wasn't good. What she did to your father wasn't good and if it wasn't good it was bad.
Pt (Patient agreeing) Well, what I was doing, during the week at times was, I was able to go back to her and than go back to her father and I was able to see, o.k. well, you know, we know this and this and that. I don't have to feel guilty about labelling it, what it is, which is ...
Th I don't have a problem if you feeling guilty.
Pt I was able to ...
Th You see, I don't want you to defend against feeling guilty.
Pt You don't want me to defend against feeling guilty.
Th Why do you feel guilty?
Pt Well, I know why I feel guilty; it's just what we talked ...
Th I don't know why.
Pt Because, we just talked about it.
Th Why?
Pt Well, because labelling, because the labelling of what happened as categorically saying that some of my mothers ...

Th But, don't you understand your using two steps when it only requires one.

Pt OK, I guess you better clarify that for me. (patient scratching head, trying to understand)

Th Oh, my goodness! (therapist, leaning forward and smacks his own forehead in surprise and laughter.)

Pt (patient responds with laughter too.)

Th If you blow the whistle on your mother as being abusive that makes you guilty, therefore you're bad. Now you have to talk about, you have to make excuses, you have to find out some mitigation of your mother's behaviour to get yourself off the hook for blowing the whistle when her evildoing. (The therapist identifies his "guilt" as loyalty to the father superego who was the maintaining factor that enabled his mother's abusiveness.)

Pt OK.

Th Now do you think that's a good use of your time? Ironically. (The therapist confronts the patient's intellectualizing.)

Pt No.

Th It's like juggling, why do you have to have three balls going, when all you need is one.

Pt Because, it seems like I'm clearing, it seems like I'm clearing, like, like …

Th Wait (therapist hand gestures to stop patient's thought), listen, think, listen, OK. You're declaring your mother sitting here, look her in the eye.

Pt OK.

Th Tell her to her face.

Pt You fucked up!

Th By?

Pt By, by your behaviour!

Th Can you be specific?

Pt By your abusive behaviour of forcing me to feel and do and be what I wasn't, because it was your need, not mine. Yeah, and it fucked me up and it's caused me um, um …

Th And what's the feeling you're expressing?

Pt Well, that I'm fu … angry.

Th Good, now tell me about how your anger feels inside, quickly. (Therapist snaps his finger with clicking sound.)

Pt Good.

Th Well, let me hear good, let me hear if it feels so good, tell me how it feels?

Pt It feels definitive.

The patient uses the defence of vagueness.

Th How does it feel, feel. Beliefs are definitive, feelings are energies. Turn your mind toward your energy.

Pt It feels clean.

The patient is encouraged to verbally express his anger as the first step to allowing the sadistic impulse to rise to consciousness.

Th Good, I'm glad but how does it feel? The energy of your anger …, where do you feel it in your body?

Pt Oh, in the centre. (Patient gestures his hand going down the middle of his body, then lets out a sigh.)

Th Good, now, that was a beautiful cleansing breath, well done. OK, it's in the centre, now give me the idea of the power of your anger, how powerful is your anger over this topic?

Pt Well it's wanted me to kill her before, so I guess it's pretty powerful.

Th Excellent, and you have a good memory of that?

The working alliance is activating the unconscious therapeutic alliance.

Pt OK, yeah it's rage it's a sensation of being trapped of wanting to, of feeling, literally of being trapped. Of being trapped in your skin.

Th I understand rage, but you shouldn't be trapped in your own skin.

Pt No.

Th So what does it look like? If you deliver it with all the force commensurate with the rage you have inside.

Pt Well, it's destructive, lethal.

Th How does it look?

Pt It looks like …

Th In your imagination, in your imagery, in your mind. What do you picture yourself doing, to release the rage? How would you have to get it out of your body?
(The patient is resisting visualization of the impulse.)

Pt Yell.

Th OK, that's what rage is to you! Now you're back to square one.

Pt It's a … yell with …

Th Listen, look at me again. Rage o.k. by definition is the desire to kill or inflict severe pain. Physical pain.

Pt The yell is kills, by blowing her apart.

Th OK, but don't do it with percussion. Use it with your own physical force, how would you use your own "physical" force, to kill her?

The therapist focuses on the physical experience of the impulse. Since we have worked together for some time, the unconscious working alliance takes over and we seamlessly move to here:
And the ego opposes the defences of repressing which his pathological superego father part commands.

We are on the roadmap to the unconscious at Figure 33, on the next page.

Pt Punching.

Th Good, tell me about it?

Pt Well, blows.

Th I understand blows, how, I can't see them. Only you can see them, describe them to me.

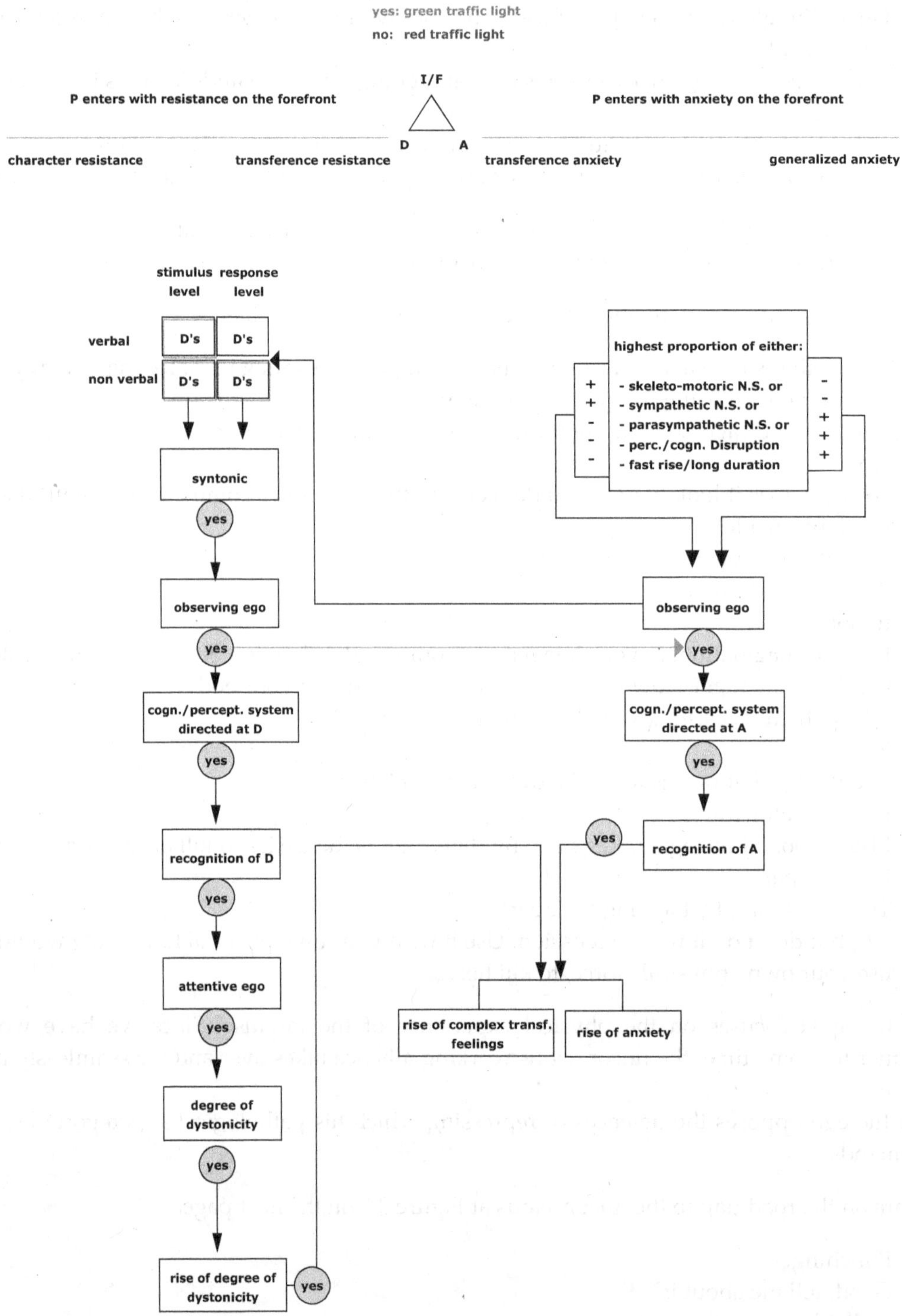

Figure 33. Depressed patient 2: road to the unconscious 2.

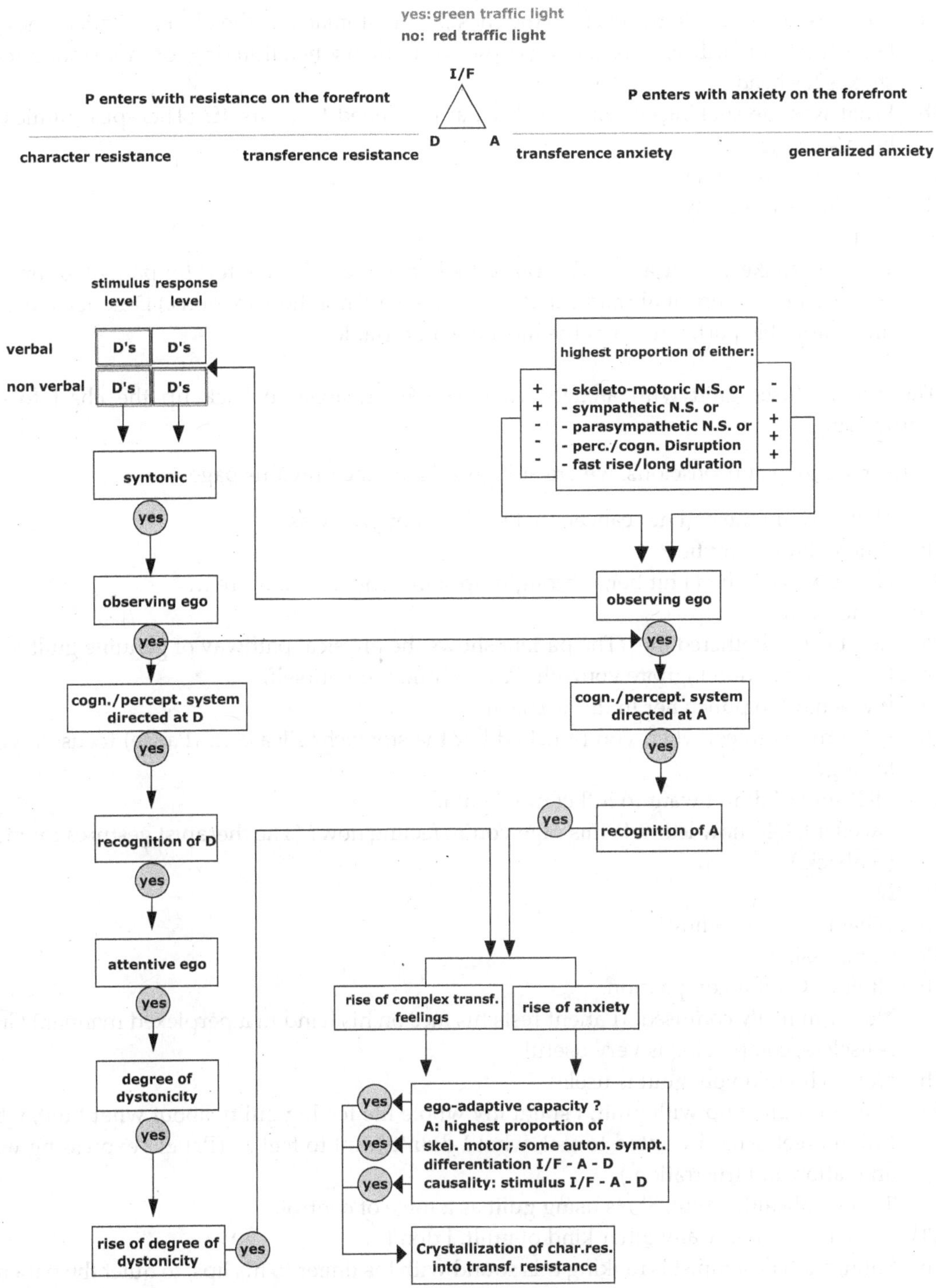

Figure 34. Depressed patient 2: road to the unconscious 3.

Pt Punches to the face, to the neck, to the chest, to the stomach, to the uhm … (Patient moving head back and forth as he is making expressions, than when thinking for more thoughts he shakes his head.)

Th What was the shaking of your head, what happened to yourself? (Therapist mimicking head shaking.)

Pt It got uncomfortable.

Th OK, that was anxiety.

Pt Yeah.

Th We don't shake anxiety away. (Therapist looks at patient, in an effort for patient to copy his actions, take a deep inhale and exhale of breath. Patient follows actions.) Describe the most uncomfortable part, what was the most uncomfortable …

(The patient fuses guilt with anxiety, causing the therapist to back up the chart to ego restructuring.)

On the road to the unconscious, we are at Figure 34, on the previous page.

Pt That's where she had her cancer, that's where her pain was …

Th Where did you hit her?

Pt Her stomach, when I hit her, it brought up some, some … re … re …

Th Some, what?

Pt Response, it bothered me. (The patient shows the physical pathway of genuine guilt.)

Th I see that, but don't ignore yourself. Pay attention to yourself.

Pt It was hard to punch her in the stomach.

Th What did you feel when you punched her the stomach? Please … (Pause) focus on your feeling?

Pt I felt sorry, I didn't want to inflict more pain.

Th Excellent, OK, now learn. Is this rage you're feeling now? (The therapist gestures for more feedback.)

Pt No.

Th What is it your feeling?

Pt Compassion.

Th Guilt … Guilt is compassion.

Pt Now, I'm really confused. (Patient rests his face on his hand in a perplexed manner.) Guilt is useless, compassion is very useful.

Th Now, who told you, guilt is useless?

Pt She did! I grew up with guilt, I spent my whole life feeling guilty about what I felt, what I didn't feel, what I wanted to feel, what I didn't want to feel … (Patient expressing with animation and frustration.)

Th That's unhealthy guilt. She's using guilt as a force of control.

Pt Yeah, I don't know any other kind of guilt. I don't …

Th Shhh, shhh (Therapist is making this sound with his finger to his lips, to quiet the patient.) Your learning, this is healthy guilt. ("Unhealthy guilt" is actually *shame* which is used by the authority figure to control the child.) You just felt healthy guilt. You just felt healthy guilt. Maybe, this the first time in your life that you felt healthy guilt. You don't need any external forces to teach you right from wrong. Your rage wants to destroy your mother, your rage wants to torture her, o.k., right. But your love for your mother, tells you, that this something that you don't feel good about doing. Those are two feelings, that's all they are, is two feelings, two opposing feelings. One feeling is rage and the desire to destroy and inflict pain. And the other feeling is guilt. Let yourself feel it, don't defend against it. She's not creating this guilt in you. She has nothing to do with this, this is you. This is your guilt, you own this, this is yours, it's in your DNA, it's yours. She didn't give this to you, she didn't teach this to you.

Pt (Patient agreeing with what is being said. At the same time having tears streaming down his face.) Well, she taught me a lot about guilt.

Th Yes, unhealthy guilt ... she abused power. A parent (Therapist reaches for props to illustrate misuse of power. A ball to signify the child and a toy gumby figurine to signify the parent.) OK, the parent is more powerful than the child. There is an imbalance of power. Wrongdoing is the abuse of power.

Pt OK, yes.

Th That is the abuse of power. Your mother used her power of her position, OK, to define for you, what was good and what was bad and to make you feel shame and guilt if you didn't conform to her will.

Pt Correct.

Th OK, now that's trauma when a parent does that. That's how you were traumatized by her. That's many ways, the ways your siblings were traumatized by her, isn't that true?

Pt Yes.

Th OK, that's unhealthy guilt when a parent controls the kid, with judgement. You see that, that is what has created your rage, which is a healthy response ...

Pt To what she did.

Th ... to what she did.

Pt Yeah.

Th But the good part of you, feels guilty about acting out your rage against her.

Pt Yeah.

Th That's all you, that has nothing to do with her. This is not her now, I'm trying to tell you, your guilt feelings are your own property now. If you beating her to death (therapist throws mother figure to the ground) and she's down there, OK, right, she's gone. She can't abuse power any more. So tell her (therapist pointing to the mother figure) about your guilt, over killing her. What would you say, sitting over her? In other words, learn about you, now. This is the opportunity to get to know yourself better. What does it feel like to kill your mother, what does it feel like, if you have a very intimate moment with her, if you tell her. (Long pause, patient looking down and looking distraught.) If you take a totally non-punitive attitude, towards you.

Pt It feels like a release.

Th Tell her. (expressing his true feelings to his dead mother)

Pt It feels good.

Th Mother ...

Pt Mother, it feels good to express my rage ... By killing you.

Th Tell her how you killed her.

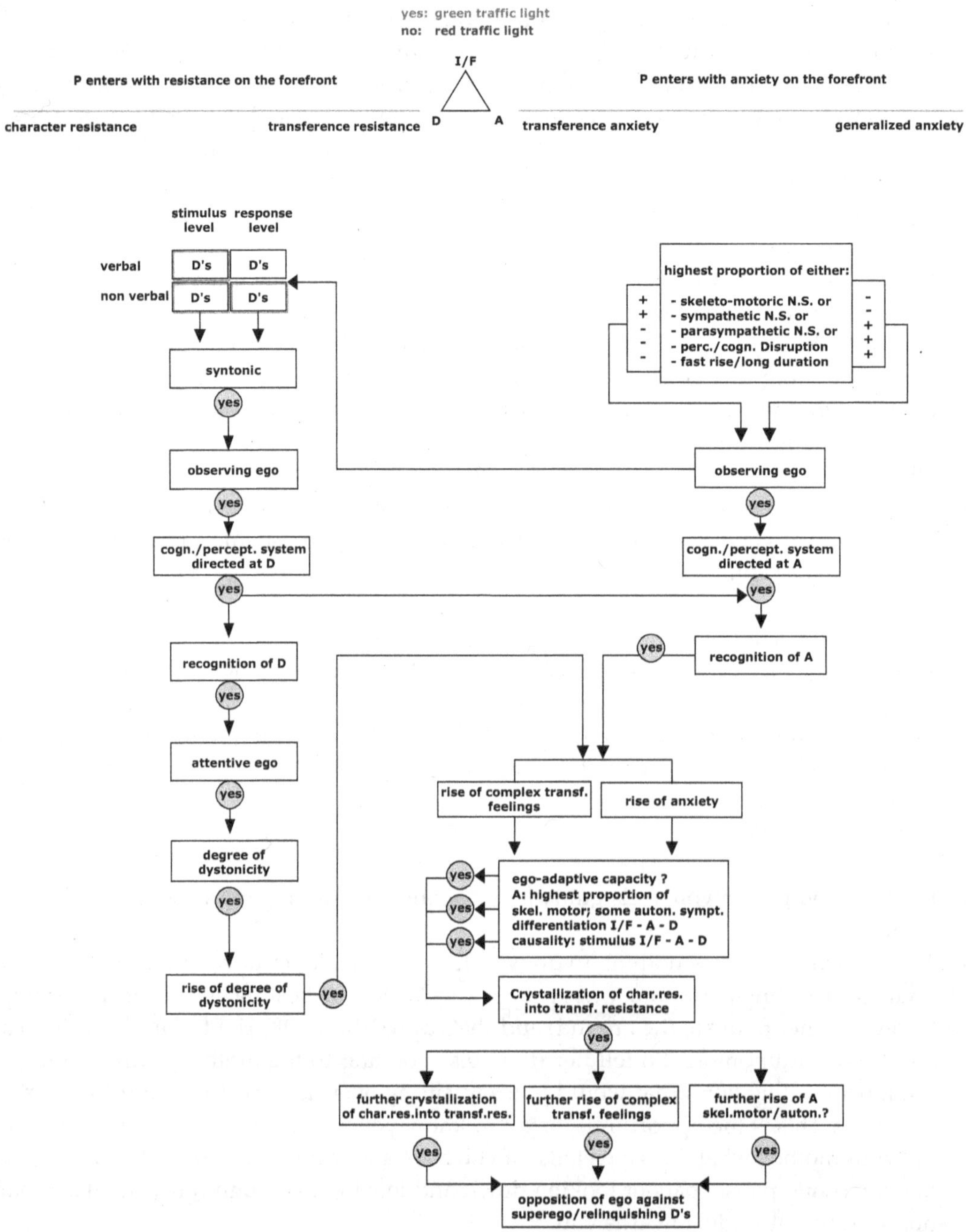

Figure 35. Depressed patient 2: road to the unconscious 4.

Pt By punching you to death … to hit you in your stomach, where the cancer killed you.
Pt No, that did not feel particularly good.
Th Why not?
Pt I wanted to inflict more pain on you and I felt guilty about inflicting more pain on you.
Th It's right, so tell her you have one hand.
Pt On the one hand, I want to kill you and on the other hand …
Th Now on the other hand I want to inflict even more pain on you … and on the other hand me, me, your son feels guilty, about my own desire. to inflict more pain on you.
Pt OK, that's true.
Th Tell, I don't need you …
Pt I don't need you to *make me* feel guilty … I feel guilty about inflicting, about expressing my desire …
Pt Acting on my desire to kill.
Th To inflict more pain on you.
Pt To inflict more pain.
Th I have lots of desire …
Pt I have lots of desire to inflict pain.
Th To be cruel on you.
Pt Yeah.
Th Yeah, and if I weren't guilty I would do what, tell her what you would do.
Pt And if I weren't guilty I would kill you. I know, I don't know, I'd probably slice you in pieces.
Th Ah hmm, yes, go ahead. You have a picture of that.

Now that the patient has insight into his complex feelings of rage, guilt, and grief, he is motivated and able to investigate his pathogenic sadism.

His ego can now oppose the defences erected against the superego's command. On the road to the unconscious we are at Figure 35, on the previous page.

Pt Yeah.
Th Well, what does that look like?
Pt Like, slicing someone to pieces.
Th Again, it's too vague for me.
Pt Eh, eh, eh, butcher's knife …
Th And what would you do with your butcher's knife?
Pt I'd slice pieces off.
Th How would you slice pieces off?
Pt By striking, like this. (Patient motioning hand in a striking move.)
Th Ah hum, OK, how many pieces to do you slice off?
Pt Quite a few.
Th Be specific again, don't trivialize …
Pt Fingers, wrist, arm, more arm, shoulders, head …
Th Yeah, that's an intense murderous and sadistic rage.

Pt Ah hmm.

Th Intense, and when you look at that picture of her, what is the feeling you have towards that image of her when you see her looking like that?

Pt At the moment, I don't get a lot of response.

Th OK, see I like that, just be yourself now. What does it look like when you look at that picture? Describe it to me, so I can see it as clearly as you see it.

Pt Slices and body parts and pieces hanging off and she's dead.

Th So, it's like a butcher went after a piece of …

Pt Meat.

Th Yeah, good, and you cut off her head too.

Pt No, it's in slices like this (Patient gesturing vertical slices), longitudinal slices.

Th OK, vertical slices.

Pt Yeah.

Th Do you notice, right now, how still you are?

Pt I feel relief.

Th Just stay still. Understand, with compassionate eyes, how deeply your mother hurt you. Because, you told me your mother sliced you to ribbons.

Pt She did.

Th That's what you're telling me. That's what her tongue did to you. (Long pause of silence.)

Pt And, I got that image of my kids and us like that. A strong eh …

Th Strong, what?

Pt Like a no, I won't, you know I won't do that to my children.

Th You got the image of your children, what do they look like?

Davanloo called this area of unlocking "the butchery factory of the unconscious". The patient had an image of his two twin infant children, one compliant and peaceful and the other fussy and restless. He worried that he would take a punitive stance towards the more difficult to parent child. We cut back in 10 minutes later ….

Pt Well, I can relax. Well, it feels peaceful.

Th Good, and what kind of picture of your Mum do you get?

Pt (Pause) It's less emotionally packed, it's just her.

Th Her, how?

Pt Smiling.

Th And describe the age you see her?

Pt Younger.

Th And what is it that you like about that?

Pt She seems happy.

Pt (Long pause, takes four deep breaths as he remembers.) She was smiling. (Taking another deep breath.)

Th And tell me what it's like to be greeted with a smile?

Pt (Takes another deep breath, begins to grieve.)

Th Go ahead, let it out, and don't keep it in that jaw, it's too much energy to put in your jaw, you'll get bruchsism, don't keep it in your jaw. That's grief.

Pt Yes.

Th What's the image of your Mum?

Pt Well she was happy when I came.

Th And why does that make you so sad, because it didn't last long enough.

Pt No, seems like it created more, just stress.

Th Or burden.

Pt Yeah. (Patient sobbing.)

Th Go to the next image, what's the first time you saw her unhappy, the very first time you failed to make her happy.

Pt I don't remember.

Th Hmm.

Pt I don't remember.

Th It's OK, just let it come into your thoughts, the first time you realized that you couldn't make her happy, whatever picture you see.

Pt My first memory is JFK's funeral on television. (Patient very emotional.) She came into the room crying, it's the first memory I have.

Th And tell me about that memory.

Pt I was just watching something on television, I had this sense that something was wrong. People seemed sad, I didn't know what death was I guess.

Th Don't worry about all that stuff.

Pt And than she walked into the room and she was crying.

Th And how did that affect you?

Pt It was sad.

Th I can see, and talk about the experience of recognizing her sadness, what was that like for you, to see her sadness.

Pt It hurt me.

Th Help me understand how it hurt you.

Pt I didn't like to watch her, be sad. And I don't think I did anything, like I …

Th But you couldn't fix it for her, there's nothing you could do to make it better. She just lost her president and it made her sad.

Pt Yeah, yeah.

Th How old were you?

Pt Three.

Th (Long pause.) So you finally were confronted with the fact that you couldn't give her complete happiness, that it was impossible for you to meet all of her needs.

Pt But, I tried.

Th I know, listen, if you didn't try as hard as any human being could try Jack, you wouldn't be sitting in this chair right now. (Patient starting deeply sob for many seconds and then slowly breathe and sob some more.) Let it out, your love couldn't fix her, it's so painful to realize that, isn't it? Your love was not enough. (pause) Can I ask you a question?

Pt Ah huh.

Th You understood, that's when you came to the conclusion that there was something wrong with you, that there you were defective.

Pt I did whatever I could to make, try to make her happy.

Th But you understand that you took on the responsibility for her unhappiness.

Pt Yeah.

Th Do you understand that? (Patient becomes very emotional, crying and than pondering for a long time, therapist looking on.) Go ahead, and tell me what's happening in your, you know heart, mind.

Pt I was a good boy (with deep compassion and tears), but I didn't, I was naturally good, I didn't need …

Th Don't externalize, you were a very good boy. But Jack don't you understand the problem that your, you couldn't accept the limitation of your own power. The problem was not all the stuff you think your mother did to you. The problem was your mother's depression and you couldn't fix it.

Pt I never thought about that.

Th Until …

Pt Now.

Th Could you try and think about it?

Pt Ah huh.

Th And tell me what you begin to understand inside when you think about it, what comes up?

Pt There's nothing I could have done

Th Do you see it clearly now?

Pt Yes (in an emotional tone)

Th Let it out, don't keep it in your jaw, let it out. Don't keep it in your gut, just let the pain out. (Patient once again cries out emotionally.) Not only for her, but also for you. Stop punishing yourself, just let it out. Keeping it in is a form of punishment, you know.

Pt Yeah.

Th What's in your mind?

Pt It feels like something letting loose.

Th Good, what are you letting loose?

Pt Heavy …

Th What's heavy? Try not to fade away.

Pt It was heavy, it …

Th What?

Pt The burden.

Th Yeah, could you use the "G" word, the guilt. You thought there was something wrong with you …

Pt Ah huh.

Th But you couldn't make her happy. (The patient is taking in deep breaths, holding in grief.) Let it go, come on, don't push it back down. Do it for you, don't push it down, the guilt, let it out. It's a heavy burden you've been carrying around in you. Imagine your life without that burden, don't burry it again. This is to hard too get to if you sabotage. That's just very punitive of you. What would you want to say to your mother's corpse, just what would you want to get off your chest. The one we sliced to pieces here, what would you want to tell her.

Pt I'm tired.

Th Go ahead, explain it. In words she can understand.

Pt I'm tired of trying to make you happy.

Th I'm tired of carrying the guilt …

Pt I'm tired of carrying the guilt ….

Th … of not being able to make you happy. (Patient begins to cry profusely.) Let it go … let it out. It was never your responsibility to begin with.

Pt No. (Patient shaking head in no response.)

Th You just bit off more than you could chew. (Long pause.) I'd love to hear.

Pt I'm tired, of the burden.

Th And the burden of course is the feeling of guilt, caused by you taking responsibility for your mother's happiness. You were a good kid, you loved your mother, you knew when she was happy and you knew when she was unhappy. And you made the mistake of thinking you were the centre of her universe. It's a normal mistake, isn't it?

Pt Yeah.

Th You got to keep those lines really clear, don't get them blurred. (Pause) You've got your wife, your wife's got you, you can tend to each other, so that the two of you can tend to them. You and your wife are the centre of their universe. Does that feel OK?

Pt Ah huh.

Th You don't want to do to them, what your mother did to you …

Pt No.

Th So could we mend the fences between you and your Mum? (Patient closing eyes and reflecting.) Tell her what you've come to understand.

Pt (Pause) I'm still angry. (Deep breath, another long pause.) It wasn't my responsibility … (Deep breaths, another long pause.)

Th It wasn't your responsibility to do what?

Pt To try to make her happy.

Th Say it … (Pointing to mother figure on the floor.)

Pt To try to make you happy. My older sister ran away to another country, so she could try to get away from it. (Patient looking down.)

Th So you're saying, "Mom you screwed up …

Pt You screwed up … by making us … centre of your universe … from the beginning … to fail … children aren't responsible for their parents' … happiness."

Th Tell her, who's responsible.

Pt You are.

Th So tell her where the legacy ends.

Pt With me.

Th Convince me, that it ends with you. Tell your mother about your guilt, mother I loved you so much …

Pt I loved you so much, I felt guilty that I couldn't make you happy. (Patient leans his face into his left hand on the armrest, looking dejected.)

Pt And I punished myself … without mercy … without compassion …

Th … by believing …?

Pt … by believing that I could do it. And then I felt … that I was defective. After that as an adult, I've blurred the lines of authority and responsibility in every situation …

Th Instead of having realistic boundaries …

Pt Instead of having a happy life … I created a miserable life for me …

Th "… just like I believed, I created a miserable life for you." (Patient doesn't repeat therapist but remains silent, contemplating. Long pause.) You paused there, I'd love to know, what happened in your mind, just objectively. What happened in there when you were hearing those words?

Pt It just resonates, makes me the realization in a different level.

Th That's what I was hoping, would you mind sharing that with me, really would be important to me to know.

Pt Is that, I never, I never knew any of this, it was impossible … situation. (Patient experiences self-compassion … crying … So after two experiences of rage, guilt, and grief, he has another episode of self-compassion, which will even further enhance the depth of the unlocking.)

On the road to the unconscious, we are at Figure 36, on the next page.

Th Could you just keep explaining that to me?

Pt There's no way anybody can make anybody else happy. And for a child to, to, to try to do it, I didn't even know what I was doing, I guess I was trying to do it, and I didn't even know what I was doing. I mean, I guess at that age. (Patient shaking his head, like not knowing.)

Th But you said, you said, I didn't even know …

Pt Didn't know …

Th … that I was even doing this.

Pt Right.

Th To who? I didn't know I was, I was motivated to try to make her happy. I didn't know that I was, I felt guilty about something. I certainly felt, felt a, a failure in not worthy of happiness. But I didn't know why.

Th But you do now.

Pt Ah hmm.

Th How's that feel?

Pt (Patient exhales.) Sadness and it's also relief.

Th So can't you feel both.

Pt Ah hmm.

Th Right, may I ask, what's the way you feel towards me, at this moment? Because your looking at me in very clear and very different set of eyes than I've ever seen you looking at me before.

Pt Just things don't seem so heavy right now.

Th So again, what I've said to you, if I just repeat it one more time for your benefit, that you've been in denial about the way in which you've been punishing yourself. Do you see that? Self-punishment.

Pt I know I've been punishing, but I didn't really understand why.

10 minutes later

Pt (Patient takes another deep breath.) Yes.

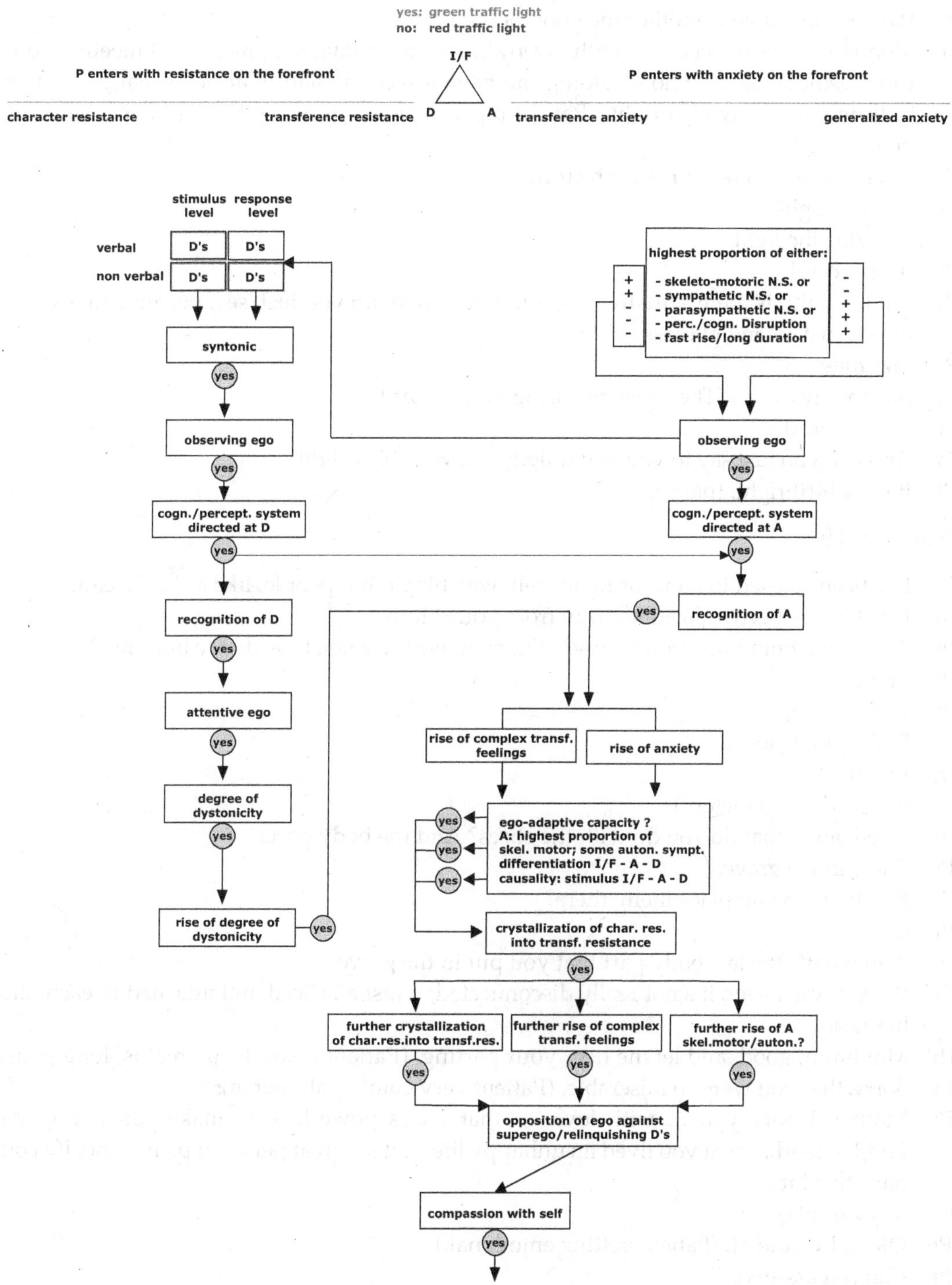

Figure 36. Depressed patient 2: road to the unconscious 5.

Th Would you tell your mother the good news. (Patient sighs.)

Pt Momma … I reconnected … with my joy… and my primal happiness … at meeting you … I met a therapist … who's helping me have a second chance, at being happy … is my birthright … is my birthright. (Patient repeats, "Is my birthright" in a lower tone and is pondering.)

Th What's it like, to reclaim your birthright?

Pt (Pause) Light.

Th Describe the light.

Pt It's peaceful.

Th But the light, is there actually a light in your brain, do you feel, see, perceive rays of light or you just mean lightness.

Pt Lightness.

Th But energy can … (Therapist gesturing movement.)

Pt Flow, warmth.

Th And can you just say to yourself quietly, it's your birthright.

Pt It's my birthright. (pause)

10 minutes later …

Pt I've been so used to monitoring myself, watching other people, like a chameleon.

Th It's all been a generalization away from your Mum.

Th So, can we bury your Mum, now? Where do we bury her, how do we bury her?

Pt In dirt …

Th Where?

Pt In the graveyard …

Th Where?

Pt In … a (local cemetery)

Th Good, and what do you do with the slices? And the body parts.

Pt There in the grave.

Th But, how do you place them, there?

Pt Gently.

Th And what's the last body part that you put in the grave.

Pt Well, it was never, it's not really disconnected, it just all sliced and attached to each other, her head.

Th Mm hmm, good, and let me hear your parting. (Patient takes deep breaths, long pause.)

Pt Sorry, that you were so miserable. (Patient very emotional, sobbing.)

Pt Mother, I bury you … with love: … that I was powerless, to make you happy. And I understand … that you lived an unhappy life … it's a great personal pain to me. If I could have fixed it …

Th … I would of.

Pt OK … I would of. (Patient getting emotional.)

Pt Can rest assured.

Th You can rest, you, you can rest assured. (Therapist pointing to patient.)

Th You have nothing to do with it, any longer. You have nothing to do with the outcome, anymore, it's out of your hands. (pause) You look shocked.

Pt I'm just processing.
Th I'm not criticizing, I'm just giving you feed … are you shocked?
Pt Yeah.
Th To hear that, well what are shocked about? Process with me.
Pt That I don't have the burden anymore.
Th Unless, you choose to …
Pt Yeah.
Th You still look shocked.
Pt There's a lot to process.
Th Well, help me with it … how do you want to close the grave? (pause) You could tell your Mum what you're going to do differently. (pause) Then she did …
Pt Yeah.
Th Or anything really, what …
Pt I feel a little disoriented.
Th OK like, anxious (Patient nods, no), dizzy (Patient nods, yes). That's anxious, what are you disoriented about?
Pt I was, just spacey.
Th Spacey, yeah, that's anxious.
Pt Oh.
Th Don't you think this is separation anxiety; you've been enmeshed with your mother, (pause) psychically. Right, isn't this like surgery, aren't I doing my best to (Therapist gesturing like he's cutting with scissors.) make you have two feet instead of four.
Pt Ah hmm.
Th So what's it like to have two feet, how many more years do you have on this earth?
Pt Well, I hope I get to see my girls grow up.
Th Give me a number; I don't care what it is.
Pt Thirty.
Pt Ah huh.
Th Right?
Pt Yeah.
Th What do you want to have happen between now and then?
Pt Happiness.
Th Could you get it out there, please?
Pt Huh (Patient getting choked up). Mom, it's my intention … It's my intention to enjoy my babies and my wife. (Patient becomes profoundly emotional.)
Th A little bit more, please. My … begins with a "l' and ends with a "e" and it has an "i".
Pt My life, my life. (Therapist nodding in agreement.)
Th Life.
Pt Life.
Th Enjoying your life is not a crime. (Patient chuckles in realization of what's being said.) It's not a crime, it's a responsibility, it's a sacred act. (Patient takes a deep breath and looks content.) Did you say about goodbye and then we'll end the session.
Pt Mm hmm, (pause) goodbye. (Patient chuckles again.) There's nothing more to say.
Th Except …

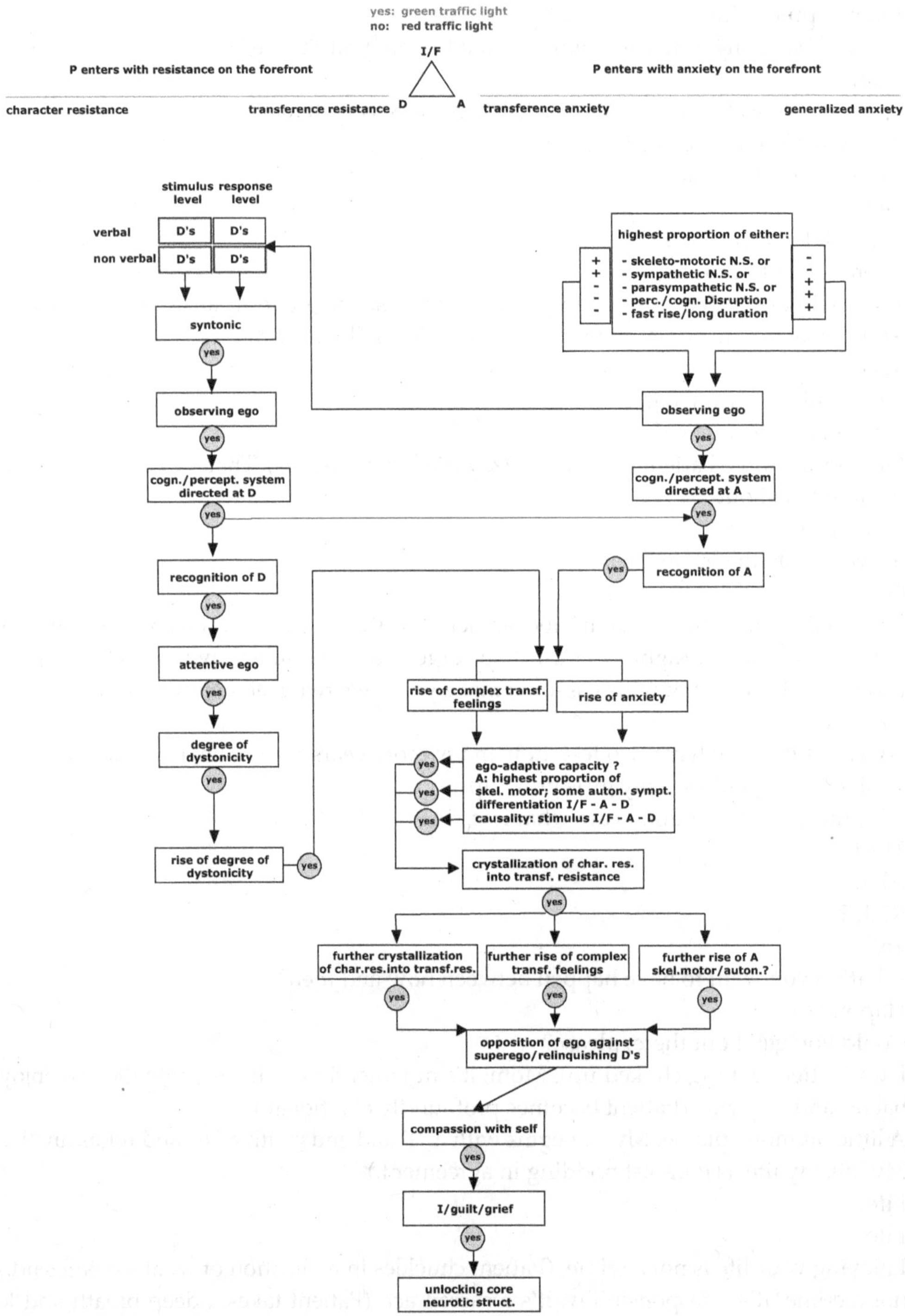

Figure 37. Depressed patient 2: road to the unconscious 6.

Pt "La Chaim" (Patient smiling.) (A Hebrew toast meaning "To Life").
Th (Pause) Any final comments before we stop today's session.
Pt Yeah, I just have to get used to feeling different. It's different.
Th But there are no excuses.
Pt No, I can't make any excuses, I've been making excuses my whole life.
Th So, you'll do your best to protect your autonomy between now and the next time we get together.
Pt Ah huh.
Th Lines of authority and lines of responsibility are crisp and clear.
Pt Ah huh.
Th If I gave you advice to focus on one part of this complex system, called your mind. That would be what I would tell you to focus on.
Pt Clear lines of authority, lines of responsibility.
Th In every system, in every interaction. In other words, don't take this old way of being with you, to the new land. (Therapist laughing.) Clear?
Pt Yeah.

After 90 minutes, we are at Figure 37, on the previous page.

We have gone full circle and the patient has developed deep awareness of his complex feelings of love, sadistic rage, guilt and grief in his relationship with his mother and links that with insight into the feelings that his twins activate in him and he understands how he must be his own therapist if he is to end the three-generational transmission of shame-based parenting.

The patient, after two more visits, terminated, and he and his wife and two children moved to a new job opportunity in another country. The patient has been free of depression and reports enjoying his career, wife, and his babies since termination for one year.

Note

1. "Adrenaline" and "noradrenaline" are the terms more commonly used in the UK and correlate to the terms "epinephrine" and "norepinephrine", which are more commonly used in the US.

Steps in the chapter

- Depression must be carefully assessed
- Positive response to trial therapy with hope is essential
- Depressed patients stabilize with a partial unlocking
- Depressed patients use instant repression
- Pharmacotherapy is a useful tool
- ISTDP may work where pharmacotherapy fails

ISTDP is both a safe and efficacious treatment for a large spectrum of depressed patients. Similar to pharmacotherapy, the patient's response to therapy must be monitored closely and appropriate interventions must be added based on the patient's response to intervention.

CHAPTER ELEVEN

Steps on the roadmap to the unconscious and its application to patients with somatization

Somatization is both a general and specific term with many definitions. Generally, it is a term used to cover a wide range of clinical disorders. Specifically, it is also a term that describes psychological process wherein an unconscious emotion is expressed through a physical pain or unexplained medical symptom. At other times, it refers to the patients who present clinically with physical symptoms in the face of psychosocial problems or emotional distress. Occasionally, it refers to patients who worry or are convinced that they are physically ill without evidence of disease; and sometimes it refers patients the pattern of frequent unexplained somatic symptoms that cause help seeking and disability (Kirkmayer, 1991).

Somatization and its various guises is an extremely common problem in all areas of medicine and mental health. It creates a major public health and economic problem since functional symptoms are among the leading causes of work and social disability. Frequently, patients with recurrent unexplained somatic symptoms may be extensively investigated with invasive, risky, and expensive medical procedures which can cause morbidity. Patients with high levels of worry about being sick also use healthcare services inappropriately (Abbass, 2009; Ford, 1983; Kellner, 1986).

History: from psychosomatic to somatization

Psychosomatic medicine is especially concerned with investigating treating the psychological causes of disease. Originally, psychodynamic theory attempted to study the role of specific psychological conflicts or personality dimensions in diseases (Engel, 1959). Unfortunately, this strategy did not live up to its promise and had the unfortunate consequence of encouraging clinicians to think of certain diseases as being especially "psychosomatic" in nature.

Contemporary epidemiologic and psychophysiologic research (Levinson, 2007) provides ample evidence of the nonspecific effects of stress on the causes and course of disease. In fact, psychological and social effects on physiology are ubiquitous and have been found to play a potential role in virtually every disease studied. Thus, the recognition that there is no unique class of psychosomatic disorders—only particular instances in which psychosocial factors play an overriding role in causing or aggravating a patient's condition—led to the elimination of the category of "psychophysiological disorders" from the *Diagnostic and Statistical Manual* of the American Psychiatric Association (1980).

We now think in terms of "psychological factors affecting physical conditions". Where psychosomatic theory is concerned with disease causation, somatization focuses attention on the experience and expression of illness. Lipowski (1988) amended his original definition of somatization as "the tendency to experience, conceptualize, and/or communicate significant psychological states or contents as bodily sensations, functional changes, or somatic metaphors". As such, somatization is properly viewed as a variation in illness behaviour and help-seeking. The relationship of somatization to psychiatric diagnoses or disorder is thus the clinical challenge.

Somatization as symptom or disorder?

Psychodynamic theory confounded a mechanism in symptom production-conversion with a clinical presentation of multiple unexplained somatic symptoms in many different organ systems—"hysteria". This was further confounded in the dramatic personality style with much amplification or exaggeration of distress—"hysterical personality" (Chodoff, 1974, 1990). With the development of DSM-III, the classic concept of hysteria was split asunder and replaced with concepts of several distinct "somatoform" disorders. In 1987 (DSM-III-R), there was a further re-classification into the categories we use today. These are conversion, somatization, body dysmorphic disorder, somatoform pain, and undifferentiated somatoform disorders, somatoform disorder not otherwise specified, and hypochondriasis. However, the diagnostic validity and clinical utility of most of these categories remains to be established.

Breuer & Freud's (1895) publication of *Studies in Hysteria* opened doors into the study of somatization but also led to confusion in their claims that the specific cause of unexplained physical symptoms were repressed incestuous sexual feelings or the result of actual trauma (molestation by a parent). Their research and ideas led to the erroneous conclusion that there are specific psychological causes to somatization, rather than a host of psychotraumata that led the patient to somatize.

Habib Davanloo's (1989) way of addressing somatization is unique in the history of dynamic psychodynamic psychotherapy. It is an excellent method of treating mind, emotion, body disorders because it is a therapy that emphasizes somatic experiencing of emotion. Davanloo's earliest observation of the moment-to-moment emergence of anxiety as the gateway to the unconscious is enormously helpful to this population, who are famous for ignoring, denying, neglecting, minimizing, and dissociating from anxiety. Furthermore, the fusion of rage, anger, and anxiety with this population is essential to be aware of and to make conscious if one is to help this population.

As noted above, in early dynamic theory, there was a bifurcation between psychosomatic disorders and the somatosensory/motoric disorders of conversion. Psychosomatic disorders were seen as the result of some form of emotional stress which caused end organ damage from a vulnerable organ. Conversion disorders were seen as symbolic in nature and resulted in deficits in function, for example, blindness meant someone didn't want to see their parents having sex. Paralysis of the arm represented the thwarted impulse to strike a loved one, and so on. These ideas were communicated to him through the writings of Otto Fenichel, *The Psychoanalytic Theory of Neurosis.* This was Davanloo's original "Roadmap to the Unconscious", and to his everlasting credit, he applied his roadmap to the clinical interview under strict criteria. He demanded that he re-create whatever symptoms the patient was suffering from in therapy so the patient could achieve cognitive affective insight into the origin of his symptoms.

In his work with somatization, he noticed a similarity in the egos of somatizing patients and those of depressed patients. Both categories of patients had far less access to their angry feelings and seemed to immediately deny or repress stimuli that might trigger them. He thus coined the concept of "instant repression" (Chapters Three and Eleven), and developed a series of techniques to overcome their interference with the patient's recovery. But most importantly, it is insistence that the patient experiences the somatic pathway of anxiety in the session, and also experience the somatic symptoms associated with the anxiety, that offers so much therapeutic hope.

Modern nosology has abandoned the dynamic system for a system that attempts to make diagnosis reliable (Hyler & Spitzer, 1978). The cost of this is we have consensus over groups but loose insights into the dynamic causes of these disorders. In short, in Davanloo's method the patient is pressured by the therapist to experience the somatic pathway of his or her core emotion (Coughlin Della Selva, 2006). This mobilizes unconscious affect which is active in the patient's subconscious. As the core emotions rise to consciousness, anxiety is mobilized. Because these patients have chronically neglected their anxiety symptoms, they frequently have excessive activity of their parasympathetic nervous system, which attempts to compensate for the excessive sympathetic arousal. The parasympathetic activity creates altered sensations such as dizziness, upper abdominal distress, diarrhoea or constipation, urge to urinate, and fatigue. Thus, the patient begins to believe that they are physically ill, and in fact may become ill because of this imbalance in their autonomic nervous system. Stress hormones like adrenaline and corticosteroids are released, causing elevated blood pressure, along with other negative consequences of chronic arousal. By using the ISTDP method of moment-to-moment observation of core emotion, anxiety, and defence, it is possible not only to observe the creation of somatic symptoms in the consulting room, but also to treat them effectively.

In this chapter, we will show the method of interviewing which allows the clinician to have significant impact on the process of somatization. Below are two cases that presented with severe somatizing disorders which were impacting the patients' social and personal lives. The first case is a consultation with only partial improvement, and the second case is a patient who underwent the whole therapy and has complete improvement.

After exploring the anxiety and symptoms, the patient is encouraged to feel the underlying rage pathway and to visualize the destructive force against the internalized aggressor and the maintaining factor. The somatic symptoms are not the result of "conversion", but are a result of a process called *projective identification*. This is used in a different way than in self-psychology (Neborsky, 2008, 2009). This term refers to the guilt over the destructive impulse being inflicted on to the traumatizing attachment figure and the corpse of the brutalized figure being re-internalized into the self, causing pain or loss of function in the victim of the original trauma (the patient). There are also other common manifestations such as projecting yourself into the other and identifying with the aggressor. Or in some cases, a patient can be hurting something of themselves to prevent using that part of the body to inflict pain like "the man that broke his fists" (ten Have de Labije, 2010).

Clinical example 1

The man who believed he had a degenerative neurologic disease

Defences at the level of the stimulus:
denial
minimization
projection
grandiosity (distortion of perception of medical input)
diversification
ignoring

Defences at the level of the response:
crossed legs
repression
selective memory loss
somatization
mislabelling
obsessions and compulsions

Partial breakthrough of anger, guilt, and grief with only limited improvement

Kevin is 56-year-old accomplished businessman and jazz musician as well as long-distance bicyclist. He had no prior psychiatric history. Two years before the consultation, he experienced searing, unbearable, shooting pain down his neck and spine. He became non-functional and suffered a disabling major depression. He has received extensive psychotherapy, but has never admitted that there was no orthopaedic or neurological cause of severe pain. He received two years of psychoanalytic psychotherapy from a colleague, and antidepressants, from which he benefited. However, he remains on the "medical magical mystery tour", seeking a diagnosis for what he believes to be a deteriorating condition. He was evaluated by a trusted colleague with all possible tests for central or peripheral neuropathic disease. He was found to have nothing more severe than mild fascial (muscle sheath) inflammation.

His marriage deteriorated as he is continuously somatically preoccupied. They have one daughter who is away at university. The wife reports that when she goes to the doctor with him, she hears that he is fine, but he distorts what the doctor said to support his own deeply held, irrational belief (somatic delusion) about his condition. The consultation was two hours. During the breakthrough, Kevin discloses a secret which he has held on to as to the "origin of his pain". He was in an automobile accident in which he was originally injured, four years prior to the interview.

Th What is it that you would like my help with?
Pt Well, my wife actually suggests that I see you and she has great faith in you and so I agreed to her that I would come and talk to you. Actually, I am seeing.
Th With what do you want my help? You are hear at 7:15 in the morning, you got up and went through some difficulty to get here which is of course very important, what are we setting out to accomplish for you?
Pt Um, well, I've got two problems and one is the fact that I am having a hard time an issue of back pain and neck pain, the second one is the real dire consequences of what is happening with our marriage.

(Patient demonstrates a rapid rise of skeletal muscle tension and squirming which he ignores.)

Th So you are having a marital problem and a pain problem, can I add a third problem to the list that I would like you to address?
Pt O.K.
Th Anxiety. Are you aware of having anxiety?
Pt Yes, um, that is kind of an interesting question because I am, but the anxiety takes the form of a, its fixational in it's first two things, it's amazing ...
Th No, with all do respect, that's obsession not anxiety. (confusion of defence with anxiety)
Pt OK.
Th No I observed you having anxiety while you are talking and I observed that you ignored the anxiety as you were talking, (the doctor clears his throat several times imitating the patient) and the fidgeting with your hands and from my observation and from my training, my belief and my professional expertise those are symptoms of anxiety.
Pt Mm hmm.
Th Are you in agreement with me that those are symptoms of anxiety?
Pt Yeah, I have some troubles seeing you now.

The patient experiences cognitive impairment with no observing ego (high rise, long duration), a red light.

We are at Figure 38, on the next page.

Th Ok, are you trying to explain the anxiety, is that what you are trying to do?
Pt Yeah, I mean I don't ... I have more anxiety right now than I normally would.
Th Whatever, you may be more or you may be the same, it's hard to tell. If you were the kind of person who had anxiety and ignores their anxiety, then you really wouldn't be aware

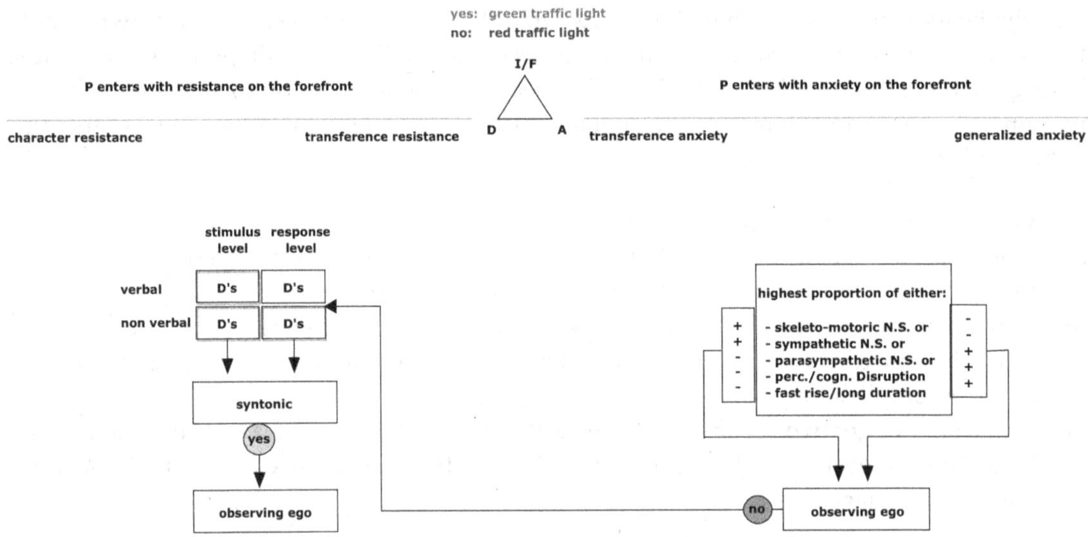

Figure 38. Somatizing patient 1: road to the unconscious 1.

of how much anxiety you are suffering from all the time, right. If the tree falls in the forest and no one is there to observe it, then how do we know that it falls, you know?

Pt Yeah, exactly.

Th So tell me what you are aware of in your body as far as, symptoms and sensations of anxiety at the moment?

Pt Well, um, I have the same issue as I have always had which is a burning in the spine from the top my neck to the bottom of the spine, and um …

Th You have burning in the spine.

Pt Yes, and so it really quite painful there to the extent that …

Th At this moment it is painful there?

Pt Right now it is um, yeah it is painful.

Th Now again in my opinion, you may be, well you are the expert in your experience not me. Ok in my opinion you are describing pain.

Pt Yes.

Th Pain is not anxiety, pain is pain. (second confusion of anxiety and defence)

Pt Yes.

Th We were saying that you were having anxiety and you immediately started talking about pain. Do you see what I am pointing out to you?

Pt Well the pain experience has made me a different person.

(The patient uses the defence of diversification.)

Th Can we stay on topic?

Pt OK.

Th What are we discussing?

Pt You are …
Th I am asking you about what?
Pt What my experience is?
Th No.
Pt And you suggested that …
Th No, no. Let's do it again, OK. This is really, really important that you and I share a common language. I observed in you anxiety as you began talking manifested by (doctor demonstrates by clearing his throat several times and fidgeting of the hands). I asked you if you were aware of being anxious and you said that you were but you didn't label (clearing the throat and fidgeting of the hands) as anxiety. I asked you how you feel the anxiety and you told me about a pain in the back of your neck, that's a pain right that's not anxiety right that's a pain. So can we just focus your attention on your symptoms of anxiety with precision?
Pt OK, um.
Th Like I said you have two problems you have pain, which I agree with, you have a marital problem which I agree with and I said can we anxiety to the list, but my observation is that you ignore the symptoms of anxiety and at times mislabel the symptoms of anxiety as something else, as pain, pain is pain, anxiety is anxiety, let's be precise.
Pt OK.
Th So what are the symptoms that you have as anxiety right now?
Pt Well I don't feel, well I guess I would feel on guard as you may say sort of stiffened.
Th Tense.
Pt Yes, I feel tense, it is not extreme by any degree, it is just not as relaxed as if I was sitting with my brother.
Th Tense and humour, tense and on guard. On guard is more like you have a state of physiological arousal a sense of danger somewhere.
Pt Yeah, exactly.
Th OK, that's good, did you feel the anxiety just through your body just then. Did you notice that?
Pt Yeah, yeah.
Th What did you notice?
Pt Maybe I'm, see this doesn't seem that extreme to me what I am doing at all but maybe …
Th I'm not saying it's extreme.
Pt What I am saying is I guess I don't notice as much, I guess a little bit, I don't feel that edgy, I guess I feel moderately edgy just because of talking to you.
Th But again, I think we are mixing two things that are different, you keep doing it over and over again, these are called in my world of practice causality errors.

(The patient's ego-adaptive capacity is poor and his observing ego is still in a coma. He fuses anxiety and defence.) A red light.

Pt OK.
Th You are mixing two different things, anxiety is physiological state of arousal, which you just described to me beautifully … on guard and tense, good. Now there is also a flow

of energy that goes along with anxiety and then you click into a defence mechanism which I call ignoring, you ignore, don't pay attention to you minimize your inner experience, you are minimizing your inner experience so that you don't get the information here (therapist points at head). I can observe the information because I am sitting here watching you, you don't observe it, therefore it doesn't register to you as happening. What I had observed was a flow of tension that went through your body and you (doctor taps his feet) did a little bit of dance there to release the tension. Do you remember doing that?

(Therapist attempts to model a healthy observing ego.)

Pt Yeah, yeah.
Th Yeah, so then to you that is just kind of nothing, to me that's significant. Do you see the difference? Right.
Pt Yeah. Sure.
Th So then I would like you to tell me what kind of anxiety you are aware of?
Pt Well, um, at this moment right now right?
Th Yeah.
Pt Um, well, you are not interested in reasons are you?, you are interested in symptoms I feel?
Th Yeah, aren't you?
Pt Yeah, huh.
Th Aren't you interested in you?
Pt Yeah, yea exactly.
Th Because my whole approach is paying attention to you with love, with compassion, with precision, with curiosity so you get a deeper understanding of you.
Pt Mm.
Th You were saying what?
Pt Well ok so how I feel.
Th The anxiety.
Pt Well so how I feel and how it is manifested is what you are interested in.
Th I hope you are interested in it too. See you keep putting it on me.

(The patient's defences attempt to sabotage the working alliance with the therapist. A red light.)

Pt Yeah.
Th Aren't you interested?
Pt Yeah, Yeah I am. What is amazing is I guess I feel like my stomach is a little too tight well I guess I don't feel that bad.
Th Your stomach is a little up tight.
Pt Probably, it is just a little.
Th There is some acidity kind of feeling or just tight?

(The patient ignores his parasympathetic anxiety manifestations.)

Pt Um, just a little.
Th Do you get acidity in your stomach ever?
Pt No, actually no.
Th OK, alright. It's just tight.
Pt It's just tight; I guess probably I feel energy just kind of going through, it's an energy surging through.
Th Alright, good.
Pt OK, I feel that.
Th See I feel that this is much more attentive than when we started, I see an improvement already and if you can connect to that feeling of energy, so you are on guard, you have a feeling of energy, you have tension and a tension fluctuates inside higher and lower right, your not always stiff as a board here, there is a moment when it will spike a little bit then it will go down a little bit.
Pt Yeah, I mean …
Th Is that right?
Pt Yeah, that is and also, you can probably tell that it is not extreme tension, so it doesn't feel extreme it is more, well I guess it is more, well it guess it is something under the surface that doesn't over take me right now, but it is still there it is kind of a feeling of electricity kind of sorts.

(The observing ego is awakening: a green light.) We are at Figure 39, on the next page.

Th Terrific.
Pt I would just kind of think, yea your right.
Th Really I mean it, so let's just summarize again, you've got tension, you've got the feeling of being on guard inside, you've got the flow of energy, do you have dry mouth?
Pt Dry mouth? I guess a little, not extreme.
Th Rapid heart beat? At this moment?
Pt Yeah, probably a little bit faster.
Th Little bit faster.
Pt I suspect.
Th You suspect or notice? I don't want you to guess.
Pt That's funny because … I'm going to say yes, if I was to feel my pulse right now I'm going to say it is up to 75 or 80.
Th How about your respirations, would you say they are relaxed and you are taking ….
Pt No, I am taking shorter breaths
Th Ok, that's what I have observed too.
Pt Little shorter breathes, yes.
Th OK, how about your bladder, do you have an urgency to urinate or is that just normal?
Pt Well, I just had a couple glasses of water before I came and I just went to the bathroom.
Th No, I am talking about right now.
Pt No.

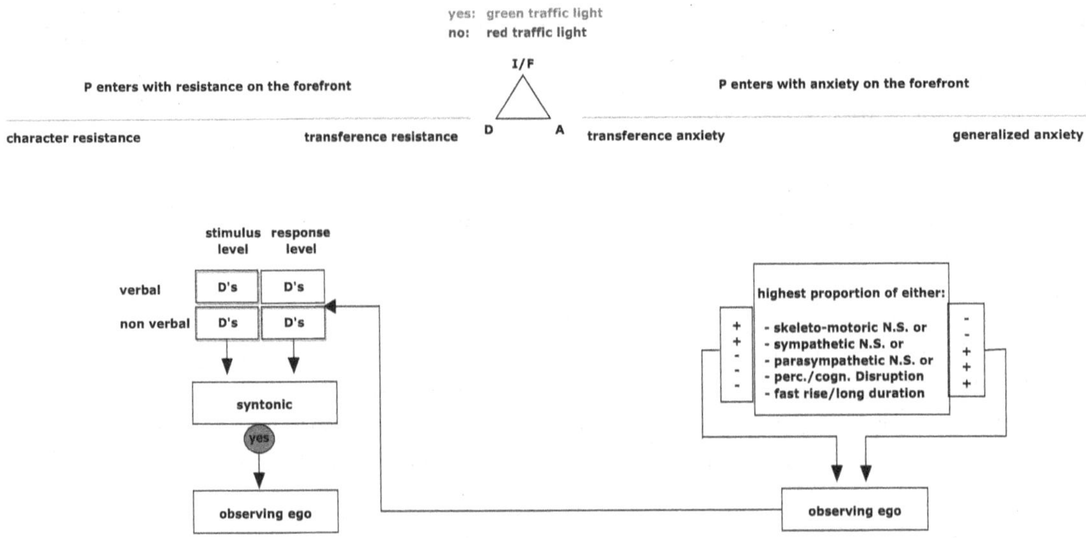

Figure 39. Somatizing patient 1: road to the unconscious 2.

Th OK, you don't have that symptom. How about nausea?

Pt No.

Th How about lower gastro intestinal disturbance like constipation or diarrhoea? I don't mean at the moment, I mean …

Pt No I don't have that problem at all.

Th OK, how abut mental symptoms of anxiety, difficulties with concentration?

Pt Do you mean right now?

Th Now or does it ring true?

Pt Yeah, I don't have the ease of concentration; I've had at points of my life.

Th OK, that's good. Not good that you have it, but good that you observe it so would you say that's been worse over what period of time that you observe it, how long has the concentration problem been with you?

Pt Well, it's actually quite a bit better in the last number of months, I've had extremely difficult times where literally ordering a coffee, I could be in line and half way through ordering I am literally my mind drifts off and I have to come back and say that's right I'm ordering coffee. Imagine that.

Th Of course I can imagine that. I've heard it many times and I can appreciate your precise observation that is one of the symptoms of anxiety that you suffer from. Losing track of your thoughts, losing track of your intention, it kind of goes away, you get distracted, it's kind of distractibility idea. Would you say that is a good description of it?

Pt Yes.

Th OK, excellent, OK, great. What I would like to do with you is get your permission on investigating what is the source of your anxiety?

Pt OK.

We have consolidated the observing ego. We are at Figure 40, below.

Th I think it could really help you an enormous amount. I immediately noticed in you a pattern that you know when I focused you on your body and your mind is grappling with the symptoms the sensations of anxiety, there seems to be association with your pain, anxiety pain. The two thing seems to have some interaction, I don't know if your aware or agree with that or not.

Pt Well, I do think that is true, I think there are other factors to but, physically to. That's a tricky circuit to understand you know the pain itself, I think it gives me anxiety as well, I think it kind of gets yea, I fill like it kind of gets me sometimes.

Th You're talking about a negative feedback.

Pt Yes.

Th Absolutely, so when is the last time that that occurred to you.

Pt Well.

Th One of those negative feedback loops. Did you see your anxiety just went up, even asking the question?

Pt Well, because it was just last night, I woke up at 3 a.m., even the slightest movement in the spine it felt so inflamed I couldn't fall asleep.

Th Again, when you said felt inflamed, you are making a causality issue and I don't want to do that?

The patient is 1) somatizing instead of 2) noticing anxiety and 3) because of ignoring anxiety and doing something about his pain symptoms result which 4) in itself causes obsessive worrying.

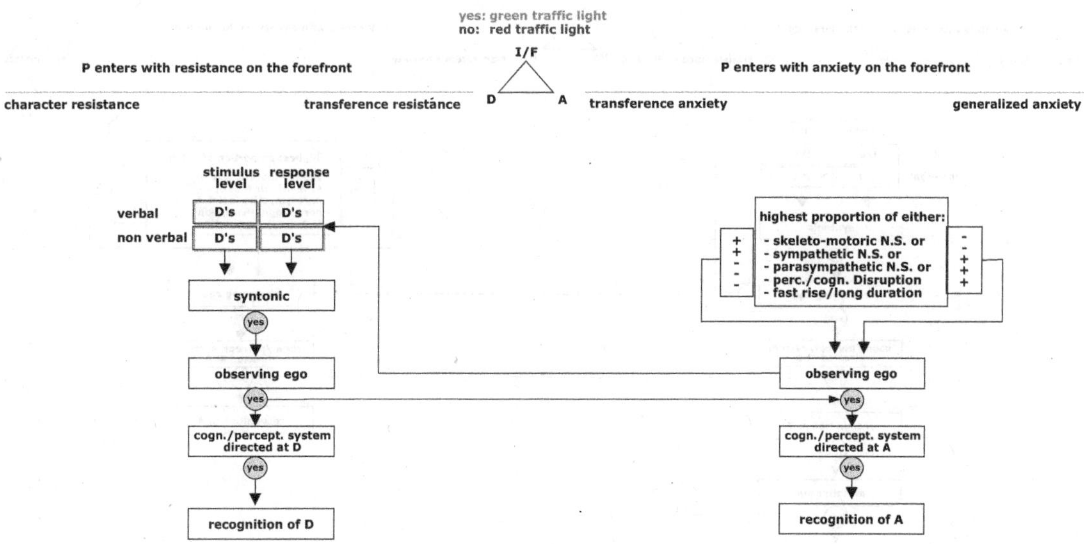

Figure 40. Somatizing patient 1: road to the unconscious 3.

Pt OK.
Th Do you follow me when I do that? Tell me precisely what you observed, what did you notice in your body without inferring any cause?
Pt Any movement exacerbated the pain, if I moved my neck …
Th To the left to the right?
Pt All movement.
Th What was the nature of the pain that you experienced?
Pt It was, it felt inflamed.
Th Inflamed, you did it again.
Pt It felt hot.
Th Hot, so you had a hot burning sensation.
Pt Yes, burning.
Th Aggravated by motion.
Pt Yes.
Th OK, was there anything else that you observed with respect to your pain, was there other manifestations of it, did it radiate anywhere?

We are at Figure 41, below.

(The therapist undoes the defence at the level of the response—somatization, moving towards somatic delusion.)

Pt No.
Th So it stayed in the back in your neck.
Pt Sometimes I felt "radiculopathy".

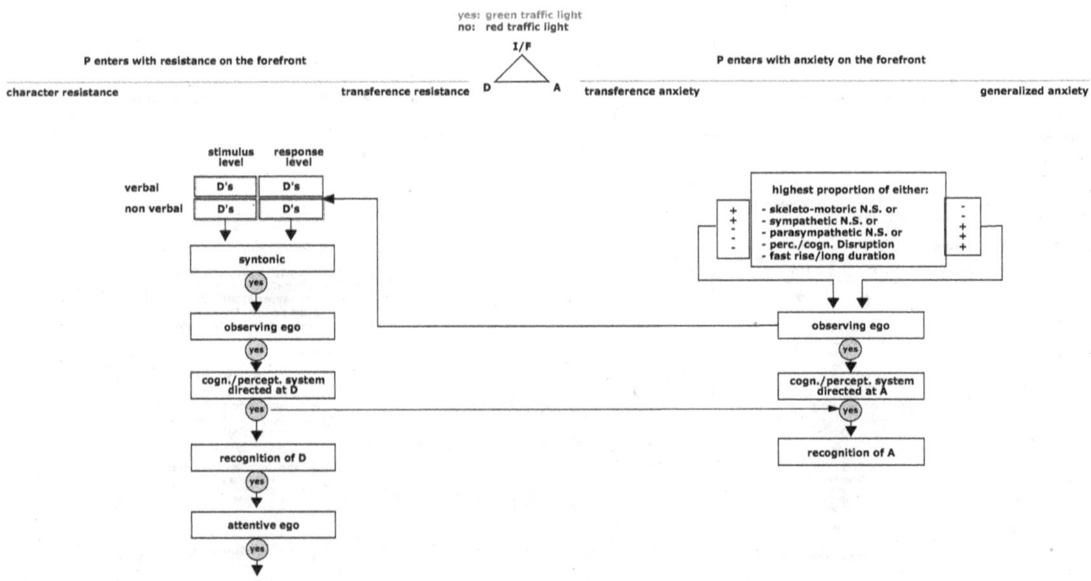

Figure 41. Somatizing patient 1: road to the unconscious 4.

(This is fascinating use of medical jargon to disguise a feeling—radiculopathy is spinal pressure on a nerve, which he does not have, the patient is again moving towards somatic delusion formation.)

Th No jargon, you can feel shooting pains down your arm, but the minute you label it with a medical term you are making causality errors.

Pt OK.

Th Do you understand that when I am saying that to you?

Pt Yeah.

Th What do I mean?

Pt While I am diagnosing, causality would mean why is it happening?

Th Your making it into a medical condition with a particular cause.

Pt Exactly.

Th Haven't you been through a diagnostic evaluation?

(A long discussion ensued of the consultant who evaluated, whom he liked and praised for his thoroughness. He, of course, ignored and distorted the findings to suit his delusion despite idealizing the consultant.)

Pt OK, I haven't seen the report but he did mention it.

Th Please, please, please when we are working together what you do on your time is totally up to you, but when you are with me, do not label things in medical terms, it is self-destructive behaviour on your part because then it makes Kevin the highest specialist on the planet and it makes Dr X and Y including me and other physicians that have seen you secondary to you and I do not think that you want to do that do you? (confrontation and identification of the patient's grandiosity—going for dystonicity of faulty conclusion formation.)

Pt Yeah, I will just not use medical terms.

Th Do you understand my point?

Pt Yeah, yeah, and yeah exactly.

Th Say what my point is please?

Pt Well you are saying that I am making statements that were not medically made by the physician who made the diagnostic test.

Th When you are doing that what am I saying to you when you do that?

Pt That I am making conclusions that the doctor did not make.

Th See I am saying more than that, I am glad that I had you repeat it. You didn't get the whole idea. You are making yourself the smartest doctor on the planet and making everyone else subordinate to you.

(The therapist is trying to make the patient's defence of grandiosity ego dystonic. The therapist focuses on his satisfaction with making himself an expert, giving himself power he doesn't have, therewith doing his best to make this defence more dystonic.)

Pt OK.

Th Would you say that back to me, not that you believe it but that you heard it.

Pt I am making myself the smartest doctor on the earth and everyone else subordinate to me.

Th Exactly! That's my point. Ok, do you agree with that point or disagree with that point?

Pt I, I guess I would have to say I'm conflicted.

Th That's a good answer actually.

Pt Thank you, I'm conflicted because I'm, well I guess I would have to say, I think your point is right on, I have had three people say "Scleropathy" (a made-up word) three physicians, and if he didn't mention, it I did have that diagnostic two other times so.

Th OK, but you went to Dr. X for a definitive opinion that was your intention of seeing him.

Pt Yes.

Th Now what is your intention of seeing me?

Pt Well I am trying to … the first two things I mentioned and of course you added something, which is I am trying to address a pain situation and understand, and then be able to handle it better and also I am very concerned about Laurel and what it is doing to our marriage and what it is doing to her.

Th What it's doing to you because if your marriage is getting hurt you are getting hurt.

Pt Yeah, exactly.

Th Right, and then I added in the observation of anxiety a problem with paying attention to it and ignoring it and that I could aggravate conditions.

Pt Exactly.

Th Now, I just want to make it clear as I get it in which you just summarized and it was well done, you are asking my help with your pain condition. You are asking this doctor here.

Pt Um well, exactly.

Th So, don't you have to take a fairly balanced view, not in the sense of that I am god or anything like that, but don't you have to take a balanced view of my opinion here.

(Trying to undo projection of his omnipotent (all-knowing) superego and the defence of reactive defiance.)

Pt Well, I think I need to absorb what you have to offer and that would be the benefit of coming here.

Th Yeah, that is what you are asking me to help you with and if you are closed … if you are the head doctor and I am the intern you are not going to listen to my opinion at all, you are going to go "ho, ho, ho, that dumb intern what does he know".

Pt OK, no, no, no you are absolutely right.

Th At time to time if I ask you for an opinion I am going to ask you to repeat it just to make sure that you haven't dismissed the opinion before you've had a chance to evaluate it and make up your own mind.

Pt OK, that makes a lot of sense to me.

(Working alliance is now consolidated.)

Th Good, so I want to get us back on track here to the feeling that you described here is very, very important to me, is the feeling of being on guard.

Pt Yes.

Th OK, so would you take a look at that with me? The stimulus for your being on guard obviously is you being here with me.

Pt Yes, it is … right now. But, it does not mean that I am not prone to being on guard in other situations.

(The therapist stimulates insight between T and C.)

Th I wouldn't doubt that for a million years.

Pt Exactly, you couldn't have put it better.

Th But since we are not in all those other situations, which are numerous, we have a great opportunity here to examine together you being on guard with me.

Pt OK, I one hundred per cent agree.

Th So if there is a pattern of you, if, this is not a conclusion it is a hypothesis, of anxiety aggravating pain, it would really be important to us to find out what the stimulus is for your anxiety and if we could address the stimulus for your anxiety, perhaps through the back door we could alleviate some maybe not all but some of your pain.

Pt OK.

Th Would you review that me that is one of thing that I want you to repeat to make sure that it got through and that we are both on the same page.

Pt Well you are wanting to determine with the feeling that the pain is exacerbated by anxiety, you would like to determine, get to the root of what the anxiety source might be in an effort to break or expose the cycle that could lead to greater pain.

Th Yes, excellent, not exactly my language but it is close enough.

Pt A rephrase.

Th A rephrase but it is good.

....

....

Pt That one was just a weird one but that one I actually did feel I just swoosh from my head but the others haven't.

Th Tell me about the energy field you just felt.

Pt The circuit.

Th Precision please, Kevin you're a precise man, precise. What energy flow did you feel and what energy flow just then?

Pt This one was from my head to my toe.

Th From your head to your toes.

Pt Mm Hmm.

Th The energy is going against whom? Who is it going against?

Pt Against me.

Th Yeah. You see, that's what self-destructive people do, is they turn their energy against themselves. So let's see what happens when you turn the energy against me. Just turn the energy against me, your tightening again Kevin (therapist shows his jaw).
Pt I don't like to do that, you're good person, I don't want to be angry at you.

(The patient now has an internal conflict over angry feelings in the T.)
We are here at 60 minutes into the consultation:

Th Listen, listen …
Pt I don't want to be angry you're great,

(The patient uses the front-door defence of idealization.)

Th Good, so where does the energy want to go now in your body if you give it permission to go wherever it wants to go? Your not in control of the energy in your body any more now.
Pt (Patient takes deep breath.) (Striated muscle anxiety confined to the rib cage, green light.)
Th Yes. Something just happened inside of you Kevin, I do not know what it was but I know something important just happened inside of you.
Pt This one wants to go out to whole world.

(The patient uses the defences of general terms mixed with denial.) On the road to the unconscious we are at Figure 42, below.

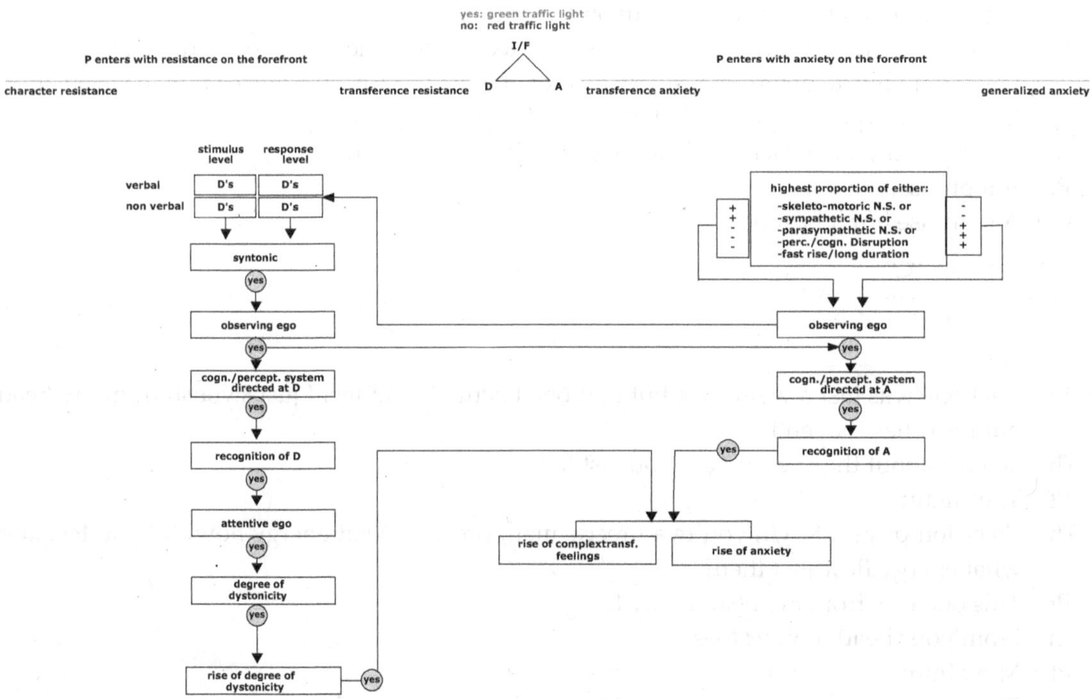

Figure 42. Somatizing patient 1: road to the unconscious 5.

Th That's good.
Pt Not you, you are just like a part of the world.
Th I agree with you, but let's start with this part of the world. Let's just start in this room and then you can take it to the rest of the world.
Pt OK.
Th So how does it start here if it comes out here?
Pt OK I will tell you what causes the anger.
Th It's fine if you want to start there.
Pt Which is a break through by the way, I wouldn't have done this.

(The therapist notices an early unconscious therapeutic alliance communication.)

Th I want you to investigate the anger, loving, caringly, with curiosity.
Pt OK.
Th But you won't do it, do you understand that's the resistance.
Th How does it come out here? Combative, I feel combative those are your words. How does it come out, describe combat.
Pt Well I create tension …
Th Repeat it.
Pt The destructive element out of my body has a rampage filled in me.
Th How does it look to you?
Pt How does it look to me?
Th That's Dr. Kevin, you learned this a long time ago Kevin, you've learned to distort at the level of input, you don't even let the inputs in. It seems like someone was very verbally abusive to you. This is a symptom of someone who was verbally abused, they don't let themselves be abused they block at the level of input.
Pt Yeah, Yeah.
Th Do you see that?
Pt Mm Hmm.
Th If you let all that combative energy out against your abuser, what would it look like? The guy who insulted you, in other words, channel the energy into a mental image.
Pt I guess I, this is quite amazing, I don't ….
Th Do you have a picture in your head, yes or no?
Pt I have a picture this is not, this not very strange here this, is not? … I don't feel angry.
Th Do you have a picture in your head, yes or no?
Pt Well naturally, I have a picture of my father. He was a military officer and he was very strict with me.
Th You have a picture in your head of your father?
Pt Yeah, he is a very strong-minded person.
Th Excellent. So you've been projecting your father onto to me and that's when you come in … Kevin please (Patient tries to cross legs), you projected your father onto me, correct? The image that image and then you come here and I am a strong-minded person that is going to do harm to you.

The therapist makes a linkage of the transference of his perception of his father (a military general P) onto the therapist (T).

Pt I project behaviours, yeah exactly, that I become expert at which is blocking input.
Th Yeah, how does it feel Kevin to understand that Kevin, that is beautiful in my opinion that understanding.
Pt It feels kind of disturbing.
Th How so?
Pt Well to think that I am so vigorously blocking access to me from the offset. So I think wow that is not good, I don't feel good about that.

(His defences at input are becoming dystonic.)

Th Kevin you just said that you had a bad feeling. Don't incriminate yourself; stop it, you're allowed to feel to bad. You're allowed to have sad feelings, you're allowed to. You just described something that is very sad that you have done to yourself. Kevin do you understand that this is not your fault?
Pt Well …
Th Kevin do you understand that?
Pt Yeah, I do.
Th Really, could you say it?
Pt Yes, it is not my fault.
Th Maybe three, four or five times.
Pt It is not my fault.
Th Say it again.
Pt It is not my fault. It is not fault.
Th How does that feel to hear those words?
Pt It feels good. It feels good.
Th Could you repeat the insight that you just had, the one that brought up all this emotion in you? This genuine insight, this incredibly valuable about this problem.
Pt Well the insight that I have is that it's a behaviour, I immediately block input the minute I sense danger associated with it.
Th That's lovely.
Pt I'm on guard for sensing harmful penetration.

(The therapist notes a clear a reference to fear of homosexual feelings.)

Th Right because you project that image of your father into the surface, the relational surface and you are fighting this battle with your dad over and over again. For how long have you been doing this?
Pt Well I've been doing it along time but …
Th How long is a long time?
Pt Since I was a little kid.
Th How many years is it?

Pt Close to my age.
Th How many years is that?
Pt I'm 56.
Th How many years have you been doing this?
Pt Probably since I've learned how to do it, since probably 3, 4, 5, 6, I don't know.
Th Yes, 53 years. Think it has taken a toll on your body?
Pt Well, Yeah.
Th Yeah, and why are you here Kevin? What do you have a problem with?
Pt Well, I have a problem with the experience of …
Th Why are you here? What are you asking my help for?
Pt I would like not to …
Th A problem with your body.
Pt Yeah.
Th Can you see that you have not been kind to your body, by making a psychological, relational issue right into a physical issue? You haven't been kind to Kevin.

(The therapist attempts to make somatizing ego dystonic.)

Pt Yeah. (Patient takes deep breath and fidgets in his seat.)
Th What happened just then? What happened inside? I saw a very strong reaction in your face, in your body.
Pt I have a lot of energy, I can feel the stimulation.
Th Yeah, I can see and anxiety is on the forefront Kevin. Five bursts of anxiety that you ignored, don't do that …. I consider ignoring a form of neglect, which is a form of violence against oneself. Neglecting yourself is a form of violence against you. So can we pay attention to what is going on in there? Can we lower your anxiety and address your emotions?
Pt Yes.
Th Can you tell me what the emotion is inside? (pause) What is creating all this anxiety inside? You have to have a tremendous amount of emotions coming out to have five bursts of anxiety come out, five we counted them.
Pt I have a hard time holding …
Th Um, Um, Um, Um. Don't do that Kevin, emotions are one word, label your feeling please.
Pt Well, I suppose I feel fear too.
Th Kevin …
Pt I feel tension.
Th Kevin, anxiety, fears, tension are all the same thing, of course you do. You suffer from chronic unrelenting anxiety. But what is the feeling that you are having with me right now? (Patient takes a deep breath.) Anxiety, say I am having anxiety with you right now Dr. Neborsky.
Pt Well, I'm having anxiety with you.
Th Lovely, could we do something about that together?
Pt Mm Hmm.
Th Could we pay attention to the anxiety? Where do you fell the anxiety? Mainly in your chest right.

Pt Right, kind of right through here. (Patient shows his abdomen area and chest area.)
Th So what other feelings are there besides anxiety, Kevin?
Pt Guilt.
Th You have guilt.
Pt Guilt.
Th You have guilt.
Pt Yes.
Th Describe it. How does it feel?
Pt Sad.
Th Sad, so you choose Kevin anxiety or sadness which do you prefer? Anxiety destroys your body and sadness heals. Which do you prefer to feel?
Pt Sadness is a tough word to think about, so I am resisting sadness.
T So tell me again what is the sad thought? (Patient takes another deep breath.) Lower the anxiety.
Pt Disappointing others.
Th You feel that you have disappointed someone?
Pt Mm Hmm.
Th Who?
Pt Lauren. (Patient begins to sob deeply.)
T Just let it out Kevin, just let it out.
Pt And Sally.
Th And Sally your daughter? You love them.
Pt (Patient nods head, yes.)
Th Let it out, you have disappointed them.
Pt (Patient nods head, yes.)
Th Yeah, I know you have.
Pt With one act.
Th With just one act?
Pt Yes.
Th I'm sorry to hear that. Is there something that you would like to get off your chest?
Pt (Patient is crying.)
Th Listen to me, listen to my words, I don't care what it is.
Pt I'm having a hard time, its actually shocking.
Th Will you let me help you with that?
Pt Well I'm getting there, I feel close, I have been working on this for two years.
Th Will you let me help you with your need to punish yourself?
Pt Yes.
Th Good, I want to. So what are you being so hard on yourself about with respect to Sally and Lauren?
Pt Well, I feel that I was cavalier? I feel that I have put them at risk.
Th I don't know what you are talking about. I'm totally clueless to what you are … what have you done?
Pt Well I um.

Th Be specific.
Pt I changed my life when I was in that car accident and I did something really bad when I did that and I really put them at risk when I did that.
Th You did what?
Pt When I had that car accident everything in my life changed at that very minute when I had that car accident.
Th Yeah.
Pt Well I … I feel really embarrassed to tell you this.

(The patient has a breakthrough of compassion for his wife and daughter, not himself. He is identified with his father and taking a self-judging stance for his accident. This is a challenging defence. The guilt is unhealthy guilt—not the healthy guilt over a murderous impulse towards an attachment figure.)

Th OK, if you don't want to tell me then don't tell me. This is only if it will give you relief, if this is going to be another weapon for you to use against yourself.

(The therapist attempts to *undo* identification with his father, the aggressor.)

Pt No, I will tell you, I just feel really embarrassed to tell you and I actually … this was a secret that I was always going to keep, but I actually confessed it a couple of weeks ago and it was a very terrible …
Pt I think I will just tell you what it is.
Th But this is what you wanted?
Pt Yeah.
Th You are not doing it for me but you are doing it for you. Aren't you doing this for you? It is obviously causing you pain.
Pt I feel like I am in excessive distress.
Th It is causing you pain isn't it?
Pt Yeah, I feel like I betrayed Lauren and Sally.
Th I understand that, the accusation of betrayal but I don't know what you did.
Pt I have this really tough time saying this one specific thing, I told myself that this is … this may sound shocking but it is the one secret thing that I have had in life.
Th Kevin, again listen to me carefully, obviously there is one part of you that wants to share and one part of you that wants to keep punishing yourself. You asked me and said I want you to help me stop being so self-punitive towards myself—"whenever I have done something I feel guilty about I am relentlessly abusive towards myself, I punish myself without mercy".

(The therapist again attempts to *undo* identification with his father, the aggressor.)

Pt This is off the charts.
Th Kevin you are trying to tell me that you are a man without mercy.
Pt Absolutely, I just can't forgive myself.

Th Yeah, Kevin do you want my help or not?
Pt Yeah.
Th What do you want my help with?
Pt Not feeling bad about this thing that I did …
Th No, I can't help you with that. You have a very unrealistic expectation, no one is perfect. Everybody screws up.
Pt I guess I …
Th Listen to me! I can help you with one thing, to stop taking a self-punitive stance. That is all I can help you with. I can help you stop punishing yourself; I can help you handle your feelings about what you have done in a different way. Would you like my help with that? OK.

(For the third time, the therapist again attempts to *undo* identification with his father, the aggressor.)

Pt (Patient nods head, yes, and cries again.)

We are at Figure 43, on the next page, at the green light.

Th So you say that you feel sad over what you have done to yourself?
Pt Yes.
Th And how does the sadness feel in your body.
Pt I feel that I am being punished for it.
Th Kevin, who is the punisher?
Pt Me.
Th You, now that is correct causality you hear? "I did something that I am unhappy with and the way I decide to punish Kevin to do something when he has done something that I am unhappy with is to punish him. I have no mercy for him, I will turn him into a psychological and physical cripple without mercy." Do you perceive that?
Pt Yeah, exactly.
Th Who are you imitating Kevin? Whose stance are you taking it towards Kevin?
Pt My father. He punished me if I wasn't perfect … if I didn't anticipate everything that could go wrong … (crying, sobbing)

(The therapist observes the patient deepening compassion towards himself.)

Th I don't think it is a reach do you? So you are not running your life.
Pt Yeah.
Th Who is running your life?
Pt Well, uh …
Th Who is running your life?
Pt Well …
Th Who is running your life? The internalized image of your father that is running your life.
Pt This confession is …

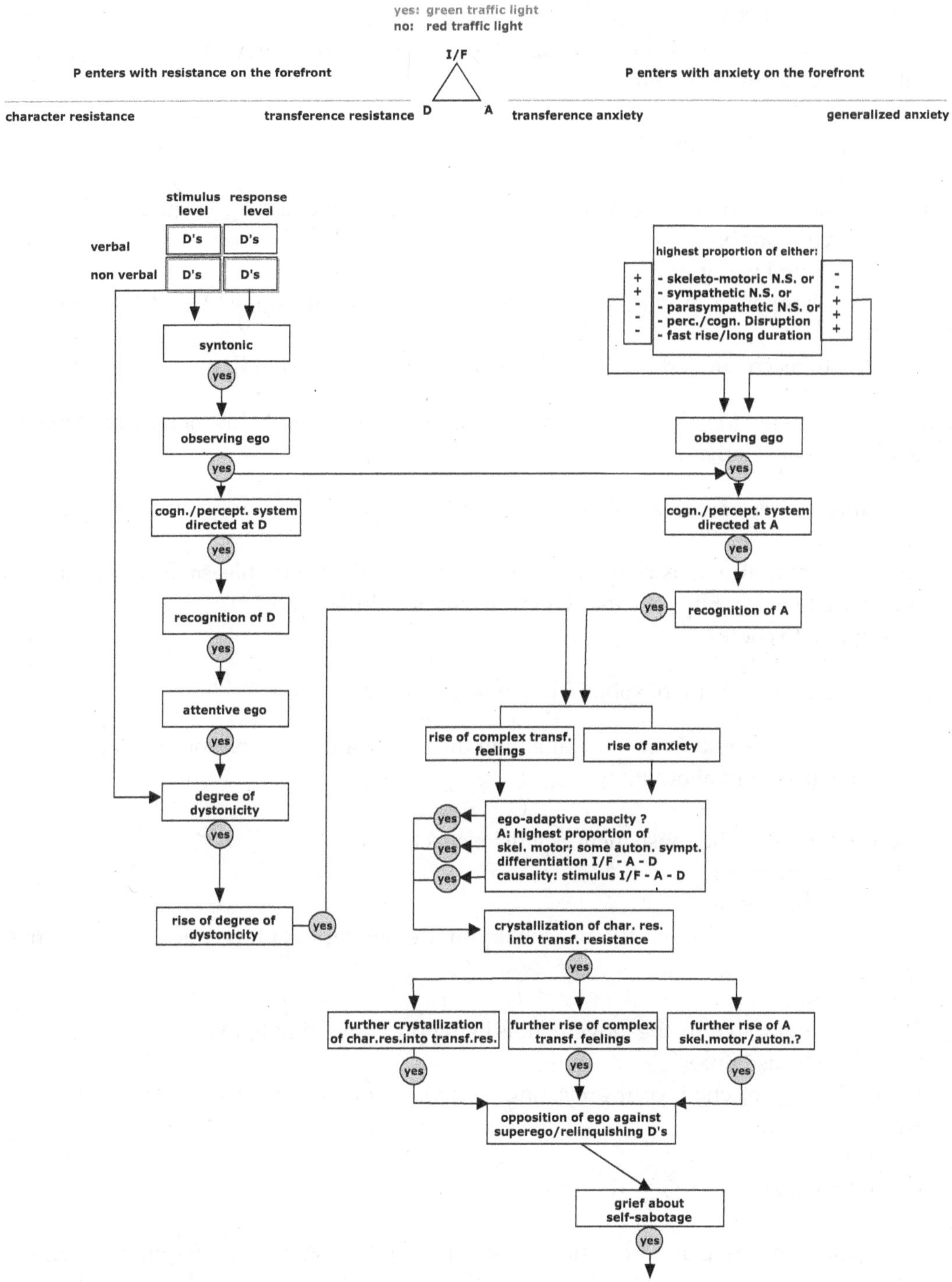

Figure 43. Somatizing patient 1: road to the unconscious 6.

Th Yeah, but don't deny the whole punishment. The punishment is to make you into a psychological, emotional and physical cripple. You have no mercy, you will not stop, you will stop punishing yourself.

Pt Well you see … (Patient stretches out in his chair.)

Th Kevin, what just happened?

Pt I'm thinking …

Th Pay attention to Kevin, he is the most important man in the universe right now. What just happened in your body?

Pt I was thinking I was going …

Th What just happened in your body, you don't think in your body? Don't intellectualize, observe.

Pt I wanted to reach out and hold your hand and felt anxiety in doing it.

(We have de-repressed longings for closeness, love, and attachment to his therapist but blocked with anxiety from his father.)

Th (Therapist agrees and gives the patient a hand shake.)

Pt Thank you.

Th You had an impulse to reach out and what was the full impulse please. In what way were you going to reach out to me that you were cut off with anxiety?

Pt I was going to confess.

(The patient uses the defence of submission to father and undoing.)

Th Of your own free will. That was something that you want to do for you, kindness.

Pt That's what's weird about it.

Th What?

Pt Because I feel that the consequences will be enacted.

Th What consequences?

Pt The consequences of …

Th What consequences? I don't know what you are talking about. Be specific, what consequences?

Pt Your disdain.

Th Oh, my disdain, so now the judgement is being projected onto to me.

Pt Everybody's disdain.

Th Kevin, this is projection, your projecting your father into me again and expecting a different damn result.

Pt Mm Hmm.

Th Do you see that?

Pt Yeah.

Th Doing the same thing and expecting a different result is the modern definition of insanity. Your insane right when you project your father into me that is an act of insanity. When you believe that I am going to sit here and judge you that's insane, all you are ding is turning me into your father and you really think that something else is going to happen in your life that is beneficial to you as a result of doing that. You project your father into me, you project your father into Lauren, you project your father into Sally, you project your father into your psychotherapist. You are not in psychotherapy; you are just in another form of a relationship with your father all the time, all the time. It's got to get old, he was a nasty man.

Th Your talking to whom right now?

Pt I'm talking to you but I hear my Dad and he's saying "you're actually an amazing guy and you actually know what you are doing, you tried really hard to impress upon me how to do things in an incredibly responsible fashion at all times, just absolutely super-responsible to the point that you can't, don't blow it". I did blow it and actually did something that … I am absolutely ashamed of myself, that I put my family at risk by driving the car down the freeway with no other cars around, thinking about something else, and the car goes into spin, I hit a curb, it rolls down an embankment and at 60 mph, I was not wearing a seat belt, and I felt like I was going to die, and I got thrown around in a car going 60 mph with no seat belt, and I was shocked when I woke up after being knocked out that I was still alive. I obviously felt great pain, there was great pain everywhere, I was thrown around going 60 mph.

Th The feelings are coming Kevin, let the feelings come. What are the feelings?

Pt (Patient begins to sob with guilt.) It was wrong the thing to do to Phoebe and Laurel.

Th Let the feeling come; don't worry about anybody else other than Kevin. What is the feeling right now? Grief isn't it, guilt and grief.

Pt Yeah, and I feel like I am constantly punished by it now.

Th What do you want to hear from your Dad?

Pt He would be so sad. (Patient begins to cry.)

Th What do you want to hear from your Dad?

Pt That's OK, Kevin, that's actually what he would say, he wouldn't be judgemental. He would be really sad.

Th Could you receive your Dad's love? Stop punishing yourself, Kevin, for making a mistake. (Patient is crying.) Can you stop punishing yourself for making a mistake? Here, your Dad does not want you to keep punishing yourself.

Pt Now I pay the price.

Th Kevin, the price is self-imposed.

Pt I do have pain …

Th Kevin! Kevin! The price is self-imposed, end of story, shut up. Hear the words, say it back to me.

Pt I …

Th Kevin look at me please, Kevin what did I say?

Pt The price is self-imposed.

Th End of story. Let it sink in, you have been punishing yourself by making yourself a physical and psychological cripple because you can't accept not being perfect, end of story, if you add another word to it you are being self-destructive, let it sink in. Let it sink in, as a little boy of three years old, you developed this idealized image of your father whom you had to perfect in order to win his love. Your real father says it is OK, but this image of your father in your head is without mercy and says that you must suffer the consequences of your mistake by being a psychic cripple, by being detached, by being alone, by being isolated, by being banished from the people you love, your wife and your child. End of story, there are no more stories, you both accept that and work with it, or you go back to the world according to Kevin. Now I can help you.

Pt I am having a hard time taking that leap.

Th I can help you if you want me to help you. Do you want me to help you? Do you want me to help you?

Pt Yeah.

Th Learn how to treat yourself better. That is what I am going to teach you how to do if you let me. Do you want me to do that you, you can say no, you don't have to come back.

Pt Well think I, I feel like I ... I have to make a decision I don't want to make that appointment yet.

Th OK.

Pt I actually feel like I need to, I am trying to see whether I need to make this confession because everything rides on me making that confession.

Th Kevin, again if you think that this problem is as simple as solving it as a simple confession. The worst thing you can do is make a complex problem simple. I am all for you making your confession, I have no problem with you doing that, but your problem is larger than that, OK, you have a wall and you project your father's eyes on to your wife and child. You think they are disappointed in you like you imagined your Dad would be. The pain is your way of punishing yourself for your act of rebellion against your Dad's instructions. We know as a child you had a lot of anger at your Dad and you were also afraid of him. So the punitive part of you is this child-like perception of your Dad. You even directly projected him onto me, and remember you had a searing pain in your back last night.

The session ends with the patient developing insight into his need to punish himself for his act of defiance against his father's instructions as well as his unexpressed negative emotions against his Dad. Following the session, he reported a significant decrease in pain and returned to biking. The patient decided to continue with his psychotherapist and promised to be more in touch with his emotions in his therapy. His pain has improved; he makes fewer causality errors; however, his relationship with his wife has not significantly improved.

We are at the end of our roadmap. See Figure 44 on the next page.

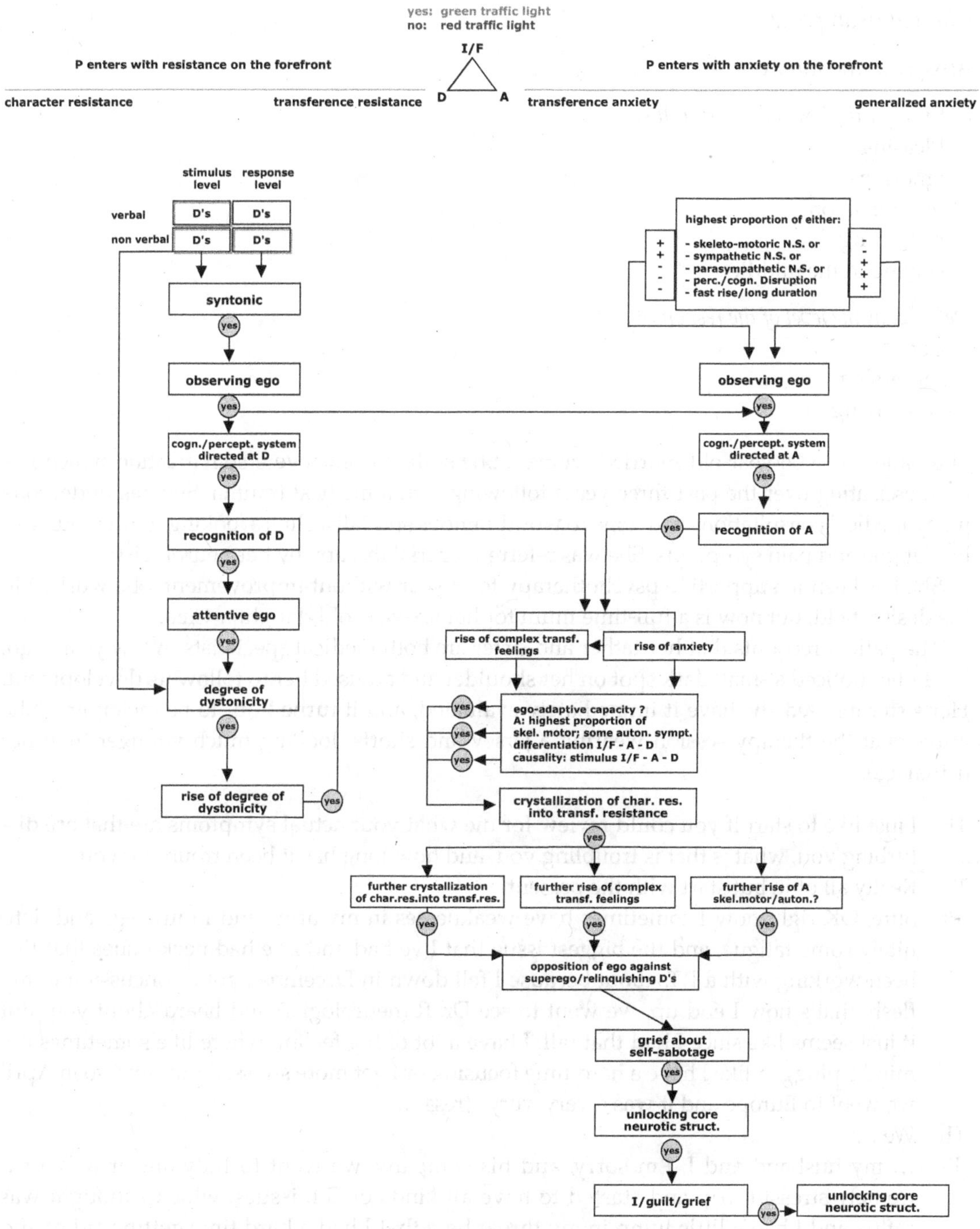

Figure 44. Somatizing patient 1: road to the unconscious 7.

Clinical example 2

Anxiety at the forefront

Defences at the level of the stimulus:

Pleasing
ignoring
minimization
neglecting
staying in the middle

Defences at the level of the response:

denial
repressing
somatizing

The patient is a 36-year-old married woman. She suffers from severe somatization which has been escalating over the past three years following actual medical trauma. She has undergone many medical consultations and gone to world-famous specialist clinics looking for the source of her fatigue and pain symptoms. She was referred for trial therapy by her neurologist.

She has been in supportive psychotherapy for a year without improvement. She worked in the design field, but now is a full-time mum for her six-year-old daughter Cleo.

The patient recounts that her father and sister are both medical specialists. A few years ago, her father noticed a small dark spot on her shoulder and advised her to follow its development. Her sister insisted she have it immediately evaluated, and it turned out to be melanoma. She appears at the therapy session wearing a jersey and shorts, looking much younger than her actual age.

Th I just like to start if you could review for me what your actual symptoms are that are disturbing you, what is that is troubling you, and how long has it been troubling you.

Th Really all of it, but start with the present.

Pt Sure, OK right now I sometimes have weaknesses in my arms and in my legs and definitely some fatigue, and the biggest issue that I've had and I've had neck issues that I've been working with a P.T. about because I fell down in December, got a concussion in my flesh, that's how I end up, we went to see Dr. R (neurologist) and heard about you. But it just seems like since I had that fall, I have a lot of fog feeling where like sometimes my mind's plugged like I have a hard time focusing or I get more stressed out. And so in April we went to Europe and it was a very, very stress …

Th We …

Pt … my husband and I, I'm sorry, and his company, we went to Italy and it was a extremely stressful trip and started to have all kinds of G.I. issues, which I thought was reflux and I had a little lump in my throat here that I had a hard time getting rid of and so I went to a E.N.T. doctor mid-June who said I had symptoms and he looked with a scope and said that I had damage from reflux and swell. And so I have been taking an anti-reflux medicine, but recently I just had an endoscopy last week and don't see any signs of reflux.

Th Good …

Pt Ah, yeah and would say that for me, I mean I've had issues before I think I was always sensitive, I had hyperventilation when I was a teenager, cause I …

Th Had you?

Pt I did.

Th That's anxiety, isn't it?

Pt Yes, yeah, you know you do and you get all, your arms and your legs get all tensed up and the breathing you know you're probably very familiar with what it is, I don't need to explain to you. But, ah, yeah I ….

Th So you've suffered from anxiety since the teenage years.

Pt I guess, what happened when I was a …

Th Why do you say, I guess, ah … (therapist, chuckling)

(The therapist highlights the defence of "in the middle".)

Pt Yes, yeah (Patient laughs also), well I didn't know if it was anxiety-related that time, hyperventilation or if it was just emotional stress. I don't really know if there's different meaning or not.

Th Well, you could call a bird a bird, or you can call it an eagle, or you can call it a sparrow, but it's still a bird. Hyperventilation is caused by anxiety, nothing else but anxiety, right. (Patient agreeing.) So you had anxiety since you were a teenager.

Pt Yes, yeah, yeah, yep, and I just, I don't know (Patient takes a deep breath), I just don't want to go on with my life like that, because I just feel my …

Th But it seems to, just that idea seems to cause you to breathe a little more deeply. What about that idea, that you have anxiety.

Pt (Patient giggles) I mean there's nothing wrong about having anxiety because we're prewired the way we are and I definitely went through a lot in my life and it's just the way I am and I have to accept it but I want to fix it in a way because …

Th Well that's what I do, but umm …

Pt Right, right, because I just think it just runs my life.

Th How can I, how can I, think it through carefully, how can I help you fix a problem if you don't want to acknowledge that you have that problem for some reason.

Pt Oh, yes I'm fine acknowledging …

Th But you know you smile when you, what is that …

(The therapist points out denial, minimization, devaluation of self, and smiling—a defence that operates at the same time at the level of the response as well as the level of the stimulus/front door.)

Pt I don't know I'm, I'm not noticing myself, I don't even … (patient laughing)

(The therapist notes silently laughing is a pleasing defence.)

Th You don't see that huh …

Pt No, I don't know, I'm not aware of my reactions; you can analyse my reactions. I don't know …

(The patient uses the defence of making herself helpless and the therapist omnipotent.)

Th Well, I can observe them, but not analysing them, I'm feeding them back to you, that, there seems to be something here that I just want to discuss with you. I not making any judgements, I'm really not, I'm really inquiring, that the idea of you suffering from anxiety, it seems to have some negative implication to you, there seems to be a negative there in your own mind about it. The way I'm assessing you and I'm wondering if I'm correct.
Pt Could be.

At the end of 20 minutes, we are at Figure 45, below.

The patient discloses that she felt secure until she was about 12, when her father started having love affairs and left her and her mother. She befriended her parent's former friends—a couple who "took care of" her and her sister. Eventually, the man sexually abused her, starting when she was thirteen, and attempted to abuse her sister a few years later.

Th Good, but you felt bad about what had happened and you were not able to go to your mother because you wanted to protect her.
Pt Yes.
Th So you carried this with you for how long?
Pt Well so, when I was umm, let's see … I think when I was around fifteen I would start to hyperventilate. When I was stressed or getting in an argument with somebody or whatever then it would just trigger and then I would just start breathing.
Th Trigger what?
Pt Trigger my hyperventilation.
Th No come on.

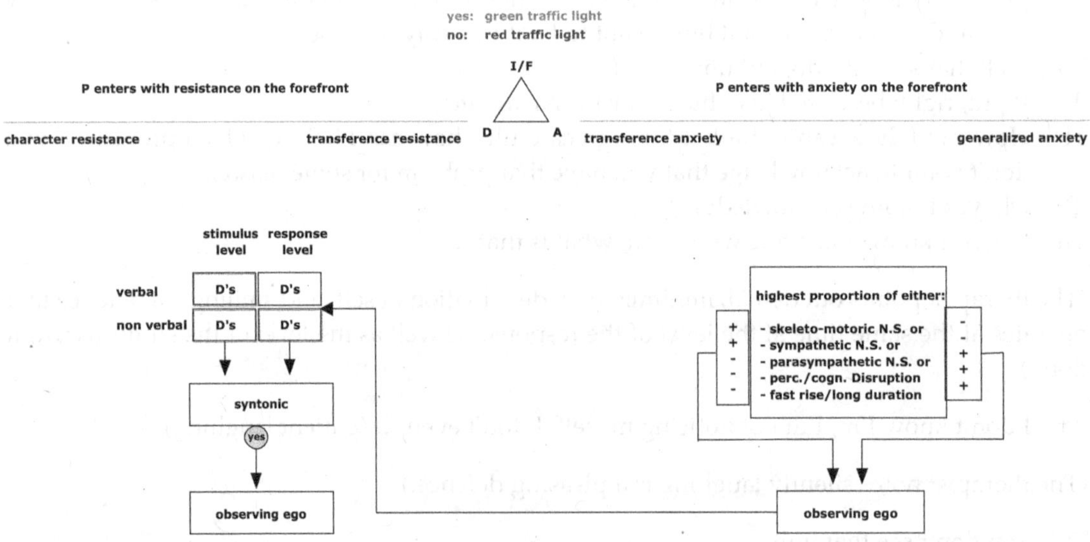

Figure 45. Somatizing patient 2: road to the unconscious 1.

Pt Oh my anxiety. (patient chuckles)
Th There you go …
Pt Oh OK, my anxiety. (patient still chuckling)
Th Please don't make having anxiety a negative.
Pt Oh OK.
Th You do have this a bit of a stance against you having anxiety. Like do you feel it is a weakness or do you feel it is a defect?
Pt I definitely, yeah I do.
Th Yeah, I get a sense that you do.

This is a classic presentation for the avoidant attachment style where the patient's parent was dysregulated by the child's distress emotions. The child is slowly taught to suppress her emotions and to please the parent. Eventually role reversal occurs, and the child becomes the parent's parent.

Pt Yeah, because I always thought, that is the thing in my teen years, I always thought "I could handle this", I know that I would look at myself in the mirror and say …
Th You can handle this meaning what?
Pt All … my parents' divorce, the fact that I got abused. I was like I will not let this impact me, this not the kind of person I want to be, I want to be a good person, and I do not want to let these events screw me up. Because I could have always gone south I guess, you know what I mean and just drinking and just you know what teenagers do, you know what I mean when they …

("Stiff upper lip" as a value which is her identification with her mother as her internal aggressor.)

Th They could act out.
Pt Yeah, I could have acted out.
Th Yeah, sure.
Pt And I didn't, I would always like very clear about the person I wanted to be but …
Th You know this is very interesting, let me comment on that. You know we all have healthy parts of our mind and we have unhealthy parts of our mind and this part of you that looks at you being in control, OK …
Pt … which is very true …
Th … of yourself at any price. I am not sure if it is entirely healthy. You know these are like a set of eyes judging you as being weak.

(The therapist points out that her "stiff upper lip" is her unhealthy obedience to the dismissive eyes of her mother.)

Pt Yes, I agree, I agree.
Th And you know and you know what it does is it discourages you from being able to be emotional and being able to get your emotions out. If you have that stance towards yourself, what you do is you tend to stuff your emotions, you put your emotions down.

When you do that, your emotions come back with a vengeance and they create anxiety. (Patient agreeing by nodding.) See if you put a higher premium on functioning than you do on feeling your emotions, even if they are very negative emotions, then that creates anxiety.

Pt Yes, yes, I guess in a way maybe I had a hard time but it depends, for the positive emotions I am very uh, uh, I am very open, I am very loving, very affectionate with my family, and I was always that way. So the positive emotions, I let them all out and …

(The patient's pathological superego requires her to be pleasant and happy for her mother's benefit.)

Th And the negative emotions?
Pt The negative emotions, I uh …
Th You notice this is when you started smiling.
Pt I just don't know what, uh, yeah in a way you put me on the spot in way, I never really realized that.
Th And how does that being on the spot here with me, how do you experience that?

(The focus is now on her experience with the therapist (T).)

Pt In a way that, wow, I don't know what to think about it, I mean how am I supposed to handle them? I don't even know. (Patient laughs.)
Th OK, you see …
Pt You know you make me think, that's what I mean, I am like wow maybe I can never … I don't know. Do you know what I mean?
Th Yes, I exactly know what you mean, but I think you are pleased am I correct that I am putting you on the spot and insisting …
Pt Yeah, you are making me think.
Th Yeah, but that is a good thing right, you don't feel bad about me do you?
Pt No, not at all.
Th Good.
Pt No, that why I am here facing the truth and dealing with it.
Th Good, I can tell. Yeah, you see how you put yourself in a bad cycle for your health. If you are discriminating against your negative emotions and stuffing them into your physical self, they are going to come back with a vengeance as anxiety like hyperventilation symptoms or vertigo, dizziness, or gastrointestinal disturbance, weakness in the arms, you can have any number of manifestations of anxiety.
Pt I have lots of pains in my body; the hard part is like should I worry about this or is that just because of anxiety or trust?
Th Well see …
Pt That's where I have a hard time.
Th But I don't want us to do is speculate on like if you have a pain, to me it's a serious matter. What I would like is for us to investigate your experiences and if we can work with them and help alleviate them, you see then you're unburdened by them and then you don't have to worry about the pain, or if we can work with the weakness and we can alleviate

the weakness then there is high degree of reassurance, a high degree of certainty that it is an emotionally based symptom.

(The therapist models a healthy superego, the two of them better investigate her problems in a precise way.)

Pt Yes, yes.
Th You see …
Pt Yes, yes, yes because you eliminate all that.
Th You eliminate it and the …
Pt Then you're left with your real symptoms and your body.
Th Right, then doesn't that make a great deal of sense?
Pt Yes, Yes …
Th Tell me about the pain, are you having it now?
Pt No, not right now just umm …
Th So right now everything feels relatively healthy in your body?
Pt Yeah, except a little weakness in my arms right now.
Th Well that's good you see we have the weakness in your arm to work with, isn't that an opportunity?
Pt Yes, yes.
Th Now you start to smile again, why do you smile when I say that it is an opportunity?
Pt (Patient shakes head no and shrugs shoulders.)
Th Are you having anxiety?
Pt No.
Th Well you might.
Pt I might but I mean I may not know because I don't know …
Th Right, because … (patient is laughing), this is what I believe …
Pt This is funny.
Th This is what you have taught yourself to do, OK.
Pt OK.
Th You have taught yourself to ignore the sensations of anxiety, until they get too high.
Pt OK.
Th So the smiling is …
Pt A nervous laugh.
Th Bull's-eye, it's a cover-up of the anxiousness. Like just then I saw your anxiety start in your hands, go up your shoulders, up your neck, down your chest, down to your pelvis, out your legs and you kicked your legs.

(Confrontation, identification, and clarification of her smiling defence at stimulus/front door—the patient is projecting her mother onto the therapist an interacting with him like she must take care of him.)

Pt I noticed my leg when up like that like uh …
Th You see so what I am going to suggest for your health is for you to pay attention to your anxiety.

Pt OK.
Th OK, but you will only do that if you don't judge your anxiety as being a sign of weakness. If you judge it as a sign of personal weakness, or if you judge yourself as being anxious as something that diminishes yourself, then you won't take the trouble to observe it.
Pt Yes, yes.
Th You will block …
Pt Yes, yes, yes.

By 30 minutes, the therapist has created a separation between the superego and the ego and has developed an observing ego. The defences have slight dystonicity.

We are on the roadmap at Figure 46, below.

At sixteen, the patient wrote to her father, who was living with his mistress, that she needed his help with something important. He ignored her. Her mother then took her to a psychologist to deal with her hyperventilation. The mother gave her no privacy with the psychologist.

We are 35 minutes into this session.

Th You know what do you feel inside? Just take a moment.
Pt Sure.
Th While you are telling me this story, let's practise by observing …
Pt (Patient grabs stomach.) I just relaxed my stomach; it was tight as I was telling you about it.
Th You relaxed your stomach.
Pt I just did it because I am being more conscious about my stomach now.
Th OK, that's good but what was the emotion that you were expressing?
Pt Of the psychologist you mean?

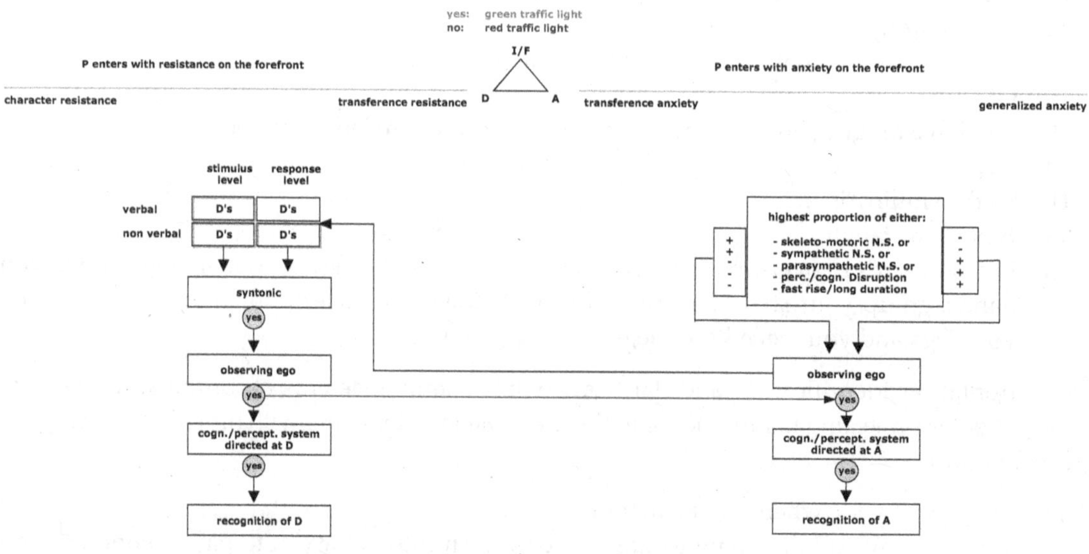

Figure 46. Somatizing patient 2: road to the unconscious 2.

Th Yes, what emotion were you expressing in your words?
Pt I didn't get to …
Th No right now.
Pt Oh, right now I'm sorry … just angry.
Th Angry.
Pt Yeah.
Th So I just wanted to point out to you …
Pt Thank you … (anxiety drops precipitously)
Th As you contact anger and as you express your anger, you notice how you started to relax a little bit.
Pt Yes.
Th Remember the whole idea while we are working here, is careful attention to your bodily experiences as you start to talk about these painful events and if we do this correctly, you see we can reprogramme your brain, you see.
Pt OK.
Th The nice thing about the brain is that the brain wants to change.
Pt And now I have the will, I want to change.

(Message that the conscious therapeutic alliance is merging with the unconscious therapeutic alliance.)

Th And you want to change you see and I am very optimistic that we will be able to make some very significant health changes for you.
Pt Yes, I am looking for answers and I am very determined to do whatever it takes.
Th Outstanding.
Pt I'm just amazed just listening to you, I'm like wow, anxiety can give all that.
Th Isn't it something? Yes, it is something. Understand I am not trying to say anything hurtful to you.
Pt I know you are not.
Th But it has been caused by a psychological self-neglect, if you look at eyes, if you have these internalized eyes that look at yourself and say that you are not allowed to have negative emotions if you do you are somehow less than, somehow defective, you are somehow a burden, if that's the stance that has been internalized …
Pt Yes, you just said two words, that were correct, a burden. Because I have people around me who say, oh you will always have something, what's next now, oh what's wrong with you now and I have felt that way like wow my health is a burden.
Th Right and we can't approach it that way, it is not accurate, it is not true.
Pt Yes my body is trying to help my mind.
Th That's correct.
Pt Yes.
Th You have to say to whosever eyes are looking at you and defining your emotions as a burden, is it your mothers eyes, is it your fathers eyes, is it both sets of their eyes, are they looking at you and saying you're a burden to me.
Pt Got you.

Th Is that you think it is or is it somebody else?
Pt I don't know.
Th Someone saying your emotional …
Pt Well, my mum would say that "you always have something definitely" definitely my mum would say that.
Th Which is s a put down?
Pt Yes, yeah.

The patient recalls that even when her mother met her husband-to-be, she told him that the patient "always had something". The therapist asks the patient what she felt about this.

We are 50 minutes into the session.

Th But what is the feeling you have when you think of her doing that, what do you notice inside?
Pt I am not really happy about it because I don't think it is helping me in any ways.

(The patient utilizes the defence of negation.)

Th OK, but you need to be a little more precise related to your feeling. If you say I am not really happy, that is a little neglecting.
Pt Oh, OK.
Th What is your feeling, what did you feel when you told me what your mum had said to your boyfriend, your husband-to-be. What did you feel inside towards her? Take a careful moment right now, take a careful moment to you, you are the most important person in the world right now and do not let anyway tell you that how you feel is not important, ok.
Pt Sure, I think I was angry and sad.
Th Right now.
Pt Mm hmm, because angry in the way that I felt, I feel in a way that maybe it is judgemental on her part.
Th I totally agree with the stimulus, but do you notice how you are slowing down your talking a little slower.

(The patient use defences of instant repression, psychomotor retardation, and intellectualization.)

Pt Yeah, I am thinking also.
Th Why, why are you …
Pt Because I have to analyse myself.
Th Why?
Pt I am very analytical; you are asking me some questions that make me think …
Th No, you were telling me I am feeling angry and I am feeling sad and then you went into your thoughts rather than … this is what causes the problem.
Pt Oh, OK.
Th You went into your analytical side.
Pt (Patient laughs) Sorry.

Th Go on, now don't apologize, you have nothing to apologize for.

(The therapist challenges intellectualization and she reverts to pleasing.)

Pt This is so interesting, I find it very good. I find it very good because I have been very analytical when I think, think, think so much and you just made me realize well what about feeling, what are you feeling? I guess I am trying to be to controlling maybe you know with my own self and I make myself laugh because it is better to laugh, I guess.
Th That's refreshing, though.
Pt Yeah, it is.
Th Don't you find it refreshing?
Pt Yes, yes, but at the same time it's all … it's all …
Th It's going to take some practice.
Pt Yes exactly, exactly.
Th Sure but I can see there is a hopefulness that just lit up in your face.
Pt No, I am just thinking about something I am sorry.
Th Stop apologizing.
Pt No, no, no, no. I just think that maybe …
Th Go with what you are thinking.
Pt OK, but is it being analytical again?
Th No if it pops into your mind …
Pt It just pops in my mind, it's a message.
Th It's like a door opening from a deeper place. It's not …
Pt This is kind of hard to say, it actually makes me emotional but …
Th Which is a good thing isn't it?
Pt Like in a way maybe (patient begins to cry) you use the word "burden" and I think maybe I feel, maybe the part of it for me to push it down and stuff, does it point to the ones I love. You know you always have "something" you just don't want to be a pain in the butt for others, you are always being drawn to negative feelings, you know what I mean, you want to be positive and just be pleasant to be around and stuff, and I was just thinking that maybe like when my mum says something like that, it's hurtful.

The patient reports that her parents separated several times during her teen years, but got back together when the patient was twenty-three. She recalls that when she tried to tell her mother about her sexual abuse, her mother stopped her.

We are 1 hour into this session.

Pt Now when I was telling the story I definitely felt some dizziness.

(She now has a somewhat attentive ego.)

We are on the roadmap at Figure 47, on the next page.

Th Bravo.

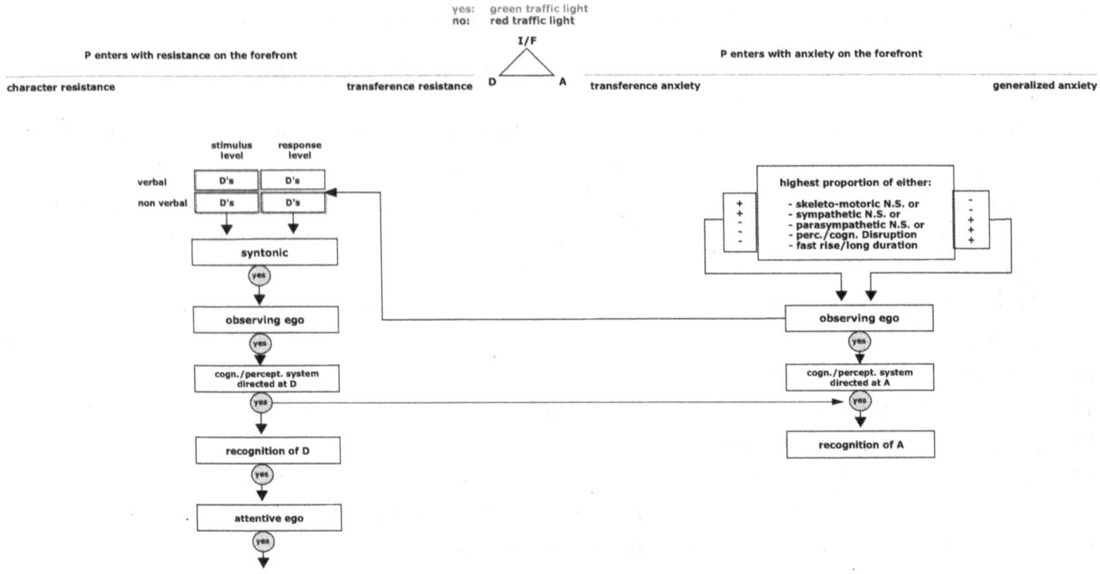

Figure 47. Somatizing patient 2: road to the unconscious 3.

Pt And I kind of feel it in the neck, coming from the neck.

Th Did you see I caught it that time, I saw it that time. I was more alert; I was more attentive to you. I am so glad that we are noticing that there is trauma here right.

Pt Yeah, I was like wow how come, whenever I get sick that it hits me so hard and just like you say "it is taking me so long to get over things".

Th Right, we are understanding how much physical infirmity anxiety can cause when it is super imposed upon medical illnesses, real illnesses, concussion was real, strep was real, and anxiety can become intertwined that is the bad news, the good news is that we can fix it by this kind of very serious systematic examination of the way your anxiety feels in your body at the moment. So what are you feeling in your body that feels odd right now, that feels anxious. What kind of sensations are you noticing inside?

Pt Right now?

Pt I feel that tingling sensation in my head right here.

Th OK, and that's called what?

Pt Anxiety.

Th Lovely.

Pt And it is OK.

Th Lovely, and again, I don't want you to forget you have strong emotions and the anxiety is here making you blind to the inner emotion that is underneath your anxiety, OK, and healing means we get to talk at the level of this …

Pt Of the emotions, yes.

Th Of the emotions.

Pt So it doesn't push anxiety up.

Th You were concealing that it was anxiety from yourself, not from me. I know it is anxiety, you were concealing it from yourself. It's a somatic manifestation of anxiety. What it is its extreme tension in your vocal cords?

Pt Yeah, I feel a little tingling in my hands right now.

Th Sure, are the hands weak or strong.

Pt It's not just weak; yeah I am probably more on the weak side but …

Th How do you like that? See that's anxiety too.

Pt I don't like it; I just feel I do not have no control over my body right now.

(The patient uses helplessness as a defence for her impulse.)

Th What do you mean you have no control over your body?

Pt I know that is part the problem I am always trying to control everything but a …

Th You are making yourself weak and helpless as if you don't have control.

Pt Yeah, we don't have to dig it to deep, it's all there (laughing).

Th Your body is getting a signal of anger; anger creates impulses in the body to act OK in an aggressive way. Rather than being aggressive, your brain is sending a signal to pull back so your body is getting two signals that are incompatible. One signal is to attack and the other signal is to pull back in order to protect.

Pt So when you say to attack, my thoughts were a little foggy, you say first to attack … to attack what the pain?

(The patient shows a rapid rise of high anxiety and goes for the defence of helplessness. We are at 90 minutes.)

On the road to the unconscious we are at Figure 48, on the next page.

Th No, to attack the person that is putting the pain on you.

Pt Oh.

Th Here, we can look at it this way. OK, this is you the child, this is you, your Dad (therapist, using figurines to illustrate), his job is to take care of you, protect you from predators. So you tell your father, daddy, daddy I have been harmed by this man, he tells you no you haven't, you are …

Pt He turns his back and walks away.

Th Right, OK, that's going to create anger and rage in you, towards him for rejecting his duty and responsibility to you. So you love him, you want to attack him, so you are in conflict. Do you protect him from your rage or do you destroy him with your rage?

Pt I don't destroy him, I protect him.

Th Who do you end up destroying?

Pt Myself, Mm hmm.

Th How is the anxiety doing right now?

Pt It just felt like it went "eertz". (Patient making a sound and gesturing that it went out.) It went through my head my neck and kind of resides.

Th Resides where?

Pt Like, it kind of just went away, like it just feel like …

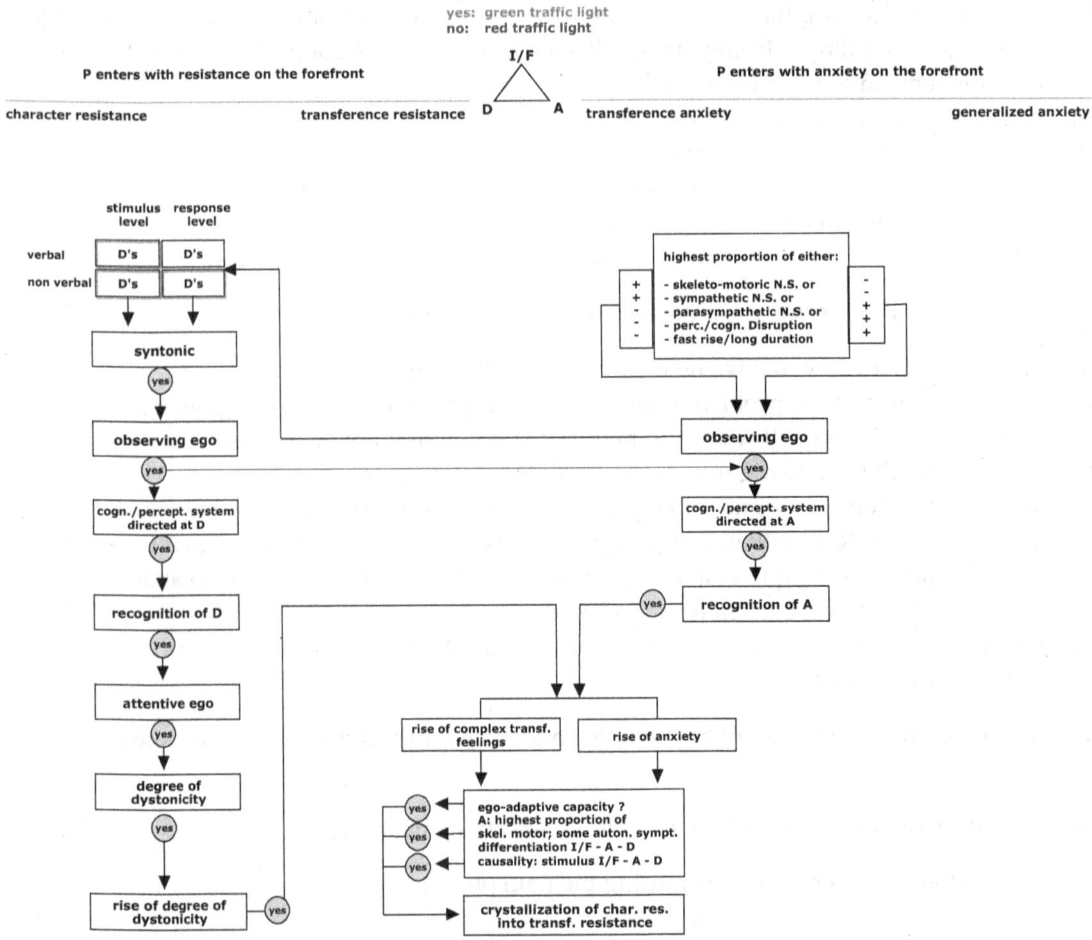

Figure 48. Somatizing patient 2: road to the unconscious 4.

Th At what point did it go away?

Pt Almost like some electrical thing, feeling sometimes.

Th Oh, sure, absolutely, at what point did it go away?

Pt I don't know, now it's back, that fog.

Th Oh, it's back, the fog is back.

Pt Well, it just seemed like every time I tried to deal with it, I had closed doors and so I learned just like pushing it down and dealing it with myself in a way and … (Patient taking deep breath and rolling eyes up and to the side.)

Th Well dealing, but not dealing, ignoring, neglecting, denying, ignoring, neglecting, denying, ignoring, neglecting, minimizing. Those …

Pt Minimizing, that's an interesting word, yep …

Th That's your unhealthy side, now your healthy side went to the lawyer.

Pt Yes.

Th And said, I was wronged, I want justice. But remember how, even when you go there, instead of you having the freedom to stand up for yourself, you worried about protecting your mother and your father.
Pt I know what the problem is I guess, is I always put everybody in front of me. (Patient's tone and body language is sad.)
Th That's brilliant that you see that and tell me about the sadness, your tightening up a little, don't create anxiety over being sad, don't do that to yourself, it's self-destructive …
Pt I don't know why I'm sad?
Th I know why you're sad.
Pt Maybe because I don't know how to put myself in front.
Th That's right; the neglect has become, you know, habitual. That's why you're sad; it's a positive sadness, isn't it.
Pt Good. (Patient laughing.)
Th Do you feel it that way or are you afraid of it?
Pt I don't know it hurts to cry.
Th It hurts to cry?
Pt Yeah, in a way.
Th Who says so?
Pt I don't know, it's like when I cry it just seems like it tightens in here, it's like a little burning sensation. (Patient pinching her skin by her throat.)

The patient has fused sadness with anxiety, resulting in tension in her vocal cords.

Th Ahh, so what you have done again is fused your sadness with anxiety. You fused sadness and anxiety, you fused anger and anxiety, you fused rage, right, with anxiety.

End of session, 1–3 hours

The patient returns ten days later, she notes that even after one meeting, she has internalized the therapist's constructive superego voice, as we shall see.

Session ten days later

We are one hour into this session.

Pt One thing though that I tried to understand because you know like whenever for these last ten days I caught myself like thinking this way, and I was like nope, my therapist would be, I would like hear your little voice "no your negative about yourself, don't be judgemental" and I would just kind of like rephrase things a little but in my head.
Th Terrific.
Pt But I realize, and I've realized since our last session I have so much anger towards my dad I really do. And there are like just so many things, it just seems like it has been one

thing after the other. I don't know how to answer still like "how does it feel to be angry"? I am just thinking more, not from a physical standpoint, its that it is more from like more, how does that feel, that emotion inside of you.

Th That is a physical standpoint, how can say not from a physical … yeah.

Pt Like right now I have knot here, if that's what we are looking for.

Th What do you mean is that we are looking for?

Pt (patient laughs) I sometimes still get confused between the emotions and the anxiety and the physical symptoms.

Th Well, you are tightening up.

Pt Yes.

Th You are creating a knot around it.

Pt Yes, yes, yes.

Th That's tension it's really quite simple, … you do with me a few times. That's tension right your throat is tightening up.

Pt Mm, hmm and it feels like pain around my throat.

Th No doubt about it, look what we've done here, we have gone from anger (feeling) towards your Dad, tension in your throat, (anxiety) to preoccupation with illness. (defence)

(Clarifying her triangle of conflict enhances her ego-adaptive capacity.)

Pt Mm, hmm.

Th I told you the whole idea for this work is us to recreate in here every single one of your symptoms and then you can decide whether they are of an emotional nature or it's something that has to be investigated for further diagnostic assessment. But right now look what you have going here it couldn't be more helpful.

Pt Yes, yes.

Th You still haven't felt the anger, though, that I have pointed out to you; you still have made feeling anger, the emotion of anger off limits.

Pt That's what you mean self-neglected.

Th Self-neglect yes, turn away. You do to yourself what your mother did with you, you turn away from your negative emotions and kind of a modelling imitation instead of learning how to investigate your emotions loving, carefully, precisely, not being afraid of them.

In the same session, the patient went on visualize her impulse to decapitating her father's mother who was the original aggressor, spoiling her son into an "entitled prince" who could have anything he wanted whenever he wanted it. The grandmother, in reality, abandoned the patient and her mother as "defective" since her son, "the prince", left them for another woman. She experienced rage, guilt, grief, and love in the session. She learned that she had punitively internalized her grandmother's eyes and had looked at herself as defective. A few months later (session 20, hour 40), the patient presented with severe body pain and fatigue. The breakthrough of rage was to her father for his rejection and for her mother who treated

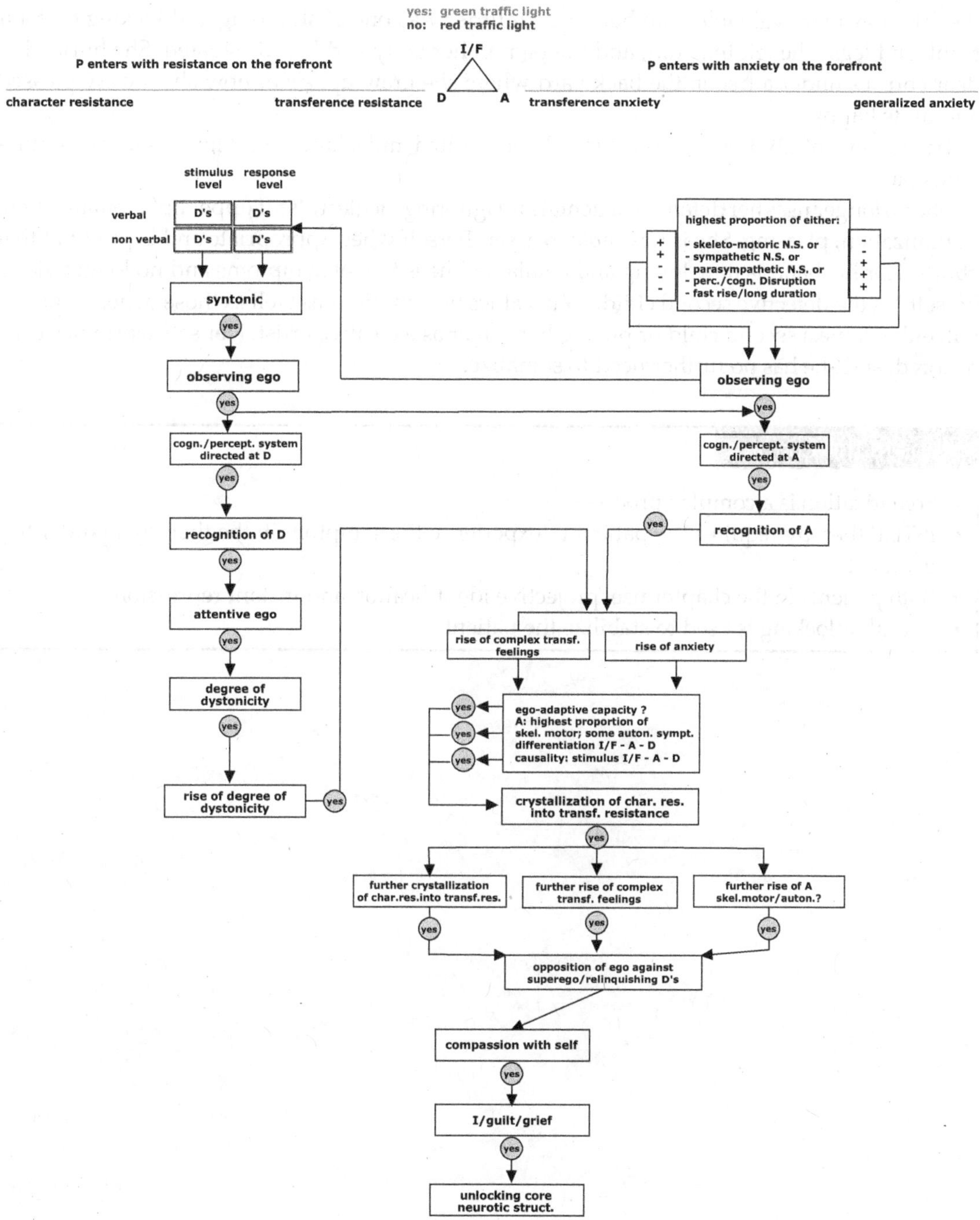

Figure 49. Somatizing patient 2: road to the unconscious 5.

the father as more valuable than her. Their murder was one of stomping and kicking on their trunk and legs. She felt the guilt, and the pain in her body and legs dissipated. She buried her dear corpses under a tree in the back yard where she grew up. As of now she is very pleased and quite happy.

At the end of six hours, we achieved the desired unlocking (see Figure 49, on the previous page).

She no longer uses her defences of denial and ignoring, neglect, "stiff upper lip", somatization, minimization, pleasing. She is now able to assert herself when appropriate and is proud of that ability. Her husband is now loving and available; she is free of symptoms and no longer views herself "as the defective second child." She values her emotions as well as those of her child and will either have a second child or pursue her career as a creative artist. Her self-worth has been restored, and she has no further need to somatize.

Steps in the chapter

- Somatization is a complex process
- ISTDP therapy requires the patient to experience the symptom in the therapy in order to get relief
- Both patients in the chapter use projective identification and instant repression
- Partial unlocking is used to stabilize the patient

CHAPTER TWELVE

Steps on the roadmap to the unconscious in a patient with transference resistance

As described in the traffic lights/roadmap diagram, patients present with either anxiety on the forefront or defences. Those patients which present with defence either use verbal and non-verbal defences in the realm of character or of transference resistance. The defences originated in order to protect the ego from some sort of dysregulation when the ego was immature. This dysregulation either represented a cumulative insecurity in the attachment relationship or an acute overwhelming threat (trauma). The ego defends itself when there is no available attachment figure to co-metabolize the trauma. Hence defences are recruited to regulate both emotion and anxiety. The unconscious is a repository of these unprocessed emotions which exist in a space where there is no time and they "sleep" under the veil of the series of defences that make up for the resistance. The art of ISTDP is to help the patient identify these defences and see them as not helpful to the self and for building an alliance with the therapist in order to not utilize them. This, of course, will provoke significant anxiety and the patient must learn to self-regulate the anxiety so it doesn't compromise the cognitive-perceptual apparatus and thus compromise self-observation. Patients who are less capable to regulate their anxiety are referred to as patients with a low ego-adaptive capacity. Mostly, they do not discriminate between the three poles of the triangle of conflict, they externalize, and they have some regressive defences in their repertoire.

Some patients who have more extreme pathology "split the ego" in order to preserve their cognitive capacities. These patients cannot tolerate complex transference feelings and vacillate between the poles of idealization and devaluation of the object. In order to "split", these patients engage in an immediate dissociation when anxiety emerges and obviously contradictory attitudes are held in consciousness without any seeming sense of contradiction. These patients are classified as borderline and also require graded exposure to their unconscious and help with tolerating love and hate towards the same person at the same time without resorting to splitting. These patients also have a paucity of sublimatory channels for their sexual and aggressive feelings, and thus frequently act out destructively towards the self as well as towards others. These patients are no better candidates for ISTDP than they are for any other form of dynamic psychotherapy, but ISTDP's results are equal to that offered by transference-focused therapy.

Let's get back to the topic of this chapter: transference resistance. Once the therapist has helped the patient recognize the role of their array of character defences in creating and sustaining the patient's problem, and once the ego-adaptive capacity is adequate, the patient sits at the threshold of a breakthrough into their unconscious. In theory, the complex transference feelings are activated by the process of moment-to-moment attention to the patient's psychic process. As the patient and therapist are working together (working alliance) to explore and understand the core of the patient's difficulties, the patient will simultaneously explore and resist. Resist means: the patient uses his defences. When the dynamic activities isolate the defences, the implicit memory of the trauma which caused the defences to be recruited in the first place is activated.

We call this feeling-memory process "transference". This is both similar and distinctly different from the way in which transference is thought of in classical analysis. In the latter, transference is seen as the emotional experience and fantasies of earlier relationships that the patient transfers onto the analytic relationship. Repressed feelings are felt towards the analyst in the relationship. And this process is encouraged. Resistance against doing it is discouraged, and then the feeling/wish/inhibition is interpreted by the analyst. In ISTDP, the focus is on the direct exploration of the feeling that wants to be transferred in real time. Again, in theory transference neurosis; that is, symptoms which the patient creates to avoid conflictual feelings, is thus circumvented and treatment is more efficient—less time, less suffering, less dependency, fewer negative therapeutic interactions. The research on outcome of this method seems to support this theory.

So let's get back to our traffic light diagram. Given adequate ego-adaptive capacity, the patient is ready to venture into his unconscious memory system. The patient and the therapist have formed a working alliance, and the patient is able to identify his anxiety with love, care, and precision. The defences are ego dystonic and the patient is now experiencing pre-consciously, rising complex (but highly conflictual) transference feelings. The character armour has been dismantled and made "dystonic", and the patient has learned that his defences are subordinated to the commands of his internalized aggressor (superego). The feelings that have been repressed are rising with a vengeance, and the forbidden murder (blood lust), sadism, or incestuous impulse is about to become conscious, and low and behold the patient retreats to the safety of *either* his former defences under the pressure of potential awareness and potential relief from his suffering.

Accomplished ISTDP clinicians see this over and over again, and this is the point which gives students the greatest frustration when cooperation of the patient ceases. This is the point which requires the greatest skill in applying adequate (appropriate) dosing of pressure, challenge, and head-on collision in order to create an intrapsychic crisis and victory over maintaining resistance. Notice on the chart that, as the therapist engages in successful, attuned interventions, there is a rise of complex transference feelings. This means rage, guilt, and grief, linked to the patient's trauma, are rising simultaneously from the unconscious to the preconscious.

First, there is pain of trauma (core shame[1]), next retaliatory rage against the offending object, next guilt over the rage and grief over the lost attachment. It is impossible to predict which emotion will rise first to consciousness, but once one breaks through, the "basement door" is now open and the others will follow on the journey to self-awareness.

But we have gotten ahead of ourselves, since we are at the rise of complex transference feelings. Notice in the next box there is a phrase: opposition of the ego against the superego. What does this mean? The patient's ego is boosted by the working alliance. However, a force described by Malan, called the "unconscious therapeutic alliance", has begun to awaken. The unconscious therapeutic alliance is an instinctual property of all humans. In theory, everyone desires "attachment security", and the precise moment-to-moment observing and attending by both parties awakens these infantile longings. Thus the patient knows they have a unique opportunity to repair a part of themselves that was damaged a long, long time ago. The consequence of that damage was the development of an alternative system which is headed by the eyes of the internalized aggressor or what we have come to call the punitive superego.

Thus, we have a battle going on between the conscious and unconscious forces of the working alliance. The patient's compliance to the dictate of his superego, his defences, are forces which operate against the establishment of a conscious/unconscious working alliance (see also Chapter Seven). The patient's conscious wish to cooperate with the therapist and the upward force of his complex transference feelings operate in favour of the conscious/unconscious working alliance. This is what we mean by an intrapsychic crisis. With adequate dosing of pressure to experience the core feeling, challenge, and—if needed—head-on collision (consequence of loyalty/obedience to the commands of the pathologic superego), an interesting phenomenon occurs. There is a breakthrough of compassion for self or grief over self-sabotage.

Why is this? Again, the answer lies in the dormant structures of the mind that have been suppressed by the series of traumas that have caused the patient's neurosis. With relief from the domination of the emotional structure by the punitive part, the patient feels the loving, caring part of their parental introject as reflected by the modelling of the healthy superego by the therapist. Thus, the patient receives the empathy and attunement that he longed for from that parent, but did not receive. This is why a true breakthrough is so powerful and transformative because a shift in the patient's stance towards himself and others occurs, and it is the momentary restoration of security of attachment in the face of traumatic emotions. In many ways, the therapy restores the patient's sense of an internal secure base. During the therapy process, his dysregulated emotions will be welcomed, contained, and digested until he feels better. In the meantime, the patient can venture out into the world again and tolerate the bruises and wounds that are part of his and everyone's daily lives.

Following compassion for self, the inquiry naturally leads to examination of the origins of the punitive system, and the complex feelings are explored one by one towards the attachment figure or figures who abused and/or neglected the patient. If time permits, the session also explores the complex feelings towards the sustaining factor.[2] After the emotions are processed through visualization (dreaming while awake); then, the memory of the original trauma is de-repressed.

If the roadmap is through grief over self-sabotage, then the unlocking is of the specific traumatic situation when the neurosis was created occurs first, and then the complex feelings towards the primary aggressor are explored and, if time permits, the secondary or sustaining factor as well.

Attachment love is the origin of all complex feelings, so it is fitting that the murdered aggressors are buried with love and the longings that were thwarted are expressed to the corpse of the parent before the grave is closed or the funeral pyre is ignited. The patient is encouraged to discuss his future plans for self-repair, self-love, self-empowerment as a way of making peace with the attachment trauma and end his personal tragedy. The patient is encouraged to develop insight into the way his presenting symptoms were a punishment for his complex feelings of love, rage/sadism, guilt, and grief towards the offending parent(s). The compassionate healthy self is now his guide through the tribulations of life.[3]

Then, the findings of the session are summarized in terms of the triangles of persons and conflict, and the origins the punitive superego are also reviewed. The treatment contract is that of continued exploration of the core emotions with love, care, and precision until the presenting complaints are resolved, and once that occurs, the expectation is that termination of the active therapeutic relationship will ensue.

The success of working in the transference is heavily dependent on the patient being able to see the realistic therapist and to separate transference perception from the perception of the realistic therapist.

A patient with a severe complex masochistic character using regressive defences

Using the roadmap: Turning character resistance into transference resistance, and transforming a patient's low ego-adaptive capacity into a strong ally: turning red lights into green lights

The patient is a 60-year-old single, attractive female social worker with long-standing anxiety and depression. She was referred by her psychopharmacologist for ISTDP treatment. She showed a highly masochistic character structure with long standing re-enactment of victimization themes with men. At the time, she was in a romantic relationship with a convicted criminal (Paulo) without money who was living hand to mouth. At the first contact, she was in a business scheme with him that put her in severe financial jeopardy. She had low ego-adaptive capacity, ego-syntonic defences of ignoring, neglecting, denying, minimizing, galloping, storytelling, ventilating, helplessness, and projecting. This is the fourth session. As a result of this session, she ended the relationship with Paulo and began dating men more appropriate to her social stature.

The character resistance has crystallized into the transference resistance by the time this session began.

Defences at stimulus and response:

making others the priority; justifying

1. projecting
2. helplessness, ventilating
3. suffering, victim

4. surrender of her entitlement to feel
5. ignoring her anxiety, denying, minimizing, neglecting
6. galloping, escape to storytelling.

Th Tell me how you're doing with your problem?
Pt Ohh ...
Th ... emotional problem?
Pt ... I'm still feeling a lot of anxiety.
Th Good, you're noticing it now.
Pt What?
Th You're noticing it now.
Pt Well, like well, I definitely do.
Th Good.
Pt And, umm, and I did have especially one episode of some pretty some unregulated anxiety umm, having to do with umm, in fact just even thinking about it now makes me anxious, having to do with some cousins that came into town and came for a Buddhist retreat that they go to every year and now it's going to be every year in San Diego, so I saw them, you know, when they had time, you know there's a schedule, but they, when they broke for lunch, I had lunch with them Sunday. And then for some reason, I had a lot of stress and sleeplessness over whether to see them again or not, umm, well, or whether, or how hospitable or to have them over for dinner at my house. It's rather weird!
Th You had some doubts.
Pt I had some doubts, umm, part of it might have been having them meet Paulo, but part of it has to do also (sigh) with just taking on ... I don't exactly what it was ...

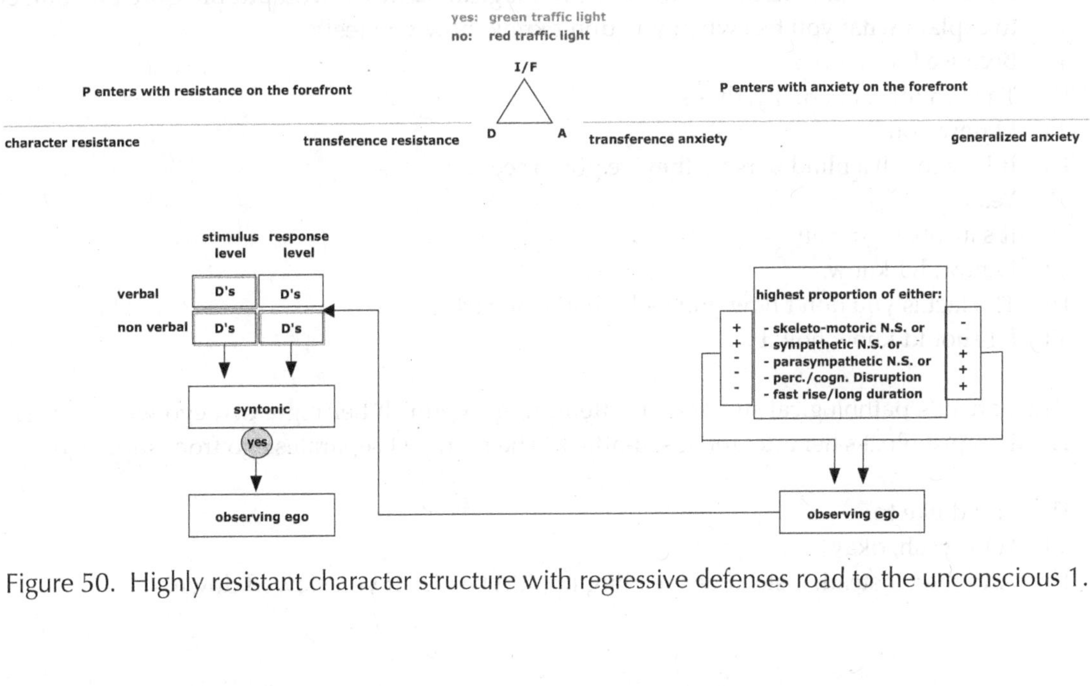

Figure 50. Highly resistant character structure with regressive defenses road to the unconscious 1.

(The patient speaks in general terms, uses helplessness, and creates a maze of confusion–chaos about the cause of her anxiety.)

We are at Figure 50, on the previous page.

Th You don't know.
Pt I can't figure it out.
Th So you're not in touch with your feelings?
Pt I'm not, yeah, I'm not in touch with my feelings. I don't see these cousins very often. They live in Santa Clara. Umm, maybe I have some unresolved anger that they don't invite me up to their house more or they're not more sociable with me, but I feel close to them.
Th You feel close, you feel close to them.
Pt Yes, this is a cousin that I've known, my cousin I've known her all my life. Umm …
Th So could we, uh …
Pt I know, I'm getting higher and higher. (The patient is complaining of rising anxiety.)
Th Oh, you know, you're doing so much better at noticing yourself. (The therapist boosts the patient's ego for noticing her anxiety.)
Pt Oh!
Th Are you pleased with that?
Pt Yeah, but I wish I wouldn't be so anxious. (laugh)
Th Well, yeah, you gotta walk before you run, I mean …
Pt Yeah, yeah.
Th You've got to observe what you're doing.
Pt I mean, I'm agitated trying to …
Th Right now you're getting agitated?
Pt Yeah, I'm trying to explain this to you and exactly how I feel.
Th How can … wait a minute now. That's not logical. How can you put pressure on yourself to explain what you feel when you don't know how you feel?
Pt Because I, I …
Th That's a form of cruelty, that's …
Pt I know you …
Th If I try to tell a blind person, they've got to see …
Pt Yeah.
Th It's just being mean.
Pt I know, I, I know.
Th The fact is you don't how you feel. That's the fact.
Pt I, I should know how I …

(The patient's pathological superego is attempting to punish her regressed ego with criticism. The therapist blocks her attempt at self-attack. The therapist separates ego from superego.)

Th You'd like to.
Pt Why, yeah, okay.
Th And then instead, instead of speeding up, it'd be nice if you slowed down.

(The therapist challenges the patient not to gallop.)

Pt Yeah, let me slow down.
Th Wouldn't that be a revolutionary thing to do?
Pt Yeah.
Th Wouldn't it?
Pt I noticed obviously that I was anxious about trying to make this decision, but I didn't analyse any further than that. I think I asked myself, Why are you so anxious about this, what's going on?
Th But can I help, would you like? We'll save time.
Pt Yeah, I would like some help.
Th Cause, again my idea for you to think about is forcing a blind person to see is cruelty …
Pt Yeah.
Th Cause they can't see.
Pt Yeah, yeah.
Th So stop doing that to yourself, it's just cruelty. Just accept the fact that you don't know how you feel right now, but I'd like to just give you an idea to work on.

(The therapist separates ego from superego for the second time.)

Pt All right.
Th Okay, you said a word here.
Pt Yeah.
Th It's a very important word called closeness.

(The therapist brings the patient's longings for closeness to her attention.)

Pt Right, right.
Th So could we start with that?
Pt Yeah.
Th Tell me about those feelings.
Pt Yeah. (sigh) This is a cousin that I've kind of idolized. She's a very interesting person. She had a very interesting job at … my, my mother came from a blended family as many families were and my mother and everyone else in that family said, no one ever talked about anything like that. It just was, even though people's ages were less than nine months apart, I guess they didn't put two and two together until later, or they just didn't think about it or discuss it. But anyway, she's my half-cousin by blood, but everyone was just cousins so …
Th I understand.
Pt Okay, so …
Th There's feeling toward her?
Pt Yeah, lot of feeling, cause …
Th Good

Pt … I always like her, we always had …

Th Why do you … you don't have to say because. (The therapist challenges "justifying" to the superego. The therapist separates ego from superego for the third time.)

Pt Okay. I always like her and I always felt warm towards her …

Th Describe …

Pt … and she always felt warm towards me.

Th … describe your, your warm feelings towards her, how they feel inside.

Pt Umm, just like I, I wanted to be more in …

Th Now you're doing it again. You see, here is where you get yourself into so much difficulty.

Pt Uh huh.

Th You try to talk …

Pt Uh huh.

Th … to explain feelings.

Pt You're just asking me how I feel.

Th How you're …

Pt I feel warm towards her and I'm …

Th How does it feel? (The therapist pressures the patient towards experiencing her warm feelings.)

Pt How does it feel? It feels good but also anxious and angry I think be … (The patient's observing ego has restored itself and the attentive ego built in the first three sessions now regulates the anxiety a bit and the patient's love, anger, and anxiety are simultaneously evoked. But she cannot experience of the poles of triangle of conflict due to low ego-adaptive capacity.)

We are on the roadmap at Figure 51, on the next page.

The therapist helps the patient attend to the rise of anxiety along with complex transference feelings.

Th Ahh.

Pt It feels good but anxious and angry too.

Th Wait, wait, wait …

Pt And sad.

Th I don't buy any of that.

Pt (sigh)

Th I believe you feel good for a split second and then you have this, uh, umm, spike anxiety and then you start to guess, to start to intellectualize. It, it, this therapy is about being in touch …

Now we are at Figure 52, on p. 318.

(The therapist moves into restructuring the ego.)

Pt Uhh, I want to …

Th … with your feelings. Look at your legs. I say in touch with your feelings …

Pt And I …

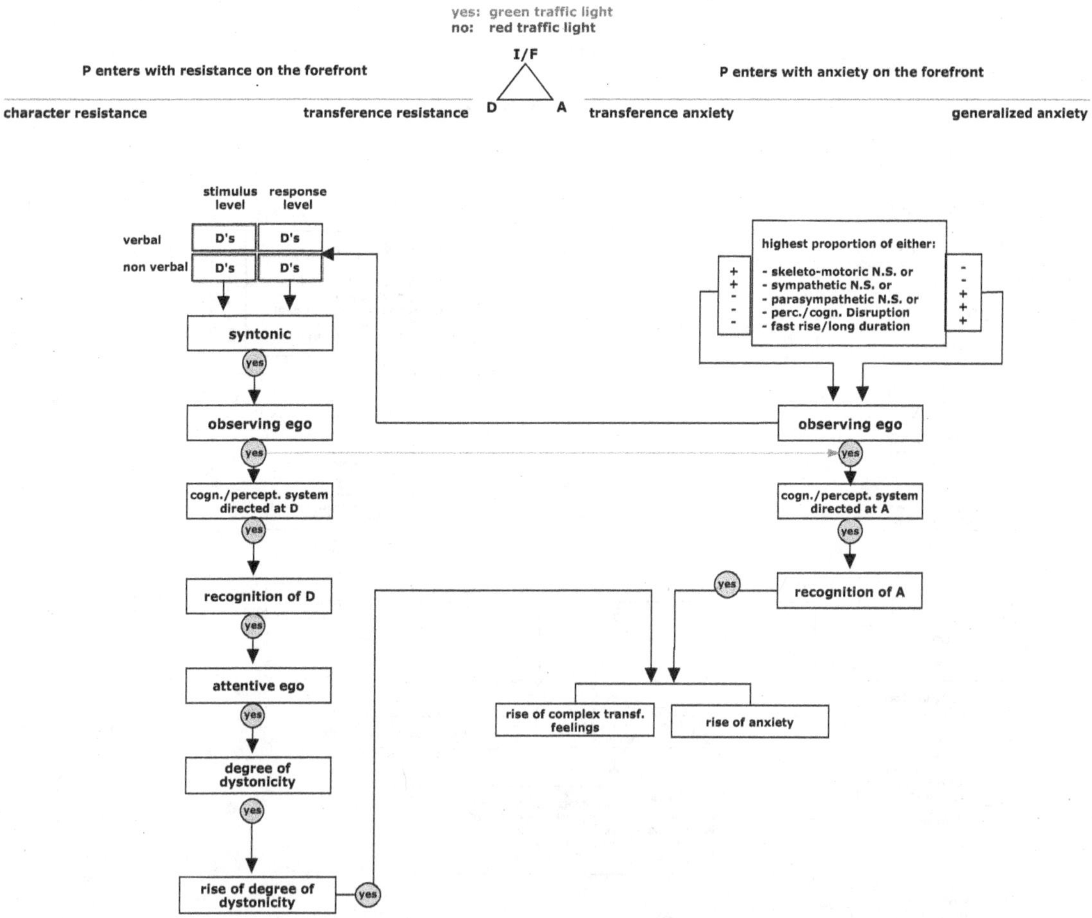

Figure 51. Highly resistant character structure with regressive defenses road to the unconscious 2.

Th … and that your anxiety goes through the roof.
Pt All right. I feel, I feel really good …
Th Yeah.
Pt … about her and …
Th Could we separate your good feelings from your anxious feelings?
Pt Okay.
Th I don't understand why you, as a woman, have to suffer from anxiety related to good feelings. I, I think that's cruelty. Er, uh …
Pt Okay.
Th Don't you have a right to enjoy good feelings?
Pt I, I, I do but …
Th Why do you have to say but?
Pt Well, because I was going to explain …

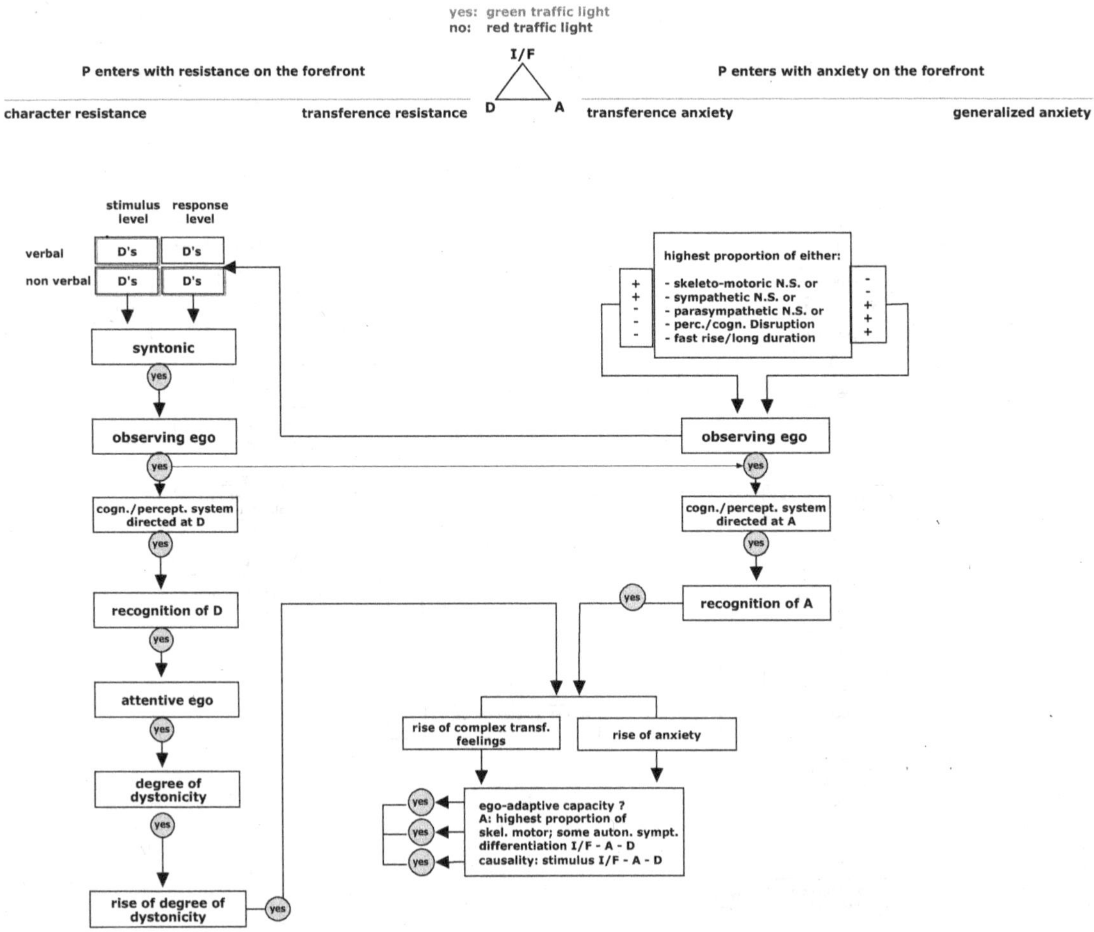

Figure 52. Highly resistant character structure with regressive defenses road to the unconscious 3.

Th Could you say I have a right?

Pt I have a right to have good feelings about this relationship with my cousin …

Th Without having to cripple myself.

Pt … without having to cripple myself …

Th With anxiety.

Pt … with anxiety.

Th Do you see that?

Pt (sigh)

Th You might have other feelings too!

Pt Well, okay, I see because I want to say to you, but it's because I want to say to you, she's always busy and I …

Th But that's what you always do. You always say but because this and but because that and because. It's like you're always having to argue with some unseen …

(The therapist shows mild disdain for justifying to the "other". The patient separates ego from superego for the fourth time. The character defences have now crystallized into the transference resistance. These manoeuvres are to keep her feelings of love, rage, guilt, and grief towards her parents locked in her confused perception.)

Pt Okay.
Th … about your right to have feelings.
Pt Okay. I, okay …
Th You have a right to have feelings.
Pt Okay, I feeling freestanding and it doesn't need to be informed polite, but on the other hand …
Th Because it has to be justified.
Pt Okay.
Th No, you don't have to justify any of your feelings.
Pt To myself.
Th To anyone. Do you? Who made you feel like you had to justify your feelings?
Pt Umm
Th Like you didn't have a right to feel what you felt? I mean you don't see the malignancy of that?
Pt Yes, I see it, but I don't.
Th Good.
Pt I, I see it, okay, that I have a right to my feelings but I feel shorted by her too, so that …
Th You're doing, now you're doing it again.
Pt Okay, I, I know I'm doing it again, I know …
Th You, you …
Pt … but can't people do that?
Th Not like you.
Pt Okay (small laugh), all right.

(The patient's ego is beginning to like its freedom from the domination of the superego.)

Th I, I mean …
Pt Okay, I really like her and I haven't …
Th No, no, I want you to see what I see.
Pt All right, okay.
Th This is you.
Pt All right.
Th And this is the part of you that has feelings.
Pt Okay.
Th Right here.
Pt Okay
Th Then you're always looking out at some higher court, justifying …
Pt Ohh.

Th … the fact that you have not only this feeling, but this feeling and this feeling and this feeling and I have to explain to you why I have this feeling or else I am going to criticize you? Is that what you think?

(The therapist is now pointing out that the patient transfers the perception of her parents onto him and that the patient cannot distinguish the real him from her transferential perception of her parents.)

Pt Uh huh.
Th Devalue you, ignore you, what is this …
Pt No, uhh.
Th … this you're doing, why are you always pleading with it? That, this is you.
Pt (laugh, laugh)
Th Your stance to me is "I have to justify to you that I have more than one feeling".
Pt See, I never looked at it that way.

(The ego is enjoying more freedom.)

Th I know …
Pt I always looked at it as, you know, I have warmth towards her.
Th Wait, wait, stay on topic.
Pt All right.
Th You say the statement, I never looked at it that way.
Pt All right.
Th Is it helpful to you to look at it that way?
Pt You know, it is, because then I can, I can experience a fullness of my feelings …
Th … because you always have to justify to a higher authority, you're going to be on the edge of anxiety every minute of your life. It's too much pressure.
Pt I didn't, I didn't …
Th It's too much pressure to live under the control of the higher authority.
Pt Right.
Th The judgement of the higher authority. I am not the higher authority you make of me.

(The therapist distinguishes himself from the patient's transference perception.)

Pt Right, right, right … So I never looked at it that way.
Th But are you looking at it that way?
Pt Now, I can see it, I can see it, I can see that.
Th Okay.
Pt But then I feel like I'm, I'm giving into not being able to feel mad at the same time.
Th Uhh?
Pt Yeah.
Th Do you understand that that has no logical basis to what you just said? You're just justifying yourself again.
Pt Yeah because I'm …
Th Cause you have to justify your right to feel mad at the same time. Who says you have to justify yourself? Who did you have to justify your right to have feelings to, in your past?

(The patient persists in transference resistance despite six clarifications.)

Pt Right
Th Who? Who was it that …?
Pt My mother. Well, I'm guessing, I'm trying to feel, I'm trying to feel.

(The patient retreats to pleasing/submission to the authority figure.)

Th You don't know just like that?
Pt Right. I, I don't.
Th Okay, that's …
Pt I don't.
Th That's, that's a fair answer. But can you …

(The therapist validates her right to not know (entitlement) and she genuinely reengages in our process.)

We are now at Figure 53, on the next page.

Pt Well, I think it's my father more because I always felt bad. (sigh)

The patient shows the deepening of emotions and increased anxiety reflecting increase CTF. We have moved past crystallization into further rise of CTF and further rise of skeletal-motor anxiety.

Th This is helpful now. Tell me about it.
Pt Yeah, I don't know why I said that exactly but …
Th Because?
Pt Because …
Th No, listen, listen, listen. You don't know why you said that. Do you know why you said it? Because you're starting to think about yourself.

(The therapist blocks self-doubt and deferring to others as the priority.)

Pt Uh huh.
Th Okay.
Pt Uh huh.
Th Okay. Think about yourself first.
Pt Yeah.
Th Not other people.
Pt Other people, how I'm coming across or what …
Th And you're saying, Oh, now you're bringing it to my attention, Dr …
Pt Um mmm.
Th I notice I note a pattern.
Pt Um mmm.

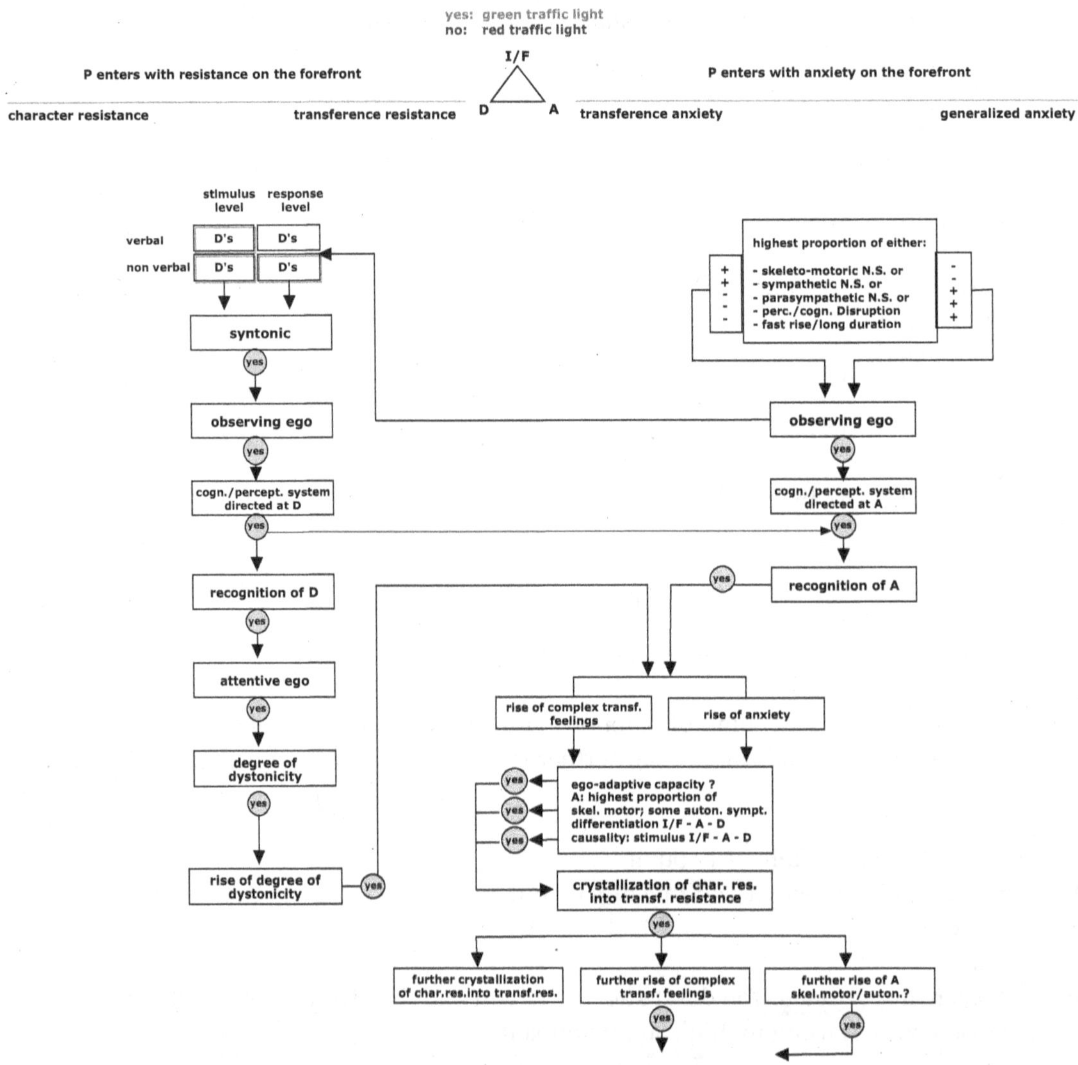

Figure 53. Highly resistant character structure with regressive defenses road to the unconscious 4.

Th That being like this in my relationship with my father …

Pt Yes.

Th … because I felt bad. You felt bad.

Pt Yeah.

Th Bad.

Pt Did I say that?

Th Yes.

Pt Because I felt bad.

Th For him.

Pt For him.
Th You felt …
Pt Yes, yes.
Th See, you felt bad for your father.
Pt Yes, yes.
Th Should we just focus on that for a minute?
Pt (sigh)

(The patient's anxiety rises in intracostal muscles, signalling CTF is about threshold!) Green light.

Th What … take your time.
Pt Yeah.
Th What did you feel about for him, what was bothering you about him?

(The therapist pressures for her emotional experience.)

Pt Well, he just never seemed to be very happy.
Th (whisper) Yes.
Pt So maybe felt I needed to mirror him or not feel better than he did or to be with him in his bad feelings. I … you know …
Th Well, that's okay. You say you felt that you had to care take him?
Pt Well, we talked about that.
Th Yeah.
Pt When he, when he …
Th Okay
Pt When he …
Th No, let me talk to you.
Pt All right.
Th So, while you're telling me in your childhood …
Pt Uh huh.
Th For whatever reasons, that you made him the priority. He was more important than you. His depression.
Pt Um mmm.
Th … okay, took priority over your right to have your own feelings.
Pt Or his craftiness, you know, his irritability, you know, he may get made, or he, you know, he might get ummm …
Th Did he frighten you?
Pt He didn't frighten me, like, we were always kind of on pins and needles in the house.
Th What does that mean?
Pt Well, that he might …
Th Could you …
Pt Get mad.

Th So could you say, he, he frightened me, his moods frightened me.
Pt His moods frightened me and also that my parents would start fighting.
Th Right.
Pt You know, because my Mum would be agitated too, you know.
Th Could you just see the burden that that placed on you?

(The role-reversal child becomes the caretaker, and the therapist asks her to empathize with herself.)

Pt Um mm. Yeah, I do see it and I feel it too. I feel this anxiety. (large breath) Green lights
Th You, you're feeling anxiety?
Pt Yeah.
Th Over what?
Pt I could see where those experience made me feel conflicted on issues.
Th You can see how that started this process?
Pt Yes and probably it started long before that.
Th And you can see how you're transferring your father onto me.

(The therapist points the transference perception out.)

Pt I'm just …
Th You not doing that only with me but with so many words you do in all of your intimate relationships men as well as women.
Pt I'm thinking something's going to go wrong or there's going to be a fight or he's going to get, he's (my father) going to turn …
Th Yes, do you understand you're walking on eggshells?
Pt All the time through life, I'm walking on eggshells through life.
Th Yeah
Pt Yeah, because I was walking on eggshells in my family. It was like being in a family of a dry drunk, although my parents never drank.
Th Okay.
Pt You know, but it's like that, you know?
Th Okay and is that fun?
Pt No, it's awful, it's awful.

(The defence of galloping returns and the therapist blocks the defence.)

Th Could you slow down now?
Pt Yeah (sigh), ohhh, okay. So then about deciding whether to invite my cousin, it's almost like taking the adult role of saying I'm the adult and I would like to invite you to my house for dinner instead of always being almost like the child going up to her house, always to her house. My brother said to me, she never comes to you, you always have to go to her. Umm …

(Green light restored—it's now time for the therapist to turn the patient's ego against her defences.)

We are at Figure 54, below, on the roadmap at creating the intrapsychic crisis.

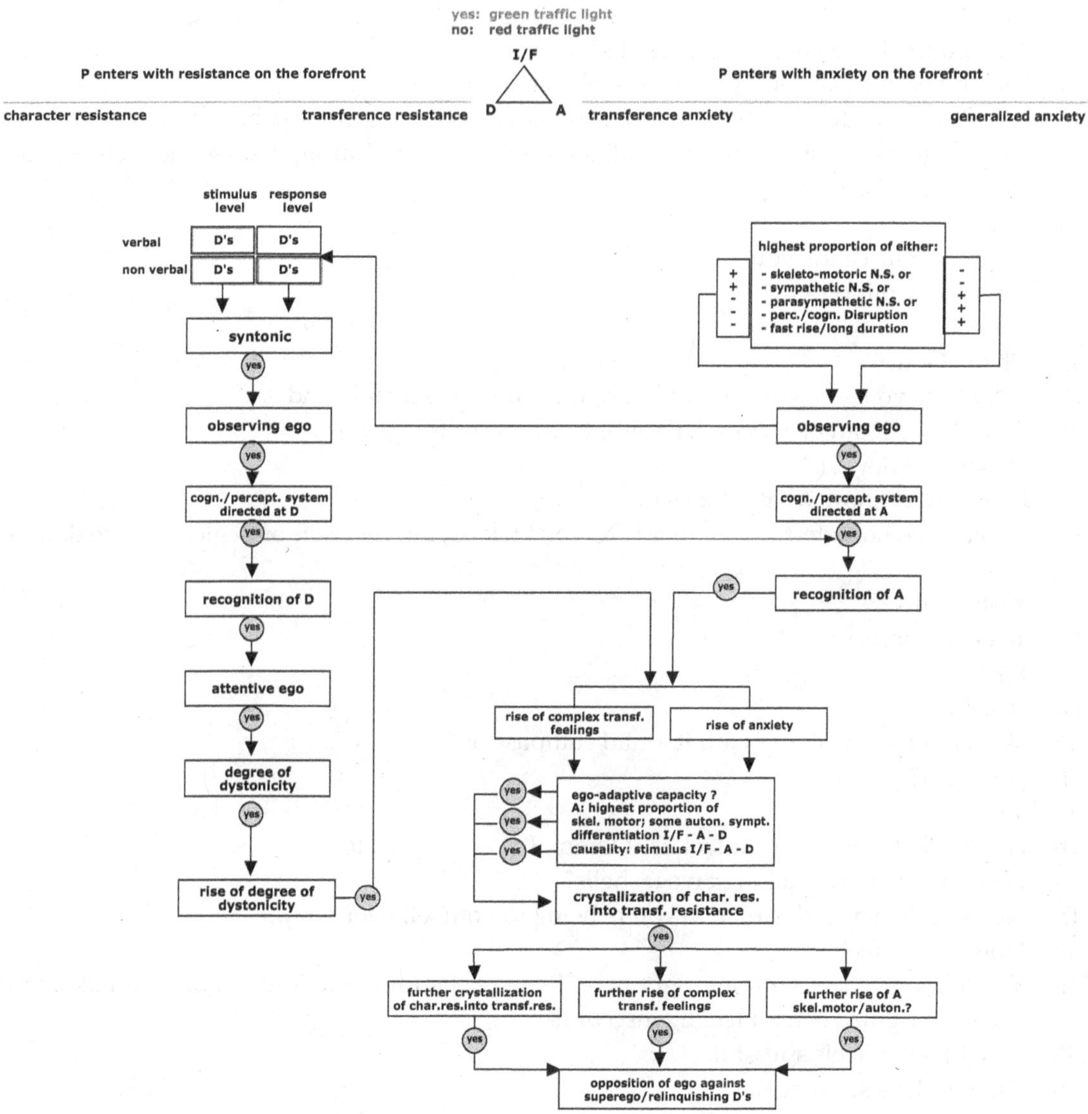

Figure 54. Highly resistant character structure with regressive defenses road to the unconscious 5.

Th Would you slow down here. (galloping again)
Pt Okay.
Th You're on an island out there.
Pt I'm island hopping.
Th Easy.
Pt All right.
Th Could we fix one problem before we address a second problem?
Pt All right.
Th I'd like to work this through.
Pt Okay.
Th Are you tired of walking on eggshells?
Pt Yes, oh yes. It's exhausting … it's just absolutely exhausting.
Th I can tell. … Yeah you're under a lot of stress. Now here's my watch. How many minutes are you going to give me of not walking on eggshells? (Turning her ego actively against chattering/discharge.)
Pt Oh.
Th Still yourself. Thank you.
Pt How many minutes?
Th Yes.
Pt Oh my God.
Th I don't see you give yourself a second, if I count the second hand.
Pt Probably 1/100th of a second. (laugh) (syntonic self-neglect)
Th Do you see now …?
Pt I don't even know what it looks like.
Th Do you see how destructive that is to you? (clarifying function of neglect and making it dystonic)
Pt Yeah, yeah.
Th To be that insecure.
Pt Like yes.
Th You do?
Pt Yeah, I'm the one living with it. (mild compassion)
Th You see it?
Pt Yes.
Th Good, good, and what's it feel like? Umm, I've got my watch.
Pt Okay, not feel like walking on eggshells?
Th No, to realize how destructive you're being to yourself every day.
Pt How does it feel?
Th Yes, to realize here with me right here. I've got the timer on. You're going to talk about a feeling, right? Without feeling insecure?
Pt (laugh) It still feels stressful.
Th Okay, so let's say it again.
Pt How does it feel …
Th No, no, no, no, no, no. You don't live for more than what was your time?
Pt 7/100ths of a second.

Th Without …
Pt Feeling like I'm walking on eggshells.
Th And I say to you, do you see how self-destructive that is?
Pt And I say, Yes I do.
Th Good. And I ask you, How does that feel? Can you expand it to 100th's of a second.
Pt No. (laugh) I'm scared of something.
Th You've got to look at this here.
Pt Okay.
Th This is crucial for you. You're here because you want my help.
Pt Yes.
Th Right?
Pt Yeah.
Th So if you continue to make yourself feel as though your father's mood is dependent on you saying the right thing or behaving the right way or making the right decisions all the time …
Pt Um mmm.
Th … the perfect decision, you will destroy yourself and our therapy will fail. Do you see that?

(The therapist applies a low-level head-on collision against the addiction to self-neglect and making others the priority.)

Pt Yes, yes.
Th You see it?
Pt Yeah, yeah.
Th Do you see that I'm not powerful enough to stop this self-destructive side of you by myself?
Pt Okay, I have to have help from you. I have to do it. Okay.

(The therapist appeals to the working alliance.)

Th Where is your father right now?
Pt Over there.
Th He's dead, isn't he?
Pt Yes, yes he is.
Th You don't act like he's dead. You act like he's sitting right here. You've transferred him on to me.
Pt Um mmm.
Th Or he's always more important than you.
Pt Um mmm, um mmm.
Th Are you willing to stop doing that?
Pt Yes, yes.
Th So how does it feel to know that you don't have to take care of him anymore starting today. You don't have to take care of him anymore. You don't have to worry about any of his reactions to anything.

Pt Huh. Oh, I don't even know how that would be.
Th Then I can't help you, you see.
Pt Yeah.
Th See, you don't believe he's dead.
Pt No.
Th Okay. What does dead mean?
Pt Dead means not around anymore, not here anymore, (short pause) okay. (longer pause) okay.
Th Okay, what? How does it feel?
Pt Well, I still feel anxiety, I feel under a lot of pressure.
Th From who?
Pt I don't know. From you, you're telling me not to do this.
Th Oh, so you took him out of the grave again? What am I telling you, you have to do?
Pt To, to have him not matter anymore.
Th Who am I to tell you that?
Pt I have to tell myself that. That he matters *but he can't dictate to me* any more on how I'm going to feel.
Th Or behave.
Pt Or behave.
Th Or what decisions you're going to make about what you're going to do, that the effect on him is irrelevant since he's dead.
Pt That's true. Yeah, that's true. Well, I, I just, I got, I have difficulty, I can't really put myself in that mindset that he's not influencing me anymore. It's, I, I just …

(The patient briefly resorts to her defence of helpless submission to superego.)

Th Is it you can't or you don't want to?
Pt Well, I do want to.
Th Well, part of …
Pt I'm afraid to …
Th Part of you doesn't want to.
Pt I think I'm just so used to …
Th Just admit it.

(The therapist confronts of allegiance to commands of the SE.)

Pt Yeah.
Th That you don't want to say goodbye to your father, instead of burying your father, all you've done is give him eternal life.
Pt Well, maybe I can bury him and say goodbye in a good way and still have his good things in me but get rid of the eggshell part. I mean I think that's possible. I can do that.
Th Well, I, not only do I think that's possible, I consider that to be the umm definition of how you mourn him.
Pt Um mm. So that's what I'd to like to do.
Th Good.

Pt You know, what I want is to remember him fondly in my relationship with him but not let him terrify me.
Th Good.
Pt Yeah, so.
Th That's a fantastically healthy woman speaking right now.
Pt Yeah, because …
Th So when you look in the eyes of the father who terrified you, what is the feeling that you have towards that man, the one that you want to bury, not the one that you felt so comforted by and so supported by and so close to, but how about the one that was so needy.

(Pressure to enhance rise of CTF.)

Pt Okay and gruff …
Th And gruff and grumpy and irritable.
Pt Um mmm.
Th And volatile.
Pt Well, I just, yeah, he's volatile, volatile. I mean I just, I see his eyes being grey, which they were.

(A spontaneous vision of the transference figure appears to the patient—the forces of the unconscious working alliance are rising above those of her resistance.)

Th Yeah, good and what do you want to …
Pt Kind of peaceful actually.
Th And what do you want to say to his eyes?
Pt I want to say, Father, I don't think you would want me to suffer like this, I know you wouldn't. I know you would be very upset if you knew that I …
Th You're having emotions while you're talking, aren't you?
Pt Um mmm.
Th Then pay attention. Is there anxiety in your mind?
Pt No, not that much.
Th Okay, what emotions are you feeling?
Pt Sadness.
Th Can you include your sadness in your discussion? Start with the feeling.
Pt Well, I do feel …
Th When I look in your grey eyes.
Pt When I look in your grey eyes.
Th I feel a deep sadness.
Pt I feel a deep sadness, and I have to say goodbye to you … (crying a little) (*breakthrough #1)*
Th Over the fact.
Pt Over the fact that …
Th That you were sick.

Pt That you were *so sick*. That I had to take care of you and put myself on the back burner.
Th Your tears are for you and all the time you spend subordinating yourself to him.

(compassion for self)

We are on the roadmap at Figure 55, on the next page.

Pt Yeah and my mother too.
Th Let's just stay with him right now.
Pt My father …
Th And your walking on eggshells.
Pt Also when I say I feel sad, it's like I, I want him to feel okay that he didn't (sigh) … (return to submission … sign of rising CTF).
Th Please, you're just going to create a muddle … (The therapist reminds the patient to quit her chaotic defences.)
Pt Yeah, okay.
Th In your mind. I'm trying to clear things up. Would you stay on my team?
Pt Yes, yes, okay.
Th Cause when I saw, what you get, keep submitting—Even for having a split second of expressing your sadness for yourself and putting yourself first, it was a spike of anxiety. Then you started dancing.
Pt Okay, okay (sighing) Sad for myself.
Th It has to be for someone else.
Pt I was feeling more sad for him. I want him to feel bad for me.
Th If you do that, you make me useless to you as a therapist. (pointing out self-defeat, submission to her superego)
Pt Yeah, okay.
Th All you're doing is the same behaviour …
Pt Over and over again.
Th … is putting him in front of you.
Pt Okay.
Th Do you want to do that?
Pt No, no, no, no, I don't.
Th Or do you want to be first?
Pt I want to be first.
Th Good.
Pt I want to put me first.
Th Could we have another look at his grey eyes?
Pt Um mmm.
Th Do you see them?
Pt Yeah.
Th What else comes up in you towards him?
Pt I see his grey eyes (whispering).
Th What's so …

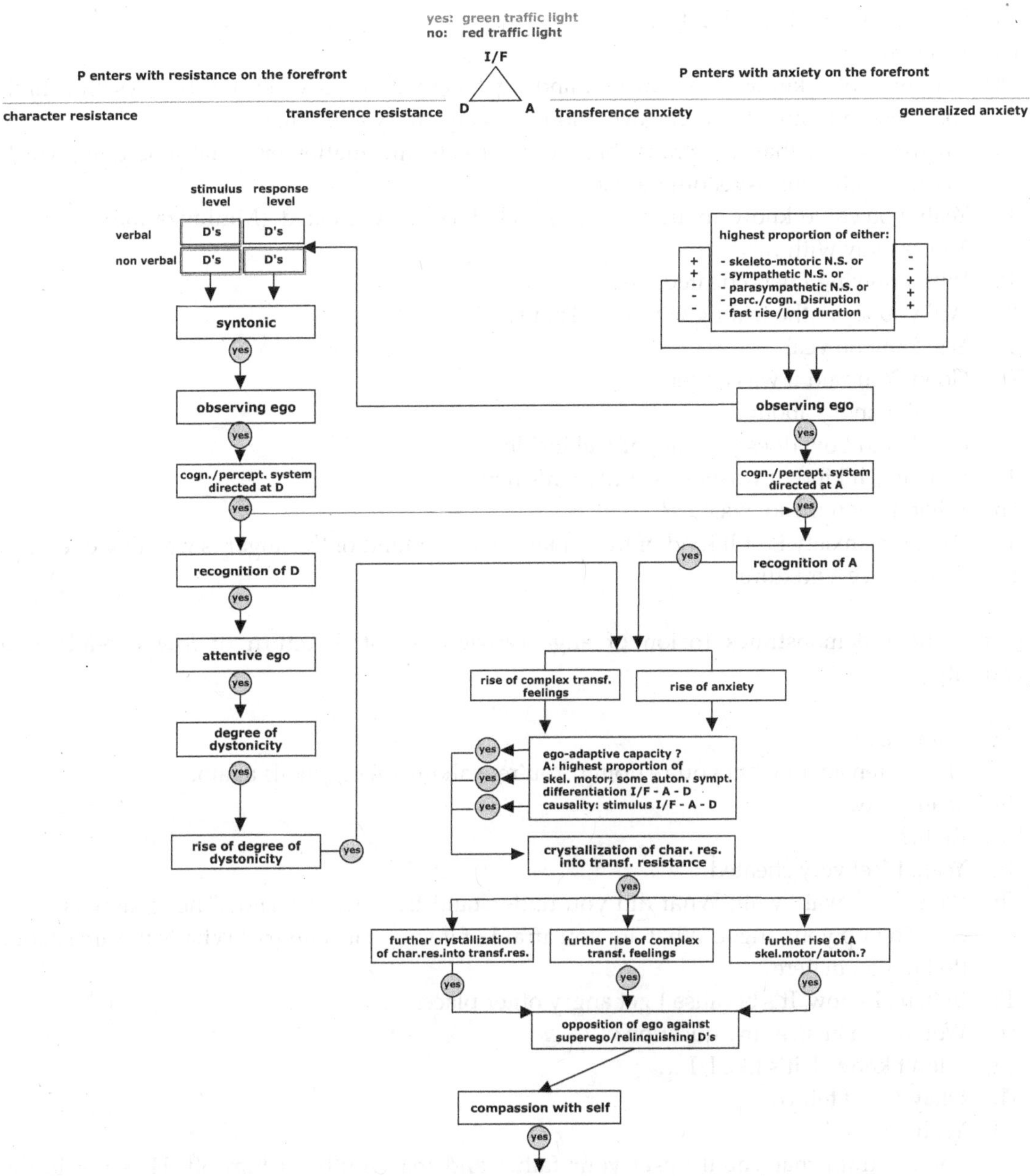

Figure 55. Highly resistant character structure with regressive defenses road to the unconscious 6.

Pt I see a line there (sigh), he looks inert.

Th Well, the guy you walked on eggshells around wasn't inert. (*confront denial*)

Pt No, he wasn't (slight laugh). He wasn't. Yeah, I …

Th Don't you feel you were cheated?

Pt I, I know I was cheated. I, I …
Th You know it.
Pt I know it, oh I know I was cheated and I get *angry* about it when I'm by myself, I think about it and I know I was cheated and I feel very angry about it.
Th Oh good, and is that something that is only private information or is that something worth sharing with your psychotherapist?
Pt Yeah, you could know about it. (laugh) Yeah. I feel very cheated. (Minimization)
Th You're okay with …
Pt With knowing I was cheated, yeah.
Th Will you share the feeling with me? That I …
Pt Yes, I am, oh yeah.
Th Good. You said it was anger
Pt Yes, I'm angry about it.
Th Good, and how does your anger feel inside?
Pt Well, it's, it kind of washes over here. It's here.
Th What do you mean, washes?
Pt Well, the anxiety is still kind of there like a ball and kind of the anger is washing over it.
Th So we have a mixture.

(The patient demonstrates fusion of anger/anxiety, so stall, return of low ego-adaptive capacity.)

Pt Yeah, yeah.
Th Now listen again what you're doing. You're walking on eggshells again.
Pt Yeah, okay.
Th Right?
Pt Yeah. I feel very cheated.
Th Wait, wait, wait, wait. What did you understand from what I said? The anxiety is there covering up your anger. What are you afraid of if you're just angry? What's the area about that to you in here?
Pt In here, I know. It's because I get angry other places.
Th Would you answer my question?
Pt I don't know. I, it's like I, I …
Th Okay. Can I tell you?
Pt Yeah.
Th You're afraid that you'll upset your father and that you'll set him off. He's not in the grave.
Pt Yeah.
Th He's projected immediately.
Pt Yeah, oh to you, yeah. Something definitely is because I really don't know you.
Th Look at my eyes. Are my eyes grey?
Pt No, they're blue.
Th Okay.

Pt Uh huh.
Th Okay, okay. So can you remember who has blue eyes and who has grey eyes?
Pt Uh huh.
Th Who has blue eyes?
Pt You do.
Th And who has grey eyes?
Pt My father.
Th And who are you angry at?
Pt My father.
Th Can you tell him?
Pt No (crying). Oh God. (Weepiness, helplessness)
Th What? You just learned something, didn't you?
Pt (crying, sighing)
Th Did you learn something valuable now?
Pt Yeah, but I can't tell him.
Th You can't put yourself first.
Pt Geez, oh. Oh!
Th What?
Pt This is such a rough road. (laughter)
Th See, I think you're in a bit of denial right now.
Pt Yeah.
Th What you're doing to yourself every day and every minute of your life is the roughest road there is. This is …
Pt Rough road.
Th This is the easy road but you won't take it. Look at me. The self-destructive part of you says you have to live the rest of your life subordinated to your father forever. It's a curse that you have put on you.

(Direct interpretation of the command of the superego.)

Pt Um mmm, um mmm. Yeah. … I fully understand and agree with that.
Th Good.
Pt I totally understand and agree and add my mother in there too please. I mean both of them.
Th Okay.
Pt Okay. I totally agree with that and understand what you're saying.
Th Good.
Pt So do you want to break the curse?
Th Yes.
Pt Yes.
Th Then look your father in the eye and tell him what you're angry at him for.
Pt I'm angry at you because …
Th You're seeing grey eyes not blue eyes, grey eyes.

Pt Okay. I'm angry because …

(The patient's anger is now separate from anxiety, which has disappeared.)

Th At you.
Pt … I'm angry at you because I had to take care of you because we never did anything fun. We didn't have fun as a family, I didn't feel love when I was young. I didn't feel secure when I was young.
Th Because you were a baby.
Pt Because you were a baby … and I had to be your mother.
Th And I had to think of you first.
Pt … and I had to think of you first and how you were going to react and if you were going to scare me and if you were going to scare my brother, and I just felt …
Th And if you were going to provoke my mother.
Pt … and if you were going to provoke my mother or my mother was going to provoke you.
Th Good.
Pt I'm angry that we just lived in a house full of anxiety.
Th And, and "I refuse," tell him.
Pt And I refuse to live this way anymore.
Th I refuse to cripple myself.
Pt I refuse to cripple myself …
Th With anxiety.
Pt … with anxiety.
Th How does that feel? I'm asking you to focus on the angry part of your feeling. You said it was down here.
Pt Right, right.
Th Right. So tell me about that part. Don't let the anxiety cover you.
Pt (big sigh)
Th You just put your father on notice with my help.
Pt Yes. That there's a new sheriff in town. And what I want. My feelings are that I come first.
Th Yeah.
Pt It's 12 noon and I get to shoot the sheriff (emotional, crying). So.
Th Isn't that an interesting …?
Pt Yeah. Right. That's a good one, huh?
Th I'm seeing lots of mixed feelings coming up in you.
Pt It's kind of a relief in a way, humour, but maybe humour is, is masking the anxiety that I …
Th Ahhh, stop talking anxiety.
Pt The anger, yeah.
Th Cause what would it take to shoot a sheriff.
Pt (laugh) It takes a quick trip, it takes a smarter person and a quick trigger person. It takes a gun.
Th So tell me what you do with your gun? Take your time.

Pt I take my gun and I go "toouu."
Th Wait, wait, wait, where do you aim it?
Pt At the heart. (Distancing)
Th At your father's heart.
Pt Yes.
Th Good.
Pt Oooh. Oooh. (The patient grimaces with guilt.)
Th What happened?
Pt That's a hard one to do, That was the hardest thing I did. (*breakthrough* #2)
Th Yeah.
Pt Okay.
Th Yeah, but what was hard about it? Talk about your feeling first. Your feeling—what was hard about shooting your father in the heart?
Pt Well, what was good about shooting my father in the heart is that it was really accurate. I've gone right in the heart the first time, so I can do it.
Th You're proud of yourself … (Pleasure in aggression restored)
Pt Yeah.
Th … for shooting your father in the heart.
Pt Yeah, yeah. Yeah, it's a feeling of satisfaction.
Th Good. You deserve that, don't you?
Pt Yeah.
Th You've been under this nasty sheriff.
Pt Yeah, for a long time. He was a corrupt Sheriff.
Th Yeah.
Pt Maybe he should be the outlaw, but no, he's the sheriff because he's the regulator, he's the law, he's the enforcer.
Th Yeah.
Pt But I don't want that enforcer anymore. I can enforce …
Pt Yeah. I don't have to …
Th If you bring him back from the dead, you'll have to do it all over again.
Pt Yeah, I'll never get over this.
Th No. Just have to do it all over again.
Pt Yes.
Th All over again.
Pt Yeah, okay, I shot him.
Th Do you want to shoot him again?
Pt (small laugh) No.
Th Why not? You can shoot him as many times as you want. Do you need more than one time?
Pt Probably will. (crying, with sobs)
Th Go ahead. Picture it.
Th You can shoot at him more than once.
Pt True.

Th So how many bullets do you want to put in his heart or his head or wherever?
Pt Three. Okay, so I did it once.
Th Yeah. Can you do it again?
Pt Yeah.
Th Where?
Pt In the same place.
Th Okay. Right in the same place or next to it?
Pt No, he was, well I mean, yes, next to it. Not in the same hole.
Th Um mmm.
Pt Where the one bullet went in and then a new hole.
Th Okay, there's three, one …
Pt And then one on the other side.
Th … two, three.
Pt So there's three, so he's dead. Yeah. (sigh)
Th I'm seeing anxiety here.
Pt Yeah.
Th If he's dead, what are you anxious about?
Pt That's true.
Th No, listen again. I think you're anxious about what you feel.
Pt I feel
Th You feel anxious. No. No. Listen to my words. You feel anxious about the feelings about what you did. Put yourself first, please woman, put yourself first. Look at your father's corpse. Three bullets in his heart.
Pt Okay.
Th And tell me where there's three bullets.
Pt Well, one for me, one for my mother and one for my brother.
Th I see …
Pt But my mother deserves to be dead too. (The unconscious working alliance is in charge now)
Th And we'll go to that in a minute. But you got very, very spikes of anxiety when you thought of shooting your father. What was disturbing to you about that?
Pt Well, I love my father. (Breakthrough #3)
Th Of course you do. Don't you have the right to have more than one feeling?
Pt That's true (crying and whispering).
Th If you make—look at me, please look at me—if you force your feelings into a black and white box … .
Pt Ahhh, okay.
Th … you won't make it through life.
Pt Okay.
Th You're not allowed to have mixed feelings?
Pt Yes (sniff).
Th Of love, hate, guilt, grief.
Pt Yeah. Eh, eh, eh, eh (clearing throat), you mean that?

Th Yeah.
Pt Okay. Maybe that's …
Th So aren't you allowed to have a lot of different feelings about this?
Pt Yeah, that makes it easier.
Th I think so. So what's the next feeling when you look at your father's corpse after you put three bullets, one for your brother, one for you and one for your mother in his heart?
Pt Hmmm.
Th Towards his corpse?
Pt (pause) hmmm. Just like one of a caring kind of, you know now in a loving way.
Th Good and tell me where you feel that loving feeling inside of you?
Pt It's kind of here.
Th Good. Just hold onto that.
Pt Um mmm.
Th Is there any anxiety about your loving feeling?
Pt I don't know if its anxiety about that. I have anxiety as I'm feeling this.
Th Okay, look at me please. You don't even have the right to have loving feeling, right, as you're taking that away from yourself about this? Do you see how cruel and sadistic that is?
Pt I'm pretty mean. Yeah.
Th Would you look at me?
Pt I'm very mean to my … means I'm mean to myself. I am mean to myself.
Th Do you hear how callous you are?
Pt I don't know why that is. (sigh). =
Th Do you hear it?
Pt It's matter of fact, kind of.
Th Yeah.
Pt I know it.
Th Go on.
Pt I know I'm mean to myself.
Th And?
Pt Probably the first thing that comes to mind is I deserve it, isn't that sick?

(The patient recognizing the origin of her need to suffer the chronic pain of disempowerment.)

Th Now.
Pt No, I know I don't deserve it! (Loud) (the function of her suffering is clear)
Th Sh, sh, sh, you're an honest woman. I love that.
Pt Yeah.
Th Don't get all anxious here.
Pt Yeah, I deserve it Kindness I deserve … . not Cruelty.
Th Now look down at your father's corpse "because I murdered my father."
Pt Because I murdered my father.
Th I have to be punished.

Pt I have to be punished with

Th Perpetual suffering.

Pt Perpetual suffering.

Th There's no space on this earth for me.

Pt There's no space on this earth for me.

Th Cause I am so …

Pt Bad.

Th That's what you've been locked into.

Pt Uh huh.

Th You see it?

Pt Well, um that and what that stands in front of me any time I've wanted to assert myself or feel a feeling.

Th To be yourself.

Pt I wasn't, I didn't allow myself or I wasn't allowed to somehow. I was very sensitive.

Th Starts off, listen. It starts off. You love your father, okay?

Pt Um mmm.

Th Your father is supposed to take care of you, but because he reverses the roles on you … And you start to see you're getting a bad deal. And you feel rage towards him, but then you feel guilt with that rage … . so you decide the solution for your guilt is to punish yourself by living your life as his perpetual caretaker.

Pt Um mmm, um mmm.

Th And there is no parole. Other than a lifetime of self-destruction.

Pt I don't want to do that anymore. I, I don't want to take care of you any more. I killed you so I can get rid of this. Because you could never be happy, no matter how hard I tried. (sigh) You were a parasite on your daughter.
And that enraged me. And you were unable to look after my brother. Or my mother. Or my mother … And so you have to go, I …

Th I'm not going to punish myself.

Pt I'm not going to punish myself. For your murder. (big sigh)

Th What was that?

Pt Well …

Th In your gut? (sigh)

Pt Well, I still identify with him.

Th In your feeling. You're very smart. I don't want to, I'm not putting …

Pt Yeah.

Th But you don't use your intelligence in the service of your mouth.

Pt (small laugh)

Th How does it feel to not punish yourself for his murder?

Pt I don't know how that feels.

Th Would you try?

Pt (sniffing) Okay.

Th Just try. Let's say the punishment ends today. How does that feel to know that when you walk in …

Pt I can't hardly even conceive of how that feels. It must feel so good.
Th But you …
Pt I can hardly even feel that and I would love to feel that.
Th Okay, but you …
Pt You know …
Th But you've got some idea that is.
Pt A little glimpse, just the tiniest.
Th Describe it.
Pt It's so wonderful to live without that burden but then comes the intrusive thought "I don't deserve it."
Th Uh huh, and what are you doing there?
Pt What am I doing here?
Th No, when you create that intrusive thought, who's …
Pt I'm cutting it off.
Th Now who's telling you?
Pt My father.
Th Yeah. Yeah, because …
Pt My mother, my father.
Th "… because you have murdered me, daughter, you have to torture yourself the rest of your life. And we want to say to him, Look?
Pt I guess I want to say to him."
Th You want to say to him?
Pt Stop bothering me!
Th No. Could you get a gun?
Pt Shoot him again?
Th And again.
Pt And again.
Th And again.
Pt (crying) I can't.
Th How many bullets does it take before he goes down?
Pt (big sigh)
Th Now …
Pt But I'm …
Th Ummm?
Pt I'm doing the bad part if I'm not the good part. I guess I …
Th I don't care if you killed the bad father along with the good father, don't hurt, if you kill them both, you kill them both. You don't have to do any kind of artificial compartmentalization. Now you said you're holding onto some grudge against your mother right now.
Pt Against my mother?
Th Yeah, what is your grudge against your mother right now?
Pt Well, I was talking about my cousin before, my mother, well my mother …
Th You kept telling me you have rage against your mother.

Pt Yes, I have rage against my mother, her support.
Th What?
Pt (sigh) She didn't support my father which. (The mother is the sustaining factor)
Th Put the burden on you.
Pt And the burden was all on me.
Th Right.
Pt Yeah, to kind of walk on eggshells with both of them. And my mother didn't accept my friends, and she just, she was just a, uhhh, she was—I start to feel anxious again as I start describing.
Th Excuse me, excuse me a second. That's the healthiest you've been in the whole session.
Pt What?
Th You just, you have noticed you started getting anxious cause you used the word describing.
Pt Yes.
Th That's the healthiest you've been the entire session.
Pt Oh.
Th You caught the anxiety early enough …
Pt Okay.
Th … before it went through your whole body and became overwhelming.
Pt Ohhh, okay, okay.
Th You're starting to care about yourself a little more.
Pt Good, good.
Th What was the feeling you were describing towards your mother?
Pt Just that she, she just was always such a downer, she made me always feel so kind of burdened that I could never quite describe. I was always never quite right.
Th Oh yeah.
Pt Never quite …
Th Yeah.
Pt … doing the right thing or …
Th Yeah.
Pt … so there was always this kind of feeling off centre. (points to her heart)
Th Yeah.
Pt Around her.
Th Yeah.
Pt And not very relaxed at all. (rage fused with anxiety)
Th Yeah.
Pt And I didn't like her really as she was raising me, so …
Th Yeah, yeah. So the feeling you were describing towards her?
Pt Is that she … (crying)
Th Do not justify to her.
Pt I'm not justifying. I just feel mad at her.
Th Okay, describe the physical part of your …
Pt I'm not too much, I'm just more saying it, but let's see.

Th Uhh, I don't believe that's true actually. I saw emotion in you and your mother's eyes, do you see her eyes? Describe what her eye colour is?

Pt Her—grey.

Th Grey too.

Pt Grey.

Th Grey too? Wait, wait, wait, wait. And what colour are my eyes?

Pt Blue.

Th Good. So you're not going to have grey eyes between you and me, are we?

Pt Okay.

Th Right?

Pt Yeah.

Th We're going to focus on her grey eyes.

Pt Yeah, okay.

Th And how did she make you feel? Like what?

Pt Just small and …

Th Worse than small. Like lead weight. That you were a burden. You were a burden to her is what you said. That's what you said. She made you feel like being a mother to you was a burden on her, not a joy.

Pt She didn't exhibit much joy.

Th Not—she made you feel as a burden, right? Look at the woman's eyes and tell me whether you feel love or hate, what do you feel?

Pt Nothing. Just, you know, cut-off-ness.

Th Okay.

Pt You know.

Th So your choice is to protect your mother from your rage by cutting yourself off. That's your choice. Is that a constructive choice? Just be true to yourself. Look in your mother's grey eyes and talk to your mother. What do you feel towards her?

Pt Anger.

Th I believe you, see.

Pt Yeah.

Th Trust yourself.

Pt Yeah.

Th Where do you feel your anger inside?

Pt Well, I'm not feeling it so much. I'm feeling anxiety, but anger is a word that came to mind. (Anxiety now replaces the angry feeling)

Th Good for you. Look at me please.

Pt Um mmm.

Th Feelings have three parts.

Pt Uh huh.

Th They have words.

Pt Um mmm.

Th A label, right? They have a sensation?

Pt Um mmm.

Th And they have an action built into them. All feelings, all feelings—you're in touch with the word anger.
Pt Right, right, right. Um mmm.
Th Look at you. You're cut off at the head. (confrontation of her submission to her maternal superego introject)
Pt Uh huh. Yeah.
Th Who's cutting herself off from her anger in this chair?
Pt I am.
Th And is it the healthy part or the self-destructive part?
Pt Self-destructive part.
Th Are you loyal to the self-destructive part?
Pt No, I don't want to be.
Th So don't cut your anger off at the head.
Pt All right, okay.
Th Include your body in your anger. How does your anger feel?
Pt I feel a lot of anger toward—well I'm saying it (sigh), let's see.
Th I think you're more than saying it.
Pt I feel angry towards my mother for ...
Th You don't have to justify it.
Pt I feel angry towards my mother.
Th How does it feel?
Pt You know and she humiliated me too.
Th How does it feel to be humiliated by your own mother?
Pt Really mad.
Th Where do you feel you're mad?
Pt Right here.
Th Where?
Pt Here.

(Lower abdomen/pelvis. This is where Davanloo places the deepest source of unconscious rage.)

Th Good. Is there any anxiety?
Pt Yeah, yeah.
Th So you're not entirely comfortable with your anger here?
Pt No, no I'm not, I'm not.
Th So perhaps it's not anger that's there. Perhaps ...
Th I'm sure it's more the humiliation.
Pt Well, she's humiliation umm by, you know, telling other kids that I liked this boy and then they tease me. You know, she humiliated me by, you know, when I told—I had this epiphany when I was about 4, I looked up at the sky and I realized for the first time that clouds actually moved. I didn't realize that. I didn't know, I just, you know, and so—she was like dismissive or you didn't know that or did you realize that.

Th Sh, sh, sh. Don't imitate her.
Pt Yeah.
Th Imitate you, what did it feel like to be on the other receiving end of that?
Pt It felt, Oh God!
Th No, what did you feel?
Pt Embarrassed that …
Th Right.
Pt You know …
Th You didn't feel loved.
Pt Yeah.
Th You felt like an object of scorn.
Pt Yeah, yeah.
Th And how does that feel to be treated that way? What does that feel like?
Pt Bad.
Th What's bad?
Pt I'm a little kid!
Th Stop with the I'm a little kid stuff.
Pt Okay.
Th What's the feeling here? Is the feeling rage, yes or no?
Pt No.
Th What is it?
Pt It's kind of mixed up.
Th Mixed up?
Pt Just a lot of anxiety and wanting to …
Th Sh, sh. Wanting to protect your mother.
Pt Yes (laughter) Wanting to justify what she did and telling how I …
Th Okay. Good. What is your goal?
Pt My goal is to put myself first.
Th Isn't that hard to do for you?
Pt Yes.
Th It is. Are you worth the effort?
Pt Yes!
Th Good.
Pt Yes, I am.
Th What would your rage like to do to your mother if she just created a …
Pt Strangle her.
Th Yeah, and do you feel the impulse to do that?
Pt A lit—somewhat, yeah.
Th What's it feel like?
Pt Like that. (The patient shows a strong forward strangling impulse towards her mother's neck)
Th Can you feel the rage from here to the hands?
Pt No.

Th Why not?
Pt I don't know.
Th Yes, you do. You're compelled to protect your mother just like you're compelled to protect your father.
Pt (big sigh) I don't know why they're more important than I am. Or they need me.
Th I can tell you why.
Pt Why?
Th Because that's the way they set it up.
Pt (laugh) The way they set it up. (laugh) That's funny.
Th It's true.
Pt Oh, man, oh God.
Th You're just having a feeling. Pay attention. What did you feel—there was the feeling.
Pt I felt Oh my God.
Th No. What's the feeling? That's an escape mechanism. What does it feel to realize that's the way they …
Pt Kind of almost hopeless.
Th What's hopeless about it?
Pt Well, I'm this little kid.
Th You were outnumbered.
Pt And they did this to me.
Th You put your mother before, well you put your mother before yourself.
Pt No, don't tell me that.
Th So why not feel your full rage like a woman instead of behaving like a child in my chair?
Pt But I feel bad for her too.
Th Oh, so we're going to use that excuse? That's what you did your whole life. So what does the murderer look like?
Pt Oh boy (sigh).
Th If you stop putting her first? Put your rage before your love for her. How does she die?
Pt Well, I would, I see myself, you know, strangling her and then her falling backwards and then me kind of almost falling on top of her, you know, strangling her like that.
Th Massive rage.
Pt Yeah. I mean I can describe this I'm t feeling it. To actually, to actually be falling on someone that you're killing, that's pretty powerful.
Th Vicious.
Pt Yeah
Th Powerful.
Pt I mean, and it shows a lack of boundaries, I mean …
Th No, no, no, no.
Pt Okay, okay. I mean it just …
Th It shows what? A very angry woman.
Pt (laugh) Yeah.
Th A violently angry woman.
Pt To do something like that.

Th Don't you think, don't you think you need to become acquainted with your violent feelings?
Pt Yeah, yeah.
Th You've been spending your whole life because …
Pt Denying them or running away from them.
Th Suppressing them.
Pt Suppressing them and feeling they weren't right to feel.
Th And punishing yourself for them.
Pt Yeah, yeah.
Th So you're in a powerful position with respect to your mother aren't you, on top of her and …?
Pt That's true, yeah.
Th How long does it take before she goes?
Pt About 30 seconds. Yeah.
Th And does her head stay on her shoulders, or do you rip it off?
Pt No her head stays on her shoulders.
Th Does she go limp in your arms?
Pt Well, she's not in my arms, but she goes …
Th Hands.
Pt Yeah, but she goes limp, yeah, she goes limp.
Th I meant in your hands.
Pt She goes like that.
Th Good.
Pt You know.
Th And do you look her in the eye and see her death?
Pt Um mmm.
Th And what does that feel like when you see her grey eyes?
Pt I don't feel triumphant or anything.
Th You don't feel triumphant.
Pt Let's see. How do I feel? Satisfied but guilty (sobbing).
Th And you got the rage out of your body.
Well, it's on her, isn't it? She's dead.
Th Is there anything you'd like to say to your mother and your father if you put them some place?
Pt Mother and Father, I know you didn't mean to do this, but boy you just caused me a complete mess. The way you set up my childhood and I know this was not your intent and you probably would do anything you could to reverse it because I know you love me, I know you love me, but boy did you fuck me up and you fucked things up really bad. You left me crippled with anxiety.
Th And set up dysfunctional relationships where I reversed the roles like with Paulo.
Pt And dysfunctional relationships where I reversed the roles. And I have to walk on eggshells. As though you were still alive. And, may I add something to this? And I have to settle for half of loaf all the time and be satisfied with that.

Th Did you feel the compassion there for a sec?
Pt No.
Th You didn't feel it? I saw it.
Pt Really?
Th What is wrong with you feeling compassion for yourself? So how would you like to bury them so that they don't haunt you, telling you, you know, daughter because you killed us, you have to suffer a life of walking on eggshells and suffer a life of being cut off from your feelings, and you have to justify …
Pt I see as you're saying these things, I'm thinking, oh my God I'm going to be all alone which is, I guess, my punishment.
Pt But, but that's the only thing I know and if I …
Th What?
Pt Is them. No, I'd rather be alone, but I'm alone when I'm suffering.
Th No, you're alone. Your suffering is self-imposed. It's incomplete separation and individuation from them.
Pt Yes.
Th Instead of saying good-bye to them, you torture yourself. I'd rather be alone every day of the week than be tortured.
Pt Well I torture myself with feelings that I'm going to be alone. I punish myself.
Th Oh, you have a million errr techniques.
Pt Yeah, true, true.
Th I'm trying to get you to lay down the hatchet against yourself.
Pt Lay down the hatchet, okay.
Th Against yourself.
Pt I know, I know.
Th So will you bury them with love?
Pt Umm.
Th How do you want …
Pt Well, they're wrapped together in the same cloth, like this, you know, a Muslim shroud.
Th Like they should have been all along.
Pt Yeah, yeah.
Th They should have been taking care of each other's needs.
Pt Yeah.
Th Not recruiting you.
Pt (sobbing)
Th You're the one who creates these symbols for them.
Pt Right.
Th You make my job easy.
Pt Yeah, yeah. No it's true.
Th The symbolic function of your mind is fabulous if you …
Pt Don't listen to it.
Th No, no.
Pt Okay

Th If you'd lower your anxiety, you would emerge.
Pt Yeah, yeah.
Th If you became more comfortable with your feeling part.
Pt Yeah.
Th That's where the symbolic part comes from is from your feeling part.
Pt Yes, yes, I agree, I agree.
Th Same stock.
Pt So they're lurking in all the little, you know … at first, it, I was, they're kind of in between facing each other and being side by side. They're actually more side by side, but they almost switch in my mind from wanting to being this way and that way and this way and that way. Okay, so they're this way and …
Th What's wrong with them being that way?
Pt Ohhh, it's two sexual or something.
Th So we have the puritan here.
Pt I don't know (laughing). I don't why.
Th Don't you think they should have had better sex?
Pt They did. I think that was what kept them together.
Th What do you mean?
Pt Well, I think that's why they stayed together.
Th Why?
Pt Because I think they had a deep attraction for each other.
Th Would you talk to them please? Tell them, Mom, Dad.
Pt Yeah.
Th All right.
Pt You had a deep attraction for each other.
Th Which was healthy.
Pt Which was healthy. But you also had things that you did to each other that did not support each other and that's where I came in and I don't want to be a part of this anymore.
Th That's where you misused me.
Pt That's where you misused me to deal with each other, to, so that you didn't hurt each other.
Th To be your caretaker, marriage counsellor, and psychotherapist.
Pt Whipping boys, whipping girl. (sigh) Where I got dumped on all the unhappy feelings of your childhood and your marriage which is not my fault, I'm a little kid.
Th So tell them your wish for eternity.
Pt So my wish for eternity.
Th Is not only that you make love to each other.
Pt That you not only make love to each other but that you love me in a way that …
Th No, but that you meet each other needs. They're dead.
Pt Okay.
Th They're never going to meet your needs.
Pt Right, right, right, right, right.
Th You're returning them to the grave.

Pt I'm returning you to the grave …

Th To meet each other's needs.

Pt In a good way so that you can meet each other's needs through eternity.

Th And I will deal with my feelings.

Pt And I will deal with my feelings on my own.

Th Of loneliness.

Pt Of loneliness.

Th After I bury you.

Pt After I bury you.

Th I'll deal with my feelings of loneliness.

Pt I'll deal with my feelings of loneliness and everything …

Th Loneliness is better.

Pt Loneliness is better than being in the iron jaws of what you did to me and how you misused me.

Th How does that feel to be a grown up?

Pt Feels kind of good, you know.

Th You like it?

Pt Yeah, it gives me hope, it gives me hope that there is a life after their death. You know, I think (sigh) I can go forward without them, without the mis …

Th How do you close the grave of your own free will?

Pt Okay, my own free will (sigh). Well, my own free will, they're like in an envelope, their tops are kind of tucked in and then side flags come over like little angels' wings.

Th That's emotional.

Pt Yeah.

Th What's the feeling when you see them?

Pt I hope they can fly on the wings of the angels. (sobbing)

Th Let it come. Don't keep your tears to yourself, just cry for your parents. Cry for them.

Pt My mother's on the wings of the angels (crying) And my father's …

Th Do you feel that they're no longer your responsibility, if they're on the wings of the angels?

Pt And I'm transferring responsibility to the angels who are much nicer than I. I can see the angels, I can see the angels carrying, carrying them off.

Th And what does that feel like for you?

Pt It feels really good.

Th Do you want to wave good-bye?

Pt Oh gee, that's hard to do.

Th It's important. You need to learn to say good-bye. They never taught you how to say good-bye, Sarah. Say good-bye. How do you want to say good-bye?

Pt (Sniffling) I can just wave good-bye to them. You're in good hands.

Th With someone who's actually qualified.

Pt To bring them happiness, and I know you'll be happy there being carried off by them.

Th And tell me where you go?

Pt You know, I kind of walk, I'm kind of on this green ball which is the earth.

Th Uh huh. Tell me how that feels.
Pt It feels good. I'm walking on the grass on this green ball, you know.
Th Now would you say out loud I'm alone.
Pt I'm alone. On the green earth. I'm free to find someone for me. No, I, I have to, I have to find someone for me and to take it seriously and to take me seriously. I know what you're saying. I've been kind of like, oh choose me, choose me and this and that. I have to go and choose somebody for me, that's worthy of me and can give me what I really want instead of the half loaf business.
Th I see a lot of feelings in your eyes. What's the feeling about?
Pt I have a big task ahead of me.
Th That's not a feeling.
Pt (laugh and sniffling) Okay.
Th There's a little anxiety which is good.
Pt But there's kind of like this freedom to that of the open road. There's an open road ahead of me if …

We have successfully completed the roadmap (see Figure 56 on the next page) and the patient experienced painful feelings towards both the primary aggressor and the "partner in crime" that functioned as the maintaining factor. In summary, we entered at the arrow as the patient's regressive defences attempted to create chaos and conceal the dual pathological superegos which cause her to use the defences of ignoring, galloping, denying, helplessness, endless submission, endless suffering (masochism) in order to thwart actualization of her sexual satisfaction and emergence into independent adulthood.

(Now, the patient is no longer frozen as a guilty, frightened, dependent child. She can spend the rest of her life as a woman.)

Th A feeling near to your heart. It's a good feeling.
Pt Oh. It's a good feeling, it's a good feeling to have this open road and to want to explore.
Th If you take your good feeling seriously.
Pt Yes, yes, I will.
Th No, no, now. Tell me how it feels in your body.
Pt It's exciting, feels exciting, but trepidatious too because I think, oh I have this task ahead. There's certain things I think I need to do.
Th What do you mean?
Pt To put my life on the right track.
Th What does it feel like to be that way?
Pt It feels welcoming.
Th Can you hold onto that place in you?
Pt Okay, yeah, yeah.
Th Can you call that place your centre?
Pt That I'm the captain here, yeah. (pause) That I want to, I want to command my own ship.
Th Yeah. How do you like that?
Pt It's pretty neat.
Th Yeah, it is.

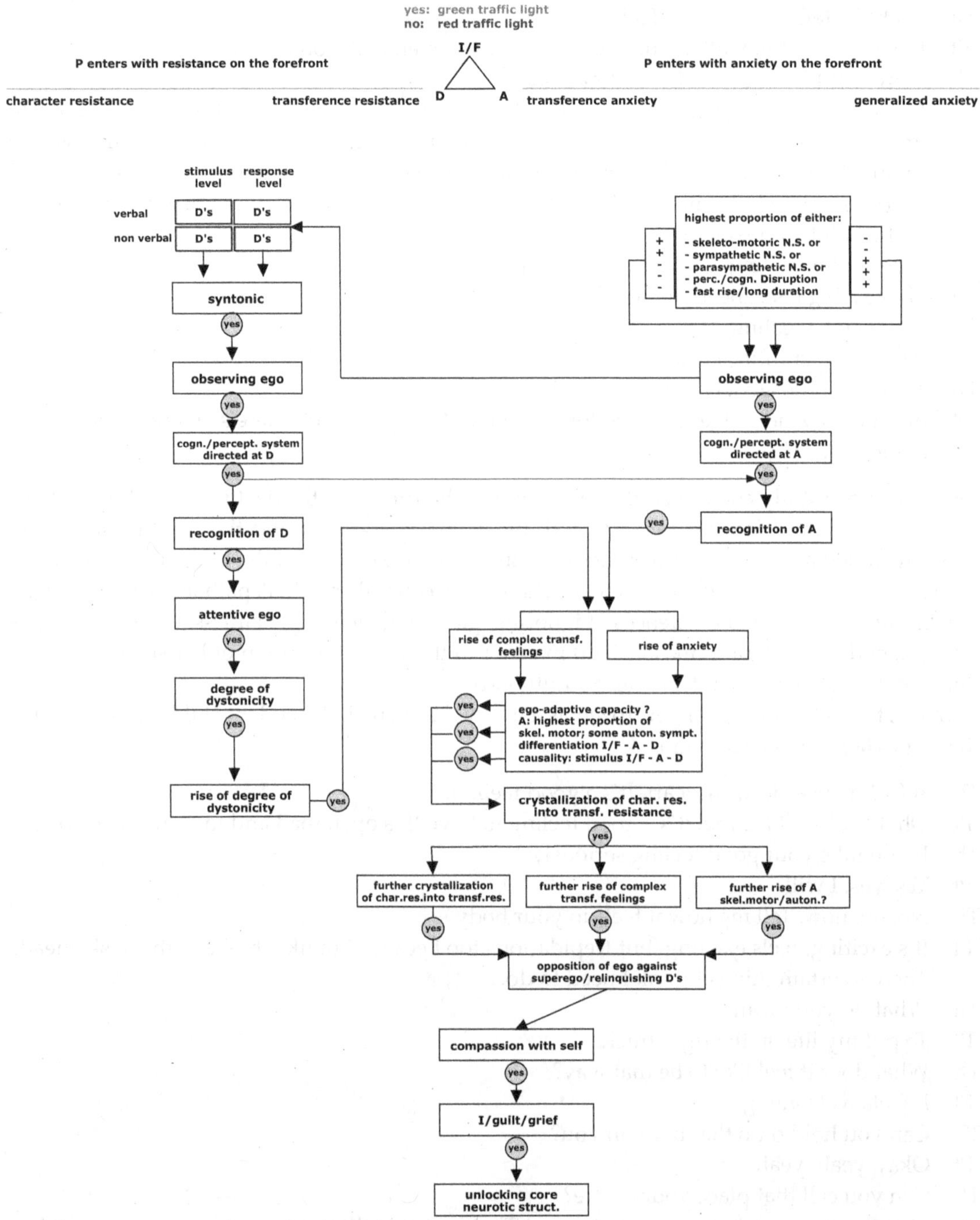

Figure 56. Highly resistant character structure with regressive defenses road to the unconscious 7.

Pt I like what you said about that it's our responsibility to find someone for ourselves. I think that's just so primary.

Th Yeah.

Pt And so important.

Th Yeah and you've been shirking your responsibility to yourself. All you've been doing is reliving your childhood in one form or another over and over again.

Pt Yeah. That's why I came here.

Th Yeah and was that a good decision?

Pt Yeah, because I told …

Th Slow down. You're speeding up. Look at me please. You're talking to me. What colour are my eyes?

Pt Blue.

Th Talk to me.

Pt I am.

Th What was a good decision about coming here?

Pt What was a good decision about coming here? That I need to start living my own life and not retreading my parent's life, what happened in my parents to me.

Th Didn't you have to put yourself first?

Pt To come here?

Th To come here.

Pt Yeah, yeah I did.

Th And has there been anything here that has ever told you that you shouldn't always put yourself first.

Pt No, no there hasn't. I need to do that.

Th All right.

Pt Now I start to feel a little anxiety like, oh what does that feel like, you know and I think it'll just happen.

Th Well, that's helplessness. You know how it feels.

Pt Okay.

Th Remember, I was just talking to the captain of her own ship?

Pt Yeah. How does that feel, you asked me and I was on the green ball.

Th Boy, you went from the green ball to the ocean and you got on your ship.

Pt All right.

Th You were the captain of your ship. I thought it was going to Hawaii but it might go some place else, I don't know.

Pt It might go to Hawaii.

Th Yeah.

Pt Yeah. It might do lots of things.

Th There's nothing wrong with giving yourself what you want, right? There's only something wrong with giving yourself what you want if you feel guilty about your murderous feelings to your parents and you feel like you have to be punished for your rage of death.

Th And whose time is it to live her life on this earth?

Pt Mine.

Th Can you, can you hold onto that as a central mission?
Pt It is a sacred mission, yes, I can. I'm going to. (sniffling)
Th Good. Now your anxiety is almost gone if you're noticing.
Pt Well, I still feel, I still feel it.
Th There's a little.
Pt Yeah.
Th There's a little but it's not like this, maybe you feel the difference in it there.
Pt Yeah, yeah. It's still here. It's still here.
Th It takes a certain degree of time.
Pt Yes, yes.
Th To make this change.
Pt Right.
Th But I see the tremendous change in you from this session from the last one.
Th How does it feel to know you're making changes?
Pt Progress? It feels really good.
Th Good.
Pt Yeah, it feels really good, yeah.
Th Okay, so we can wrap it up and I don't have to smash my watch?
Pt No, don't smash it. (laughter)
Th You're going to hold onto your feelings.
Pt I am, I'm going …
Th Between now and the next session?
Pt Yes, yeah.
Th You'll report back to me.
Pt Yes, yes.
Th What it's like to live from this place.
Pt For me, for me.
Th With your feet on the earth.
Pt Yes, yeah.

The patient subsequently blossomed as she recognized that she was suppressing her sexuality out of guilt and fear over competing with her mother for her father's affection. She not only held on to her gains, and but also successfully terminated her therapy four sessions later. She has a new partner whom she attracted at a dancing class after overcoming her inhibition of her repressed childhood exhibitionism. At the end of therapy, she was free of anxiety and depression and was able to request what she wanted from relatives and say no when she meant no without suffering.

Notes

1. There is semantic confusion about pain of trauma. Davanloo (Neborsky, 1986) "Where in the structural model is pain?" Modern theorists see pain of trauma as shame (Shore,1998) which Shore posits as a simultaneous firing of the sympathetic and parasympathetic autonomic nervous

system in the immature unloved infant. The authors prefer pain of trauma as it differentiates from "shame" as an inhibitory defense when the ego is judged or devalued by the pathologic superego. (Neborsky, 2003)

2. Sustaining factor (ten Have de Labije, 2003) refers to the parent who allowed the abuse or neglect to continue. Frequently the rage/guilt grief is more intense toward the parent who "knew but did nothing".
3. Sroufe's (1990) research on attachment security reveals that securely attached children are able to avoid victimization or perpetration schemes throughout the life cycle.

Steps in the chapter

- Patients with character pathology will eventually use these defences to deactivate the CTF
- The therapist must be active in order to prevent the establishment of a transference *neurosis*
- The therapist must appeal to the patient's desire for freedom in order for them not to experience the therapist as the traumatizing figure
- The therapist helps the patient distinguish between their desire for help, the therapist's desire to help free them from their compulsion to repeat, and the necessity to face their own true, albeit painful, feelings

CHAPTER THIRTEEN

Exiting the roadmap to the unconscious in the phase of termination

Approaching the phase of termination

The end phase of therapy is determined by the beginning. The therapy began as a problem-solving relationship wherein all the treatment goals are agreed upon in the initial interview. Once the ego starts to separate itself from the superego and the resistance is defeated, the unconscious part of the working alliance starts to develop (Davanloo, 1990). The therapist has activated the patient's attachment longings and they have driven the patient to accept the therapist's help to explore and revisit the trauma based feelings from the past. The patient has hopefully unmasked the eyes of his internal aggressor(s), understood his/their commands, the ways he submitted to these commands, and declared his freedom from the conditions which were imposed upon the self by his pathological superego. Through internalization of the constructive superego that was modelled by the therapist, the patient gained access to his complex of transference feelings which were associated with past traumatic experiences. In cooperation with the therapist, he has worked these feeling through. The process, as described by Davanloo (1978, 1980, 1984, 1990, 2000), itself, when administered correctly, ignites the termination phase of therapy.

In short, the patient has defrosted from his frozen state and the powers of personal growth are freed. When this happens, the patient experiences himself in a new and constructive way, from a position of earned secure autonomy. Because of his liberated curiosity and inherent desire to explore the world, his need to build and maintain nurturing and autonomous relationships takes over; it thus becomes time to say goodbye (see Table 8).

Table 8. Signals of movement into a termination phase of therapy and of a constructive goodbye.

1.	Symptom remission (Axis I, DSM-IV)
2.	Separation of ego and superego parts
3.	Attentive ego and capacity to understand self in terms of the two triangles
4.	Ability to investigate longings, feelings, behaviour, norms, and values with love, care, and precision
5.	Capacity to act upon one's own longings, feelings, behaviour, norms, and values with love, care, and precision
6.	Building and sustaining of constructive relationships.

Thus, once the patient has become his own therapist, it is time for the therapeutic relationship to end. He is as expert as is the therapist at understanding his problems in terms of the triangles of person and conflict. He monitors his anxiety, his old defences have become dystonic, and his feelings as well as his anxiety are healthily regulated.

As all endings of relationships involve loss; one has to accept the farewell, one has to mourn the end of the good aspects of that particular relationship, and one also has to have faith in one's own capacity to continue without the other. The relationship of the patient to the therapist is not an exception to this fact of life.

Emergence of defences against termination

Sometimes a patient may regress to helplessness to defend against saying goodbye to the support of the therapist. Sometimes a patient may regress to helplessness because of deeper activation of past traumatic experiences. For instance, a patient who has lost his most beloved parent to death, and is then left with a dismissive abusive parent by himself, or a patient whose competitive parent never allowed the patient to be successfully independent from him or her, could again take refuge into his defences around termination. Another example might be the patient who was blamed by his helpless and single raising parent whenever he enjoyed contact with other people. The therapist must be aware and alert to these phenomena because they refer to the issues that were not addressed sufficiently by the patient and therapist.

Occasionally, patients who have made positive changes in all kinds of relationships come to a session and surprise the therapist with their wish have this as the last session and to say "goodbye" in an abrupt way. This would be an example of acting out defences to avoid painful feelings of loss. In our view, it is, as a general rule, a mistake of the therapist to comply with this. It would be better to investigate with the patient which feelings he wants to avoid in himself and of the therapist.

Termination phase of patients: some vignettes of sessions

The following transcripts show two different termination sessions in which the patients say their goodbyes and discuss why their therapies succeeded and wherein their prior therapies did not seem to work. The diagram of red and green traffic lights is not included since there have been multiple unlockings, workings through, and the attentive egos of these patients are operating, their resistance is low, and the unconscious/conscious working alliance is at the forefront.

Termination 1

The man who reclaimed his power

The patient is a 60-year-old consultant who was referred by his psychopharmacologist for a block of ISTDP. He was highly traumatized during a recent assignment overseas. He was hired to establish higher educational guidelines for Third World developing countries. When he started working, he soon became aware he was in a politically corrupt system. He found himself on the losing end of every issue with the head authority figure of the country where he was consulting. He found himself getting progressively more anxious and depressed. After a year, he returned to the USA and sought therapy to address lingering depression and self-doubts. It also became apparent that he was stuck in a loveless marriage. The therapy had focused on his longings and painful feelings, which were underneath his need to please his internalized highly abusive father (part of his pathological superego) and the consequences of this need on his relation with his wife. His father, a practising alcoholic with no desire for either sobriety or recovery, had frequently beaten him into abject submission as a child and did not tolerate any autonomy of his son.

The therapy took twelve hours. In the therapy, we firmly established criteria 1, 2, 3, 4, partly criterion 5, but 6 was forestalled secondary to his decision to leave his loveless marriage after a failed attempt at marital therapy. His wife stated she has no interest in therapy or in continuing the marriage, and in fact she did not love him. They had had no sexual intimacy for four and a half years.

Pt I'm doing really well .... .

Th I'm pleased to know about the progress of your emotional recovery, how are you doing? In that regard, are you still paying attention to yourself?

Pt Yeah, and it has, it's having, um, um, it manifests itself, and to me in interesting ways.

Th Um mm.

Pt Which I attribute to this process.

Th Um mm.

Pt I don't know, you know, I could go on and on about it, it's cause and effect and everything, but, uh, for example, just to give you an example which, which I noted to myself last night, I'm watching a studio movie last night and which I know, I actually own and I'm watching the slap stick part where the parrot gets away, and the gang try to return the parrot. Do you know, do you?

Th Yes. Um mm.

Pt And I actually became hysterical with laughter.

Th Um mm.

Pt And I thought to myself, Why am I, was actually goofying at this, uh. Then I thought to myself, Wow, that's really, umm, more kind of a happy experience, It's been a long time since I felt happy. You know, I, became quite sad at my own reaction. I couldn't stop myself from just, uh, almost rolling on the floor with laughter at the well- known and, and quite familiar scene.

Th Well, irrespective of the cause?

Pt Yeah.

Th That's wonderful, its wonderful news that you're able to feel both happy as well as sad ...

Pt I would actually say it was almost I was laughing hysterically. My wife was on the couch, and she doesn't laugh aloud much at anything, and I just said, Gee, that thing, isn't that funny? (laugh) So haven't been thinking much about my dad, haven't been uh ...

Th Before we go onto what you haven't been doing. Right now I'm just seeing a lot, your hands.

Pt My fingers ... yeah.

Th I wasn't sure if you were nervous.

Pt No, I went for a ride. My riding partner had lumps that actually bent with his fingers which are not normal riding gloves and I look at them very enviously. And I thought if he were a decent person he would share one of them. (laugh-joking)

(The patient reassures me it's not anxiety, and I believe him and his attentive ego.)

Th (laugh) So one thing that you've noticed is deepening of feelings of happiness.

Pt Yeah, let me give you some other umm, umm symptoms, would you say, symptoms, would you?

Th Yes.

Pt Umm, I'm, uh working on a paper for publication on my Third World consulting experience and I'm, I've gained some emotional distance from that ... .

Th Trauma.

Pt Trauma. But not, but in addition to that, I had a revelation in the writing of a piece of it last week and I, and I'm having gotten them sort of the middle of this emotional turmoil which characterized my reaction through the whole thing, I just felt myself completely at sea emotionally and even, well very much emotionally, not intellectually because I felt that I was an expert and then, that I hadn't been challenged, but I didn't quite know what had happened. And then thinking more deeply about the, the whole episode and how it came to be, I was reviewing my whole thinking about it as I was writing. I realized that the thing was very, very badly conceived and I was *incredibly naïve* to have accepted the position in the first, in the first place. In addition to that, I was reflecting on how the position, the work that I'd, the role that I had been given over there, I'd been giving me a real, uhh, boost, a real umm boost to my low self-esteem and my ego. Get this?

Th Um mm.

Pt I'm thinking about my ego and what a good thing it was to have been given that job. And here I was stroking my ego and thinking that this is the kind of acknowledgement and recognition that I've always wanted, in a sense that I'm being given this kind of a role.

Th Yes, yes, I understand.

Pt And then I thought afterwards, when I was reviewing it, I thought, Well, here I was really out of touch about, what really I was experiencing. If I really had been smarter and more detached and not so needy, in the sense of "I need this to feed my self-esteem". I could have just stepped back and said, "This is really a cockamamie job and if I had my head screwed on straight I wouldn't accept it."

Th Um mm.

Pt And I'm, I'm umm, kind of, being considered for another job in Serbia, almost identical, and I've now taken the, a com, believe me this is not a perspective that I had three weeks ago. I think in the perspective now that I think this is going to be another cockamamie job which, if I took for reasons of psychological need, and …

Th Vanity.

Pt … vanity or bolstering my own self-esteem, I'd jump at the job, whereas now I say, I've looked very critically at this job to see if it bore any of the same earmarks of the train wreck I had just been on.

Th And what could you negotiate …

Pt How I would negotiate it or I would say, Look, you're going to send me over here and I'm going to have a look-see. I would like to be thinking about this yesterday. You're going to pay me and I'm going to fly first-class to Serbia and I'm going to have a long talk with all the key people that would be, you know, that I would be working with and would be instrumental in making this thing a success, and if I don't find it, if I'm not getting the right feedback, I'm just going to walk. I would say that would be absolutely the terms of, with my taking this next job. And that hadn't, that idea and the strength upon which I would be able, the psychological foundation upon which I would be making the set of terms was not in me three weeks ago.

Th What you're, what you're saying is umm, not exactly directly, but indirectly is that there's been an improvement in your sense of self-esteem.

Pt Correct. Now, you see, I link a lot of that to your reminding me and helping me come to the, the realization or the epiphany, or what did we call it? I said this was a real breakthrough. It was that, umm, if I can get that off my back and also throw off, the, the mantle of self-deprecation and, and self-flagellating that I allow my internalized father do to myself. I see that problem as life long and with complete clarity.

Th Right.

Pt If I can do that, maybe, I, I wasn't thinking clearly, I wasn't thinking one plus one equals stronger self-esteem, clearer headedness professionally or anything else, but I believe that that's actually happened, this sense of having thrown back, umm, the job to some extent and beginning to read, beginning to read myself more clearly and caringly. And that's had one back to the kind of effect that it has, that you can see yourself more clearly, professionally, you could understand the kind of times of delusional sense of Hey, this is really the compensatory stuff that I needed to hear about getting my job in former job in Kosovo, to do what? To fix dam, damage, or, or to prove yourself to, prove myself to my dad. I'm not proving anything to my dad. In fact, I walked into this stupid train wreck, trying again to prove myself to him!

Th But you realize, like visiting your dad, how trying to prove yourself to your dad is a fool's errand.

Pt Yeah. Funny you use that word. I've said, I've been using that phrase "fool's errand" in the last couple of days.

Th Oh really?

Pt Over and over again in my head. I say to myself, and in fact part of the phrase in talking to a good friend of mine and collaborator of this paper was that the whole thing of Kosovo was to use your word of a fool's errand. But I'd been suckered into it by my psychological need to prove something to my Dad and to myself.

Th Could be amalgamation of the two.

Pt Could be amalgamation of …

Th Every person looks at himself or herself initially …

Pt Yeah.

Th … through their parents' eyes. Now …

Pt So, so … I think that's for just a rip to me. Now, I'm kind of a star. So I can write a different paper based on this and not see myself as you know, this poor victim.

Th You can see your part.

Pt Yeah, I can see myself and what kind of unfortunate turn it may take and, and the lack of clarity I did have and envision what I should have had and applied when I took the job.

Th To me, what you're describing and I don't mean to dramatize things, it's, it's not what I'm saying, but to me, what you're describing is the essence of tragedy, it's just to hear well in any story, does it recognize what their air to flaw is, their character flaw ultimately dictates their demise.

Pt Yeah. Yeah. Yeah. I make those connections. I don't know if they're, I'm sharing them with you.

Th Which connections?

Pt My connection about my character flaw that resulted in the, my diminished capacity professional to see what I was walking into and dealing with the corrective in a way that's simply unprofessional, although I should have asked.

Th But you were saying something to me.

Pt Well, I'm, I'm just testing all that with you, I'm testing it in here, now … . Does that sound right to you, because I need that connection in my head for it to really feel different

Th You know the phrase, "The truth seems to be self-evident?"

Pt Yeah, yeah.

Th You, you, the idea of you questioning it, uh, it's veracity, it seems a little bit more like the old you.

Pt It's not impressing me in thought right now, I mean, how long does it take for this stuff to become embedded and part of my …

Th Yeah, yeah. To me, uhh, it's so uhh psychologically accurate. There's nothing more I can do, uh, to give it the stamp of authenticity.

(As the patient declares disloyalty to his former aggressor, he *regresses* by transferring his power to the therapist and the therapist affirms that the patient is indeed powerful and capable.)

Pt You can't? I need a little?. (laugh) I'm anxious now about accepting my own power, aren't I?

Th (laugh) Indeed, it's understandable that you would be anxious taking the power away from your Dad. Previously he would destroy you if you tried.

Pt (Nods ...) Observation No. 4. Correct for me. Couple of other things to throw out here.

Th Clearly you and I can celebrate the fact that that feels really good to have that blind spot expunged.

Pt Yeah, and it's given me a different sense of my, it's really bolstered my sense of, uh and given me a different perspective on how I would go into and do go into many, umm professional endeavours, when I have an opportunity, a good professional opportunity, very, very often I'm now looking back, I'm reflecting back, a couple weeks, I've been reflecting back on how I diminished myself in these professional relationships on, for reasons I haven't been clearly, I haven't been clear about, I understand why have I not been more assertive, okay. So this is sort of this question, okay ...

Th Sure.

Pt ... comes up because what did we come away with from the last experience? An assertiveness on my part to recognize, umm dad sitting on my back and, and flagellating me, let me take over the whip when he's not around and saying, Well that's not right, that's not right. Let's just, you know, that's, that's not going anywhere. So, what, what triggered that? What, what gave me the strength and the conviction and the, and the tenacity or whatever it is to say, Dad, enough of this, enough and stop it, because I ...

Th And you don't have to live with it.

Pt I don't live with it. I don't know how, I don't know where that came from.

Th Oh, I do.

Pt But I'm going to apply it again on another ...

Th May I just throw something out and you can respond to it with ...

Pt Yeah.

Th To me was, the obvious in talking to you, is that you had a mixture of feelings around your anger or your rage towards your dad. In other words, on one hand you know that your rage toward your dad was uhh, uhh a normal response to being an abused animal, right, okay?

Pt But you're going to see through it, and in addition to that, it wasn't right. Well, these are, these are bad feelings and impulses ... I would say, "I shouldn't have this. I shouldn't be out of control."

Th That was the mixed feeling ... right on. Therefore with you putting it in cognitive terms, I will put it in emotional terms, and I would say that you felt guilty about the extent of your anger towards your dad, so rather than, you know, learning from the experience of being under the thumb of a critical bully, instead you put yourself into situations of where you were put in harm's way and expected some different outcomes, you know, rather than being victimized. The cards were so stacked against you in Kosovo that there was no way that you could prevail in that situation. All you were going to do was either get crushed or assassinated, you know. You were outmanned and outnumbered.

Pt Yeah. But there was your insight that before that you directed, that you ... .

Th Your mixed feelings.

Pt And the sense that I was punishing myself for feelings of guilt for being angry at, at umm the punisher, you know, the guy who was dad, who was making my life a misery. And I felt guilty about feeling bad and angry. Wow, isn't that …

Th See, what that does, in my opinion, is truncates your natural proclivities toward self-assertion. In other words, the drive toward self-protection, which is know where your rage is coming from, right, cause your dad's supposed to protect you. He's not supposed to, you know, whack you around for good things, uhh, for good things that you're doing, he whacks you around, gives you some ridiculous response, that just twists your whole instinctual system around, it just turns it on itself.

Pt So let me give you another for instance.

(The therapist and the patient have a strong working alliance, so the patient himself makes a P-C link in the triangle of persons.)

Th Love to hear it.

Pt Uh, I had a, an exchange with my wife and I've been watching my wife's patterns of behaviour, response, and our communication in the last three or four weeks. I've been observing them, you know, in different things, let's just say that. Things have changed, it's flipped its switch with dad and the work breaks and all that other stuff, and she said something to me a couple of days ago that was *so derogatory* and, and expressed her distress with me, real disgust, real, *ad homines* and I thought to myself immediately, I, a trigger went off in my head and I said, "Isn't she like dad in the sense that there's, I've been looking for approval from dad, I've been wishing my life, my married life was more fulfilling and had more, umm approving and rewarding messages, in addition to a completely different style of what we're doing with our lives than??" And, then, something inside of me said, I'm going to end this. Just instantly and there was no question about it. There was absolutely no doubt, there wasn't any umm, "maybe she'll change, maybe we could have months or years of therapy or family counselling". No, Maybe, maybe, maybe. None of that came up at all. It was just almost like the epiphany when I, when you, what we had in here that said, I've been complicit in allowing dad to stay on my back and flaming this way, I was complicit in that and I thought, The same dynamic here. I'm, this is a very punishing, personally punishing, personally difficult, painful experience for me to be told that I'm an absolute worthless worm, a human being. And I thought, Am I complicit in this because I have the choice that I could make in this respect? And I did say, I'm going to take steps now to end this relationship and exit it if it's not right. And that happened again kind of an epiphany, a moment of epiphany that said, When, and the messages are all wrong, the facts are all wrong. I'm not a shit. Why am I, why am I, what's the conflict here? Why am I conflicted about this? The trouble of taking fuller, embracing the idea that I don't have to put up with this and it wasn't there. It wasn't the habitual, conflicted, guilt ridden sense that Yeah, she's probably right and it's probably all my fault and I probably am a shit and there's nothing I can do about it. That kind of dialogue was not in my head, *it just didn't happen*. It always has happened for many, many, many years. What do you make of that?

Th I don't have anything other to say than to, I'm delighted, I mean I'm so pleased for you.

(The therapist celebrates that the patient had dethroned his pathological superego.)

Pt Yeah.

Th What do you have to say?

Pt I thought of you and the whole reason for your practice and why people should be doing this! If is there no intellectual curiosity that you'll cope by yourself with your illness … just suffer. And, I thought to myself, Well … that's really interesting. I was really startled and umm, curious about how that had happened to me. I actually reflected on it afterwards, because I just thought. Wow, I am really a different person thinking and processing these experiences then the guy who was there a month ago. I was actually, Wow, this is so nice! I was very, very personable, surprised at my ability to take that stand about my wife and well obviously, uhh, anxious. What is in the future, you know, what does the professional and social future hold for me? I mean, it opens up. It's good for her, but also for me. It's like the dad on your back. You don't have to have dad on your back and you certainly don't have to umm weld the same burden with your wife.

Th And so, you married your dad.

Pt Yes! And I don't have to be married. There's a choice, and of course, I went through the self-doubt of "what will people say? No, you can work it out and she'll change, you know, she'll understand what she's doing and counselling will work." And I know just the same insight that I had about Kosovo. … That's another fool there. I'm not going to go down that road because I know this woman after twenty-two years of marriage. She's not changing. She's not being acceptable to the good services of people like you or a counsellor or anything else. It's not going to happen and I can tell you based on my knowledge of experience. Maybe I'm totally wrong, maybe people of your calibre and skills could work some sort of miracle with her, but …

Th You're, you're getting your finger on the key you're able to change and that's motivation.

(The therapist blocks the defence of self-doubt from returning.)

Pt Motivation, yeah.

Th It's your motivation to look at your inner emotional problem, take a strictly honest view of it and take steps on your own behalf once you understand what your problem is. That's the critical miracle in my field. The talent of the psychotherapist obviously is part of that equation, but without that first part of emotional integrity and you know, strict honesty towards what one is doing in one's life is self-destructive, umm, nothing good comes out of it.

Pt And it, and it's consistent without it. Your insight about, about both the dynamics in Kosovo and the people that I was working with (*the therapist had pointed out they were criminals with only personal profit as their goal*), also apply here. I could, I could run at them all day, you know, and grab them by the lapels, you know, figuratively and say, "Please, listen to me. Let's find common ground. Let's, this is a problem, let's solve it." But I now see they have no commitment, no interest, no personal—that wasn't part of their game plan, and the same would happen here again. I mean I would say to myself, I've got to make that effort. I've got to beat myself up. I've got to throw myself at that wall over and over and over again until I'm bloodied and despondent and suicidal because they're not playing, they're not going to meet me, they're going to come to the table and negotiate in good faith. And that's not going to happen here with my wife. She's not going to, and I know that and so I actually have fresh from the battlefield in Kosovo and fresh from the epiphany here with, "Hey, who's this other guy sitting on your back, and by the way it's your dad ...", What would I do that for? Why would I go into another situation with all of my instincts and my intellect and my experience with my wife? This is another fool's errand!

The patient reveals a long history about his wife's history. Her father was a talented professional but an alcoholic man who died of self-neglect and self-abuse. They were at first independent spirits, but as the relationship progressed, she became controlling, devaluing, and distant, and withdrew emotionally and sexually from him. She calls him an alcoholic although he does not drink, and publically disparages him. It became clear that she projected her pathological superego on her husband and has punished him and herself with isolation. He is absolutely determined to leave her despite economic disadvantages.

Pt Future. Where do I live? How do I sleep? Do I have enough money, I mean, however—just the mechanics of, like getting out, relocating. I'm not loved to work here by the way, so at the moment I don't have, uh, without work fees anymore. Starting to work ... things like that. These are the mechanics of it. Remarkably, though, the part that was absent which goes back to what we talked about, that you've helped create was, where's the guilt? Where's the flagellating, the self-flagellating guilt on my part that doesn't allow me to embrace the idea that I don't have to do this? I don't have to perpetuate the situation and that I'm fully responsible for it. I'm guilty as charged by my wife of this, you know, but not the "isms", dereliction, and all the rest of it. I'm not, I'm not. It actually didn't pop into my head.

Th Well, that's a big change.

Pt It's a huge change.

Th Yeah.

Pt It's absolutely huge. (Happy) The absence of it ...

Th Yeah.

Pt ... startled me. I said, Wait a minute, where's the, where's my all of what putting the brakes on anything that would change this dynamic, right?

Th Right.

Pt I don't have to sit here with my dad on my back and also take the whip when he's not around. Wait a minute, I ... wait.

Th What do you mean?

Pt I don't have to (laugh). That was the ...

Th You were being whipped by your wife.

Pt Or being, be whipped by my wife.

Th Right.

Pt And also to accept on the face of it, all of this stuff that is to me, emotionally untrue, it's psychologically dishonest and untrue and it's on, on the, the facts don't bear it out. She has conjured her dad as an alcoholic in his entire life and I'm now an alcoholic.

Th It's, its ...

Pt These aren't the facts, these aren't the facts, cause I know them.

Th It, it's, actually it's a delusion in a certain sense, a soft delusion.

Pt Yeah, yeah. And when, if I were to say to my wife …

Th I mean this is a little reminiscent of some of the things she dealt with, with your sister too.

Pt Uh, not only that, but part of the real emotional payoff or the, the real emotional core of that epiphany about dad and about how I'm, you know, the tool that to beating me up at the same time, was the sense of relief, where relief can bring me to tears. The sense of relief, the acknowledgement that relief is possible and um …

Th Well, it, it—from my point of view, you know, based on your integrity and your ability to see things clearly, it seems to me like it's a very straightforward decision.

Pt Yeah.

Th It's a sad decision in a sense of, you know, having to say goodbye to something that I'm sure you had hoped at one time would last forever but uh, the reality is that most things don't last forever.

Pt Well, not only that, but that's very true. It's very dumb, dumb. There are very mixed emotions, of course, and there will be grief.

Th Um mm.

Pt And then sadness and? It's not easy, it's not an easy thing to go through.

Th No.

Pt And …

Th You kind of, you went through the loss of uh, uh the woman that you loved earlier in your life. That was very difficult.

Pt Extremely.

Th And (pause) …

Pt And in the sense of, of um (pause) anticipating, um, navigating difficult emotional circumstances, I have a lot of anxiety just about that.

Th It's normal.

Pt Of course, it's normal. I didn't think was normal. I never gave myself permission to feel um turbulent emotions and even emotions as you said, if you counted out, rage and.

Th Complex feelings.

Pt Very complex feelings. They're both that this is not right, or this is unfair and this is cruel and uh, and that I'm supposed to love this person, but I hate this person at the same time in the same instant, and at the same time, those kinds, being able to navigate those and see the complexity of an emotional situation is both bad and liberated towards hoping to enforce. It holds up the …

Th The hope.

Pt But I'm also knowing that by creating a different environment, I can actually relieve myself of the pain that is being inflicted, the emotional pain that is being inflicted, the emotional pain that is being inflicted in that moment. I don't want to be in a dining room listening to my wife disparage me.

Th I would even add the adjective oppressive, that there's a oppressive environment. If I heard you correctly, the relationship was, came together based upon a kind of free spiritedness that the two of you had.

Pt The adventuresomeness, yeah.

Th Yeah.

Pt And her courage to go off on these sort of, you know, I didn't know what she was going to come up with.

Th And, and I'm sure you must desperately miss that person.

Pt And we'll have, I also have felt a very, very …

Th No, I mean already. It doesn't sound like she's there anymore.

Pt No. Already, it uh, you're right, you're absolutely right. I already made that decision that this is no longer tenable. It, it's, that actually was the moment when it became past. Funny that I didn't realize that, but that's exactly actually nailed it. There was a moment when it is over.

Th That's right.

Pt It is over and it's now, we're now in the transition period between it being emotional and psychologically over and it being physically over, right. And now the mechanics of?? and move out and move here and you set up, however, your life. But it's over because I said I won't, I'm not here anymore for this. Funny, I didn't realize is that second, the actual cross, you cross a line …

Th Exactly.

Pt You actually cross the finish line. Dad, it's over. I'm tossing you off the back and throwing you with you. With that then it's over. And, but I didn't speak to my father over Christmas and didn't want to speak to him. I didn't feel bad that I didn't want to speak to him, which was a completely different than it had ever happened before.

Th Right.

Pt It was completely different, and he belatedly sent us a Christmas card. When my wife said, Oh here's a card from your dad and I said, I really don't care to read it. We don't have anything to say to each other anymore. I'm not going to read the card hoping that it has a good word in it for me. I don't care. He doesn't have that power over me anymore to make me hope it has something nice to say to me in it. I just said I don't care and it's been lying on our dining room table, the card, and I've never picked it up. And I'm not forcing myself to …

Th ???

Pt I'll take a peak, I'll take a secret peak, I can hope.

Th It's emancipation.

Pt It's emancipation. Funny, I did, it's absolutely gone, I mean that power my dad would have over me to, you know, please feed me a crumb of, of approval and affection. Completely gone. For me, it's kind of, it's new and it's startlingly new and it's, again, I'm have to get used to is, to get used to the new me. It's taking a little bit of time but it's slowly but surely things are beginning to sink in.

Th It sounds like you like this guy.

Pt Sure, sure. Not a bad fellow at all, actually not a bad chap, and but more importantly there's more of a sense of a of a tenuation of my sense of self-worth with my, um …

Th Behaviour.

Pt Behaviour.

Th And thinking.

Pt And thinking and the way I think about things like writing an article about Kosovo. The whole tenor of the article, I wrote a previous piece with my collaborator and I look back on it now and it's all full of a self-pity and victimization of a poor guy who got treated badly by a bunch of bad people and now it's a completely different kind of detached, intellectually clear and I think, more professionally useful article about certain insights that I now have of both how it was set up wrong and ??, but it doesn't, I'm not the centre of the whole story and it's, it doesn't focus on me being this hapless victimized expert. That's not the story at all. It's a completely different story. I think, wow, where did that come from and it came from our work in here.

Th Yeah.

Pt That's where it came from and I'm, that's very, very gratifying for me because I need to keep telling myself that I do still have my intellectual chops, that I still have, despite all the discouragement and the personal, the sense of degradation that I feel in my marriage and I fell into the hands of, that I inflicted upon myself with my dad, I really now feel there could be a, a integration of both my professional and intellectual skills and my social and psychological health. It seems to be uh returning. Psychological health recovery. I'm going to go, I'm a recovering masochist, whatever you want to call it.

Th (laugh)

Pt Now I'm saying, it's really, there is this integration now that there is a different emotional self and it strengthens my ability, which I've always put so much store in which is intellectual, professional, those are the certain markers of my own self-esteem.

Th Great. You've restored the pursuit of happiness.

Pt Yeah.

Th As a virtue.

Pt Yes, and a legitimate, a legitimate part of my personality, the legitimacy of my personality traits that have been um distorted, or, or truncated, or hidden or something through all these years of …

Th Abuse.

Pt Abuse.

Th Yeah.

Pt Yeah. And I don't understand this very well, but I, but it's (pause)—the question has just popped into my head occasionally and it hasn't gone away. It's popped in a couple of times. How much of what my, my dad and I were doing to me collectively this thing, this creature that was punishing me, how much of that was being, um um like to my marriage? What was I looking for in a marriage if it had any of those kinds of similar um dynamics? Is there any possibility that I was in fact looking for someone who would um emotionally withholding or …

Th Punitive.

Pt Punitive. Uh, what do you make of that? I don't really know cause I wouldn't have known anything, any of the things at the outset that I would have said, Oh, this is the right person for me because she's going to be withholding?

Th Well, part of it is philosophical.

Pt Yeah.

Th Remember, there's always free will.

Pt Yeah, yeah.

Th You don't want to get away from free will to create uh um uh uh, that people have free will. However, what we know is when you a history of abuse in your childhood and that it's unresolved as yours has been up to now, then a structure of mind is created that supplants free will, so what I would suggest to you that you were traumatized and unresolved and you married a woman who has been traumatized and is unresolved and each of you were following a script that led to mutual unhappiness.

Pt Right. Okay.

Th So if, remember, there's a co-participation on her part.

Pt Right.

Th In this process. She had free will to not indulge the part of you that needed to be punished. She had free will, but it was compromised.

Pt Yeah.

Th Just like your free will to do due diligence about Kosovo was compromised.

Pt Yeah.

Th See the way I …

Pt Yeah, I, I do.

Th So what we're celebrating here …

Pt Yeah.

Th … is the restoration of your free will.

Pt Yeah. Yeah.

Th To it's proper place in your psychological makeup. It, it, it had been subordinated to seeking your master's approval.

Pt Which was of course never fate to come. (laughter)

Th It was like, I think of those donkeys in Tijuana that are motivated by holding a carrot on a stick in front of their eyes. They work but never get the reward.

Pt Carrots on a stick (laughter). Right.

Th So the story about the card is, you know, the Christmas card is "I'm no longer chasing the carrot on the stick."

Pt Yeah.

Th And then you feel empowered but with that empowerment comes a sense of, you know, now responsibility because you've got to, you know, use your own noodle here.

Pt Right.

Th To decide what course you want to, you know, follow here and you are given choices, a lot of choices, a lot of decisions to make, a lot of research to make, uh, uh, of positive decisions in your life.

Pt And …

Th Hence, the anxiety which is totally normal. It's a very good …

Pt Yeah.

Th … signal for you.

Pt Yeah.

Th There's danger out there.

Pt There's lots of work and danger out there. And one of the, one of the locks that you could have in this, in navigating this is to um um backslide in a sense that you'd revert back to the point of belief that you don't have free will, whether you are in fact a bad person fundamentally.

Th Well it's not that you don't have free will, it's that your free will is coopted or subordinated by this coalition between your father and you that does need to be abused to, to, you know, to take on more and more responsibility to meet unreasonable expectations in order to be loved.

Pt Yeah.

Th That could take over between you and Serbia, that could take over between you in any situation that you're trying to prove your, your value through uh more and more impossible beings. That would be called a compulsion.

Pt Right.

Th And then you'd, you know, you'd put on whatever blinders you need to put on in order to, you know, take on your next mission which would be, of course, Mission Impossible. That's the way I think about it.

Pt Well, uh, I, uh agree with your insight and uh, uh find it um incredibly value and um refreshing. That's the kind of thing *that I need on a card to carry around*, what you just said about, about how you could remanufacture these, these tortuous, the co-dependencies on this and to sever, or what you said, subvert. The free will that you do have, but you're going to part for awhile while you go do one of these, another one of these relationships where you're trying to find certain kinds of psychological and emotional rewards in, in from people. You're going to give them the power to give them, bestow them and um??, you know, what's the point of that, what was the point of that? Go back into, and that would be the kind of a warning saying I would have, with a few words, a few code words on a card or something, pull out my wallet, Am I doing this again? I'm telling you that's the kind of thing that the drives and anxiety that I would have, yeah, I could really see myself falling back into that.

Th But, again, let me just ask you the question from the other side of what is the attraction?

Pt Yeah, what is the attraction again? Yeah, you really liked it there?

Th (laugh)

Pt The torture, the flagellation and whatever and whatever.

Th You know the expression, "Been there, done that"?

Pt Yeah. Dumb shit.

Th T-shirt.

Pt Yeah.

Th Yeah. What, no I don't think so. Uh actually, I don't think it's as big of a risk as you think cause once the reward system of your brain has been restored, would you ever give it up again?

Pt Right. That's very, uh uh, hopeful for anybody that comes into this office. It's really an amazing, that's a very powerful insight for, for your patients and I'm speaking, you know for myself, but I speak on behalf of others. It's not, this isn't um biological. This isn't, this isn't wiring, this isn't hard wiring.

Th Oh no.

Pt To be in these relationships that are …

Th It's acquired, it's software.

Pt Yeah.

Th You look emotional to me right now.

Pt Well, I can tell you that you changed doubts that I had is that they I could ever work myself out of these blinds. I am very grateful and have loving feelings towards you. You have changed my life and I am sad that I will not be seeing you anymore. (cries openly) I wanted to tell you a couple of things.

Th I just didn't want to not ignore the emotion that I saw in your eyes there for a second. What was it eh?

Pt It is again the acknowledgement of, both it starts confidently and then it works its way emotionally into me.

Th Um mm.

Pt That we aren't trapped. It's not biologically, it's not, we aren't set up this way. It's not like me having schizophrenia like my sister.

Th That's right.

Pt This is in a way self-inflicted.

Th First environmentally, then self-inflicted …

Pt Environmentally?

Th Which then becomes perpetually.

Pt Right on, right on. And it, I, first of all I process in intellectually or cognitively and then finally it just sinks right in and says, Yeah, that's a true.

Th But what's your feeling?

Pt Again, relief, I am very happy.

Th Relief?

Pt I'm not destined to be like this, you see, that was the thing that I couldn't, when we said, "Okay let's throw dad in the wood pile." (after grinding him in a wood chipper) What's that? You're kidding. And what, that became such a powerful hope and possibility because they are many, many years ahead of not having dad on me. That's a very, very remarkable prognosis or something that you.

Th And not having his assistant named your wife.

Pt I hadn't, I hadn't ever allowed myself to believe that. (pause) I, I mean really, you've actually kind of nailed the internal dilemma that I have all my life. Someone bestows happiness on me or gives me the, the …

Th That's called approval.

Pt Approval. But you need that that registered so good.

Th But you thought that was happiness.

Pt The happiness got pressed because I got somebody else's approval.

Th Right.

Pt And that is completely different than what I know to be the truth and that you, is the pursuit of happiness is in fact is the end in itself because we of course we can't guarantee anything.

Th Yes!

Pt We don't know what's going to happen when we take our holiday and it could be a disaster, it could be wonderful, a fine experience. But it's the pursuit of that matters, and I know that deep inside me, intellectually and cognitively, that I haven't ever allowed myself to act on it for some reason because it was not … I wasn't allowed to do that, I wasn't allowed to do that. And that means, in fact.

Th Your dad went of its way to break you.

Pt Correct. And that in fact means that you're not allowed to do things like manipulate your environment or change your environment or change the dynamics of your environment in the pursuit of your own happiness.

Th Or assert your intellect.

Pt Assert your intellect.

Th In doing due diligence to avoid situations that are risky …

Pt Now you're going to love to do that. Now, you're going to love to go down the road and say, Oh gee I don't think this is going to be a very healthy situation for me and it will probably curtail my pursuit of happiness. Now you're going to want to explore that. Amazing. Amazing what we do to ourselves. Absolutely remarkable! And, and these kinds of, say these epiphanies, these breaks, I mean, I don't have to put this.

Th Wait, remember, you do to yourself in many ways what was done to you originally, you know, by your faulty parenting, and it takes a certain degree of psychological, emotional, cognitive effort to undo those original patterning experiences. Now, on the other hand, it has to be stated you've done remarkably well with very little, that you've fought the greatest majority of this battle on your own before you ever met me. I mean you didn't end up, a street person, alcoholic, suicidal mess. You broke away as best as you could from a toxic situation with your dad on your own.

Pt Well, you're skilled and insightful, but what is it about the structure of your practice that's helped this, helped create this or mobilized this, uh, this work?

Th I don't understand the question.

Pt Well, I'm, I'm.

Th Uh, I'm happy to answer, I just don't understand what you're asking basically about the structure of my practice. That sounds very …

Pt I've seen other psychiatrists and psychologists, and we didn't get anywhere, we didn't get into this, we didn't get down to this, we didn't get this far. Why not? What is it about the mechanics of your, of your practice that you think sets you apart? I know that you, you know, there's a name for the, for the, for the …

Th Approach? (ISTDP)

Pt Your approach is in fact—is it the approach or is it you? I mean you should think about this because Dr. Carl (his referring doctor) wants to know. I said to him, you know, I've just can't believe what we've, what I've been going through with this guy and he says, "Well, do you agree with the approach?" And I said, Completely, and, why don't you study it since you refer patients to him?

Th (laugh)

Pt If you like what he's achieving, why don't you figure out what he's got, or if he's got something that's just particular to the man or is it the approach?

Th Well, you know, that is a very interesting question that many researchers have tried to address is it the specific psychotherapist or is it the specific approach and obviously you just can't separate the two. But I can tell you until I used this approach I wasn't getting the results that I am getting presently.

Pt There is something in the approach.

Th Yes.

Pt Yeah.

Th Sure. So remember the whole basis of this has to do with a certain degree of mindfulness on your part, to pay attention cause we're really emphasizing on you is paying attention to a couple of different things. No. 1, know your anxiety. What is the stimulus for your anxiety? What is your response to the anxiety? Are you attentive to the anxiety as opposed to being judgemental? Are you attentive to the anxiety as opposed to being dismissive? Okay. When you pay attention to the anxiety, you question with curiosity. What is the emotion underneath the anxiety that you're feeling? Is the emotion anger, is it rage, okay, is it grief, sadness, guilt, happiness? What is the emotion, okay? And then you, beginning to develop a bit of connection between the present and the past if you're having anxiety over your inner emotions, okay, why are you having anxiety over your inner emotions, what happened to you in the past that caused you to suppress your inner emotions and accept less you deserve for yourself? That's the most succinct I could …

Pt Yeah.

Th So that's the key in my mind is maintaining a psychological focus on the moment, not going into all the different, "ya ya ya dada dads" about this and that, that the mind can just take you endlessly in a thousand different meaningless directions. But don't do that. "Stay focused on the present moment and investigate with love, care and precision the present moment." Because that's where we all live.

Pt I'd love to have the last five minutes on a tape.

Th Could you give me a bit more about that? What's the feeling around that summary, I mean, I understood that you admire it, but I think I'm seeing more feeling coming up in your face, so …

Pt Well, because it's, it's something to remember. It's the guidepost and I tend to think that I need.

Th It's that flashcard.

Pt It's the flashcard! And one of the funniest things you ever said to me (lovingly spoken) in the short time we've known each other, you said, "Well, how do you get to Carnegie Hall?" Well, you *practise.* Well, how do you get mental health? Well, *you practise*. You practise, and what you're describing is what you're practising.

Th That's right.

Pt You know, this uh, this attention, this focus and then the way you approached that past anxiety into emotion and then without judgement, just keep being curiously attentive. Brilliant. It's a flashcard.

Th Well, that's what you requested.

Pt I'm a flashcard kind of guy. I really am. I really like to think, that I've got a flashcard in my wallet and it's, it provides sort of a little backstop. Well, I'm not going to forget all of this because it was all just today in this office and when I left I forgot it all and it merely went over my head when I first, you know, came up to a stop light. No, no. Invented,? practise, practise, practise, practise.

Th You know there was another topic that you were going to bring up um …

Pt I was going to say, I just find these things everywhere. I look now. I'm reading Keith Richards autobiography which I highly recommend, a remarkably pleasant read, really, really remarkable. He never got any approval from his dad, still cries about it. (ironic laugh) Why would you think, what more does he need in his life? Well, he never got his dad's approval and still? (laughing and crying himself) To this day he cries.

Th See, he's not where you're at.

Pt I'm not there. Well, that's refreshing when we're all in these different kinds of boats at the same time. I just finished reading a big profile in the *New Yorker* about Ely B …, you know the big financier of the arts in L.A. and I thought to myself, that's the guy who didn't treat anybody very well and one of the guys who he mistreated who worked for him as a lawyer who became a director of one of his galleries for years. He actually complained a lot in this article to the writer. "You know I never got a thank you for a well done from Ely B …" And I thought to myself, we're all, everybody on earth is looking for a that *at-a-boy* at some point (laugh), you want some affirmation or approval. No matter who we are, no matter how high you get, how, how your life seems to be, you know, so well put together and you've got everything you could possibly want.

Th So you're, you're feeling more of a connection to your colleagues who have been under the thumb of these punitive and authoritarian, withholding people?

Pt Correct.

Th And, a, and it's not, there's no shame obviously they're not humiliating themselves to say it in public that they were abused.

Pt You know I worked for this Ely B … for five years pro bono, and I never got a thanks from him. I said, Wow, you'd never know, the sting never leaves does it?

Th No.

Pt I just thought wow!

Th You know, I would like to have your um input as to your future here. I'm pleased you've turned the corner and I'm fine with us ending this today, or you can come back for as many visits that you feel would be helpful to you to keep you on the right trajectory. I have to trust your judgement as to what you need in that regard, so what is your response on that?

Pt Why don't we wait for a while and I will make an appointment, but if I feel I'm getting really fuzzy headed or I'm feeling myself looking at world again through dark grey goggles, I'll give you a call.

Th That would be absolutely fine.

(The therapist reflected on whether more termination sessions were required. But after reviewing the session in his mind and realizing that the patient's father never accepted his sons autonomy, the therapist determined that the patient needed support for his autonomy.)

Pt All right. That'd be fine with me, and to you, how do I express my appreciation? I mean I'm paying my bill, but you've got to know this is just a transformative conference, it's remarkably transformative and I have huge amounts of gratitude.

Th I can see it on your face.
Pt Yeah, I can't thank you enough. Goodbye.

In a follow-up session, the patient reported he had ended his loveless marriage, published another paper on his experience in Kosovo, and was now in Serbia, creating an educational programme with a receptive and cooperative administration.

Termination 2

The woman who found her worth and created healthy boundaries

The patient is a 32-year-old female psychotherapist who presented for anxiety, and loss of self in relationships manifested by addictive pleasing of her partners. Her mother was described as an emotional wreck who was draining and unstable. She and her husband, the patient's father, had divorced when she was four. She had a distant relationship with her father, who showed favouritism for his children that he bore with his next wife—her stepmother. The patient was abused by her stepfather.

When she came to therapy, she was in a love relationship with a partner who had violated significant boundaries to pursue her. Her health care was in chaos, and she was in a bad professional situation where she was being victimized by administrators and faculty of her clinical graduate programme. Furthermore, she was being manipulated into doing potentially destructive activities involving patient care by a disturbed supervisor. The therapy took eight months of regular block therapy sessions. She had been discussing termination in the prior two sessions because she was feeling so much better and being able to sustain boundaries in personal and professional relationships. Here is a vignette from her next to last therapy visit.

In her termination process, she reflects on the origins of her multifocal character pathology and the change process.

Pt What I needed all along is for people to model appropriate boundaries and attachments and to protect me and that is what I needed and I didn't get that and I spent …
Th From?
Pt My Mum, my Dad, Stepdad, and others, and I feel like I've just lost so much time and have gone through various versions of hell.
Th I think that is true, that is painful but true.
Pt Yeah, so like I said I am sad that because of the way everything happened and because of how clouded my judgement was and everything else, I ended up in this position at the clinic and ended up taking this abuse and I said this to someone that was thinking about taking the position and I said that I honestly feel that I lost a year of my life and I do.
Th In one respect, yes, but you know what we are celebrating …
Pt Yes, exactly I agree the other side …
Th The other side of that you—found yourself.
Pt Right, exactly.
Th And your voice, and your self-respect, and your self-worth.

Pt Right.

Th So we go from victim to survivor to victor, you know so it may have taken a year of your life but that is better than taking a lifetime.

Pt Yeah, and the other side to that and I wouldn't have gotten to you if not for what had happened and I wouldn't have had the resources to see you if I hadn't been the work that I had been doing, so I see that.

Th Life is a complex bag, isn't it?

Pt Yeah, you know when we talked about this time with the doctors and the patient situation replicating my real life and that I couldn't have created that situation, yet and there it was.

Th I saw more feelings coming when you said that, was there wonderment?

Pt Yeah.

Th Its wild isn't it when you see it that way.

Pt Yes it is. Oh and I talked to my Mum about this issue of replication of things that are seemingly beyond our control because she had something at work that was replicating her former stuff and she said that she doesn't remember my Stepdad ever spanking me, and she said that she never would have allowed it, and I said well it must have happened when you weren't there, I don't remember that part but I know it happened. It was interesting, and her adjective for him was "an asshole and dictator", those were the two things that she immediately said about him so it was interesting to hear her talk about that.

(The stepfather had spanked her for minor infractions, but more to the point, he made her remove her underwear and expose her buttocks. The patient and therapist came to understand that she was a victim of sexual abuse that she had denied.)

Th In what way was it interesting for you?

Pt Because it validated my inner sense because I can't remember a whole lot of him, I remember being very afraid of him, but I can't remember a lot, but for her form her own perspective before I said anything about that, for her to say those adjectives about him, which I said was very validating.

Th Did you believe her when she said that she would have never allowed it?

Pt Yes.

Th When you hear that how does that make you feel?

Pt Well, I mean this is a thought not a feeling but it made me feel like she really did have (patient begins to cry) the best intentions and even she had lines that she wouldn't have allowed people to cross.

Th You're valued.

Pt Yeah.

Th That you are worth standing up for.

Pt Yeah … yeah.

Th And if I could just now go full circle with you for a second, you stood up for her as well.

Pt Yeah, but *she doesn't see it that way*, but yeah.

Th (laughs) Who cares how she sees it.

Pt Absolutely, I know and by my saying I will not allow this to continue.

Th That's a win, win.

Th Yes, but this talk you had with your mother actually sounds healing.

Pt Yes, it was, I don't know what happened but she started to go to a therapist, well I shouldn't say I don't know what happened because she started to going because I wouldn't be her therapist and …

Th Oh, a boundary.

Pt Yeah, and she went and got someone. It was interesting, I don't know if it was that day where we had the step father conversation, but I had called her up and she said that I am not going to go see my therapist today because I don't have the money and I said why don't you just go and tell her that you don't have the money and ask her if you can pay her next week. She says no there are signs on the door that says you have to pay or you can't come to therapy. I am telling you if one of my patients came I would much rather have them come and pay me next week then not come at all, so I would think about that and that is all I said. Then she went and told the woman and she had her session.

Th Ok, what about that, what does that mean to you?

Pt Well, one it shows, this is where I learned my defeated, helpless, weepy defence thing first of all.

Th Yes, powerlessness.

Pt Yeah, but then at the same time if I just state my opinion and then just drop it, that she will either take that advice or not but at least I can give it and not making her feel controlled or anything else, just that I had an opinion and I just said it.

Th Like two adults.

Pt Yeah. (laughs)

Th What is the laughter?

Pt Well, yeah, that has not been the interaction style, so that I can just say things.

Th Well you got anxious when I, said "two adults".

Pt Yeah.

Th What made you anxious when I said "like two adults".

Pt Because it hasn't been.

Th My experience is anxiety is created by feelings.

(The patient knows this very well but is regressing to old defences around the stress of terminating therapy as well as a dysfunctional frozen child state.)

Pt Fair enough.

Th You just restated the fact.

Pt Yeah, fair enough. It was sadness, a twinge of sadness that I felt as in it was really … I don't know, other than just saying again it is just really disappointing that our communication has been so flawed for so long.

Th Well, again communication is one thing ok, its relationship to me, remember it been this your mother was this and you were the needy the child who was attached and then at a certain point in the time the roles got reversed then you became the parent and she was the child ok, now its equal to equal, adult to adult.

Pt But that only happened because I changed and set boundaries.

Th Your mother needed a mother so she turned you into her mother.

Pt But that does spark anger in me though that I am the one who had to do this.

Th Why do you say but? Of course it sparks anger, why does sit spark anger in you?

Pt Because it was inappropriate.

Th Inappropriate doesn't cut it.

Pt Well, no I was getting started.

Th It is worse than that.

Pt As we talked about it, it is role reversal, it's … I don't know what words to use, but it …

Th Goes against the laws of Mother Nature.

Pt Right.

Th It's a perversion: it sets in motion tragedy after tragedy after tragedy because that's the working model of that is being laid down for you.

Pt That was being played out all over the place. Right, yeah. It is so weird for me to not be anxious all the time.

Th Do you feel that you have permanently changed your working model of attachment to a secure model?

Pt I feel like we have, I mean yeah, I feel like we have. It is different this time, it is not like the last time when I said "we'll see" because I had a sneaking suspicion, but, I mean what has happened over the last couple of days was basically the Mt. Everest of my challenge.

Th Could I just mention something to you about my understanding of attachment and I think this is so important … there is no such thing as secure attachment, it's secure autonomous attachment, it's a balancing that secure people can do and they know that within themselves they will be OK, their standing up for themselves upon their values, their beliefs, and their principals, and that their security as an individual is not on the line. I mean bad shit may happen because there are bad people in the world, but your inner sense of self is not being risked when you stand up for yourself. As a matter of fact, an autonomous person doesn't even know the concept of not standing up for themselves, it is not an option. They may have to develop skills that will help them to stand up for themselves effectively, but that's practising, that's different.

Pt Well, it's a fundamental shift in my belief as you were saying, about your self-worth, about your stance, and there is this inherent confidence, I don't know it just shifted, like I said months ago, if I had not had … if I were in this position where I had 12 weeks left of a paid job and I was going to quit in protest, I would have been not sleeping, freaking out, and trying to find anything, and now I am saying to myself, something will work out, I only have to keep putting forth effort and something will work.

Th So how exciting is that, that shift within your working model of attachment in your own self … it is wonderful.

Pt Yeah, yeah, it's great.

Th You're pleased.

Pt I am. I feel this little bit of sadness too. I don't know what that is, but uhm …

Th That's OK, just take a look at that and see what's coming up.

Pt (long pause) I mean the only thing I think, and maybe this isn't sadness, but I am not used to appreciation being …

Th It's sadness, go ahead.

Pt I don't know, it's not sadness per say, it's that I am feeling appreciative that I am here but for whatever that brings … it brings a wave of grief along with it, that like I said before, that it has taken this long for me to get there. (sobs)

Th Well, I can understand that interpretation, but can I propose another cause other than the past … this can be sadness regarding the future in the sense that you don't require my services any more.

(The therapist increases the here and now intimacy to their mutual feelings of loss at finishing their work. There is also happiness that they are able to part as equals.)

Pt Yeah, and maybe that's what I am labelling as appreciation but yeah.

Th It's both.

Pt Yeah, that may be.

Th Go ahead what's coming up for you?

Pt Well …

Th This is a really important time for you to process these feelings; this is all new territory you have never been in a secure position leaving before.

Pt Right.

Th Isn't that a cool idea.

Pt It is. (Patient smiles) I think this is one of very few relationships where I feel that you one hundred per cent put me first and help me really get to the goal that I wanted to get to and you also thought I needed to get to and …

Th To a hundred per cent level, yeah, I thought you needed to get to that goal.

Pt And so when you have someone like that around you will miss them when you are not interacting with them in the same way so I think that is why I am sad.

Th I do too.

Pt But I do feel confident that I can go out and create these kinds of relationships now.

Th As do I, there is not a doubt in my mind, and as a matter of fact I would be angry at you if you didn't.

Pt Yeah, I just really appreciate what we have been able to accomplish in our work together.

Th I really value your thoughts and your impressions, I would like to hear your … what has been helpful, what aspects of the way we approached this process were unique for you, that were different than what you have experienced in other forms of therapy.

Pt Well there's a lot, but I mean there is first the characteristics of you, which is that you're patient but you held a very clear focus and a very clear line about what was happening when I was defending off here and anxiety off there, you held that focus but in a very compassionate way. When I told you how strongly I reacted to the kind of the mocking technique, you just said ok, I am not going to do that again. You were very non-defensive and were focusing on me and what was going on and you really were able to see things that and point them out to me in clear ways that I wasn't exactly seeing them in that way, whether it was my own interpretations or whatever …

Th Your blind spots.

Pt Yeah, so I mean all that together is what I needed. I do think that the longer sessions especially in the beginning were very helpful because I could watch it happening because for the first hour I was just deflecting, defending and fighting especially in the beginning and that it really took time to start chipping those back. I think also there was a fluidity that it didn't have to be that we are talking about this or we are doing this, again you had some kind *of roadmap* and I was willing to go with it. I think all of those things.

Th That's wonderful to hear and thanks for recognizing the flexibility that's it's not one suit of clothes that fits everybody.

Pt Yeah, and I think that there was one point where you said "I don't care what you do" and that was one of those comments that made it really … I knew you were genuine in it and it really made me feel safe and communicated that I really was the focus and accepted.

Th Well when you say, I don't care what you do?.

Pt You said to me.

Th Yeah, what … refresh my memory?

Pt I think we were talking about jobs and where I was going to be, what I was going to do and you said something like you can be a plumber, I don't care, but it was something like that.

Th Right.

Pt And it was in that way that I would have wanted my Dad, my Mum to have said to me and that was …

Th Pursue your passion.

Pt And that it is ok to be whatever you want and that you don't have to go get the big name job, just go do what is going to make you happy.

Th So that would be undoing the role reversal and the transference that you weren't here to add points to my accomplishments. It was about you finding your way in the world and you pursuing this with love, care, and precision, the goal of finding out what it is that would give you the most satisfaction in your life.

Pt Right, so those are the ones that really stick out.

Th It seems like to me not because I said it, but it seems like that is what you are really doing. Now you are seeking out the right environmental fit.

Pt Right, there are no shoulds any more, really. It's what do I want to do and what is going to be nice for me? That is very different from … because several months ago I remember when my Mum was visiting we were trying to figure out all this job stuff and now I'm saying I am just going to do what I want to do.

Th It seems to me that to be able to say those words there is a centre of self-worth from where that.

Pt Yeah, you cant say, and do I really genuinely mean it, what do I want to do unless you believe you have a right to it and that is the difference, before …

(The under-entitled child has found her sense of healthy entitlement.)

Th It's not simply a right, but that you have value that will be recognized by the world.

Pt Right, and that has fundamentally shifted in my head to. Just because the clinic is moronic, I can't base myself and my worth and my value off of their devaluing manipulative statements.

Th You have a little smile on your face there.

Pt Because I can see it now, I mean I couldn't see it before.

Th There was a fusion between their eyes and your pathological part and now there is a separate self between them and you.

Pt Right and that's like I said," the should" is the people pleasing, it's that other part that is *not there now*. But it ruled my actions for a long time.

Th That is so fantastic to hear, I mean think about it the creative energies that are now freed up in you to really be creative, it's not for secondary gain any longer.

Pt Yeah, yeah.

Th I see happiness.

Pt Yeah, and satisfaction.

Th You mentioned quitting your research job, you had an association to that I wanted to hear.

Pt Yeah, because we were talking about good byes. I had decided to take the job at that the public clinic as a defence so that I didn't feel "bad"—every other time I quit a job, I would feel bad, I was *hurting the people that I was leaving behind*, (*mother*). In my eyes, I wasn't being a good soldier and this time I was like, "I don't want to do this!" I have been doing it for quite awhile and don't want to drive forty miles back and forth in a day, I don't like the job and I wish them all well and they will find other people. This is the first time I have left and not felt sad, regret, bad, shame nothing I was glad I was leaving and had true appreciation for the people I liked and that was it.

Th So the mother of projection doesn't exist any more, and your mother doesn't get depressed every time you say goodbye.

Pt Apparently not.

Th Isn't that a good way to think about it.

Pt Yeah, it was fundamentally different. I gave them two weeks' notice and there was no way that they would fill that position in two weeks and I didn't fill anything negative toward myself about it.

Th So you didn't engage in the role reversal and you didn't fill like you were abandoning a family that needed you.

Pt Right, and which is pretty exciting.

Th Go ahead the excitement is leading you where?

Pt No it is really, I just felt this warm kind of happy feeling.

Th About?

Pt Just feeling free.

Th About your future?

Pt Yeah, that I am not tied into a bunch of rules and again not being shamed and manipulated into uhmm …

Th So your exploratory system is now liberated.

Pt Yeah, which it hasn't been.

Th You talked about relational longings, which are incredibly healthy parts of you. Do you have any thoughts about how that is going to unfold, are you are going to give yourself opportunities?

Pt It is a multiple step process in that I have to not work so much first to be able to have time.

Th Twelve weeks of work.

Pt Exactly.

Th I accept that, duty and responsibility is part of the burden of being a psychotherapist.

Pt Yeah, and then after that, I don't know where I will be but wherever that is I am going to start getting in engaged in things I like to do and then hopefully meet people in those things.

Th And that would be like? What are the things you like to do?

Pt Meditation, going to group sitting, joining something where there is like tennis where I can play socially stuff like that, then hiking clubs, skiing or something and just getting out and hanging out with people more. Yeah, and just being more social because I have so exhausted, constricted and insular that I have really been interacting with people in the world very much, like I do my thing but then I … you know. Even interactions with people in line at the coffee shop or whatever, things that are normal social things that I have done in the past. I mean I noticed today that I am more interactive.

Th So it sounds to me that you will be sending out a different vibe.

Pt Right, exactly.

Th Can you characterize that vibe?

Pt It is a sense of self-confidence.

Th And I am always going to say value.

Pt Yes, and value and feeling secure in that I don't need someone, there isn't this desperate pull but it is just coming from a place of genuinely wanting to interact and know people.

Th Yeah, in other words, there is availability and a happiness a playfulness, also a curiosity about getting to know another member of the species and how they think and how they feel, and how they operate.

Pt Yeah.

Th And how do you feel your selectivity organ is operating.

Pt Oh, I think a hundred per cent differently, it's just becoming automatic to not put up with inappropriate behaviour and inappropriate treatment.

Th (laughing) I am just laughing because it is music to my ears.

Pt The fact that it was so automatic that I picked partners who required me to take care of them. I mean that is what is going to happen is that … I have plenty of diagnostic skills so I can pick stuff up and say no I am not going to be dealing with that. So I feel like I am going to be able to attend to it and now that I am not constantly anxious that when I have anxiety I will listen to it because it is telling me there is something underneath that I need to pay attention to.

Th If the integrity of the attachment system is restored, then when you have that feeling, that means there *actually is* something dangerous.

Pt That's what I mean.

Th Right, but if it's not restored, then it's about your emotions or your own projections getting activated. Normally, the attachment system is designed to help you explore the environment until there is danger and only then run back to secure base.

Pt Right.

Th That's when it is working well, but we as human beings of course coopted and use for it other purposes than nature designed it to be used for.

Pt So, that is my sense of it, anyway.

Th That's great that you have that selective judgement capability to make sure that you are only going to create vulnerability with people that are trustworthy. That seems to be a whole new skill set.

Pt Yeah, yeah, absolutely. Rather than take in everything that comes so that you are not alone, just like I said, that pull.

Th I don't think that this is entirely so that you are not alone because you are compelled to re-enact the role reversal, you just keep re-enacting the role reversal over and over again, so you have to have somebody who is really screwed up to re-enact your former mother and child role reversal. As for our work on restoring and rebuilding the working model of attachment …?

Pt That's done …

Th You've worked your way up to the F (earned-secure) category, you should be very, very pleased.

(The patient is an accomplished student of the AAI and understands the categories.)

Pt I am, I was very tired yesterday but I was very happy, to just watch myself sitting in that meeting and saying to my boss "well I don't know what you are going to do but it's not going to be me", again to just not to have any anxiety, no mixed feelings and just to be so resolute in my convictions and my values it's just great! So, thank you.

Th And the feeling is mutual, it's just a pleasure to work with someone like yourself who has such integrity even though your mind can be screwed up, you are always willing to look how it was screwed up.

Pt Yeah, well and one of thoughts that I had as I was coming down this morning is that who I am didn't change but how I approached myself and what I thought about myself did in very positive ways. I just thought that was cool, that your basic values, your basic beliefs and everything else, everything that I have ever felt and thought about everyone *else now applies to me.* (emphasis patient's)

Th Yeah, that's nice and you know there had to be and sometimes I think that we don't do enough of this but there had to be something about your relationship with your mother that had to do with creating some of these positive values.

Pt Yeah, oh yeah and I think I have said that before she always said to me that I can do whatever I wanted to do that I just wasn't even a question and when she is not in that powerless mode is very self-confident and very self-assured in realms other than relationship or to self. So those things I definitely got from her and they were reinforced very clearly, those areas have never been tarnished.

(The patient can now maximize on her mother's positive contributions now that the pathologic introject of her is expunged.)

Th Any other interactions with your Mum come up and any other ones that you felt were particularly meaningful in building a positive part of yourself?

Pt Well, she never forced me to do anything, she let me do whatever I want, which had positive sides and negative sides to it in that I missed a third of my fifth grade year just because I didn't want to go to school and she let me—not necessarily a good thing, but that I in some ways I felt that … she trusted me, that she wasn't hovering, that she wasn't checking in to excessively but she kept me … some of that I did myself, though.

Th The supportive part was what again? What was the supportive part of your interaction with her?

Pt Again that she let me be autonomous, even though I wasn't emotionally autonomous, I had free range, I was trusted, and I don't think that I was ever punished by her, I was just talked to and told like, "you can't do this again". And if someone overstepped the line, she would say just ignore them. I remember this one time, I was about seven or eight, and we were in Toys R Us, and I saw these pencils I liked and I put them in my back pocket and I walked out of the store with them, and she found them later and asked, and I told her, yeah, this is what I did and so I didn't consider it as stealing but anyway, she brought me back to the store with the store manager and the guy said, well alright, I am going to call the police and she said, "no that is going too far". I just wanted her to learn the lesson that you just can't take things and that there are consequences for doing stuff like that, but you are going over the line, this is to far, and so we left because I was crying and freaking out …

Th Wait why were you crying and freaking out?

Pt Because he told me that I was going to jail.

Th For?

Pt Stealing the pencils, and I am like 7. (laughter)

Th What is that again called?

Pt Uh, cruel or are you thinking something in specific?

Th No, your behaviour. What is stealing?

Pt Bad.

Th (makes a face and patient laughs) Why is stealing bad?

Pt Because you are taking something from someone else.

Th Right, so you are violating … boundaries.

Pt Right, yeah. So in that instant she showed me that was not ok.

Th Just think about that. Go ahead what's coming up?

Pt Uhm, it just feels a little ironic, that's not a feeling but …

Th No, it's ok you're comparing something to something, what's the irony …

Pt That she can't set boundaries for herself, nor did she set them with me in emotional ways but in these more societal ways she did.

Th I appreciate the irony, but yeah, that's the way it is, that's the way these things happen is that there is dissociation when it comes to the emotional maintenance and care of personal boundaries, and that the same values sometimes more frequently than not don't apply.

Pt Right, which is what I did within myself?

Th And you re-enacted with?

Pt Everyone.
Th And with?
Pt Well with my former lovers. Yeah, yeah, yeah.
Th Go ahead share the humour with me.
Pt Well, no its just …
Th I feel it to the ironic humour.
Pt No, but I think I … the thought coming into my head is a second chance but I just …
Th Second chance?
Pt I don't know, it that same … like you were talking about, synchronicity, how things occur, I don't want to say recreate …
Th Second chances.
Pt Yeah.
Th It is not ok to dissociate and knockout personal agendas when it is suits you.
Pt Right.
Th So does it feel too onerous to implement this plan of healing for you.?
Pt It is my highest duty and responsibility to me to build and maintain healthy boundaries in my love relationships and my professional relationships. My father abandoned me, my mother seduced me into being her mother, and my step dad violated my Mum's authority and then abused me sexually for his needs. You have restored the parts of me that were damaged by these relationships, and you have given me the psychological tools to succeed at maintaining healthy boundaries because I now value me. I am deeply grateful to you beyond what words can convey.

The patient successfully terminated her therapy having addressed all six criteria of termination. She has launched her new career with grace and confidence, and we completely believe the days of being a co-participant in victimization are over and her future is bright for love, intimacy, and prosperity.

Both of the transcripts demonstrate the patients' opinions about what changed their lives from a continued compulsion to repeat their past traumas. They each independently found the focused use of attention as crucial to their improvement. In addition, experiencing their deepest feelings with a stance of "love, care, and precision"—*sans* judgement—freed them from anxiety and allowed their unconscious guilt to be exposed. This enabled them to separate from their internal aggressors and experience freedom to choose lives and relationships that they wanted based on their own instinctual needs and longings.

It is fitting that we end this chapter with a quote from Sigmund Freud when he addressed analysis "terminable or interminable". His words apply as much to intensive short-term dynamic psychotherapy in today as they did to analysis in 1937. The ideal circumstances for termination occur when:

> two conditions have been approximately fulfilled: first, that the patient shall no longer be suffering from his symptoms and shall have overcome his anxieties and his inhibitions; and secondly, that the analyst shall judge that so much repressed material has been

made conscious, so much that was unintelligible has been explained, and so much internal resistance conquered, that there is no need to *fear* a repetition of the pathological processes concerned. (p. 219)

Steps in the chapter

- Internalization of a constructive superego—access to complex transference feelings related to past trauma—working through
- Signals of the start of the termination phase and of saying goodbye
- Emergence of defences against the pain of saying goodbye
- Some vignettes

APPENDIX

Assessment forms

Evaluation initial interview (fill in after maximum 3 sessions of 90 minutes)

Name of supervisee: date of initial interview:

Name of supervisor:

Patient's initials: M/F Age

Patient's complaints at arrival
(patient's words)

Ego-adaptive capacity at beginning of initial interview?

a) Does the patient differentiate between I/F - A - D?

yes/no

if yes: between what? (give examples)

if no: between what not? (give examples)

b) Does the patient make the correct causality between his perception of T or C or P and I/F - A - D?

if yes, example

if no, example

c) Anxiety manifestations of patient?

striated	yes/no
sympathetic	which
parasympathetic	if yes, which
cognitive/perceptual disturbances	if yes, which
rise and fall of manifestations	short/long rise
short/long duration of manifestations	short/long fall

d) Is the patient projecting, or does the patient understand that he transfers the perception of P on to T and C?

example:

Which defences at beginning of interview?

syntonic	**dystonic**
....	....
....	

Nature of superego pathology (the patient identifies partly/fully with which introjected characteristics of which parent)

(e.g., the patient ignores, denies, devalues, etc. as his mother did)

Degree of superego pathology at beginning of initial interview?

low - fairly high - high - very high

Location on spectrum of structural neuroses at beginning of initial interview?

extreme left ....
the middle of the left half ....
the middle ....
the middle of the right half ....
extreme right ....

explain why

Where on the road to the unconscious are you after 3 x 90 minutes? (use the Roadmap diagram)

explain and illustrate with example
....
....

Did I establish some degree of unconscious/conscious working alliance (after 3 x 90 minutes)?

explain and illustrate with example

Did your patient have a breakthrough (after 3 x 90 minutes)?
yes/no

if yes, about what?

– grief/anger about self-destruction
– complete: sadistic impulse/guilt/grief towards Th or C or P
– partial: sadistic impulse (no guilt, no grief)

illustrate:

Was there an unlocking?
yes/no

if yes, illustrate:

Did I manage to make C-T-P links with the patient?
yes/no

if yes, illustrate:

date of supervision:

(maximum 3 x 90 minutes = initial interview) ...

After that ...

Interim evaluation (each time after 10 x 90 minutes)

Interim evaluation

Name of supervisee

dates of sessions 1 to 10:
(after initial interview)

Name of supervisor

Patient's initials M/F Age

Ego-adaptive capacity (at the time of this interim report)?

a) Differentiation between I/F - A - D?
yes/no

if no: example

if no: what is the reason?

b) Correct causality between perception of Th or C or P and I/F - A - D?
yes/no

if no: example

if no: what is the reason?

c) Anxiety manifestations?

d) Does the patient understand that he transfers his perception of P on to Th and C or is he still projecting?

yes, he sees the transfer/ no, he still projects

if still projecting: example

if still projecting: what is the reason?

Are there still syntonic defences?
yes/no

if yes: which ones?

if yes: what is the reason?

Did your patient have complete breakthroughs with unlockings?
yes/no

if yes: example

if no: none or partial (circle)
What is the reason?

Summary of the therapeutic process?

Therapy: results up until now

Does the patient understand that he has an intrapsychic problem and that his interpersonal problems are the consequence of his intrapsychic problem?
yes/no

Is the patient working in the triangles of conflict and persons?
yes/no

Which are the positive results?

In his relation with partner/children:
example

In his relation with friends/colleagues:
example

In his relation with superiors (work):
example

In his relation with siblings:
example

In his relation with parents or other persons from the past:
example

Which are my problems in the relationship with this patient?
example

I will focus on the following aspects of my therapeutical functioning in relation with this patient:
example

Date of supervision:

GLOSSARY

Anxiety

In patients with a high capacity to regulate anxiety, signs of anxiety will be reflected by a pattern of facial muscle behaviour, by tension of other striated muscles, by a pattern of sympathetic reactivity and sensory vigilance. The proportion of somatomotor manifestations will be higher than the proportion of autonomic manifestations. The rise of the respective manifestations will be slow, the duration relatively short. The patient will accurately perceive these manifestations and will label them as anxiety.

Attentive ego

see under *Ego*

Biofeedback

In the mid-1960s, the technique of biofeedback was invented. The technique is essentially one in which a selected physiological activity is monitored by an instrument which senses, by electrodes or transducers, signals of physiological information such as heart rate, blood pressure, muscle tension. The sensed information is amplified, then used in the instrument to activate a display that reflects changes in the physiological activity. The information is actual feedback about the internal process that the person can use to increase control of the internal process. Over time, the goal is to be able to control such processes without the use of the machine. In ISTDP, in using the techniques of confrontation, identification, clarification the psychotherapist functions as a provider of external biofeedback when aiming at the patient's *anxiety* and feelings.

Breakthrough of the impulse, guilt, grief, love

A term of Habib Davanloo to describe the emergence of deeply conflicted emotions (rage, guilt, grief, love) into consciousness, following the defeat of the patient's defences along with lowering of the patient's *anxiety*.

Central Dynamic Sequence (CDS)

A term coined by David Malan to describe a set of clinical interventions, devised by Davanloo, to access the patient's unconscious in order to have a direct view of the patient's *multifoci core neurotic structure*. Classically, Davanloo considers his CDS as consisting of the following phases: inquiry, pressure to feel, clarification and challenge to defences, transference resistance, intrapsychic crisis, systematic analysis of the transference, further inquiry exploring the developmental history, breakthrough to the unconscious, exposure of the core neurotic conflict, followed by consolidation.

Challenge

A technique, taken from cognitive therapy, to motivate and challenge the patient's constructive *ego* to quit his repertoire of self-destructive defences.

Character resistance

see under *Resistance*

Confrontation, identification, clarification

The techniques of confrontation, identification, clarification can be aimed at impulses and feelings, at *anxiety*, at defences. Confrontation: directing the patient's cognitive/perceptual system to some aspect of his intrapsychic problem. Confrontation is immediately followed by identifying the target, and subsequently the therapist will clarify the function of this target.

Conscious and unconscious working alliance

The conscious component consists of the patient's conscious will to get well, to cooperate with the therapist, to face the truth no matter how painful, to drop his defences, to face disturbing feelings. The unconscious component consists basically of the repressed impulses and feelings, which are pressing for expression and are therefore on the patient's side. The conscious working alliance takes four components requiring activity and cooperation between therapist and patient: 1) the emotional bond, developed between therapist and patient, that allows the patient to make therapeutic progress; 2) the therapist and patient have the same vision of the patient's problems and the same definition of its constituting elements/aspects; 3) an agreement between therapist and patient about (intermittent) goals of treatment; 4) an agreement about the division of therapy tasks to accomplish these goals.

Defences

see under *Resistance*

Ego

One of the three major subdivisions of the mental apparatus, which has both conscious and unconscious components. The ego mediates between the instinctual needs of the person, the challenges of the external world, and the demands of the superego.

Attentive ego: the patient's cognitive/perceptual system is curiously and actively directed towards his intrapsychic processes out of intrinsic motivation.

Observing ego: the patient's cognitive/perceptual system is passively present to a certain degree.

Ego-adaptive capacity

The quality and degree to which the ego deals with external and internal pressure. External pressure can be seen as the demands of the external world. Internal pressure can be seen as the downward pressure of the superego and the upward pressure of impulses and feelings.

Restructuring the ego-adaptive capacity: helping the patient to discriminate between the three poles of the *triangle of conflict*, to recognize physical concomitants of feelings and anxiety, and to label them correctly, to help the patient to attain a healthy anxiety regulation, to see correct causalities, and to make his defences dystonic.

Ego-dystonic

see under *Resistance*

Ego-syntonic

see under *Resistance*

Emotion regulation

Refers to the conscious and unconscious processes by which human beings influence at what time they have which emotion(s) or impulses, with what intensity and duration, and how and when they are expressed.

Assessment of degree and quality of emotion regulation: assessment of the degree and quality of a patient's healthy regulation of his feelings, impulses, anxiety should include assessment of manifestations of 1) the somatomotor, 2) autonomic and endocrine, 3) cognitive and perceptual patterns, as well as assessment of the extent to which these three subsystems are involved.

Empathy

The capacity to recognize and, to some extent, share feelings (such as sadness or happiness) that are being experienced by another sentient or semi-sentient being. Empathy is a necessary precursor to the capacity to feel guilt. Someone may need to have a certain amount of empathy before being able to feel *compassion*.

Grief

A multi-faceted response to loss, particularly to the loss of someone or something to which a bond was formed. While the terms are often used interchangeably, bereavement often refers to the state of loss, and grief to the reaction to loss.

Guilt

A *cognitive* or an *emotional* experience, based on the capacity to have empathy and love, that occurs when a person *realizes* or *believes*—accurately or not—that he or she has harmed another person by his behaviour and has the action tendency to undo this harm. It is closely related to the concept of *remorse*.

Head-On Collision (HOC)

A powerful technique, consisting of several components, that is essentially addressed to the unconscious part of the working alliance, with the aim of mobilizing this against the *resistance*. The dosage of the HOC can be varied by the number of repetitions of the components and the therapist's tone of voice.

Identification, imitation, introjection

Identification—an unconscious process by which an individual imitates and introjects his ways of thinking and acting after those of an important figure in life such as a parent. The roots of the concept can be found in *Freud's* writings. The three most prominent concepts of identification as described by Freud are: primary identification, *narcissistic* (secondary) identification, and partial (secondary) identification. When there is hundred per cent identification with a superego, there is no self.

Impulse

There are murderous and sexual impulses. An impulse is considered a desire to act in a certain way, typically in order to ease instinctual tension or gain pleasure. Impulses are seen as life-preserving.

Modelling

Later findings, based on Miller and Dollard's research, made it clear that virtually all learning, resulting from direct experience, occurs on a vicarious basis by observing other people's behaviours and by observing the consequences of those behaviours to other people.

Multifoci core neurotic structure

Buried in the unconscious, this is considered to be responsible for the patient's symptoms and character disturbances. The multifoci core neurotic structure consists of the coupling of the representation of the patient's perception of traumatic experiences with important persons in childhood with the representation of a complex of mixed feelings (sadistic and sexual impulses, love, guilt, grief towards these persons).

Omnipotence

Thought to be a function of an infantile belief in being all-powerful.

Pathologic bereavement

An important concept in ISTDP, in that Davanloo conceptualizes psychoneurosis as a variant of pathological bereavement in which the patient's grief and normal mourning processes are frozen at the time of the developmental trauma or loss. His method and techniques seek to convert pathologic mourning into acute grief.

Projection

A defence mechanism in which an individual attributes to another person an unacceptable thought, feeling, or attribute (e.g., superego) which is his or her own.

Projective identification

Davanloo coopted this term from Melanie Klein: intolerable aspects of the self are projected into another person accompanied by the fantasy that this aspect controls the other person from within. Davanloo sees projective identification differently. The patient identifies with a former aggressive attachment figure and projects himself onto the other person in the interaction. Or the patient identifies and introjects the damages he inflicted with his impulse upon the other person. Or the patient damages certain parts of himself in order to prevent expressing his unconscious destructive impulse. These unconscious mechanisms of projective identification are particularly relevant to patients on the right side of the spectrum of psychoneurosis and are believed to be the mechanisms of symptom formation.

Resistance

Takes the form of a series of defences (which Davanloo classifies as obsessional, regressive, and tactical), put into operation by the ego in interaction with the id and the superego to oppose the rise of the complex transference feelings, the triggering mechanism for unlocking to become operative, the process of unlocking the unconscious, intimacy, and the development of the *conscious/unconscious working alliance*.

Defences are commonly conceptualized as managing anxiety from both internal and external threats. The more defences are automatic, chronic, and the more there is satisfaction with them, the more they are considered syntonic and maladaptive. The more defences are non-automatic, variable, and the more there is dissatisfaction with them, the more they are considered dystonic.

Character resistance: a series of syntonic defences that is habitual and can be seen as a set of representative reactions to everybody. Characteristics of former (aggressor) caretakers are constantly, chronically projected onto all persons in the present, the ego's discriminating function is absent, reality testing is poor.

Transference resistance: see under *Transference process.*

Role play, modelling, and role reversal

Techniques developed in behaviour therapy. Via role play, modelling of the therapist, and role reversal (after the therapist's modelling, roles are reversed and the patient takes over), the vicariously derived information is actively codified by the patient as best as he can. The patient can gain a coherent view of, e.g., sequencing steps in expressing a feeling in a constructive way. Overt practice and corrective feedback can refine the patient's understanding of the steps to be taken. Practice and performing the modelled behaviour outside the therapist's office will stabilize the patient's competence.

Separation of ego/superego

A process demonstrated by Davanloo which was codified and emphasized by ten Have-de Labije to free the *ego* from the implicit obedience to the commands of the superego. This process enables the development of an observing and attentive ego and reduces the dosage of power of later interventions to access the patient's unconscious.

Shame

An affect linked to a sense of being judged as bad or unworthy by another. The roots of the word "shame" are thought to derive from an older word meaning *to cover*; as such, covering oneself, literally or figuratively, is a natural expression of shame. In ISTDP, shame is a result of a pathological superego judging and blaming the self and is dealt with as a defence.

Superego pathology

Refers to a sadistic superego, leading to the patient's need to suffer as a punishment for violent and murderous impulses. The superego has taken over the ego, has paralysed its functioning, and has replaced the normal search for satisfaction and fulfilment with an ever-present need for suffering.

Transference process

A process first discovered by Freud in which unresolved conflictual feelings are transferred to the therapist. In ISTDP, the transference could be defined as a process in which the following five interacting components comprise the transference: 1) the patient's perception of a person in the present; 2) the representation of the introjected and repressed perception of an important person from the patient's past; 3) the repressed complex of the impulse and mixed feelings towards the representation of this important person from the past; 4) the *anxiety*, aroused by the repressed complex of the impulse and mixed feelings; 5) the set of defences, making up the *resistance.*

Triangle of conflict

First described by Freud as "signal anxiety" but systematized by Ezreil and Malan.

The triangle of conflict depicts the pain- and guilt-laden impulses and feelings that are kept out of consciousness by anxiety and various defence mechanisms.

Triangle of persons

First described by Menninger and adapted by Malan, depicts the patient's perception of persons in the past, the therapist, and persons in the current life of the patient.

Unlocking of the unconscious

A term invented by Davanloo referring to a state when the patient has defeated his defences and has access to complex feelings of rage, guilt, grief, and love that are related to past trauma, caused in the interactions with past attachment figures.

Working through

In the process of working through, the links between present and past and the origin of the patient's pathological superego structure are repeatedly made. The conflictual emotions of the past are re-experienced and released, and motives for self-sabotage are removed and replaced with self-love, and compassion for former attachment figures.

REFERENCES

Abbass, A. (2002a). Modified short-term dynamic psychotherapy in patients with bipolar disorder preliminary report of a case series. *Canadian Child Psychiatry, 11(1)*: 19–22.

Abbass, A. (2002b). Office-based research in ISTDP: data from the first 6 years of practice. *Ad Hoc Bulletin of STDP: Practice and Research, 6(2)*: 5–14.

Abbass, A. (2002c). Intensive short-term dynamic psychotherapy in a private psychiatric office: clinical and cost effectiveness. *American Journal of Psychotherapy, 56*: 225–232.

Abbass, A. (2002d). Short-term dynamic psychotherapies in the treatment of major depression. *Canadian Journal of Psychiatry, 47(2)*: 193.

Abbass, A. (2005). Somatization: diagnosing it sooner through emotion-focused interviewing. *Journal of Family Practice, 54(3)*: 231–239.

Abbass, A. (2006). Intensive short-term dynamic psychotherapy of treatment resistant depression: a pilot study. *Depression and Anxiety, 23*: 449–452.

Abbass, A., Campbell, S., Magee, K. & Tarzwell, R. (2009). Intensive short-term dynamic psychotherapy to reduce rates of emergency department return visits for patients with medically unexplained symptoms; preliminary evidence from a pre-post intervention study. *Canadian Journal of Emergency Medicine Nov, 11(6)*: 529–534.

Abbass, A., Kisely, S. & Kroenke, K. (2009). Short-term psychodynamic psychotherapies for somatic symptom disorders: systematic review and meta-analysis. *Psychotherapy and Psychosomatics, 78*: 265–274.

Abbass, A., Lovas, D. & Purdy, A. (2008). Direct diagnosis and management of emotional factors in chronic headache patients. *Cephalalgia Dec, 28(12)*: 1305–1314.

Ainsworth, M. D. S., Blehar, M. C., Waters, E. & Wall, S. (1978). *Patterns of Attachment: A Psychological Study of the Strange Situation.* Hillsdale, NJ: Erlbaum.

American Psychiatric Association (1987). *Diagnostic and Statistical Manual of Mental Disorders. Third Edition, Revised.* Washington, DC: American Psychiatric Association.

American Psychiatric Association (2010). *Practice Guideline for the Treatment of Patients with Major Depressive Disorder* (3rd ed.). Arlington, VA: American Psychiatric Association.

Anthony, S. J., Piper, W. E., Ogrodniczuk, J. S. & Klein, R. H. (2006). *Termination in Psychotherapy: A Psychodynamic Model of Processes and Outcomes.* Washington, DC: American Psychological Association.

Bandura, A. (1977). *Social Learning Theory.* Englewood Cliffs, NJ: Prentice Hall.

Bandura, A. (1982). The self and mechanisms of agency. In: J. Suls (Ed.), *Psychological Perspectives on the Self* (Vol. 1). Hillsdale, NJ: Erlbaum.

Bandura, A. (1985). A. model of causality in social learning theory. In: M. J. Mahoney Freeman (Ed.), *Cognition and Psychotherapy.* New York, London: Plenum Press.

Beck, A. T., Rush, A. J., Shaw, B. F. & Emery, G. (1979). *Cognitive Therapy of Depression.* New York: The Guilford Press.

Benoit, C. (1990). Management of transference resistance in Davanloo's intensive short-term dynamic psychotherapy. *International Journal of Short-Term Psychotherapy, 5*: 277–296.

Benoit, C. (1991). Management of transference resistance in Davanloo's intensive short-term dynamic psychotherapy, Part II. *International Journal of Short-Term Psychotherapy, 6*: 145–161.

Bleuler, R. (1996). Anxiety as an indicator of initial transference resistance and its handling in intensive short-term dynamic psychotherapy. *International Journal of Short-Term Psychotherapy, 1(1)*: 1–20.

Bordin, E. S. (1979). The generalizability of the psychoanalytic concept of the working alliance. *Psychotherapy: Theory, Research and Practice, 16*: 252–260.

Bowlby, J. (1969). *Attachment and Loss. Vol. 1. Attachment.* New York: Basic Books.

Bowlby, J. (1980). *Attachment and Loss. Vol. 3. Loss.* New York: Basic Books.

Bowlby, J. (1988). *A Secure Base: Parent–Child Attachment and Healthy Human Development.* London: Routledge.

Brenner, C. (1991). A psychoanalytic perspective on depression. *Journal of the American Psychoanalytic Association, 39*: 25–44.

Breuer, J. & Freud, S. (1895). *Studies in Hysteria.* In: J. Strachey (Ed.), *The Standard Edition of the Complete Psychological Works of Sigmund Freud,* Volume 1. London: Hogarth Press, 1975.

Cardoso, S. H. & Sabbattini, R. M. E. (2002). The animal that weeps. *Brain and Mind Magazine, 16*: 7–22.

Carpenter, M. B. (1972). *Core Text of Neuroanatomy.* Baltimore: The Williams and Wilkins Comp.

Chodoff, P. (1978). The diagnosis of hysteria: an overview. *American Journal of Psychiatry, 131*: 1073–1078.

Cooper, S. H. (1998). Changing notions of defense within psychoanalytic theory. *Journal of Personality, 6*: 947–964.

Coughlin Della Selva, P. (2001). Dynamic assessment of ego functioning in Davanloo's ISTDP. In: Have de Labije, J. ten (Ed.), *The Working Alliance in ISTDP: Whose Intrapsychic Crisis*? (pp. 1–40). VKDP-Amsterdam.

Coughlin Della Selva, P. (2006). Emotional processing in the treatment of psychosomatic disorders. *Journal of Clinical Psychology, 62*: 539–550.

Cramer, P. & Davidson, K. (Eds.) (1998). Defense mechanisms in contemporary personality research. Special Issue, *Journal of Personality, 66*: 879–1157.

Davanloo, H. (Ed.) (1978). *Basic Principles and Techniques in Short-Term Dynamic Psychotherapy.* New York: Spectrum.

Davanloo, H. (Ed.) (1980). *Short-Term Dynamic Psychotherapy.* Northvale, NJ: Jason Aronson.

Davanloo, H. (1984) Short-term dynamic psychotherapy, In: H. Kaplan & B. Sadock (Eds.), *Comprehensive Textbook of Psychiatry* (4th ed., Chapter 29.11). Baltimore: Williams & Wilkins.

Davanloo, H. (1987a). Intensive short-term dynamic psychotherapy with highly resistant depressed patients. Part I: Restructuring ego's regressive defenses. *International Journal of Short-Term Psychotherapy, 2(2)*: 99–132.

Davanloo, H. (1987b). Intensive short-term dynamic psychotherapy with highly resistant depressed patients. Part II: Royal road to the dynamic unconscious. *International Journal of Short-Term Psychotherapy, 2(3)*: 167–185.

Davanloo, H. (1987c). Clinical manifestations of superego pathology. Part 1: *International Journal of Short-Term Psychotherapy, 2(4)*: 225–254.

Davanloo, H. (1988a). Clinical manifestations of superego pathology. Part II: The resistance of the superego and the liberation of the paralyzed ego. *International Journal of Short-Term Psychotherapy, 3(1)*: 1–24.

Davanloo, H. (1988b). The technique of unlocking the unconscious. Part I. *Major Unlocking of the Unconscious. International Journal of Short-Term Psychotherapy, 3(2)*: 99–121.

Davanloo, H. (1988c). The technique of unlocking the unconscious. Part II: Partial unlocking of the unconscious. *International Journal of Short-Term Psychotherapy, 3(2)*: 123–159.

Davanloo, H. (1989a). The technique of unlocking the unconscious in patients suffering from functional disorders. Part I: Restructuring the ego's defenses. *International Journal of Short-Term Psychotherapy, 4*: 93–116. [Reprinted in Davanloo (1990), pp. 283–306.]

Davanloo, H. (1989b). The technique of unlocking the unconscious in patients suffering from functional disorders. Part II: Direct view of the dynamic unconscious. *International Journal of Short-Term Psychotherapy, 4*: 117–148. [Reprinted in Davanloo (1990), pp. 307–338.]

Davanloo, H. (1990). *Unlocking the Unconscious*. Chichester: John Wiley.

Davanloo, H. (1995). Intensive short-term dynamic psychotherapy: spectrum of psycho-neurotic disorders. *International Journal of Short-Term Psychotherapy, 10 (3, 4)*: 121–155.

Davanloo, H. (1996a). Management of tactical defenses in intensive short-term dynamic psychotherapy, Part I: Overview, tactical defenses of cover words and indirect speech. *International Journal of Intensive Short-Term Dynamic Psychotherapy, 11(3)*: 129–152.

Davanloo, H. (1996b). Management of tactical defenses in intensive short-term dynamic psychotherapy, Part II: Spectrum of tactical defenses. *International Journal of Intensive Short-Term Dynamic Psychotherapy, 11(3)*: 153–199.

Davanloo, H. (2000). *Intensive Short-Term Dynamic Psychotherapy: Selected Papers of Habib Davanloo, MD*. Chichester: John Wiley.

Davanloo, H. (2001). Intensive short-term psychotherapy: extended major direct access to the unconscious. *European Psychotherapy, 2(1)*: 35–70.

Davis, D. (1988). Transformation of pathological mourning into acute grief with ISTDP. Part II. *International Journal of Short-Term Psychotherapy, 3*: 279–298.

Davis, D. (1989a). Resistance and transference in ISTDP and classical psychoanalysis—similarities and differences, Part I. *International Journal of Short-Term Psychotherapy, 4*: 313–331.

Davis, D. (1989b). Resistance and transference in ISTDP and classical psychoanalysis—similarities and differences, Part II. *International Journal of Short-Term Psychotherapy, 5*: 1–24.

Decety, J. & Moriguchi, Y. (2007). The empathic brain and its dysfunction in psychiatric populations: implications for intervention across different clinical conditions. *BioPsychoSocial-Medicine, 1*: 22.

Driessen, E., Cuijpers, P., de Maat, S., Abbass, A., de Jonghe, F. & Dekker, J. J. (2010). The efficacy of short-term psychodynamic psychotherapy for depression: a meta-analysis. *Clinical Psychology Review, 30*: 25–36.

Drury, N. (1988). Some technical aspects of the pre-interpretive phase of trial therapy in highly resistant patients with ego syntonic character pathology, Part I. *International Journal of Short-Term Dynamic Psychotherapy, 3*: 213–235.

Drury, N. (1989). The problem of resistance in dynamic psychotherapy. *International Journal of Short-Term Psychotherapy, 4*: 217–248.

Drury, N. (1990). Handling resistance in a patient with major character pathology. *International Journal of Short-Term Psychotherapy, 5*: 25–57.

Engel, G. (1959). Psychogenic pain and the pain-prone patient. *American Journal of Medicine, 26*: 899–918.

Englert, H. (2004). Sussing out stress. *Scientific American. Mind, special edition. 14(1)*: 56–62.

Fan, L. Y. & Chiu, M. J. (2010). Pharmacological treatment for Alzheimer's disease: current approaches and future strategies. *Acta Neurol Taiwan, 19(4)*: 228–245.

Feather, B. W. & Rhoads, J. M. (1980). Psychodynamic behavior therapy. I: Theory and rationale/II: Clinical aspects. In: J. Marmor & S. M. Woods (Eds.), *The Interface between the Psychodynamic and Behavioral Therapies* (pp. 293–331). New York: Plenum Press. [Reprinted from *Archives of General Psychiatry*, (1972) 26: 503–511.]

Fenichel, O. (1945). *The Psychoanalytic Theory of Neurosis*. New York: W. W. Norton.

Ford, C. V. (1983). *The Somatizing Disorders*. New York: Elsevier.

Fossella, J. A., Sommer, T., Fan, J., Pfaff, D. & Possner, M. I. (2003). Synaptogenesis and heritable aspects of executive attention. *Mental Retardation and Developmental Disabilities Research Reviews, 9(3)*: 178–183.

Freud, S. (1917). *Mourning and Melancholia*. In: J. Strachey (Ed.), *The Standard Edition of the Complete Psychological Works of Sigmund Freud*, Volume 4. London: Hogarth Press, 1975.

Freud, S. (1937). *Analysis, Terminable or Interminable?* In: J. Strachey (Ed.), *The Standard Edition of the Complete Psychological Works of Sigmund Freud*. London: Hogarth Press, 1975.

Frijda, N. H. (1986). *The Emotions*. Maison des Sciences de l'Homme and Cambridge University Press.

Frijda, N. H. (1993). *De Emoties*. Amsterdam: Bert Bakker.

Gaillard, J. (1991). Importance of phenomenological approach in patients with depression. *International Journal of Short-Term Psychotherapy, 6*: 95–112.

Gallese, V. (2005). Embodied simulation: from neurons to phenomenal experience. *Phenomenology and the Cognitive Sciences, 4*: 23–48.

Gallese, V. (2006). Intentional attunement: a neurophysiological perspective on social cognition and its disruption in autism. *Brain Research: Cognitive Brain Research, 1079*. 1079: 15–24.

Gallese, V. & Goldman, A. (1998). Mirror neurons and the simulation theory of mind-reading. *Trends in Cognitive Sciences, 12*: 493–501.

Gallese, V., Keysers, C. & Rizzolatti, G. (2004). A unifying view of the brain of social cognition. *Trends in Cognitive Sciences, 8*: 396–403.

Gelso, C. J. & Woodhouse, S.S. (2002). The termination of psychotherapy: what research tells us about the process of ending treatment. In: G.S. Tryon (Ed.), *Counseling Based on Process Research: Applying What We Know*. Boston, MA: Allyn & Bacon.

Goadsby, P. J., Lipton, R. B. & Ferrari, M. D. (2002). Migraine—current understanding and treatment. *New England Journal of Medicine, 346*: 257–270.

Goldstein, A. J. & Chambless, D. L. (1978). A reanalysis of agoraphobia. *Behavior Therapy, 9*: 47–58.

Gottwik, G., Orbes, G., Tressel, F. & Wagner, G. (1998a). Application of Davanloo's intensive short-term dynamic psychotherapy in the treatment of patients with agoraphobia, fainting attacks, anxiety, panic, somatization and functional disorders. Part I: Technical and metapsychological roots of the technique; initial phase of trial therapy. *International Journal of Intensive Short-Term Dynamic Psychotherapy, 12*: 77–103.

Gottwik, G., Orbes, G., Tressel, F. & Wagner, G. (1998b). Application of Davanloo's intensive short-term dynamic psychotherapy in the treatment of patients with agoraphobia, fainting attacks, anxiety, panic, somatization and functional disorders. Part II: The first break-through. *International Journal of Intensive Short-Term Dynamic Psychotherapy, 12*: 105–123.

Gottwik, G., Orbes, G., Tressel, F. & Wagner, G. (1998c). Application of Davanloo's intensive short-term dynamic psychotherapy in the treatment of patients with agoraphobia, fainting attacks, anxiety, panic, somatization and functional disorders. Part III: Partial unlocking of the unconscious. *International Journal of Intensive Short-Term Dynamic Psychotherapy, 12*: 125–149.

Gross, J. J. (1998). The emerging field of emotion regulation: an integrative review. *Review of General Psychology, 2(3)*: 271–299.

Guidano, V. F. & Liotti, G. (1985). *Cognitive Processes and Emotional Disorders: A Structural Approach to Psychotherapy*. New York, London: The Guilford Press.

Have-de Labije, J. ten (1999). Maintaining Davanloo's discovery for uncovering the unconscious: an attempt at formulating operational definitions of the dependent variables. Parts I and II. *Ad Hoc Bulletin of Short Term Dynamic Psychotherapy: Practice and Theory, 3(1)*: 4–21.

Have-de Labije, J. ten (2001). Red and green traffic lights on Davanloo's road to the unconscious, Part I. In: Have-de Labije, J. ten (Ed.) *The Working Alliance in ISTDP: Whose Intrapsychic Crisis?* (pp. 41–50). Amsterdam: VKDP.

Have-de Labije, J. ten (2003a). The racehorse that identified with her rider's whip. *Ad Hoc Bulletin of Short Term Dynamic Psychotherapy: Practice and Theory, 7(2)*: 48–68.

Have-de Labije, J. ten (2006). When patients present with anxiety in the forefront. *Ad Hoc Bulletin of Short Term Dynamic Psychotherapy: Practice and Theory, 10(1)*: 35–69.

Have-de Labije, J. ten & Neborsky, R. J. (2005). Understanding and overcoming instant repression. Parts I, II, III. *Ad Hoc Bulletin of Short Term Dynamic Psychotherapy: Practice and Theory, (10)*: 10–34.

Hesse, E., Main, M., Abrams, K. Y. & Rifkin, A. (2003). Unresolved states regarding loss or abuse can have "second generation" effects: disorganization, role inversion, and frightening ideation in the offspring of traumatized, non-maltreating parents. In: M. F. Solomon & D. J. Siegel (Eds.), *Healing Trauma* (pp. 57–107). London: W. W. Norton.

Janowsky, D. S., el-Yousef, M. K. & Davis, J. M. (1972). A cholinergic-adrenergic hypothesis of mania and depression. *Lancet, 23(2) (7778)*: 632–635.

Janowsky, D. S. & Overstreet, D. H. (1994). The role of acetylcholine mechanisms in mood disorders. In: F. E. Bloom & D. J. Kupfer (Eds.), *Psychopharmacology: The Fourth Generation of Progress*. New York, NY: Raven Press.

Joyce, A. S., Piper, W. E., Ogrodniczuk, J. S. & Klein, R. H. (2007). *Termination in Psychotherapy: A Psychodynamic Model of Processes and Outcomes*. Washington, DC: American Psychological Association.

Kalpin, A. (1994). Effective use of Davanloo's "head-on collision". *International Journal of Short-Term Dynamic Psychotherapy, 9*: 19–36.

Kandel, E. R. & Kupfermann, I. (1995). Emotional states. In: J. H. Schwartz & T. M. Jessell (Eds.), *Essentials of Neural Science and Behavior* (pp. 595–613). New York: Prentice Hall.

Kellner, R. (1987). Psychological measurements in somatization and abnormal illness behavior. *Advanced Psychosomatic Medicine, 17*: 101–118.

Kirmayer L. J. & Robbins, J. M. (1991). *Current Concepts of Somatization*. Washington, DC: American Psychiatric Press.

Konzelmann, C. (1995). Head on collision with resistance against emotional closeness in ISTDP. *International Journal of Short-Term Psychotherapy, 10*: 35–51.

Korff, P. von (1998). Early management of unconscious defiance in Davanloo's ISTDP. Part I. *International Journal of Intensive Short Term Dynamic Psychotherapy, 12*: 183–208.

Lebeaux, D. (1999). The rise of the transference in Davanloo's technique of ISTDP: principles, technique and issues for training. *International Journal of Short-Term Dynamic Psychotherapy, 13*: 3–16.

LeDoux, J. (1996). *The Emotional Brain: The Mysterious Underpinnings of Emotional Life*. London: Simon & Schuster.

Levinson, J. L. (2007). *Essentials of Psychosomatic Medicine*. Washington, DC: American Psychiatric Press.

Lewis, H. B. (1971). *Shame and Guilt in Neurosis*. New York: International Universities Press.

Lipowski, Z. J. (1988). Somatization: the concept and its clinical application. *American Journal of Psychiatry, 145*: 1358–1368.

Malan, D. (1979). *Individual Psychotherapy and the Science of Psychodynamics*. London: Butterworth.

Mauss, I. B., Bunge, S. A. & Gross, J. J. (2007). Automatic emotion regulation. *Social and Personality Compass, 1*: 1–20.

Menninger, K. (1958). *Theory of Psychoanalytic Technique*. New York: Basic Books.

Miller, N. & Dollard, J. (1941). *Social Learning and Imitation*. New Haven, NJ: Yale University Press.

Neborsky, R. J. (2003). Shame and guilt from a developmental neuroscience perspective: implications for technique in ISTDP. *Ad Hoc Bulletin for Short-Term Dynamic Psychotherapy, Practice and Theory 7(1)*: 54–75.

Neborsky, R. J. (2005) Understanding and overcoming instant repression. Part III: *The Wailing Prisoner: Self-Punishment to Self-Pardon. Ad Hoc Bulletin of Short Term Dynamic Psychotherapy; Practice and Theory, 9(2)*: 10–34.

Neborsky, R. J. & Peluso, E. (2008). Understanding and overcoming projective identification. Part I. *Ad Hoc Bulletin of Short Term Dynamic Psychotherapy: Practice and Theory, 12(2)*: 29–46.

Neborsky, R. J. & Peluso, E. (2009). Understanding and overcoming projective identification. Part II: The man with the ghost in the basement and the nursery. *Ad Hoc Bulletin of Short Term Dynamic Psychotherapy Theory and Practice, 13(3)*: 8–33.

Neborsky, R. J. & Snyker, E. (1986). A workshop experience in short-term dynamic psychotherapy. *International Journal of Short-Term Dynamic Psychotherapy, 4*: 257–263.

Netter, F. H. (1994). *The Ciba Collection of Medical Illustrations*. Volume 1: *The Nervous System: Anatomy and Physiology*. New York: Basic Books.

Ochsner, K. N. & Gross, J. J. (2005). The cognitive control of emotion. *Trends in Cognitive Sciences, 9(5)*: 242–249.

Olds, D. D. (2006). Identification, psychoanalytic and biological perspectives. *Journal of the American Psychoanalytical Association, 54*: 17–46.

Perry, B. D. (2001). *Violence and Childhood: How Persisting Fear Can Alter the Developing Child's Brain*. In: D. Schetky & E. Benedek (Eds.), *Textbook of Child and Adolescent Forensic Psychiatry* (pp. 221–238). Washington, DC: American Psychiatric Press.

Quintana, S. M. (1993). Toward an expanded and updated conceptualization of termination: implications for short-term, individual psychotherapy. *Professional Psychology: Research and Practice, 24*: 426–432.

Quintana, S. M. & Holahan, W. (1992). Termination in short-term counseling: comparison of successful and unsuccessful cases. *Journal of Counseling Psychology, 39*: 299–305.

Reitav, J. (1991). The treatment of character pathology with Davanloo's ISTDP. Part I: Management of resistance. *International Journal of Short-Term Psychotherapy, 6*: 3–25.

Rizolatti, G. (2005). The mirror neuron system and its function in humans. *Anatomy and Embryology, 210*: 419–421.

Rizzolatti, G. & Arbib, M. A. (1998). Language within our grasp. *Trends in Neurosciences, 21*: 188–194.

Rizzolatti, G. & Craighero, L. (2004). The mirror-neuron system. *Annual Review of Neuroscience, 27*: 169–192.

Roe, D., Dekel, R., Harel, G., Fennig, S. & Fennig, S. (2006). Feelings during termination of psychodynamically oriented psychotherapy. *Bulletin of the Menninger Clinic, 70(1)*: 68–81.

Rogers, C. (1959). A theory of therapy, personality and interpersonal relationships as developed in the client-centered framework. In: S. Koch (Ed.), *Psychology: A Study of a Science*, Volume 3 (pp. 184–256). New York: McGraw Hill.

Rosenberg, P. (1987). Resistance in psychoanalysis and ISTDP. *International Journal of Short-Term Psychotherapy, 2*: 35–54.

Said, T. (1988). Trial therapy with clinically depressed suicidal patients. *International Journal of Short-Term Psychotherapy, 3*: 241–267.

Schafer, R. (1968). *Aspects of Internalization.* New York: International University Press.

Schildkraut, J. J. (1965). The catecholamine hypothesis of affective disorders: a review of supporting evidence. *American Journal of Psychiatry, 122*: 509.

Schildkraut, J. J. (1995). The catecholamine hypothesis of affective disorders: a review of supporting evidence. *Journal of Neuropsychiatry and Clinical Neuroscience, 7*: 524–533.

Schore, A. N. (1994). *Affect Regulation and the Origin of the Self: The Neurobiology of Emotional Development.* Hillsdale, NJ: Erlbaum.

Schore, A. N. (1998). Early shame experiences and infant brain development. In: P. Gilbert & B. Andrews (Eds.), *Shame: Interpersonal Behavior, Psychopathology, and Culture* (pp. 57–77). New York: Oxford University Press.

Schore, A. N. (2003). Early relational trauma, disorganized attachment, and the development of a predisposition to violence. In: M.F. Solomon & D.J. Siegel (Eds.), *Healing Trauma* (pp. 107–168). London: W. W. Norton.

Schubmehl, J. (1995a). Management of syntonic character resistance in ISTDP: Part I. *International Journal of Short-Term Dynamic Psychotherapy, 10*: 3–19.

Schubmehl, J. (1995b). Management of syntonic character resistance in Davanloo's technique: Part II, The rest of the trial therapy. *International Journal of Short-Term Dynamic Psychotherapy, 10*: 63–84.

Schwartz, G. E. (1982). Integrating psychobiology and behavior therapy: a systems perspective. In: G. T. Wilson & C. M. Franks (Eds.), *Contemporary Behavior Therapy: Conceptual and Empirical Foundations.* New York, London: The Guilford Press.

Siegel, D. J. (Ed.). *Healing Trauma.* London: W. W. Norton.

Sroufe, L. A., Egeland, B. & Krentger, T. (1990). The fate of early experience following developmental change: longitudinal approaches to individual adaptation in childhood. *Child Development, 54*: 1615–1627.

Trivedi, M. H., Rush, A. J., Wisniewski, S. R., Nierenberg, A. A., Warden, D., Ritz, L., Norquist, G., Howland, R., Lebowitz, B., McGrath, P., Shores-Wilson, K., Biggs, M., Balasubraman, G. K. & Fava, M. (2006). Evaluation of outcomes with citalopram for depression using messurement based care in STAR*D: implications for clinical practice. *American Journal of Psychiatry, 163(1)*: 28–40.

Trunnell, T. (1987). The management of the mechanisms of depression in ISTDP. *International Journal of Short-Term Psychotherapy, 2*: 1–15.

Whittemore, J. (1998). The application of Davanloo's ISTDP to a complex masochistic patient with panic, functional and somatization disorders: from the "frying pan" into freedom. Part I. *International Journal of Short-Term Dynamic psychotherapy, 12*: 151–181.

Whittemore, J. (1999a). The application of Davanloo's ISTDP to a complex masochistic patient with panic, functional and somatization disorders: from the "frying pan" into freedom. Part II. *International Journal of Short-Term Dynamic Psychotherapy, 13*: 17–48.

Whittemore, J. (1999b). The application of Davanloo's ISTDP to a complex masochistic patient with panic, functional and somatization disorders: from the "frying pan" into freedom. Part III. *International Journal of Short-Term Dynamic Psychotherapy, 13*: 49–79.

Wickens, A. P. (2005). Chapter Five. In: *Foundations of Biopsychology*. Essex, UK: Pearson Education.

Worchel, J. (1986a). Transference in ISTDP. Part I: Technique of handling initial transference. *International Journal of Short-Term Psychotherapy, 1*: 135–146.

Worchel, J. (1986b). Transference in ISTDP. Part II: Technique of handling initial transference resistance. *International Journal of Short-Term Psychotherapy, 1*: 205–215.

Zois, C. (1986). Handling resistance in depressed patients. *International Journal of Short-Term Psychotherapy, 1*: 17–30.

INDEX